The ENCYCLOPEDIA of the
CAT

The ENCYCLOPEDIA *of the*

CAT

BRUCE FOGLE, DVM

FIREFLY BOOKS

DK

A DK PUBLISHING BOOK

Project Editor
CANDIDA FRITH-MACDONALD
Art Editor
URSULA DAWSON

Editors
TRACIE LEE DAVIS, SHARON LUCAS,
SARAH WILDE
Designer
HEATHER DUNLEAVY
US Editor
CONSTANCE M. ROBINSON
US Consultant
SOLVEIG PFLUEGER

Managing Editor
FRANCIS RITTER
Managing Art Editor
DEREK COOMBES

DTP Designer
SONIA CHARBONNIER

Production Controllers
RUTH CHARLTON, ROSALIND PRIESTLEY

Picture Researcher
SAM RUSTON

Breed photography
TRACY MORGAN, CHANAN,
MARC HENRIE, TETSU YAMAZAKI

First published in Canada in 1997
By Firefly Books Ltd.
3680 Victoria Park Avenue
Willowdale, Ontario M2H 3K1

Candian Cataloging in Publication Data
Fogle, Bruce
    The encyclopedia of the cat
Includes index.
ISBN 1–55209–164–3
1. Cats – Encyclopedias. I. Title.
SF442.2.F63 1997   636.8'003
C97–931164–0

Reproduced by Colourscan, Singapore
Printed and bound in Italy

CONTENTS

CHAPTER ONE
THE CAT FAMILY

CHAPTER TWO
CATS AND PEOPLE

INTRODUCTION

Early evidence
The cat probably reached Britain with the Roman Empire; this terracotta tile from Reading dates from the first century AD.

IN MANY REGIONS OF the world the cat is now our most popular animal companion, yet it is still the least understood. All of the species that we have domesticated, either as livestock or for companionship, are sociable by nature. The dog is called "man's best friend," not just because it has been adapted to serve us but because it shares our need for attachment. This need to care or be cared for is an instinct in all sociable species and an engine of behavior in domesticated animals other than the cat. Unique among our animal companions, the cat still lives its own life.

Descended from the North African wildcat (*see page 18*), the domestic cat evolved to be a solitary hunter. It does not come from a cooperative culture, where individuals live and hunt together, as exists in some larger cat species such as the lion. With small rodents, amphibians, and birds as its food sources, the wildcat's meal is large

Religious acceptance
The cat's role in Christianity has varied. It was treated favorably in the Lindisfarne Gospels (see left), but was later associated with heresy.

enough to fill only its own stomach, so it developed natural independence, being content to live and hunt alone, and to meet other cats only during territorial disputes or mating. When cats moved into new human

Witch's cat
By the 14th century, Europe was gripped by religious fervor. The cat's nocturnal habits condemned it as evil in the eyes of the Church.

communities, those that were cared for discovered a source of ample food. Natural selection favored more sociable individuals, slowly transforming the wildcat into the domestic cat that we know today.

FORM AND FUNCTION

Since that domestication over 4,000 years ago, the cat has been both deified and persecuted by turns. Some cultures have been fascinated by its natural fertility, while others saw in its behavior the signature of the devil. A misunderstanding of the cat's ability to survive on instinct as a nocturnal hunter is at the root of many of the misconceptions that developed, and some survive even today. In fact, the cat is one of nature's most successful products. All aspects of its anatomy result from evolutionary logic, but the total is an animal of grace and beauty. Its eyes dilate fully for night vision but shut down to slits in bright sunshine.

Cartoon favorite
Cartoon cats have shown enduring popularity. Felix, one of the first, became a U.S. Air Force emblem and is still well loved worldwide.

Artists' models
Théophile Alexandre Steinlen (1859–1923) became well known for his brilliantly accurate portrayals of cats. Many other artists have found a highly successful niche by specializing in felines.

Touch-sensitive whiskers help the cat to "feel" its way when it hunts in low light levels, while its delicate hearing permits it to hear the tiny, high-pitched sounds of a mouse squeaking. An accurate sense of balance permits it to climb away from danger, while its righting reflex allows it to regain its balance if it accidentally falls. All of these characteristics create an animal that is appealing to our eyes and to our minds.

THE SOCIABLE CAT

Although biologically predisposed toward a solitary life, in certain circumstances, when food is plentiful, the cat can alter its solitary behavior. Female groups share maternal responsibilities such as feeding and protecting the young. As the male kittens mature, fights with female relatives intensify until they leave the colony, forming an informal brotherhood with other male cats. These patterns are seen clearly in colonies of feral cats, and are also found in household cats. During the 20th century, the cat has moved from a minor role in human society to a more commanding position as one of the most popular of all animal companions. By the 1980s, it was the most popular animal companion in North America, a position it

Naive art
Folk art has incorporated many motifs from everyday life. This feline figurine is an example from the rich tradition of American folk art.

also reached in many European countries in the mid-1990s. The variety of new breeds that have been developed in the last 50 years is perhaps equal to the number of breeds that have evolved throughout all the preceding centuries, and such trends will continue. Selective breeding for sociable temperament is now almost as important as breeding for shape and color.

The cat is a perfect animal companion for us. Quiet, self-cleaning, content to snooze whenever the opportunity arises but capable of astounding episodes of activity when its brain is engaged, it is also aesthetically pleasing. Perhaps the cat's most important characteristic is its independence. A cat may live in your home as a result of your choice or its own, but if left to its own devices, its chances of surviving on its own decrease only slightly. The greatest value of the cat is that by living with us it gives us an opportunity to view the natural world in our own homes. In the future development of our relationship with the cat, that integrity is what we should strive to maintain.

One of the family
As it spread eastward, the cat basked in the reflected glory of the tiger, which held symbolic importance in Asia.

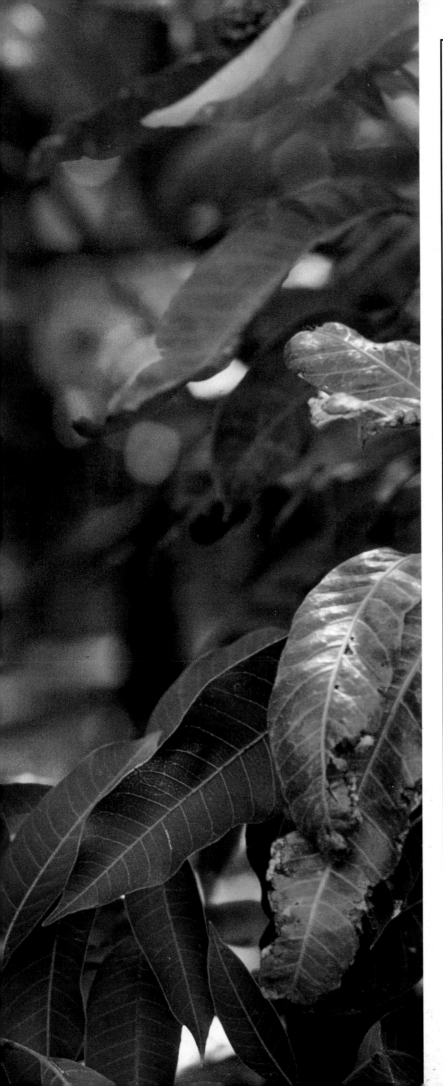

CHAPTER ONE

THE CAT FAMILY

MILLIONS OF YEARS AGO, MEAT-EATING mammals evolved – species with unique shearing and cutting carnassial teeth. The cats' dependence upon eating the flesh of other animals has been at the core of their evolution. They developed matchless hunting capabilities, making them the most efficient land-based carnivores. Some of the large cats worked cooperatively to capture food. Most of the smaller cats evolved as lone hunters, preying on animals large enough to fill only a single stomach. Three million years ago, a species not unlike the modern domestic cat first emerged, but it was only within the last few thousand years that members of this species chose to live in close proximity to people.

ABOVE MALE RED TABBY AMERICAN SHORTHAIR

LEFT FEMALE INDIAN TIGER

ANCESTORS OF THE CAT

TODAY'S CAT FAMILY COMES FROM THE SAME ROOTS AS ALL OTHER predator mammals. The world's first mammals were small, with limited brain capacity, but in the evolutionary process these were replaced by newer species with more refined abilities. Over tens of millions of years, primitive cats evolved, adapting to climate, to available prey, and to competition from other evolving carnivores. Successful adaptations have occurred, been lost, and then recurred as the environment altered. Educated guesswork is used to map evolution, but recently genetic fingerprinting has been employed to calibrate a "molecular clock" for the evolution of today's species.

The history of modern mammals, including the cat, is traced from fragments of ancient bone and teeth. These shards of evidence do not, however, give us any clues about the two most fundamental traits of mammals, their fur and their skin glands. Fur offered insulation while skin glands allowed mammals both to sweat and to manufacture nourishment for their young in the form of milk. These are simple adaptations but are at the root of the mammal's success in a variety of environments.

THE EARLIEST ANCESTORS OF THE CAT

After the dinosaurs died out 65 to 70 million years ago, they were survived by, among others, the mammals. The earliest mammals were the fish-eating creodonts, and one of their forms evolved into smaller, forest-dwelling miacids. For unknown reasons, the creodonts became extinct and the miacids thrived. It has been assumed that this evolutionary change occurred because the miacids had larger brains, although there is no fossil evidence that this is so.

The early miacids were long-bodied, short-legged animals that evolved into the variety of modern families of carnivores we know today. Each family fits into its own ecological niche, from the bears at the largest end of the scale to the civets and mongooses at the smallest, and the cat family spans the range from tigers and lions to tiny sand cats. Among the carnivore families, the cats are most closely related to the civets. Paleontologists look at structures at the base of the skull, in particular the structure which acts as a bony case surrounding the

The spread of the cat
Australia and South America separated from the ancient land-mass called Gondwanaland before feline evolution began. The cat family evolved in Eurasia and North America, and when South America linked with its northern neighbor, cats entered that continent. With no land bridge available, the cat did not enter Australia.

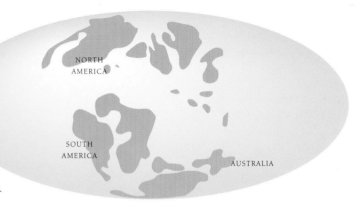

middle ear, to help differentiate one species from another. Unfortunately the fossil record for small cats is sparse, in part because many ancestral species inhabited forested regions where conditions for preserving fossils were poor. Fossil records for larger species are more abundant and show that cats lived worldwide.

THE FIRST CATLIKE CARNIVORES

The early "cats" are classed as *Proailurus*. They shared many characteristics of the *Viverridae* family, including walking plantigrade, or flat-footed, and can be considered half-cat, half-civet. About 20 million years ago, *Proailurus* gave way to *Pseudaelurus*, walking digitigrade, on the tips of its toes, and possessing stabbing canine teeth. Experts consider this group of animals as the first members of the modern cat family. Within this group there were both larger and smaller species. They were light, agile, and varied in sizes between the modern puma at 220 lb (100 kg) and the lynx at 64 lb (29 kg).

Out of the *Pseudaelurus* group emerged the direct ancestors of the modern cat family, *Felidae*, as well as other "dead-end" branches, such as *Smilodon*, the saber-toothed cats that survived until less than a million years ago in Europe, Africa, Asia, and the Americas. Saber-toothed species evolved independently at least four times, as creodonts, as marsupials, and twice as ancient species of cats. Their jaws opened 50 percent wider than other cats', and the long teeth were flattened and serrated for more efficient cutting. The species evolved to hunt large grazing mammals and probably died out when their food supply diminished, having become too selectively adapted for other prey.

EARLY CAT DISTRIBUTION

The early big cats inhabited most parts of the world. Lions lived not just in Africa, but in Europe, throughout Southeast Asia, across Siberia, and throughout North and Central America down to northwest South America.

Cat evolution
The evolution of modern cats does not follow a simple plan. During 60 million years of carnivore development, evolution created and rejected numerous varieties of "proto-cats." Fossil evidence is used to track evolutionary developments, but it can be misleading. Fossils from arid regions tend to remain intact, while those from damper regions disintegrate. One consequence is that experts disagree on the details of cat evolution, although they do agree on the broad picture. Feline evolution has taken many dead ends, one of the most spectacular being the saber-toothed cats (Smilodon), but it has led inexorably to the variety of cat species that survive today.

Creodonts
The predominant carnivores 53–60 million years ago, creodonts were rather small, no more than 12 in (30 cm) high at the shoulder. They had thick necks and long bodies in relation to their legs. All of today's carnivores evolved from creodonts.

Miacids
Miacids evolved around 60 million years ago and survived the creodonts. They were up to twice the size of the creodonts, with longer legs and slender heads.

PALEOCENE

EOCENE

Leopards and jaguars lived throughout western, central, and eastern Europe, Africa, Asia, on the island of Java, and throughout the Americas. The lion and the lynx are thought to originate in Africa, while the leopard may have evolved in India. Jaguars evolved in Eurasia and spread into the Americas. Tiger fossils two million years old have been found in China; the oldest fossils of cheetahs were found in France, and of pumas in North America.

Small cats never populated North America. The small predator's niche was already filled by carnivores from the Mustelid family, including the mink, marten, wolverine, and skunk. The domestic cat's extinct ancestor, Martelli's wild cat (*Felis lunensis*), evolved in Europe or the Middle East.

NEW EVOLUTIONARY EVIDENCE

Traditional classifications of cats have been based on the geographical distribution, size and shape, and behavior of species. Cats are divided, on the basis of where they are found today, into Old World and New World species. Small cats that did not roar were further classified as *Felis*, while big cats that did roar were classified as *Panthera*: an arbitrary but useful division, with only a couple of misfits – the cheetah (*see page 12*) and the clouded leopard (*see page 13*). However, recent studies of DNA and the ancient viruses found in body cells have cast this system into confusion.

The old geographical divisions have been undermined as cats from different continents are found to be closely related. Even more surprisingly, cats that appear very different physically have been shown to share almost identical DNA and virus-resistance patterns. Several cats currently classified as *Felis*, including the serval and golden cats (*see page 16*), are now thought to belong in the *Panthera* genus, despite their inability to roar.

In the future, the traditional classifications will be replaced with new, accurate groupings that will tell us more about the history of the cat family. For now, however, the old names remain in use, in this book as elsewhere, to avoid a confusing variety of classifications.

The saber-toothed cats
Skeletons recovered from the Rancho La Brea tar pits in California show that the Smilodon *had canine teeth over 6 in (15 cm) long. While deadly in appearance, the teeth were too fragile for use in attack and probably were used to subdue and kill prey after it was brought down.*

AUSTRALIAN "CATS"

Australia, New Guinea, and New Zealand separated from the major landmass called Gondwanaland about 85 million years ago, long before cats evolved. In these regions, animal evolution was isolated from the rest of the world. While no indigenous mammals had arrived in New Zealand, marsupials – mammals that give birth to young that develop fully in a pouch in the mother's body – existed in Australia. In the absence of true cats, a marsupial evolved to fill their predatory niche. The tiger cat, *Dasyurus maculatus*, became one of Tasmania's and eastern Australia's small native predators.

Carnivorous marsupial
In Australia, the absence of true cats allowed this marsupial carnivore to fill the cat's environmental or ecological niche.

HOPLOPHONEUS

NIMRAVINUS

DINICTIS

SMILODON

Pseudaelurus
By 20 million years ago, carnivores that looked like modern cats had evolved. The Pseudaelurids were larger than miacids and typically feline, with flexible shoulder blades, spines, and tails. These species walked almost on their toes and inhabited open plains in North America and Europe.

MACHAIRODUS

ACINONYX

FELIS AND PANTHERA

Felis lunensis
Felis lunensis, a species that lived in Europe about 12 million years ago, is thought to be the direct ancestor of today's wildcat family, *Felis silvestris*. They were smaller than their predecessors and, considering their European habitats, probably had thick coats with spotted tabby markings.

Modern cats
Cats radiated into two groups, Old World and New World, between 8 and 12 million years ago. Scientific developments have led to genetic fingerprinting, which reveals the close relationship between the domestic cat and other species like the Pallas' cat.

MIOCENE

PLIOCENE

PLEISTOCENE

BIG CATS WORLDWIDE

THE BIG CATS SHARE THEIR ORIGINS AS WELL AS MANY ASPECTS OF their behavior with their smaller relatives, although most of the big cats are members of the *Panthera* genus, while the small cats are members of the *Felis* genus. There is, however, a fundamental distinction between the two groups: big cats have the ability to roar, but cannot continuously purr, while small cats can purr continuously, but do not roar. Members of the big cat group naturally inhabit Africa, Asia, the Indian subcontinent, and South America. With the exception of the Masai subspecies of lion, these relatives of the domestic cat are classified as vulnerable or endangered species.

The classification of the big cats still varies according to different authorities, but with the development of genetic fingerprinting the genetic identity of each species is now being investigated. Without doubt, the results will lead to some reclassification of the species.

Like the domestic cat, all big cats are born blind and helpless, covered with fur, in litters ranging from one to six individuals. Unlike other carnivores such as bears or wolves, which supplement their meat diets with vegetation, cats feed exclusively on vertebrate prey. They cannot survive without eating animal protein and fat, and each species of big cat has evolved its own technique for capturing its meal. The lion uses cooperative social behavior and brute force to catch and kill mammals that are often considerably larger than itself, the cheetah employs speed and an under-the-throat death bite to kill, while the tiger, leopard, and jaguar all stalk and pounce on their prey.

LIVING WITH HUMANS

To humans, the big cats have often held social and religious significance. Tigers and jaguars have been worshipped in their native lands, while lions and leopards have been used by many nationalities as symbols of royalty. Other than the domestic cat, the cheetah has the longest history of living alongside people. From Ethiopia through the Arabian peninsula to Mogul India, cheetahs were used for centuries as hunting companions, raised to hunt antelope and other herbivores.

In India, the cheetah's role was similar to that of the falcon in Europe: it was taken, blindfolded, to the hunting area and freed when the quarry was sighted. India's other big cat, the tiger, has never been tamed. Although tigers rarely make contact with humans, in the absence of other prey some do learn to kill people, and the man-eating tiger has become embedded in Indian folklore. Labeled a "man-eater," it was hunted extensively in the 19th century and is now an endangered species.

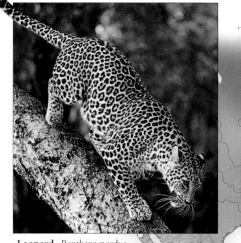

Leopard *Panthera pardus*
Most leopards, found from Africa through the Far East, have black spots on a fawn coat. The black panther, previously thought to be a distinct species, is now known to be a black-coated variety of leopard. This natural variation in coat color has been deliberately increased in domestic cats.

Cheetah *Acinonyx jubatus*
Perhaps the most distant of all the domestic cat's living relatives, the cheetah is the fastest animal on land. It shares the hunting territory of lions and leopards, but prefers to hunt for its meals in the morning and early afternoon, when other predators rest. To assist with rapid acceleration, its claws, unlike those of other cats, do not retract into sheaths.

Jaguar *Panthera onca*
The only big cat to be found in the Americas is a New World equivalent of the leopard. Although classified as a big cat, it grunts and growls but seldom roars. Jaguars are lone hunters, preferring dense forests and swamplands with easy access to water. Now exterminated in the United States, subspecies exist from Mexico to northern Argentina.

LION AND TIGER HYBRID

Lions and tigers have been cross-bred in captivity, producing new hybrids referred to as "tigons" or "ligers." The viability of matings shows how closely, in evolutionary terms, these two distinct species are related, but the fact that the offspring are usually sterile indicates the degree of divergence that has occurred within the cat family.

Infertile offspring
Like matings between the horse and the donkey that produce the sterile mule, the lion and tiger hybrid cannot breed.

Tiger *Panthera tigris*
Found in isolated pockets from India to Siberia, the tiger's habitat ranges from tropical forests to rocky mountainsides. A male's territory covers that of four or five females but never another male's. When prey is plentiful, tolerance of other tigers increases, but when it is scarce, tigers live alone and meet only to mate.

Clouded leopard *Neofelis nebulosa*
Found from Nepal to Taiwan, the clouded leopard hunts in trees, preying on monkeys, squirrels, and birds. Its rigid hyoid bone is like that of the small cats and prevents it from roaring, but its resting posture is that of a big cat.

Lion *Panthera leo*
The most sociable members of the cat family, lions live in "prides" of related females, a characteristic also found in the domestic cat. The lion is restricted to Africa, although a small population of Asiatic lions exists in the Gir Forest of northwest India. Expansion of agriculture has forced several subspecies into extinction, although lions recently found in the Addis Ababa zoo in Ethiopia may be survivors of the extinct Barbary lion of North Africa.

Diminishing habitat
The broad geographical distribution of big cats, living in so many varied habitats, gives an impression of stability and success, but big cat numbers are declining almost everywhere. This is partly due to hunting for pelts and the Far East animal products trade, but also through loss of natural habitat. A hundred years ago, tigers ranged from Turkey to Korea and Bali. Without active human intervention, the habitat of the big cats will shrink even more.

SMALL CATS IN THE AMERICAS

ANIMALS ADAPT AND EVOLVE SO THAT THEY MAY SURVIVE IN THEIR environment. Due to the rich diversity of topography and climate in the Americas, a wide variety of species in the genus *Felis* has developed there. The largest of the small cats, the puma, has been successful throughout all the Americas, while the medium-sized lynx and bobcat found a niche in North America, although their future is not certain. In South America, a number of smaller cats evolved. Many of these are similar in size and appearance to the domestic cat, but they are intrinsically wild. None is as potentially tamable as the ancestors of the domestic cat.

Evolving cat populations became separated when continental drift created landmasses that were surrounded by ocean. Because this effectively halted the spread of animals to some areas of the world, regions such as Madagascar and Australia have no indigenous cats (*see page 11*). The Americas have only one big cat, the jaguar (*see page 12*), but a diverse range of small cats in the genus *Felis* evolved. Scientists think that many of these cats developed in North America and then migrated south when continental movement brought South America back into contact with North America. In South America, cats successfully diversified into the variety of species that exist today.

The domestic cat's American relatives are of similar size but of shy temperament. Few have been studied in any detail, and very little is known of their biology or social behavior. Many of these small cats prefer to live in dense underbrush or in trees, where they hunt at night, and these habits make them far more difficult to observe than cats that live on open plains and hunt by day. Genetic tests of these American small cats have not been performed, but it is very probable that many are closely related to each other. The ocelot, margay, tiger cat, kodkod, and Geoffroy's cat are now all thought to be strains of one species. The bobcat and lynx are often classified as another single species.

HUMAN CONTACT

Due to the secretive lifestyles of the smaller cats, there are few native stories about them. The one exception is the jaguarundi, which, according to some authorities, was tamed by local Indians before the Spanish arrived in South America. Both the jaguar and the puma are thought to have played significant roles in the mythology of pre-Columbian civilizations. Artifacts left by Aztec and other societies suggest that these cats were respected, even venerated. In North America, the bobcat was characterized as a trickster by the Native Americans, making appearances as such in their folklore, but it was never tamed.

Lynx *Felis lynx canadensis*
The only member of the cat family that lives on both sides of the Atlantic, the lynx is widespread throughout its native habitat. While European lynxes are large (*see page 17*), some adult American lynxes are no bigger than domestic cats. A taste for snowshoe hare is detrimental to the species: fluctuations in the hare population directly affect lynx numbers.

Bobcat *Felis lynx rufus*
A subspecies of the lynx family, the bobcat or red lynx inhabits vast areas of North America from Nova Scotia down into Mexico. Its black-spotted, brown coat serves as camouflage in the rocky, bushy terrain where it hunts. Slightly larger than the lynx, with a longer tail, the bobcat has large ears, but less dramatic ear tufts than its relative.

Ocelot *Felis pardalis*
Once widely distributed, the ocelot has suffered the misfortune of having a handsome orange-yellow coat, black-striped and spotted, for which it has been hunted to extinction in parts of North America. A superb climber, it hunts in trees and sleeps during the day.

Jaguarundi *Felis yagouarundi*
Sometimes called the otter cat or weasel cat, this feline inhabits dense undergrowth from Arizona to Argentina. Because its fur has never been popular, it has escaped the hunters, but little is known about its behavior. Most active in the morning, jaguarundis eat rodents and rabbits, and frogs and birds as well. South American Indian stories tell of taming jaguarundis for use in rodent control.

Puma *Felis concolor*
Ranging from southern Canada to Patagonia in South America, the puma is also known as the cougar, panther, and mountain lion. The largest member of the genus *Felis*, it preys on animals from rodents to deer. Because it kills domestic livestock, it has been hunted to the point where both the Florida panther and the Eastern puma are now endangered species.

Threat from humans

The most serious threats to small cats are the fur trade, the exotic-pet trade, and loss of habitat. Public awareness of how wild animals are killed has led to a dramatic reduction in the trapping of wildcats, and legislation now protects endangered species, but both came too late for some species. For fashion items, skins needed to match: once there were not enough skins from one species, hunters simply moved on to the next species. The result is that some populations of spotted cats may never recover. In the face of habitat loss due to agriculture, the remaining populations must adapt or decline further.

Tiger cat *Felis tigrinus*
Also known as the little spotted cat, ocelot cat, and oncilla, the tiger cat is often mistaken for its close relative the margay. Its habitat extends from Costa Rica to northern Argentina, but it is rare because it is hunted for its coat, which varies in color from cream to rich ochre. Although a forest dweller, it does not live in trees as much as the margay. It preys on birds, mammals, lizards, and insects, but little is known of its social behavior.

Margay *Felis wiedi*
The margay, sometimes called the long-tailed spotted cat, looks much like a small ocelot. Although a close relative, it is considerably smaller – about the size of a large domestic cat. Its habitat extends from Mexico to Argentina, although it has become extinct in vast areas of the Americas.

Mountain cat *Felis jacobita*
This rare cat inhabits the high areas of the Andes. It is the same size as the average domestic cat, although males can be slightly larger. Its silver-gray coat, spotted or striped with brown or orange, is dense, and makes it well adapted for the bitter weather of its high-altitude habitat. It has been seen at altitudes of up to 16,000 ft (5,000 m) above sea level.

Pampas cat *Felis colocolo*
Also called the "gato pajero" or grass cat because of its favored habitat, the pampas cat ranges from Ecuador to northern Chile and Argentina. It is a nocturnal predator, and preys on ground-nesting birds and small mammals. The size of a domestic cat, the pampas cat arches its back dramatically and its fur stands on end when it is excited or aggressive.

Geoffroy's cat *Felis geoffroyi*
Sometimes called Geoffroy's ocelot, this tiny cat is closely related to the kodkod and the much larger margay. An excellent climber and swimmer, it preys on small mammals and birds. Its habitat extends from Brazil and Bolivia south into Argentina. The color of the coat varies from ochre to silver, but spotted gray is the most common.

Kodkod *Felis guigna*
The smallest of the American cats, the male kodkod, or guiña, is never more than 7 lb (3 kg) in weight and 21 in (52 cm) long. This spotted, gray-brown tree-dweller is found mostly in central and southern Chile, but populations also exist in western Argentina. Very little is known about its social behavior or hunting habits, although farmers claim that it attacks poultry.

SMALL CATS IN AFRICA AND EURASIA

MOST AUTHORITIES NOW CLASSIFY THE SMALL AND MEDIUM-SIZED cats of Africa and Eurasia as members of the genus *Felis*, the domestic cat's close family. There are many similarities in the sizes, looks, activities, and even, when they are known, the genetics of these cats. Like the domestic cat, the lifestyle of its close relatives is one of prolonged inactivity punctuated by bursts of activity when in search of food. Little is known about the social behavior of these species, but those that have been observed have displayed habits similar to those of the domestic cat. Few, however, carry the potential for domestication in their natural form.

The individual anatomical and behavioral characteristics of each species of wildcat are the result of evolutionary adaptations to take advantage of available sources of food. Some species, such as the fishing cat, have adapted to life on the water's edge, where they feed on shellfish, snakes, and rodents. Others, like the Chinese desert cat, have had to adapt to life in an arid climate, and more typically prey upon small mammals.

All cats have developed coat colors and markings that camouflage them from their prey in their particular environments. Generally speaking, spotted cats live in forests, while less vividly patterned cats live and hunt in tall grass or open territory. Regardless of their habitat, however, all of the domestic cat's close relatives share common characteristics. In the wild, most cats are solitary and keep to their own territories, which they mark with scent. A male's territory may overlap the territories of several females but male and female rarely meet, except to mate after a brief courtship.

SMALL CAT HYBRIDS

Small cats can successfully interbreed, although cross-species matings are unlikely to take place in the wild. Just as a lion mated to a tiger produces a "liger" or "tigon" (*see page 13*), hybrid small cats are born. The difference between these matings and those of the big cats is that, with the correct cross-species alliance, the resulting kittens are fertile, capable of perpetuating the new hybrid. Some species have been bred with the domestic cat, creating handsome hybrids. However, the resulting hybrids are often intractable, especially in early generations. Tameness, developed through generations of breeding, is quickly diminished by breeding with species that have not undergone the biofeedback or hormonal changes associated with tameness (*see page 58*).

Jungle cat *Felis chaus*
This cat is misnamed, for it prefers open country, reedy marshes, and woodland, and is also known as the reed cat, swamp cat, and marsh cat. Mummified jungle cats have been found in Egypt.

Sand cat *Felis margarita*
This cat's territory stretches from Saharan Africa to the deserts of Baluchistan in Asia. It has thick hair between the pads of its feet to keep it from sinking into the sand, and it is able to survive without water, obtaining moisture from its prey of desert rodents.

Caracal *Felis caracal*
A member of the lynx family that has adapted to the heat of the tropics, the caracal has distinctive ear tufts. Its habitat ranges from Africa to the Arabian Peninsula and India.

African golden cat
Felis aurata
This rare cat inhabits the high forests of Africa, although it is not a tree dweller. Its prey includes rodents and birds, which it hunts by night and day. Its coat varies from brown to gray.

Serval *Felis serval*
A native of the African savannas, the serval's coat is tawny with black spots. It can leap twice its own length to bring down birds.

Black-footed cat
Felis nigripes
The smallest of the African cats, this spotted cat is found in the savannas of southern Africa, where it preys on lizards and small rodents.

Rusty spotted cat
Felis prionailurus rubiginosus
The smallest of the Asian cats, this tiny feline, which is smaller than a domestic cat, inhabits the scrub and grassland of southern India and the humid mountain forest of Sri Lanka. This cat is nocturnal and hunts small mammals, birds, and insects.

Lynx *Felis lynx pardina*
The largest of the European cats, the lynx can be up to five times heavier than the domestic cat. Ranging from Scandinavia to Siberia, lynx populations vary. Extinct in France and Italy, the smallest population is found in the desert area of central Spain, where around 1,000 survive.

Pallas' cat *Felis manul*
From Iran to western China, the Pallas' cat inhabits mountainous and rocky terrain, where it preys upon rodents. It has evolved with small ears and a very dense coat in order to survive subfreezing temperatures.

Asian golden cat *Felis temmincki*
Also known as Temminck's golden cat, this close relative of the African golden cat lives in rocky terrain from Nepal and southern China to Sumatra. Its markings are pale in the south, but in the north it is spotted and striped.

Asian leopard cat *Felis prionailurus bengalensis*
Similar in size to the domestic cat, the leopard cat inhabits an area from northern China to the islands of Indonesia – where its success is aided by its ability to swim and catch fish. It has been bred with the domestic cat to produce the Bengal (*see page 208*).

Fishing cat
Felis prionailurus viverrinus
With slightly webbed toes and less retractile claws than other cats, the gray-brown, spotted fishing cat lives in the mangrove swamps of India, Sri Lanka, China, and Myanmar. It preys on fish, shellfish, snakes, and small mammals.

Marbled cat
Felis pardofelis marmorata
The marbled cat is found from the eastern Himalayas to Borneo. Very rare, it is now protected in India and Thailand. Its coat resembles that of the clouded leopard, but it is considerably smaller in size.

Flat-headed cat
Felis prionailurus planiceps
Also known as the marten cat, this red-brown cat's most distinctive feature is its long, flat head. Throughout its habitat in India, Sri Lanka, Indonesia, and southern China, it prefers proximity to water, where it hunts small mammals, birds, and fish.

Iriomote cat
Felis prionailurus iriomotensis
Discovered in 1967 on the Japanese island of Iriomote, this small nocturnal cat lives by the water's edge, eating birds, crabs, and small mammals. Probably fewer than 100 survive, each hunting in its own territory.

Vanishing species

As do many of their relatives, a number of the small cats of Africa and Eurasia face an uncertain future. Fortunately, species such as the caracal, serval, African golden cat, and Pallas' cat exist in viable numbers in secure wildlife refuges. Others, like the Iriomote cat, the Asiatic golden cat, bay cat, and flat-headed cat, are vulnerable and in danger of extinction. Governments realize the value of "ecotourism" and now invest in protecting the habitat of many of these species, but unfortunately for both the ecotourist and the dedicated biologist, many of these cats are too wary of human presence to be seen. Wildlife films continue to be the only way of seeing many of these relatives of the domestic cat.

Chinese desert cat *Felis bieti*
Inhabiting the steppes and mountains of western China and southern Mongolia, this domestic cat-sized species has a dense coat, and thick hair on the soles of its feet. Its yellow-brown coat offers camouflage in its dry habitat.

Bay cat *Felis pardofelis badia*
Extremely rare, this close relative of the marbled cat is also known as the Bornean red cat. It has a chestnut brown coat with spotting on the underbelly. Most rare are individuals with bluish fur. It inhabits rocky, forested regions of Borneo, where it preys on small mammals and birds.

CLOSEST RELATIVES

THERE IS A GROUP OF SMALL, INDEPENDENT WILDCATS SCATTERED across Africa, Europe, and Asia that are members of the genus *Felis*. They are so similar in appearance that experts are unable to agree whether each is a distinct species, or simply a regional race or subspecies adapted for its environment. These wildcats have proved to be the domestic cat's closest relatives: recent genetic studies suggest that the domestic cat is virtually identical to the African wildcat, and that these two varieties are appreciably different from both European and Asian wildcats. All of these cats can be interbred, producing fertile offspring.

The wildcat, *Felis silvestris*, is the domestic cat's closest relative. Until recently, taxonomists have failed to agree on the significance of differences within this species of small, lone hunters. There are visual differences between varieties, with coat color and texture varying according to habitat, and there are also differences in temperament between the wildcats of Africa and those of Europe. In Somalia, for example, African wildcats live close to human settlements, even scavenging within the boundaries of villages. In Britain, Scottish wildcats are virtually never seen, although some have adapted to hunting the plentiful supply of rabbits that are found on agricultural land.

Recent studies carried out by Professor Eric Hurley at Cape Town University in South Africa have indicated that there are distinct genetic differences between the European wildcat and the African wildcat. The study suggests that although physically similar, they diverged into two different species hundreds of thousands of years ago. Genetic studies are likely to reveal that all the regional varieties of European wildcats are isolated populations of a single species.

DISTINCT DESCENDENT

The studies of the African wildcat show that it has "genetic fingerprints" almost identical to those of the domestic cat, giving sound evidence that the domestic cat is an emigrant from Africa.

Sufficient subtle differences remain between the genes of African wildcats and domestic cats to identify an individual as one or the other, even in mixed populations. Experts have disagreed about whether the scavenging African wildcats and adapting Scottish wildcats are full-blooded wildcats or wildcat-domestic hybrids: genetic testing may answer this question.

The wildcat family

Wildcats have thrived in climates ranging from the harsh winters of Scotland to the burning scrub of Africa. They have evolved into a range of types, with differences subtle enough for some to argue that they are closely related, diverse enough for others to see them as separate species.

Scottish wildcat *Felis silvestris grampia*
Once prevalent throughout Britain, wildcats had disappeared from England by the 1800s, retreating to Scotland, where they survive north of a line drawn from Glasgow to Edinburgh. With protection, their numbers have begun to recover. The Scottish wildcat has a broader head and shorter tail than the domestic cat.

Spanish wildcat *Felis silvestris iberia*
Looking like heavily built domestic tabbies, the wildcats of Iberia are a remnant of the wildcats that once lived throughout Europe. Hunted for their pelts and persecuted because they are believed to prey on livestock, they survive today only in isolated regions.

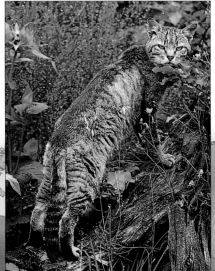

European wildcat *Felis silvestris europeus*
After declining almost to extinction, the populations of European wildcats are now stable in many countries. Intractable and virtually untamable, this indigenous wildcat is now a protected species in many regions, including Germany, the Czech Republic, and Slovakia.

Indian desert cat *Felis silvestris ornata*
Also called the Indian desert wildcat, the habitat of this cat ranges south from Russia down to central India. It is smaller than its African and European relatives, and its coat is spotted rather than striped.

African wildcat *Felis silvestris lybica*
The African wildcat, like its European relatives, has a larger brain than the domestic cat, which is probably due to the demands of survival. Unlike European wildcats, it can be relatively tame if raised in captivity. Genetic investigations indicate that this is the true ancestor of the domestic cat.

HYBRIDIZATION OF THE WILDCAT

Wildcats in Europe have been threatened by human persecution and the spread of agriculture. Less obviously, they may also have been endangered by hybridization with the domestic cat. It is possible, even likely, that male wildcats have fathered kittens with female domestic cats. At adolescence, these hybrid kittens exhibit the father's wild ways and move away from human settlements. As a result, wildcats are unlikely to play a role in the development of the domestic cat, but domestic cats may play a role in the evolution of the wildcat. Genetic testing suggests that hybridization between the African wildcat and the closely related domestic cat is uncommon. Although tests have not yet been carried out on the European wildcat, its natural reclusiveness suggests that hybridization is not a serious threat to its survival.

Truly wild
Unlike the African wildcat, which can be domesticated if raised from kittenhood, the wildcats of Europe appear to be innately fearful of humans. This trait is so strong that even a hybrid of wildcat and domestic cat, such as this one, will be a lifelong "spitfire," unable to adapt to life with people.

FROM WILDCAT TO DOMESTIC CAT

UNLIKE OTHER DOMESTIC ANIMALS, THE CAT IS SELF-DOMESTICATED. It chose to live in close proximity to people because it was in its interests to do so, a natural selfishness that remains at the core of domestic cat behavior to this day. This self-domestication was relatively recent, occurring long after we had domesticated the dog. The cat's ancestors needed specific psychological and physiological traits to help them to infiltrate the new and unique ecological niche of the human settlement. Under the altered environmental pressures, both physical and behavioral changes occurred, creating the most successful ever of all the species of cat: the domestic cat.

The history of the cat is best documented in ancient Egypt, but Egypt was not necessarily its first domestic home. A cat's tooth from 9000 BC has been found in a settlement site in Jericho, Israel. Wildcats did not inhabit Cyprus, so feline remains from before 5000 BC found on the island (*see page 24*) suggest that cats were taken there, perhaps even as pets. Remains from before 4000 BC have also been found near Harappa, in the Indus valley.

The earliest remains from Egypt that show a possible affectionate relationship between cats and people are as old as those from Harappa. At a burial ground in Mostagedda, Middle Egypt, a man was buried with a gazelle near his head and a small cat by his feet; Egyptologists believe that the gazelle was intended to serve as his funerary meal, and the cat was his pet.

Egypt's first permanent human settlements, with their granaries and silos, appeared around 4000 BC. This unique development offered concentrations of rodents and edible waste, together with abundant shelters and safety from larger predators, to any cat willing and able to take advantage of them. Two small cats, the jungle cat *Felis chaus* (*see page 16*) and the African wildcat *Felis silvestris lybica* (*see page 19*), lived in this region. With a less fearful nature, the African wildcat was prepared to enter this new environment in search of its preferred rodent prey. A further minor genetic mutation, perhaps involving the hormonal control of emotions (*see page 58*), created a population with a unique survival advantage – an ability to live and breed in human settlements.

Birth place of the domestic cat
Although there is evidence that cats lived alongside humans in other places, the floodplains and delta of the Nile have yielded the most abundant records of feline domestication.

NILE BASIN

• BUBASTIS

EL LISHT •

• BENI HASAN

• MOSTAGEDDA

ABYDOS •

Records of domestication
The development of settlements and agriculture along the fertile floodplains of the Nile provided the indigenous wildcat with the potential of a new environmental niche. From this time onward, burials and paintings provide tantalizing scraps of evidence for a growing relationship between felines and humans. The absorption of the domesticated cat into Egyptian society seems to have been complete by about 2000 BC, and was followed by its recognition as the symbolic embodiment of a deity.

The African wildcat's natural lifestyle
In its natural environment, for which it has evolved over millennia, the African wildcat has very little stress from overcrowding, but it faces fierce competition for mates, prey, and territory: few kittens live to adulthood. Domestication suits stress-tolerant animals that can accept more crowding.

Living in two worlds
The development of agriculture around 4000 BC (*see right*) opened up a new world of possibilities to the wildcat; here was an unprecedented abundance of ready prey gathering around crop fields and granaries. To take advantage of this bounty, however, the cat had to be able to tolerate living not only at higher densities of population, but also in close proximity to other species. The first feline remains in a human tomb, found at Mostagedda, date from around this significant time. Others exist from the following millennia, although it is hard to say exactly how domesticated these cats were.

ADAPT AND SURVIVE

Under these new environmental pressures, the wildcat evolved into the domestic cat. There were enduring changes in its character. Placidity became an increasing asset, since only the most placid and least fearful could survive in close proximity to so many people and animals. Sympathetic people became substitute parents for motherless kittens. Uniquely, compared with other wildcat subspecies, kittens raised by people during the critical first seven weeks of life did not develop a fear of them on reaching adulthood; they remained willing companions.

There were also physical changes. Camouflage was no longer needed, so coat pattern and color mutations that would not have survived in the wild were perpetuated in the settlement cats. The gastrointestinal system changed to cope with a more varied diet; the domestic cat's intestines are longer than the wildcat's. The brain became almost 30 percent smaller because the cat was no longer so dependent upon its senses for survival.

THE ROAD TO SUCCESS

People recognized the value of the newly domesticated cats as vermin killers, but they probably also served a less well-known purpose. Rats and mice were devastating pests, but poisonous snakes, both indoors and outdoors, were lethal. There was little that people could do to safeguard themselves from cobras and vipers, so supreme, fearless hunters such as wildcats were tolerated or even openly welcomed in settlements for their willingness to hunt snakes as well as rodents. The cat became overwhelmingly popular because of its humble origins and its doubly protective role.

The ancient Egyptians developed a deep respect and understanding of cats and their behavior, in time even turning them into symbols of deities. Some researchers claim that the cat itself eventually became a deity of sexuality or fertility in Egypt, but such direct worship of felines is unlikely. What is certain is that the cat's natural behavior ensured that it became a prominent symbol in religion and superstitions, and its image became incorporated into a huge variety of objects. The domestic cat was now exportable; at first, only stories and images of the domestic cat were carried around the Mediterranean, but these reports were soon to be followed by the cats themselves.

Direct descendent
Today's pets remain close to the ancient stock of self-domesticated wildcats – at heart, virtually nothing has been either added or taken away. Without socialization in kittenhood, even the most selectively bred pedigreed cat will turn its back on countless generations of domestication; given the chance and a little practice, it will hunt and defend its territory just like a wildcat.

In the heart of the home
Those cats that could overcome natural timidity and solitary habits found the human home to be a safe and comfortable niche. By 2000 BC, the cat was well established, appearing in hieroglyphics from El Lisht. The first artwork to show a cat in a domestic setting dates from c. 1950 BC and was found at Beni Hasan. In keeping with the elaborate coding of later Egyptian art, the mistress of the house is indicated by the cat crouching beneath her chair (see left). It was in the Ptolemaic period, from 333–30 BC, that cat worship reached its peak, centered on Bubastis in the Nile delta.

HYBRID THEORIES

Among the many mummified feline remains found at Beni Hasan, thought to have been offerings to Bastet (see page 26), are several large skeletons of the marsh-dwelling jungle cat Felis chaus. This has led some to speculate that the domestic cat is in fact an evolutionary hybrid of the African wildcat and the jungle cat. However, Professor Eric Hurley's genetic studies of the cat, which use minute examinations of gene sequences, suggest that the domestic cat is genetically far too similar to the African wildcat to be a hybrid with any other species, including the jungle cat.

Discredited ancestor
The role of Felis chaus in the development of the domestic cat has long been disputed; the first scientific evidence appears to rule it out.

CATS
AND PEOPLE

HISTORICALLY, CATS HAVE PLAYED A remarkably ambivalent role in human society. Worshipped as beneficent gods in some cultures, they were castigated as the agents of evil in others, including Western Christianity. In the last 150 years our relationship with the cat has changed dramatically. Although in literature and art it is sometimes still equated with witchcraft and immorality, in the modern culture of advertising and entertainment the cat now represents sensuousness and refinement. The great success of the cat in surpassing the dog as man's most popular animal companion in North America, Britain, and elsewhere is ample evidence of its universal appeal to modern sensibilities.

ABOVE FEMALE RUDDY SOMALI

LEFT MEDIEVAL MANUSCRIPT PORTRAYING CATS AS HUNTERS

THE SPREAD OF THE CAT

THE DOMESTIC CAT HAS BEEN A REMARKABLY SUCCESSFUL MIGRANT; in a relatively short space of time, it has spread from the Near East and Africa to all the continents except Antarctica, and on to many islands. Early in their dispersal, cats may have been transported simply to satisfy people's curiosity, but the cause of their continued success was the spread of the mouse and rat. Cats became a valuable commodity in the war against rodents, and it was in this "terminating" role that they traveled across the world's trade routes, eventually reaching the New World. In total, the domestic cat population currently numbers hundreds of millions worldwide.

Language studies offer interesting clues about where cats originated and when they traveled. In his classic work, *A History of Domesticated Animals* (1963), naturalist Frederick Zeuner claimed that the cat came from the Near East and Africa, and discussed the origins of its various names. He theorized that the word "cat" was of North African descent and came from the Berber word *kadiska*, which corresponds with biological evidence that points to this region as the origin of the domestic cat. In other parts of North Africa and the Middle East, the domestic cat was known as *kadis* in Nubian, *qato* in Syrian, and *quttah* in Arabic.

FELINE NOMENCLATURE

The ancient Egyptians used the onomatopoeic word *miou* for the domestic cat, now reinstated in the modern breed name Egyptian Mau. When cats first arrived in Greece they were called *gale* (the Greek name for polecats), while the Latin word *felis* was used to denote any yellowish carnivore, which included the weasel, the polecat, and the cat. By AD 100, the word *katoikidios* was attributed to the cat in Greek texts, and 200 years later *cattus* had supplanted *felis* in Latin. Variations of these words entered many other languages, including French with *chat*, Spanish and Portuguese with *gato*, Italian with *gatto*, Swedish and Norwegian with *katt*, Danish and Dutch with *kat*, German with *katz*, Czech with *kocka*, and Russian with *koshka*.

CONQUERING THE WORLD

In mapping the spread of the cat, one of the most significant finds comes from a tomb in Cyprus, thought to be the remains of an African wildcat, *Felis libyca*, dating from about 5000 BC. This cat, which must have been imported, was a domestic animal but still as large as a wildcat.

It seems that the cat reached India, probably with Phoenician traders, by 500 BC, and in all likelihood even earlier: the two Indian epics, the *Mahabharata* and *Ramayana* both mention the cat, and are dated *c.* 300 BC. It is, however, much harder to map the arrival of the domestic cat in countries of Asia. Dates vary between 2000 BC and AD 400 for the cat's arrival in China and Southeast Asia, while the traditional date of

AD 999 for Japan (*see page 30*) does seem rather late considering the proximity of these lands. The comparatively late arrival of the cat in Europe was undoubtedly due to the embargo that the Egyptians placed on this sacred animal. But with the advent of Christianity, the cat traveled north with the expanding Roman Empire, eventually reaching southern Russia and northern Europe around AD 100. A cat skeleton excavated from a Roman villa at Lullingstone in southeast England supports this theory. Around the same time, cats arrived in Norway under a different escort, possibly accompanying returning mercenaries from Byzantium (now Istanbul). Surprisingly, it took another 400 years for the cat to reach Latvia, by which time cats were being traded freely throughout most of Europe.

There was then a very long period before the cat embarked on its voyage to the New World. Although French Jesuits took cats to Quebec in the 1500s, and at least one cat accompanied the Pilgrims to America on the *Mayflower* (1620), it was not until the 1700s that cats appeared in the New World in appreciable numbers, when settlers in Pennsylvania imported them to control a plague of rodents.

Domestic adaptation

The majority of skulls from Egyptian cat cemeteries resemble Felis libyca *(see page 20). Since the first cats were domesticated, subtle, gradual changes in coat color have arisen through climate, terrain, and artificial selection. American and Australian coat colors show that cats traveled here from British ports in the 1700s and 1800s respectively. Cats with an almost white "Van" bicolor originated in Byzantium (later known as Constantinople, now as Istanbul), but became isolated in Scandinavia after being taken there by returning traders and mercenaries.*

Spiritual effigy

This wooden feline effigy, dating from around 1450, was found at Key Marco in southwestern Florida. It is believed to be a ritual item symbolizing a spiritual connection between the human and animal kingdoms. The Key Marco feline could be mistaken for a domestic cat, except that it predates the cat's arrival in the Americas and is more likely to be a Florida panther.

NORTH AMERICA 18TH CENTURY

French funerary stele

Similar to modern-day tombstones, funerary steles were once erected to commemorate the dead. One theory suggests that it was customary for the Romans and Gauls, who buried their dead children with their toys, also to show them with their pets – such as in this stele of a boy called Laetus (*c.* AD 100). The pet, in this case a cat, was thought to assist in a safe journey to the afterlife.

Scandinavian figurine
This rudimentary cat, carved in amber, was found in an archaeologial excavation of a site in northern Sweden. It is thought to date from the 9th century. Such artifacts indicate that the domestic cat was established, if not commonplace, across Scandinavia by this time.

Canine confrontation
When cats first settled in mainland Greece they were probably viewed with curiosity. This Greek marble relief (c. 500 BC), shows a cat and a dog being introduced. The interest shown by the observing men indicates that the intention was to see the outcome of this controlled confrontation, while the use of leashes indicates that the animals were regarded as personal property.

Middle Eastern statuette
Found in Lachish, Israel, this ivory cat carving dates from around 1700 BC. Although the Egyptians forbade the exportation of their most revered animal, regular commercial traffic between Egypt and other Middle Eastern ports would have assisted the cat's eventual migration.

RUSSIA
AD 700

BRITAIN
AD 100

JAPAN
C. AD 600

INDIA
500 BC

Protective feline spirit
The inscription on this Buddhist scripture warns, "If you dream of a kitten and your small child lolls out its tongue, then you may know that this spirit is the cause of the trouble. Sacrifice to it and all will be well." This script was originally part of a set depicting 16 female spirits with animal heads, all of which were concerned with protecting the young, from Dunhuang, Chinese Central Asia (9th century).

Turquoise pottery
Only this tiny fragment remains from a piece of glazed Persian pottery, dating from around the late 13th century. Although the nose is missing, the embossed head is recognizably that of a feline, and positioned slightly above it is the figure of a bird.

AUSTRALIA
19TH CENTURY

Fertility talisman
The increase in the popularity of the cat deity Bastet (see page 30) in late Egypt (c. 600–200 BC) was reflected in the large numbers of cat talismans which were produced at that time. This bronze female cat with kitten may have been presented to Bastet as an expression of gratitude or in expectation of future favors, especially in connection with matters such as fertility and child care.

CAT-VENERATING RELIGIONS

ALTHOUGH IT IS NOT AS COMMON IN MODERN CULTURES, ANIMAL worship was once widespread. Deities who were not depicted in animal form usually had a sacred animal that typified their attributes, and cats of all sizes were among the animals that played such a role. The big cats, such as lions and jaguars, were often associated with protective forces, whereas the domestic cat symbolized more "feminine virtues," especially fertility. Because of its natural nocturnal inclinations, the cat also came to be seen as a guardian of the night and sometimes death's companion, which may have led to its later associations with magic and the devil.

Many religions have incorporated cat worship in one form or another. It is generally agreed that the domestic cat originated in North Africa, which is probably why the ancient Egyptians were the first to recognize its religious potential. In South America, where big cats were prevalent, early societies similarly incorporated the jaguar and cougar into their pagan rites.

Religious charm
Small cat amulets, such as this one (c. 305–30 BC), were probably worn as jewelry by Egyptian worshippers of Bastet.

EGYPTIAN CAT CULTS
Cult activities reflecting the ancient Egyptian fascination with felines focused chiefly on two anthropomorphic deities – the lion-headed goddess Sekhmet and her sister, the cat-headed Bastet. Religious or royal associations with "the king of the beasts" were common worldwide, but a cult based on the domestic cat was unique.

Bastet was a contradictory figure because she held the dual associations of life and death. This connection was taken to the extreme with the mummification of large numbers of domestic cats. During the late 19th century, excavators at the temple of Bast at Beni Hassan, Egypt, discovered over 300,000 mummified cats at a single site – unfortunately they were shipped to Britain, ground up, and sold as fertilizer. This extraordinary find shows the prevalence of cat worship.

After the mummies had been offered to the gods, priests gathered them up, and buried them in nearby cat cemeteries. When a cat died, its owners would try to give it a decent burial. They went into deep mourning and shaved off their eyebrows. Temple priests even killed and preserved specially bred cats, then sold them to pious pilgrims as cheap versions of the highly desirable cat statues cast in bronze.

In Egypt, to kill a cat, even unintentionally, was punishable by death. Historian Herodotus (484–424 BC) told the tale of an unfortunate Greek who did just that. Extreme veneration for the cat contributed to the eventual downfall of the Egyptian empire.

WILD FELINE DEITIES
Domestic cats did not reach the Americas until after the arrival of the European immigrants, but the jaguar and other cats of the New World had their place in the pantheons of its early cultures. Beliefs among South American peoples included the idea of medicine men turning into jaguars after death, and the concept of the cougar as *amigo del christiano*, or the Christian's friend, after a young Spanish girl's life was said to have been saved by a cougar.

Egyptian funeral stele
On this tomb stele, or stone, from about 1250 BC, two cats are stationed over a man and his wife. The inscription is a hymn to the "great cat" Atu, and the "perfect god," known as the sun god, Ra.

Mediterranean painted vase
Domestic cats and their habits were undoubtedly well known in the classical world. On this vase (c. 600 BC), two figures – the seated one may be Aphrodite – play with a ferocious-looking cat and a white pigeon.

CLASSICAL IMAGES
Greek mythology reveals a wealth of symbolism concerning the lion, but very little involving the domestic cat. But there is some ambiguity in the mythical tales concerning the multifaceted goddess, Artemis. She was originally regarded as a lioness, but was credited with creating the cat, and later fled to the moon in cat form.

The Roman equivalent of Artemis was Diana. Both were revered as great hunters as well as moon goddesses – the moon is said to rule fertility, which links these deities with Bastet (*see page 30*). The Romans imported many of their cultural inspirations from Greece; Venus, goddess of love and sexual pleasure, also equates with the Greek Aphrodite, Egyptian Bastet, and Norse Freya. Venus is at once an affectionate little kitten and a savage cat armed with teeth and claws, an embodiment of maternal emotions. Paintings of Venus as goddess of love frequently depict her with a cat.

Fertility instrument
Bastet, a goddess of pleasure, music, and dance, is linked with the ancient musical instrument called the sistrum, a form of rattle consisting of four beaded rods held in place by a loop, often used in fertility worship.

CATS IN PRE-CHRISTIAN EUROPE

Celtic and Nordic cultures integrated cats into their customs and folktales, which in turn became part of the early Christian faiths. For example, the Welsh pagan goddess Cerridwen (*c.* 800 BC) has a link with the fertility cat cult through her son, Taliesin, who changed himself into a grain of wheat to hide from her wrath. Cerridwen swallowed the wheat grain and nine months later her son was reborn. During a description of his other fantastic incarnations, Taliesin said, "I have been a cat with spotted head upon a tripod."

In Nordic legend, the fertility goddess Freya arrived in a chariot drawn by a team of cats. These legendary felines symbolized the twin qualities of their Scandinavian mistress, namely fecundity and ferocity. Like real cats, they were normally affectionate and loving, but could be fierce when aroused. Far up in the north, Finnish people also believed in a cat-drawn sledge, but this time it was sent to fetch their souls. An account of this can be found in the epic Finnish poem *The Kalevala*.

Not all cat associations have been benign. After all, the giver of life was equally connected with the realms of the dead. In the Germanic myth of Thor and the Midgard Serpent, we get a glimpse of the cat's more sinister associations when the Midgard Serpent, who is bent on destroying the earth, is disguised as a cat. In Christianity, the serpent represents evil and betrayal. This story may have been a forerunner of the many tales of perfidy and evil concerning the cat in later religions (*see page 28*).

ISLAMIC BELIEFS

Neither the ancient Sumerian nor Babylonian religions had records of a cat cult as such, although an ancient Persian legend maintained that the cat was born from the lion's sneeze.

Widespread cat appreciation came later, due to a variety of tales associating cats with the Islamic prophet Muhammad. One legend tells of a cat that saved the Prophet from almost certain death from a snake bite. Another tells of a cat, Muezza, that lived with Muhammad in Damascus. After completing his work one day, Muhammad saw that Muezza had fallen asleep on the flowing sleeve of his garment. Out of respect for Muezza, Muhammad cut away the

Babylonian lion relief

The lion is an ancient symbol of royalty. For example, this lion relief – dated between 604 and 561 BC – was excavated from the Babylonian city of Ishtar and is now on display in the Archaeological Museum in Instanbul.

Sacred golden puma

From about 600 BC onward, Peruvian peoples have worshipped a puma god, which their early artists made in a variety of stylized forms.

sleeve rather than disturb his sleeping companion. To this day, because of this story, cats are allowed to enter all mosques freely. Stories such as this were brought from the Holy Land to Europe by crusaders from France, Italy, Germany, Spain, and Britain. The cat became associated with Islam, and this is one reason why the Catholic Church was so successful in its efforts to equate cat ownership with heresy (*see page 28*), and later with evil.

SACRED CATS OF ASIA

The Hindu and Parsee religions are known for their respect for all living creatures. In theory, at least, each orthodox Hindu household is expected to feed and house a cat. The Parsees – established from a group of Persians that settled in India during the 8th century – considered it a serious crime to kill a cat, although it did not attract the death penalty as it had in Egypt.

In the original canons of Buddhism, the cat is excluded from the list of protected animals because of an incident that took place at the time of the Buddha's death. All the animals gathered, weeping, around the sacred remains; only the snake and the cat remained dry-eyed.

Venerable temple cats

In Buddhist temples across Asia, cats are kept as mousers. The Siamese breed is said to be descended from these temple cats, and many show the typical pointed pattern.

Then the cat pounced on the rat and ate it, proving its disregard for the solemn event. Today, cats can achieve nirvana (the attainment of ultimate serenity) like all other beings.

Early Chinese Buddhists revered the cat's self-containment. Its tendency to "meditate" gained it respect and protection, and its ability to see in the dark was thought to be of value in warding off evil spirits. Throughout China, cat figurines and amulets were used to keep both evil spirits and rats away from homes. In Japan, an analogous Buddhist tradition evolved. When a cat died, it was buried in, or near, the owner's temple. On the same day, a painted or sculpted likeness of the cat was offered at the temple altar. By doing this, the cat's owner gained assurance of tranquility and good fortune during the whole of his or her lifetime.

This overview of cat-venerating religions highlights many shared beliefs. Cats often hold an equivocal position; they can both bestow life, and they can take it away.

CATS AND CHRISTIANITY

MANY EARLY CHURCHES OCCUPIED PAGAN SITES, AND RELIGIOUS festivals often incorporated pagan symbols, particularly at the time when Christianity first spread across to Rome and northern Europe. The cat had many roles in the old religions, and these were sometimes incorporated into the new faith. The Church's ambivalent attitude toward cats has its roots in these beginnings. Some parts of the Church ignored their presence; others, such as the Russian Orthodox Church, valued and respected cats, and there are records of early Catholic Popes who treasured their cats. But in 1484 the Church turned upon cats, and for hundreds of years they were persecuted.

As independent and nocturnal creatures that lived alongside humans, cats became the subject of myth and folklore in many cultures. Deified in Egypt, they were associated elsewhere variously with the supernatural, evil, and fertility (*see pages 30–32*). It is perhaps unsurprising that when looking for enemies within, the Christian Church turned on the cat.

EARLY ACCEPTANCE

Although African wildcats are known to have lived in Israel thousands of years ago, there is no mention of cats in either the Old or New Testament. Christianity is unlikely to have inherited a position on cats from Judaism, which made no reference to them until around AD 500, when the Talmud briefly praised feline cleanliness. It was as Christianity spread to the

Middle East, North Africa, and the European continent that cats and other animals became part of the religious symbolism. Some pagan symbols were adopted by the early Church, while others were demonized. Jesus became known as "The Lion of Judah" while the snake, which was previously venerated in some North African religions, became the image of evil. One of the first Christian sects to evolve were the Egyptian Copts, in the first century AD. Their gospel included cats that were judges after death. This may be linked to the fact that the Egyptian god Osiris, the Lord of the Dead, was often represented in feline form.

In northern Europe, the early Celtic Church encouraged conversion to the new faith by accepting and adapting pagan traditions that did not conflict with the new teachings. The pagan reverence for the natural world was often incorporated into early Church teachings, and several saints from this period are associated with cats. For example, St. Gertrude of Nivelles is often depicted with a cat and is the patron saint of cats, gardeners, widows, and travelers. In France, February 5 was St. Agatha's feast day, when women were supposed to refrain from working. Those who were caught doing so were said to be confronted by the saint in the form of an angry cat. Another story that originated in France has it that the cat was the only creature who was privileged with knowing the path back to the Garden of Eden after Adam and Eve's expulsion, and this cat later took Jacob to the gates of heaven.

MEDIEVAL PERSECUTION

The earliest Christian association of cats with evil began in the 600s, when the Gnostics preached dualism. Dualism allowed the equal importance of the teachings of Jesus, Buddha, and Zoroaster. The Gnostics were considered heretics by the Church and were accused of placating the devil in the form of a black cat.

Feline martyr
Artists often used cats to represent evil. In this 1554 engraving, a cat dressed as a priest is hanged at an anti-Catholic demonstration in London.

Philosophical cat
St. Jerome is sometimes portrayed with a cat, rather than a lion, because cats were the traditional companions of philosophers. This 16th-century Flemish roundel is in Begbroke Church, near Oxford.

Five hundred years later, similar accusations of heresy were becoming common in Europe. In 1232, Pope Gregory IX established the Inquisition in order to detect heretics who, it was declared, worshipped the devil in the form of a black tomcat. In 1344, during an outbreak of St. Vitus's dance (a disease of the nervous system) in the French town of Metz, cats were blamed and publicly burned. In 1347–1348, the Black Death (bubonic plague) swept across Europe, reducing the population by a third. The disease was spread by rats, but cats were blamed. The Lord Mayor of London was one of many officials who ordered all cats to be destroyed, unwittingly removing the greatest barrier to the continuing spread of the disease.

Mother and child
Cats often feature in art and sculpture with the Virgin Mary. This may be due to the Italian legend about a cat whose kittens were born in the stable at the moment Jesus was born. Their descendents all have crosses on their backs.

Witches' companions
The association of cats with witchcraft has persisted in our imagination. The artist Théophile Steinlen, famous for his perceptive cartoon illustrations of cats, drew this fantastical picture of witches and cats in the 20th century.

Holy decoration
Heathen temples were often adorned with images of cats and birds. In the 20th century, these images appear in Christian places of worship. This carving is seen in a new cathedral in Washington, DC.

In the early 15th century, the Knights Templar, founded 250 years earlier to protect pilgrims on their way to the Holy Land, were accused of worshipping the devil, who appeared in the form of a black cat. The Church's persecution of people with principles that varied from orthodox Christian beliefs, and the association of these people with cats, led inevitably to the cat's association with paganism and witchcraft.

The shrieks of cats as they mated were interpreted as the cries of innocent people consumed by the "familiars." In Hungary, it was said that all cats automatically become witches between the ages of seven and twelve years unless a cruciform incision was made in their skin at birth. Old women were accused of turning themselves into black cats at night to slip into stables to harm cattle. The witch hunts spread through Europe and across the Atlantic to the American colonies, where they culminated, in 1692, in witch trials in Salem, Massachusetts; here, 150 people were accused of witchcraft and 20 were executed. In Europe, the association of cats with heresy and witchcraft led to cat "festivals" in which cats were tortured and killed. The Ypres Cat's Parade in France, which originated around AD 962, is an example. Cats were thrown from the belfry for being associated with witches.

Today, the rehabilitation of the cat is so well established that the Ypres Cat Parade is a popular attraction for cat lovers, who come to see models of cats paraded through the streets and cloth toy cats thrown from the belfry.

ACCEPTANCE OF CATS
During that period of intense persecution, cats were also beloved companions. In Russia, cats were the only animals that were permitted to live in nunneries and monasteries. Throughout Europe, many individuals, including members of the Church, kept cats, although most had to do so secretly for fear of persecution. With the Act of 1736 abolishing all witchcraft laws, the Catholic Church's antipathy toward cats began to diminish. In the 19th century, Pope Leo XII's cat, Micetto, was born in the Vatican, and later Pope Pius IX's cat sat on his knee while he gave audiences.

Demon cat
Flauros, a feline-headed demon, was invoked by those who wished to take revenge on other demons. This illustration is from the 1864 edition of Dictionnaire Infernal by occultist Collin de Plancy.

CATS AND WITCHCRAFT
In the 15th century, in Germany and elsewhere in Europe, there was a revival in pagan rites. The cult of Freya (*see page 26*) honored the fertility of cats. Cultists were first accused of heresy, but accusations of witchcraft soon followed. In 1484, Pope Innocent VIII decreed that witches worshipped Satan and that they took on the form of their animal helpers, called "familiars." The usual "familiar" was a cat.

Throughout Roman Catholic Europe, people were tortured and killed because they owned or cared for cats. A lack of understanding of cat behavior perpetuated the myths. Cats slept, or pretended to sleep, all day so that they could wake at night to guide evil spirits.

Peruvian fiesta (left)
This 18th-century drawing depicts a saint's day celebration in South America, in which the local inhabitants adorn themselves in various forms of feline-based costume and parade through their village.

St. Cadoc's cat (right)
A common European myth relates how the devil constructed a bridge and claimed for himself the first living being to cross over it. Here St. Cadoc is seen duping the devil, presenting him with a tiny cat instead of the human being he had hoped for.

CAT MAGIC AND SUPERSTITIONS

THE VERY NATURE OF THE CAT LENDS ITSELF TO IDEAS OF SORCERY and divination. Its large eyes dilate fully to see in the dark, causing the mirrorlike retinas to give a ghostly reflection, and its nocturnal habits have always been shrouded in mystery. Another puzzle is the cat's ability to live through plights that would be fatal to other animals, making it one of nature's best survivors. Combined, these factors have worked both for and against the cat. In some places it has been celebrated, even treated like a god, while in others it has been feared and treated with contempt. In short, wherever the cat has traveled, stories of magic and superstition have followed.

Although the cat is no longer worshipped and revered, as it was by the ancient Egyptians, many customs and superstitions that built up around it still exist in other cultures today.

FERTILITY ASSOCIATIONS

The domestic cat became associated with the Egyptian goddess Bastet (*see page 26*) about the Twenty-second Dynasty (945–715 BC). But it was not until the Ptolemaic period (332–30 BC) that the cat-headed Bastet's popularity reached its peak, when she was worshipped at a huge annual festival of revelry and sacrifice for bestowing the gifts of life and fertility.

Cat protection
This mummified cat is an unfortunate relic of the old European practice of bricking up a cat into the wall of a building as a charm against rodents or evil spirits.

Portent of nocturnal powers (below)
In early Tarot cards, the Fool is often a vagabond being bitten on his leg by a cat; today a dog is more usual. Symbolically, the cat warns of the powers of darkness.

Centuries later, in many parts of the world, cats were either buried beneath newly sown crops or beaten to death as a symbol of threshing and smoothing of the grain. This was to encourage a stronger crop next spring, and is perhaps testament to Bastet's fecundity. With the advent of Christianity the cat lost its position as a deity (*see page 28*). Instead, cats were often persecuted in the name of religion, which may be why the Church perpetuated ritual cat sacrifices. Based on the original Egyptian superstition that fire symbolized purity and fertility, cat sacrifices by fire became a part of the Halloween and Easter festivals. These feast days are still important to the Christian Church but luckily for the cat, sacrifices are not.

AGENTS OF FORTUNE

Superstitious beliefs persist that cats, and especially black ones, can bring both good and bad fortune – a belief that is often based on geography and ownership. As Moncrif, the first

Witch with magical cat
The notion of magical, witch's cats has died out as a superstition, and now only survives in semi-humorous illustrations like this one.

naturalist to rehabilitate the cat, wrote in his *History of Cats* (1727): "the color black works very well against cats in unsophisticated minds; it heightens the fire of their eyes, which is enough to make people believe they are witches at the very least." Black cats were said to be in league with the devil and as a result were often sacrificed. Later, the unfortunate black cat became a portent of good luck in Britain when it crossed your path; this was based upon the idea that evil had passed you by unharmed. In North America this is reversed on the basis that the black cat is an evil spirit: its mere presence is dangerous.

The cat's legendary introduction to Japan is said to have occurred on the tenth day of the fifth month of the year 999, when a Chinese mandarin presented the emperor, Ichijo, with a white female cat. The birth, shortly after, of a litter of five kittens in the imperial palace of Kyoto was a harbinger of a benign future for the cat in Japan. Today, the image of a cat with one paw raised in a beckoning movement is a

Good luck symbols (above)
The black cat on the right of this card is wearing a swastika, an auspicious sign associated with Buddha. In Britain, the black cat is viewed as a lucky omen.

Shooting stars (right)
In 1805 the cat-loving French astronomer Lalande introduced the cat in the sky map, with a constellation for ailurophiles called Fælis, since lost to us.

Japanese symbol of good luck and prosperity. It is known as the *Maneki-neko*, or Beckoning Cat. The legend began when some samurai followed a beckoning cat to a shrine, where they took shelter from a storm. They spread the fame of the shrine, and people brought their cats to be buried there and prayed for their feline souls and for luck in their own lives. The national cat of Japan, the Japanese Bobtail (*see page 196*) is also associated with fortune. It has been adopted by sailors, because its naturally occurring bobtail resembles the royal family's emblem – the chrysanthemum – and it is used as a talisman to ward off sea storms.

Talisman for success
Here, the raised left paw of the Japanese Maneki-neko, *or Beckoning Cat, promises* sen ryo, *or great wealth. A raised right paw promises* fuku, *or luck and happiness.*

MAGICAL POWERS

There is a long-standing tradition that cats can affect the weather, which perhaps stems from their earlier association with crop fertility. For example, in Cambodia an ancient custom involves taking a cat from village to village, where it is sprinkled with water to persuade Indra, the compassionate Vedic god, to send the rain necessary for a good harvest.

Throughout Europe and beyond, a cat with its paw behind its ear was a portent of rain. There may be some truth in this; one theory is that changes in air pressure before a storm may affect the cat's ears, causing it to paw at that area. Many other weather predictions have arisen from cat behavior, such as a cat purring and rubbing its nose for good weather, or yawning as a sign of rain.

The origin of the widespread superstition that a cat has nine lives, because of its amazing ability to survive, probably started in ancient Egypt, where the number nine held magical values. This idea was later adopted during the 17th century, when accusations of witchcraft were rife (*see page 28*). It was believed that a witch could take the shape of a cat nine times, and so a cat could effectively be reincarnated nine times as well. Maltreatment of cats was never institutionalized in China, as it was in Western Europe. This was perhaps because superstition gave cats the power to avenge themselves on their killers after death.

Medieval engraving
In this earliest surviving Western representation of the ages of man, the 70-year-old is shown with a cat. Both the cat and the dog have been linked with age and wisdom.

CLAIRVOYANCE

Astrology and alchemy were tolerated by the early Church, and practitioners used the cat in some horrendous rituals. However, it was believed that a harmless way to acquire clairvoyance was to live from early childhood with a tortoiseshell cat. Western astrology ignored the cat, but in the Chinese horoscope it is sometimes a substitute for the Rabbit, which represents the fourth sign of the zodiac. The cat has also appeared in the Tarot – the art of divining the future from the fall of cards. In early sets of Tarot cards the Fool is often shown as a vagabond with a cat biting his leg. In the Tarot the cat is linked with nocturnal powers.

ANCIENT BURIAL RITUALS

One superstition for which there is much material evidence was that if the body of a cat was built into a house wall, it would keep away rodents. This belief survived as late as the 18th century, and the dried, mummified corpses of cats have been found in many buildings in Europe.

In Thailand, the ritual burial of cats is based on religious creeds in the ancient manuscript scrolls, known as the *Cat Book Poems*. They state that when a man of great spiritual advancement dies, his soul enters the body of a cat, and then ascends to heaven on the death of the animal. At one time, this belief was part of the ritual burial of members of the Thai royal family, when a live cat was left in the tomb. There was a small hole in the tomb's roof, and when the cat emerged from it the monks knew that the departed soul had passed into the body of the cat.

This Thai ceremony, like all the other rituals mentioned here, is no longer performed. However, it seems that cat-based superstitions are still a large part of many cultures, and such old prejudices, especially against the black cat, die hard. In truth, cats are harmless animals – unless you happen to be a mouse.

Japanese shapeshifter
This picture is based on the story of a witch cat at Okabe, on the Tokaido road. In this scene, a demon cat with a typical double tail dances with the witch's attendant, watched by a huge spectral cat in the background.

Legendary creature
Sightings of a cat-headed creature with a snake's body, reported to attack livestock, reached legendary status in Italy, probably because it was never caught.

CAT FOLKLORE AND FAIRY TALES

WHEREVER CATS HAVE LIVED, STORIES AND PROVERBS HAVE EVOLVED around their behavior. Cats carry an air of mystery along with an aloof attitude, and these attributes have captured our imagination. One feature that is peculiar to the cat, more than to any other animal, is an association with magic, which is often manifested through the cat's ability to transform itself into different guises. Across the world, these magical cats, both good and bad, have become immortalized through pantomimes and plays. Cat stories, proverbs, and sayings enrich many languages, but most countries will have their own unique examples as well.

In all cultures, stories have been passed down through the ages by word of mouth, until certain gifted story-tellers decided to record these tales in print only a few centuries ago.

POPULAR FABLES AND PANTOMIMES

Many well-known fables are attributed to the Greek author Aesop (c. 6th century BC). Although these tales were rarely written down, they traveled verbally around the world until the French poet La Fontaine (1621–1695) adapted and embellished many of them. From this large collection of stories, the cat is often portrayed as a sly and devious creature, whose predatory greed is always at the forefront.

One fable in particular – *The Cat, the Weasel, and the Rabbit* – was an obvious criticism of human behavior. The rabbit and the weasel go to the elderly cat Raminagrobis to ask him to settle a dispute. In order to do this, the cat asks them to move closer and stand on some scales so that he can weigh his judgment for their case. When they do this, he lashes out and kills

them, thereby settling the dispute. La Fontaine neatly concludes: "This strongly resembles the squabbles which petty rulers sometimes have among themselves, before they are swallowed up by mighty kings." La Fontaine's Rodilard is a more sprightly version of Raminagrobis. In order to catch mice, he plays dead and also camouflages himself with flour.

Not all stories paint the cat in a bad light. There are tales of reciprocal kindness between humans and cats, as shown in the story of a Tuscan woman who is considerate to cats and is rewarded with gold, whereas her sister, who has no time for them, receives only scratches.

Traveling tales (left)
Many countries illustrate their folktales on national stamps, such as this Mongolian cat-and-mouse fable. The other stamp features a giant cat from the Faroe Islands, a figure from a traditional ballad.

Grimm's musicians
Around 1812, the Brothers Grimm recorded various stories, including The Bremen Town Musicians, *who are a troupe of animals, among which is a cat. They combine their vocal skills and natural weapons into a fearsome "monster" to scare robbers away from their spoils.*

Pantomimes are a theatrical amalgamation of the most popular folk stories and fairy tales, and two famous ones, *Puss in Boots* by the French author Charles Perrault (1628–1703) and *Dick Whittington*, both feature cats prominently. These cats, through cleverness, even magic, bring good fortune to those who are associated with them. Dick Whittington's cat is usually depicted as black, because in Britain black cats are a good omen (*see page 30*).

Cinderella is another well-loved pantomime. In modern productions the fairy godmother is played as a kindly woman, but in the original Italian version the part was written for a cat.

The world turned upside down (left)
For many centuries, before reading was widespread, moral stories were recorded in pictures so that people could understand them. Man Shoeing a Cat *is one of about 1,500 wall paintings from Taagerup Church in Denmark dating back to the early 1500s, in which the order of nature is reversed so that animals and people engage in strange, unexpected, and unreasonable behavior.*

Unlikely story (below left)
Little is known about the Egyptian "working classes" who were employed in the construction and decoration of royal tombs. Images such as this tabby cat herding a flock of geese, taken from a practice sketch (c. 1150 BC), may be part of some long-forgotten fable, or simply the artist's attempt to inject some humor into the scene.

Cautionary tale (right)
Aesop's tale of Venus and the Cat *is vividly illustrated here as the cat-maiden spies a mouse and gives chase. This fable is perpetuated in proverbs, such as the Biblical saying* "A leopard cannot change its spots," *and the succinct German proverb,* "The cat cannot leave the mouse."

Metamorphic cats

From ancient times, stories have been told of cats that are transformed into humans, often becoming beautiful women. Aesop's tale of *Venus and the Cat* concerns a cat who falls in love with a handsome young prince. Venus, the goddess of love, agrees to transform the cat into a beautiful girl, and when they meet the couple eventually marry. But Venus is not convinced that the cat's transformation is complete, so on their wedding night, she introduces a mouse into the couple's bedroom. Forgetting herself, the girl pounces on the mouse and devours it. The goddess, confirmed in her suspicions, decides she must turn the girl back into a cat.

In Japanese folklore, the shapeshifting cat is of a more sinister nature. In a tale similar to Western vampire myths, a demon cat attacks a fair maiden and sucks out her lifeblood. It then assumes her identity. In its new female form, the cat turns its attentions to the maiden's lover, Prince Nabéshima. By gradually extracting his life force, during nightly visits, the vampire cat weakens the prince to the point of death. He is saved just in time through the vigilance of his

Japanese vampire cat
A combination of the cat's finely honed predatory skills and its mysterious nocturnal movements may have inspired the story of The Vampire Cat of Nabéshima. *In Japanese fiction, devil cats are recognized by a bifurcated tail.*

faithful servant, and the impostor is eventually destroyed. A similar fable comes from Spanish-Jewish folklore. Lilith, Adam's first wife, leaves him to become a vampire in the form of a black cat, who then descends upon helpless, sleeping babies and sucks out their blood. This story may have contributed to the widespread belief that a cat may lie on a sleeping baby, causing suffocation.

Favorite proverbs and stories

All languages are rich in cat proverbs and cat sayings, many of which can be applied to feline or human behavior. The following selection cites only a few, out of hundreds of examples: from Spain "A cat with gloves cannot catch mice," from Italy "Old cats mean young mice," from the Netherlands, "The man who does not love cats will never get a pretty woman," from Britain, "Curiosity killed the cat," and finally from Russia "A cat and a woman are for the house, a man and a dog are for the yard."

Romantic tale (left)
In the late 17th century, Comtesse D'Aulnoy wrote Le Chatte blanche, *or* The White Cat. *Its roots probably lie in the "Venus" story, although in this version the prince cuts off the cat's head to turn her into a princess, and they then live happily ever after.*

Magical cat (right)
Dick Whittington, *one of the most popular British folktales, is also a splendid subject for pantomime. According to the legend, Dick came to London as a poor boy and, with the help of his magical cat, made his fortune.*

A well-loved but wily trickster
Of all the illustrations showing Perrault's amoral feline, Puss in Boots, *this one by Gustave Doré (1832–1883) is among the best. It is easy to believe that a cat portrayed in such a commanding manner could con his way into the king's court.*

There is an African folktale that neatly explains how the cat came to be the favorite companion of women all over the world. A cat is seeking the best animal to live with for protection. Each time the cat chooses a new protector, that animal is preyed upon by a stronger one, so the cat keeps moving on until finally it settles with a man. When the man goes home he is confronted by his wife, who in anger chases him from the house. From then on, the cat took shelter under the woman's protection.

Apart from the proverbs and stories, the cat has found its way into many words and colloquialisms. Most of these are directly related to cat behavior, such as "cat burglar" – a nimble thief, good at scaling walls, or "cat house" – a brothel.

Every language has its own particular feline stories, proverbs, and sayings, and if space allowed it, they would all be illustrated here. But as time moves on, it is more than likely that there will be a new range to choose from.

7. La Chatte Blanche

CATS IN CHILDREN'S LITERATURE

CHILDREN'S STORIES ARE OFTEN REMNANTS OF FOLKTALES, DISTANT myths and legends, and ancient pagan beliefs. In the 18th century, after centuries of persecution in Europe, the cat's reputation began to improve; as a consequence, it appeared in many a tale. Some children's stories are true to the real nature of cats, teaching young minds to recognize and understand typical feline behavior, but many tales are fictional, and were created purely for children's entertainment and delight. Stories of mysterious, fantastic, and magical cats have become particularly popular, and the cat is now an enduring figure in children's literature all over the world.

It was probably through fables and folk stories that the domestic cat first made its appearance in literature (*see page 32*). Because many of these tales were of a didactic nature, they came to be regarded as "morality tales" for teaching children, and became the basis for well-known fairy tales and children's stories.

PROTOTYPE CATS

In its original form, *The Adventures of Pinocchio* by Carlo Collodi (1826–1890) was a morality tale for adults, which later became classified as children's literature. In the original version, the cat was used to represent human hypocrisy, but first and foremost he was a street cat, surviving on his wits, and scavenging for food.

The real nature of the domestic cat is best described by Rudyard Kipling (1865–1936) in his classic story *The Cat that Walked by Himself*. Kipling tells the tale of how Woman tamed a number of animals to serve her and Man, and how she and Man almost, but not quite, tamed the cat. After a while, the cat went to them of his own accord and they eventually struck up a bargain. In return for milk and shelter, the cat agreed to kill mice and be kind to babies when he was in the house, but essentially "he is the Cat that walks by himself, and all places are alike to him."

A little-known British children's story from the 18th century is *The Life and Adventures of a Cat*, in which the hero is a cat named Tom. Until it was published, male cats were called "boars" or "rams," but ever since, in English-speaking countries, male cats have been known as "toms."

HUMANIZED CAT HEROES

The celebrated children's author Beatrix Potter (1866–1943), in common with the cartoonist and illustrator Louis Wain (*see page 50*), found success by humanizing her animal characters. Her tales began life as a series of letters to the children of a former governess, but are now household favorites across the

Dual nature
This confident feline is from The Cat that Walked by Himself, *written and illustrated by Rudyard Kipling. In the story, the cat is part tame and part independent.*

world. Her characters have faults, just like real people; Mr. McGregor's white cat is someone to be avoided, according to Benjamin Bunny in *The Tale of Peter Rabbit*, but in *The Tale of Tom Kitten* and *The Tale of Samuel Whiskers*, cats are portrayed as likable characters who are naughty but nice.

In the mid-20th century, new feline heroes appeared in children's literature. The American author Kathleen Hale (1898–) based the marmalade cat Orlando, his wife, Grace, and their kittens, Pansy, Blanche, and Tinkle, on her own cats. Orlando's adventures grew into a series of 18 books that, with their humorous

Famous grin (above)
In Alice in Wonderland, *as Alice talks to the Cheshire Cat, it slowly disappears until only a disembodied grin remains. Among the many possible origins of this cat is a brand of Cheshire cheese, which featured a cat's grin on its packaging.*

Marmalade cat (right)
For over 30 years, the children's author Kathleen Hale wrote and illustrated her Orlando *adventures, in which her affable marmalade cat takes a trip abroad, becomes a doctor, celebrates his wedding, and, in 1968, even goes to the moon.*

CHARLES FOLKARD /11.

The ultimate survivor (left)
This illustration from The Adventures of Pinocchio *shows the cat escaping from an altercation between Pinocchio and his creator. The story of a puppet that becomes a boy is now a children's classic, but originally it was an Italian morality tale in which the cat represented hypocrisy.*

Lear's seafaring characters (below left)
While living and working in Italy, Edward Lear was inspired by his beloved tabby, Foss, to write the magical verse of The Owl and the Pussycat. *Edward Lear illustrated all his work with simple line drawings that were strikingly modern for their time.*

Cautionary tale (below)
The lessons to be learned in children's literature are often harsh. In the French story La Boîte d'allumettes, *or* The Box of Matches, *a young girl plays with matches, accidentally sets herself on fire, and burns to death. Her two faithful cats extinguish the flames with their tears.*

plots and distinctive illustrations, are now classics of children's literature. Since Hale's long-running success, the fashion for the "cat series" appears to have died out. Although modern cat protagonists such as Mog, the witch's cat, and the ghost cat Fred have their fans, the current trend in children's literature seems to be for unusual animals, fantastic creatures, and even teddy bears.

POETIC CATS

Many creative people have gained inspiration from their cats, and poets are no exception. The British-born artist and humorist Edward Lear (1812–1888) based his famous verse, *The Owl and the Pussycat*, on his much-loved tabby, Foss. However, it was possibly through rose-tinted glasses that Lear addressed Foss: "What a beautiful Pussy you are," because Foss had a stocky body and a shortened tail. Despite these unconventional looks, Foss made a perfect model for Lear, and is now also immortalized in cartoon form.

Another devoted cat fan, T.S. Eliot (1888–1965), based his collection of 14 cat poems, *Old Possum's Book of Practical Cats*, on his numerous cats. Each poem is a play on the English language – which can be lost through translation – with characters such as Growltiger, Rumpuscat, and the mystery cat Macavity. Eliot gave his cats human traits, while managing to keep the essence of their feline nature.

Moral lesson
In the 19th-century morality tale Poor Minette, *good and bad cat spirits fight over the tempted soul of the ingénue cat, Minette.*

MISCHIEVOUS CATS

The cat's association with magic and sorcery has long been utilized in children's literature. Lewis Carroll (1832–1898), author of the *Alice* books, put the famous Cheshire Cat among the characters found in Wonderland. When Alice sees a large cat, grinning from ear to ear, she asks, "Please would you tell me why your cat grins like that?" The answer she receives is, "It's a Cheshire Cat and that's why." This opaque reply may have come from the saying to "grin like a Cheshire caterling"; caterlings were deadly swordsmen, who protected the Royal Forests in the reign of Richard III. Over time, caterling became shortened to cat, and anyone seen with a notably evil smile was said to be "grinning like a Cheshire cat."

Writing under the pen name of Dr. Seuss, Theodor Seuss Geisel (1904–1991) created perhaps the most successful and undoubtedly the most mischievous of all modern literary cats in *The Cat in the Hat*. A gawky, subversive cat in a stovepipe hat decides to keep two bored children entertained while their mother is away. Chaos ensues, but this magical feline manages to return everything to normal just before the mother returns. If only reality were as anarchic, and at the same time as controlled, as in these bewitching cat books.

CATS IN LITERATURE

DOMESTIC CATS PLAYED A MINOR ROLE IN THE HISTORY OF EARLY writing, appearing more often in fables, proverbs, and children's stories than in major works of literature. This began to change in the 19th century as the cat's popularity increased and it became an acceptable literary subject, even starring as the central character.

Cats, with their associated charm and mystery, have proved to be universally captivating – writers as diverse as Pierre Loti, Anton Chekhov, H.G. Wells, and Don Marquis have all paid tribute to them in stories, essays, or poems. Today, a wealth of publications are available to suit the tastes of every kind of cat lover.

Cats and writers often live together, perhaps because these individuals are temperamentally suited. Unlike dogs, cats never interrupt the creative flow with loud barking or demands for a walk; instead they are quite happy to amuse themselves or sleep quietly nearby.

PROVERBS AND APHORISMS

Cat proverbs are found in all languages; some make reference to the cat's prowess and special instincts, a few to its grace and beauty. From China comes the comment, "A lame cat is better than a swift horse when rats infest the palace." The Irish say, "If a cat had a dowry she would often be kissed." A proverb from the American South has it that "The cat is mighty dignified, until the dog comes by." From Britain comes the saying, "In the cat's eyes, all things belong to cats."

Many cat-loving writers have made memorable comments about their admired felines. Canadian novelist Robertson Davies (1913–1995) wittily described the mutually beneficial relationship in his line, "Authors like cats because they are such quiet, lovable, wise creatures, and cats like authors for the same reason." Davies was not alone in his fond feelings for cats. The novelist Sidonie-Gabrielle Colette (1873–1954), author of *Gigi*, was one of the literary world's great cat lovers. "By associating with a cat," she wrote, "one only risks becoming richer." Another commentator was the British Prime Minister Sir Winston Churchill, who was awarded the Nobel Prize for Literature in 1953.

Commemorative stamp
Russian author Aleksandr Pushkin (1799–1837) almost always kept feline company. He included many in his stories, and sketched them for relaxation. Issued by his homeland, this stamp commemorates his literary works and acknowledges his affection for cats.

Generally known as a commanding orator, he reportedly said, "All dogs look up to you. All cats look down to you. Only a pig looks at you as an equal." Théophile Gautier rather pithily added that "The cat is a dilettante in fur."

The American writer of books for adults as well as children, Samuel Langhorne Clemens (1835–1910), better known by his pen name Mark Twain, was devoted to his cats. He was often photographed with them and liked to give them whimsical names such as Apollinaris, Blatherskite, and Zoroaster. He explained that the names were not given "in an unfriendly spirit, but merely to practise the children in large and difficult styles of pronunciation."

THE CAT AND THE POET

One of the earliest, and perhaps most beautiful, homages to the cat was written in Gaelic by an anonymous Irish monk during the 8th or early 9th century. Famous throughout Ireland as *Pangur Bán*, meaning "whiter than white," the poem describes their life, with the monk hunting for words while the cat hunts mice.

> Oftentimes a mouse will stray
> Into the hero Pangur's way;
> Oftentimes my keen thought set
> Takes a meaning in its net.

The Italian poet Torquato Tasso (1544–1595) succumbed to delusion and was interred in an asylum, as was the British poet Christopher Smart (1722–1771). Strangely, both found the environment conducive to feline verse. Tasso produced the work *Sonnet To My Cats*, whereas Smart penned *Jubilate Agno* – with a section to *My Cat Jeoffrey* – which was turned into an operetta by Benjamin Britten (1913–1976). Other famous poets from Wordsworth to Baudelaire have eulogized their feline friends.

Gruesome story (left)
This illustration, from The Black Cat *by Edgar Allen Poe (1809–1849), shows the gruesome moment when Pluto, the black cat, reveals his master as the murderer of his wife. Oddly, Poe was reputed to be a cat lover.*

Poetic sphinx (below)
In his epic poem, The Sphinx, *the Irish writer Oscar Wilde (1854–1900) extols the feminine traits of this mysterious, mythical creature.*

Portrait of an artist (left)
This portrait (1910) of the French writer Pierre Loti (1850–1923) was made shortly after the success of his book Au Maroc, *or* In Morocco, *which probably explains why he is wearing a fezlike hat. He is shown with a cat because Loti was well known as a great cat lover, and wrote repeatedly about his feline pets.*

Feline sleuth (right)
Like many authors, American-born crime writer Patricia Highsmith (1921–) chooses feline company, and like others in her genre, she chooses a Siamese. This breed has a peculiar attraction for the sleuthing novelist, possibly because of its age-old reputation for almost human intelligence.

Catlike behavior
Colette loved cats. She was photographed with them, she included them in her works, and even portrayed them herself in the theater. As well as portraying an excellent sphinx, she played a cat on stage in La Chatte amoureuse.

Don Marquis (1878–1937), the American writer, is known for *archy and mehitabel*, the verse adventures of the cockroach archy and the cat mehitabel, written entirely in lower case. As the story unfolds, mehitabel emerges as an aspiring lady whose natural "alley cat" inclinations prevail in the end.

REVEALING CAT STORIES

Fiction is often based on autobiographical material and many authors have reconstructed their "cat experiences" to great effect. Anton Chekhov (1860–1904) wrote of how his uncle Pyotr tried to train his kitten to kill mice. Each time a mouse was caught in a trap, Uncle Pyotr grabbed the kitten and pushed its face toward the unfortunate rodent. Naturally, when it was released, the terrified kitten ran away. Forever after, on catching sight of a mouse, the cat trembled and took to ignominious flight. Chekhov was taught Latin by the same uncle, and afterward always reacted to the Classics much as the cat reacted to mice.

In her short story *The Cat*, Colette recounts the short-lived marriage of the petulant Camille to the doting Alain. Sadly, Alain's doting affection is for Saha, his Russian Blue cat, and in a jealous rage Camille attempts to kill Saha. Alain guesses Camille's wicked deed, and, faced with an ultimatum, chooses Saha. This tale is not unlike the author's real-life experiences with men.

People have a lasting fascination with the idea of the human in animal form, as seen from folklore and fairy tales (*see page 32*). Humanized cats make interesting characters. One of the most outspoken is Tobermory, the feline creation of Saki (1870–1916), whose real name was H.H. Munro.

Tobermory acquired the gift of speech and, with a feline disregard for the consequences, used his gift with devastating effect on members of a high-society house party.

GENRE FICTION

For those with a combined love of cats and mystery, there is a specific genre of books available – the detective novel. At the turn of the 20th century, Guy Boothby, an Australian novelist, based his books on the sleuthing skills of Dr. Nikola and Apollyon, a black cat. A little later, Dorothy L. Sayers (1893–1957) gave her detective Lord Peter Wimsey a crest, featuring a cat with the motto "As my whimsy takes me."

The contemporary American author Lilian Jackson Braun began writing her *The Cat Who...* mysteries when one of her treasured Siamese cats mysteriously fell to its death from an

Farmyard tales
The story of Turi and Kamphau'ern, two cats from adjacent farms, was told and illustrated by Norwegian artist Olaf Gulbrannson (1873–1958). The dramatic tale of love and death reads like an account of human intrigues.

apartment window. There are now more than a dozen books to choose from, all featuring the highly talented Koko and Yum Yum, Siamese cats with a bent for detection. Another contemporary author, Akif Pirinçci (1959–), this time from Germany, wrote the compelling novel of cats and murder, *Felidae*, later made into a cartoon film (*see page 46*).

The ultimate genre, for fantastic invention, must be science fiction. In *The Invisible Man*, one of the first writers in this genre, H.G. Wells (1866–1946), made his ill-fated scientist try out his new drug on a cat before taking it himself. Cats find a more comfortable home elsewhere in science fiction. C.J. Cherryh (1942–), for example, based one of her alien races on cats in her *Chanur* series of books. Robert A. Heinlein (1907–1988) was also a fan of felines. He immortalized his own cat, Pixel, by giving that name to the title character in *The Cat Who Walked Through Walls* – a cat who does just that, because he thinks that he can.

During the 1980s, publishers discovered that "the cat book" sells, and consequently a glut of them appeared on the market. Of these, many are either fictional or anecdotal, but some are prized for originality or comprehensive coverage. Serious tomes, such as *The Literary Companion to Cats* and *The Cat in Ancient Egypt*, now vie for the book buyer's attention with many more recreational titles, including *The Internet for Cats, Testing Your Cat's IQ*, and *Yoga for Cats*. All of these books have their own particular appeal. In fact, hundreds of new titles are published worldwide each year, and before too long the "cat book" may well qualify as a separate genre in itself.

CATS IN EASTERN ART

LARGE CATS SUCH AS LIONS AND TIGERS WERE FREQUENTLY PAINTED or sculpted as images of power and leadership, from Persia to India and on to China. In Persia, lions were symbols of royalty and can often be found on the walls and pillars of ancient palaces such as the magnificent ruins of Isfahan. In China, the tiger is considered the "Lord of the Beasts," and features heavily in myth and symbolism. As the cat spread eastward, it naturally basked in the glory of its larger relatives, and consequently found its own related niche in art. Artists had little difficulty in capturing the essence of these relatives of the venerated lion and tiger.

Eastern art forms, although highly structured and stylized, can be vividly natural and much truer to feline behavior than contemporaneous Western art. In Eastern art, bicolors and tortie-and-white cats are by far the most commonly portrayed, suggesting that those patterns were preferred by the travelers who took the cat to Asia, or by the people who lived there.

Artistic license
The swirls and gilding on this 13th-century cat from Rayy, Persia, indicate that this is a typical example of Islamic art.

PERSIAN ART
Muslims regard the cat with favor because it was the pet of Muhammad (*see page 26*), but there is no tradition of representational art in Islam. Therefore, cat images from the Middle East – where cats were plentiful and longhaired cats evolved – are extremely rare. Only a few small figurines, paintings on tiles, and bottles and boxes in the shape of cats have been found. It is in the works of visiting Western painters that we first see cats lazing luxuriously at the feet of Arab scribes or being fed tasty morsels by Arab women.

However, in the 14th century, anonymous Ottoman artists did paint striking narrative scenes of national folktales and stories from the Bible, often including domestic cats in an incidental role in their tableaus.

INDIAN AND FAR EASTERN ART
In India, most early interpretations of cats are found in carved or painted religious images; for example, a goddess of fertility may be seen riding a cat. In painted scenes that told a

Breed beginnings
By the 19th century, cats that could be the forebears of the Japanese Bobtail (see page 144) appear in Japanese art. This example, by Hokusai, shows the characteristic short tail, long hind legs, and the preferred coat pattern.

story, perhaps of a feast day or the arrival of Western visitors, cats signify high status and wealth. Other proof of the cat's exalted status in India exists in local folk art traditions, including portraits, still lifes, and observations of animals. The house cats in these paintings resemble the exclusive pets in court portraits, implying that there may have been little or no effort to create pedigree-type breeds.

Farther east, in Thailand, cats were highly regarded, and their wide variety of coat colors and postures were recorded in vivid paintings. The many manuscript copies of the *Cat Book Poems* (*see page 92*) depict pointed cats – ancestors of the Siamese – copper-brown "Sopalak" cats and silver-tipped blue "Si-Sawat" cats, as well as tabbies, bicolors, and patterns that would baffle geneticists and breeders. The most famous manuscript copy is now in the Thai National Library in Bangkok, but others exist in museums around the world.

Cats did not became widespread in Chinese art until the Sung Dynasty (AD 960–1279). They appeared in many court portraits, suggesting that, as in India, cats were status symbols.

Human-looking cat (left)
An anonymous Indian artist in the 19th century created this anthropomorphic cat. Its dark-lidded eyes, showing an expanse of white around the irises, appear far more human than feline.

Indian trading scene
In a vivid "story" painting from the 17th century by an unknown Mughal artist, wealthy traders are portrayed in opulent surroundings. An alert white cat sits contentedly beside the chair of the most important Westerner.

Cats at play
Much Eastern art has been lost because it was worked on fragile paper, or, like this 18th-century painting, on silk. These tabbies are typically Oriental, being striped; Western cats at this time were often blotched tabbies.

Most Chinese artistic renditions of the cat are expressively natural. *Spring Play in a T'ang Garden*, attributed to the Chinese Emperor Hsuan Tsung, who reigned from 1426 to 1435, depicts kittens frolicking among flowers in a garden. On silk and in woodblock, cats stalk bees or climb trees to avoid bug-eyed dogs. By the 1500s, the cat was a popular subject for *cloisonné* figures and, because of its superb nocturnal vision, for lamp designs. These lamps took the form of crouching cats in painted porcelain. The models were open at the top, with hollowed-out eye sockets, and the light from a candle within shone through the eyes, both to illuminate and to ward off evil spirits.

JAPANESE ART

The cat achieved lasting fame in Japanese art, where it was represented in scroll paintings, pottery, bronzes, and ivories for almost a thousand years. From the 1700s onward, cats became even more widespread in Japanese art. As in China and throughout Europe, the cat was associated with evil spirits (*see page 28*), and Japan's double-tailed witch cat of Okabe was a particularly common subject.

Feline opportunist

Kuniyoshi's cats are strikingly real. The boldness of the tabby as it steals a fish in Girl Chastising a Thieving Cat is familiar to anyone remotely acquainted with felines.

Most Japanese paintings and woodblock prints show cats in the typical tortie-and-white *mi-ké* patterning, seen in the Japanese Bobtail today, but in earlier works the cats tend to have longer tails. Through the 18th and 19th centuries, bobtails and predominantly white cats appear more and more in illustrations.

The most accessible renditions of cats in Japanese art are those portrayed in woodblock prints. Beginning with Utamaro (1753–1806) and Koryusai (late 18th century), through to the magnificent portrayals by Ando Hiroshige (1797–1858) and Utagawa Kuniyoshi (1797–1861), cats are portrayed with a reality seldom seen in Western art.

Utamaro included cats as the companions of beautiful women, while Hiroshige portrayed cats in scenes, such as the series *Famous Sites of Edo*, in vividly realistic attitudes. But it was Kuniyoshi, more than any other Japanese artist, who depicted cats with supreme accuracy and acute observation. He adored cats, and his studio was overrun by them. As a young boy, Kawanabe Gyosai (1831–1889) was Kuniyoshi's pupil, and he later sketched Kuniyoshi holding a cat in one arm and painting while other cats washed themselves and frolicked at his feet.

Perhaps Kuniyoshi's most famous work is the triptych woodblock print of the *Fifty-three Stations of the Tokaido Road,* with each station represented by a cat. Most of the cats are short-tailed and particolored, but there are also striped tabbies and solid-colored cats, as well as the double-tailed witch cat of Okabe.

Untamed hunter (right)
The kitten in this Japanese scroll is happily trawling a fish bowl in search of an extra snack. The pretty bow around its neck reveals that this kitten is well loved, and presumably well fed, but despite its comfortable life the feline's natural hunting instinct remains intact.

Tiger netsuke
The Japanese used netsuke toggles, often carved in the form of an animal like this ivory tiger, to fasten containers to their kimono sashes.

Cats also play a significant role in Kuniyoshi's other works. In his theatrical scenes, demonic and spectral cats from *kabuki* plays are invested with recognizable feline characteristics, while his portraits of actors, nobles, and courtesans often include incidental cats. In one of these, he portrays a beautiful young noblewoman painting butterflies while a kitten pounces on her finished paintings. Although it is intended to be an homage to the skill of the young woman, Kuniyoshi's portrait is also an astute comment on the natural predatory instinct of cats. This is typical of the best of Eastern art, revealing acute natural observation within an apparently rigid, stylized medium.

CATS IN WESTERN ART

IMAGES OF DOMESTIC CATS HUNTING, FISHING, SUCKLING THEIR young, and playing with children are abundant in Egyptian art, but Greek and Roman artists ignored the small cat, preferring to portray the more spectacular lion and tiger. The cat's association with the old religions from antiquity until the Middle Ages brought them into disfavor with the Christian Church, and they rarely show up in art of that period. During the Renaissance, the cat began to appear in allegorical paintings, often as a symbol of perfidy and evil. Later, in American and European art, cats came to symbolize beauty and harmony, often appearing in domestic scenes and family portraits.

With the exception of the illustrators of the Lindisfarne Gospels in AD 700 and the Irish Book of Kells in AD 800, European artists and artisans throughout the Middle Ages disregarded the cat, although cats occasionally appear in carvings in Celtic churches (see page 28). These carved cats may owe more to fables and pagan stories known to the carpenters and masons than to Christian influence.

CATS AS SYMBOL AND ALLEGORY

The Christian Church's hostility toward cats is the most likely reason for their infrequent appearance in early Western art. When a cat does appear, it is often as a symbol of treachery or evil. The Italian artist Domenico Ghirlandaio (1449–1494) followed an artistic tradition of portraying a cat sitting at the feet of Judas in his painting *The Last Supper*. The cat is thought to indicate Judas's treachery. Jacopo Tintoretto (1518–1594) also included a cat of rather sinister appearance in his version of the same scene; in another painting, *The Annunciation*, Tintoretto painted a wicked-looking cat on its guard under a menacing cloud. The Venetian artist Jacopo Bassano (c. 1517–1592) was one of the few artists of this period to use animals in a natural manner, and included two black-and-white cats in his *Animals Going into the Ark*.

Family psalter
Psalters were prayer books commissioned by wealthy families. Illustrated with both Christian and folklore narratives, they were often used to teach children Latin. A Lincolnshire knight, Sir Geoffrey Luttrell, commissioned his psalter around 1330. It is filled with an unusually large profusion of figures and foliage, including this cat and mouse, all rendered in exquisite detail.

The German painter and engraver Albrecht Dürer (1471–1528) produced the intricate woodcut *Adam and Eve*, in which a number of animals appear. The mouse is caught by Adam's foot, and may represent human weakness and vulnerability, while the cat is linked by its tail to Eve, and is likely to symbolize sexuality and evil. The great master of fantasy, Hieronymus Bosch (c. 1450–1516), painted demonic cats in *The Temptations of Saint Anthony*, and in many of his paintings the demons resemble the feline form. As the 18th century approached, the association of cats with the devil waned. In his paintings *The Skate*, *The Thief in Luck*, and *The Dead Hare*,

Jean Baptiste Chardin (1699–1779) showed cats as thieves and gluttons rather than symbols of the devil. During this period, the English artist William Hogarth (1697–1764) produced a series of works named the "Stages of Cruelty," which includes depictions of cruelty to cats. This suggests that the cat was no longer regarded as the perpetrator of evil, but as the victim.

CATS IN DOMESTIC SCENES

The cat rarely appeared in naturalist painting before the 18th century, although Leonardo da Vinci (1452–1519) appears to have found the anatomy of the cat fascinating. Some of his sketches are as accurate as photographs in their portrayal of cats in action and asleep, while others are more fantastical and dragonlike. As European artists moved away from the old subjects of religion, history, and mythology, and turned to illustrating scenes from daily life, cats began to appear in domestic scenes. In England, William Hogarth painted his famous portrait *The Graham Children*, which includes an alert cat, and the great animal portraitist George Stubbs (1724–1806) painted his only known study of a cat, *Miss Anne White's Kitten*. In France, artists Antoine Watteau (1684–1721)

Allegory or realism? (left)
In The Last Supper *by Francesco Bassano the younger (1549–92), son of Jacopo, the cat is positioned facing a dog – a typical symbol of treachery opposed to fidelity. However, this cat and dog appear in several paintings by the Bassano family, and it is likely that the animals were domestic pets.*

Reluctant plaything (right)
Dressing the Kitten, by Joseph Wright of Derby (1734–1797), shows a kitten suffering the indignity that has befallen many family pets through the ages. This sentimental scene is a model of lighting and composition in portraiture.

Feline delight
In his Garden of Heavenly Delights, Hieronymus Bosch painted, among his typically monstrous beasts, a sleek cat with its freshly caught meal. He often used the feline form in his illustrations of fantastical demons, and although at first glance this cat appears to be a normal representation, on closer examination the cat's teeth are rather fearsome and its claws resemble talons.

Languid beauty

Perhaps better known for the cat adventures in the comic strip Images sans paroles, *Théophile Steinlen was an accomplished artist. This study of a reclining brown tabby,* L'hiver: chat sur un coussin *(1901), is a testament to his skill at capturing the essence of the feline nature.*

and Jean Fragonard (1732–1806), and in Italy Giovanni Tiepolo (1696–1770), all included contented cats in their paintings, curled on the laps of shepherdesses, in the arms of mistresses, or simply idling in luxury with their owners. A portrait of a boy, *Don Manuel Osorio de Zuniga* by Francisco Goya (1746–1828), shows three plump cats eyeing the young boy's tethered magpie. Few of these representations come close to the anatomical perfection of Leonardo da Vinci's best sketches, and it was not until the influence of the famous French painter and naturalist Jean-Baptiste Oudry (1686–1755) spread that realism was once more achieved.

CAT PORTRAITURE

During the 19th century, the Swiss-born artist Gottfried Mind (1768–1814) produced many carefully observed watercolors and skillfully executed pen studies of his cat Minette and her kittens. The works of Dutch-born Henrietta Ronner (1821–1909) were thought sentimental at the time, but are highly prized today for their accurate observation of cat behavior, while the Swiss-born artist Théophile Steinlen (1859–1923) produced thousands of drawings of cats that, although intended as comic strips, brilliantly caught cat behavior (*see page 44*). Other European painters were using cats to symbolize the sexuality of their subjects. For example, Edouard Manet (1832–1883) put a self-contained and serene cat at his subject's foot in his painting *Olympia*, perhaps as a subtle code for sensuousness, a technique used in portraits of geishas in Japan. Auguste Renoir (1841–1919) was far more robust in his affinity with cats.

In many of his paintings, such as *Madame Julie Manet*, *Girl with a Cat*, and *Sleeping Girl with Cat*, his cats are playful, spirited, and sensual, much like the women he portrays. In Russia, the poet Aleksandr Pushkin (1799–1837) drew subtle pencil sketches of his cats, and these can now be seen at Boldino, his house near Pskov.

AMERICAN FOLK ART

For almost 150 years, beginning in the early 18th century, folk art was the dominant indigenous form of painting in the United States, although it was often underestimated

Companionship (right)
In Girl with a Cat, Auguste Renoir illustrates the close relationship between cats and humans. The cat appears relaxed and trusting in the girl's arms, while she bends her head toward it in a touching demonstration of affection.

Domestic bliss (below)
American folk art often shows family groups or single portraits. A typical example is Girl in Red with Her Cat and Dog, by Ammi Phillips.

and undervalued until recent times. Portraitists, often self-taught, traveled around the country painting middle-class families. The names of many of these artists are unknown but some, such as Ammi Phillips (*c.* 1788–1865), left what are now treasured bodies of work. Both dogs and cats were regularly portrayed in these family paintings, and they communicate a vivid impression of domestic security and stability in the early years of American settlement. No longer associated with paganism and the devil, the cat had become a modern symbol of beauty and peaceful civilization.

CATS IN MODERN ART

DEVELOPMENTS AWAY FROM REALISM IN THE TWENTIETH CENTURY have produced a rapid succession of styles, and the popularity of the cat as a suitable model for painting and drawing has never waned. Practitioners of every movement, from German Expressionism to Pop Art, have been drawn to the cat's natural beauty and unique presence, and have attempted to capture the cat on canvas, in print, or in three-dimensional form. Cat art now abounds in both traditional and modern styles, and mass reproduction has ensured its popularity worldwide.

Until the advent of World War II, many artists regarded Paris as the mecca of art, choosing to settle and work there. From this large, creative melting pot various contemporary art styles arose, and within each genre are innumerable fine works of art that depict the cat.

CAT-LOVING ARTISTS

A tradition for living with feline companions and creating representations of them has been established during the 20th century. One of the first artistic ailurophiles to emerge was the British painter Gwen John (1876–1939), who surrounded herself with cats in her home and painted them on many occasions. She was artistically overshadowed during her lifetime by her more famous brother Augustus, but her paintings are now highly sought after. The Japanese painter Tsuguharu Foujita (1886–1968), the British Surrealist Leonora Carrington (1917–), and the media-aware Pop artist Andy Warhol (c. 1928–1987) have all produced a variety of cat studies simply because they were

Cubist cat
Pablo Picasso's interest in the wild, untamed qualities of all cats is evident in La Technique *(c. 1962), in which a domestic, or possibly feral, cat clearly shows its savage nature as it contemplates an assembly of food.*

enamored of this fascinating animal. In the work of the early German Expressionists there was a declared and deliberate distortion of reality, and cats began to appear in works of art that exaggerated aspects of their form to convey their unique feline qualities. The chief subjects for the Expressionist Franz Marc (1880–1916) were animals and nature, which included cats. The Swiss painter Paul Klee (1879–1940) was

extremely fond of cats and painted them frequently in imaginative scenes. Klee was influenced by the Expressionists, although he never affiliated himself fully with any one style.

MODERN CAT STUDIES

The development of Cubism – another great art movement – is often credited to the master of form and volume, Pablo Picasso (1881–1973). Of his works depicting cats, he is quoted as saying: "I want to make a cat like those that I see crossing the road. They don't have anything in common with house pets; they have bristling fur and run like demons." It was clearly the cat as stalking hunter that inspired his portrayals.

Later came Surrealism, which was concerned with exploring and illustrating the workings of the unconscious mind. The Spanish artist Joan Miró (1893–1983) was a Surrealist, and his work *Tête* (*Le Chat blanc*, 1972) shows a feline animal, whose whiskers are in the form of eight spider's legs on a mottled background. Certain artists are not easily identified with the various movements that proliferated during the early decades of the 20th century. For example, Marc Chagall (1887–1985) preferred to take from each the lessons that were useful to him. In 1910, Chagall left Russia for Paris, where his Jewish folk background fused with modern French techniques to produce highly

Ceramic icon
This 1980s raku cat portrait by Jill Crowley (1946–) is part of a series based on Crowley's own Burmese and a neighbor's tom that used to pester it.

Perfect balance
Martin Leman, the most sophisticated of "naive" painters, has earned an international reputation through his widely sold gift books, containing cat images such as this interlocking pair named Winsor and Newton.

Behavior study (left)
This early 20th-century Franz Marc cat sketch may appear stylized, but it superbly captures the fervid intent of these circling felines. Marc made an intensive study of animal anatomy in order to arrive at a system of rules of form.

Feline high jinks (right)
Working in Europe, Japanese-born Ryozo Kohira (1947–) combined traditional wood-block printing, modern techniques, and vivid colors in this imaginative study of drunken, gluttonous cats, The Cat's Voyage *(1964).*

Curious portrayal
In Girl with a Kitten (1947) by Lucian Freud (1922–), a kitten is held in an unusually tight grip by Kitty Epstein, a close friend of the painter. The girl's overtly anxious expression and the kitten's direct stare combine to unsettle any viewer of this portrait.

andy Warhol

Animal observation (right)
The graphic artist Tsuguharu Foujita made numerous, closely observed cat studies, and Le Chat (1939) is a typical example of his meticulous style. He was highly proficient in lithography and used many of his own cats as models for his behavioral observations.

Personal gifts
During the 1950s, Andy Warhol frequently sketched his favorite cats in frivolous poses. The results were originally printed as presents for his close friends, but have now been published posthumously in gift books, as well as appearing on mass-produced mugs and T-shirts.

stylized images filled with nostalgic, fairy-tale qualities. He utilized this skill in the 1930s with illustrations for the *Fables of La Fontaine* (*see page 32*), many of which involve cats.

COMMERCIAL CAT ART
Following World War II, the art world shifted its center to New York, triggering the next major wave of art styles. Some of the artists that flourished in this atmosphere found a niche in new mass-market ventures such as posters and gift books, even collectible plates. Andy Warhol was one of these purveyors; perhaps best known for his colorful lifestyle

and Marilyn Monroe screen prints, he was also passionate about his cats, reproducing them in thousands of witty, whimsical drawings. The British painter, Martin Leman (1934–) has built a highly successful career with his many books featuring sleek and sophisticated cats.

Although cats are not the central theme of paintings by the American artist Will Barnet (1911–), Madame Butterfly, the beloved family cat, is often included in his uplifting family portraits. Similarly, the Scottish artist Elizabeth Blackadder (1931–) has been inspired mainly by everyday subjects, such as domestic items, flowers, and her cats. At one time three cats

joined the household and she began to record their unexpected and independent movements. But probably the best-known scene to include a cat is the portrait *Mr. and Mrs. Clarke and Percy* (1971) by the British artist David Hockney (1937–). Seated in designer Ozzie Clarke's lap, Percy was so named only for the portrait.

The cat has been a celebrated subject in the modern art scene, and with its ever-growing popularity as a domestic companion there is every reason to believe that it will remain so.

Fantastic creatures (right)
Leonora Carrington's mysteriously named painting Tuesday (1964) is peppered with felines and cat-headed females, all presented in a dreamlike, Surrealist style.

Watercolor portrait (below)
In this Expressionist portrait, Zu Apollinaire (1935) by Hannah Höch (1889–1978), the form of the sleeping cat is stretched to convey its extreme comfort and relaxation.

CARTOON CATS

FROM THE EARLIEST FELINE IMAGES PENNED BY ARTISANS IN ancient Egypt, through the humanized characters of the early 1900s, and the more recent comic strips, the domestic cat has been an ideal medium for caricature, satire, and humor. Some cartoonists have used cats to convey political or social comments, whereas others have drawn attention to the obvious similarities between feline and human behavior. During the 20th century, a host of imaginative cartoon cats has been unleashed on a delighted public, creating an extremely lucrative and internationally successful form of entertainment.

Cartoonists often give cats a valuable dual role in their work, as representations of both feline and human behavior. The cat's fluid, sinuous movements translate effectively onto paper, allowing cartoonists to capture the essence of the feline, but the cat's facial features are ideal for conveying human expression, making it possible for cartoonists to portray human characteristics in a feline guise.

HISTORICAL CARICATURES

The divinity of the cat in ancient Egypt ensured that it played a prominent role in Egyptian art. Stonemakers, sculptors, and painters were employed by the state to decorate the tombs of the New Kingdom pharaohs (1540–1196 BC). In addition to their work on official monuments, these artisans created the first "cartoon cats" – humorous, satirical drawings on papyrus (reed paper) and ostracon (smooth white limestone). At Deir el-Medina, in the region now known as the Valley of the Kings, a wealth of papyri and ostraca have been discovered. Now spread throughout the museums of the world, these informal drawings provide a fascinating window on the irreverent and appealing cynicism of that time (see page 32). Some ostraca are simple cartoon sketches of cats, but others are scathing commentaries on aristocratic, ancient Egyptian life.

In Russia, an unknown cartoonist portrayed Czar Peter the Great (1672–1725) as a cat in the cartoon, *The Cat of Kazan*. In 1698, the czar was reviled by the old aristocracy and church hierarchy because he outlawed the wearing of beards. Facial hair in the form of a mustache was allowed, however, mainly because the czar sported a fine specimen – known as his "whiskers" – which was considerably exaggerated on the cartoon cat.

Political burlesque
The Russian ruler Czar Peter the Great made himself so unpopular during his reign that, on his death, he was lampooned as a large cat, inelegantly lying on its back with legs and tail in the air, being buried by mice.

In recent years, the cartoon cat has played a less political role in Russia, starring in light-entertainment comic strips such as *Holidays in Prostokvashino* and *The Adventures of Leopold*.

ORIENTAL OBSERVATION

For centuries, Japanese artists (*see page 38*) have been able to capture the true nature of cats in their woodblock prints. The accuracy of their observation and illustration has been profound. This is also true of many modern Japanese cartoonists, who often employ the fierceness and frailty of cats to symbolize these same aspects of human nature.

Clean and tidy
By nature, cats, as well as humans, are fastidious in their hygiene. Ando Hiroshige has artfully captured this shared attribute in his anthropomorphic drawing.

Early satire
Although the Egyptians duly revered the cat, they were not without a sense of humor. This satirical papyrus (c. 1150 BC), was penned by Theban scribes. It shows a procession of cats acting as household servants, attending to a seated lady mouse or rat and her young offspring.

The popular Japanese artist Ando Hiroshige (1797–1858) created humanized cats that not only conveyed human actions and emotions, but also retained their feline nature. Western influences permeate current Japanese cartoons, with the escapades of the atomically powered *Doraemon*, and the celestial cats Luna and Artemis in the comic book *Sailormoon*.

COMMERCIAL CARTOONS

In the West, humanized cats were often used for satirical commentary until sentimentality became a popular theme in Victorian Britain. The second president of the British National Cat Club was the artist Louis Wain (1860–1939).

Early cartoon hero (left)
Although its heyday was the 1920s, Felix the Cat is still well loved today. Felix Kept on Walking was his theme song, ideal for a cat that always seemed to attract trouble.

Purrsonalized logo (above)
The French artist, director, and cat lover Jean Cocteau (1889–1963) artfully combined a few symmetrical ink blots with flowing calligraphy to create this highly distinctive cat emblem for the Club des amis des chats.

Stories without words (above left)
Artist Théophile Steinlen is best known for his picture stories, Images sans paroles. *These three sketches conclude an amusing comic strip story, which shows how the cat's inherent curiosity can end in disaster. Steinlen was probably the first artist to successfully show cats in violent motion.*

His innumerable caricatures of clothed, semi-human cats were, and still are, highly popular (*see page 50*). His characters have distinctly human features and enjoy many human pastimes, including smoking cigars, drinking tea, and playing cards.
Later in life, suffering from schizophrenia, his humorous, gentle images evolved into intricate, psychedelic patterns.

Another deeply cat-conscious artist was Théophile Steinlen (*see page 40*), whose Parisian home was known locally as "Cat's Corner," because of its large colony of former strays. These cats were the inspiration for Steinlen's posters, advertising commodities ranging from tea and milk to cafés and veterinary clinics.

FAMILY FAVORITES

Since the images of Wain and Steinlen, there have been many other cartoon cats to delight us. The prototype was the cheeky rogue *Krazy Kat*, by American cartoonist George Herriman (1880–1944), who first appeared in 1910. Krazy Kat paved the way for the highly successful *Felix the Cat*, penned by Otto Messmer (1892–1983). Felix's character was that of a resilient survivor in a hostile world, conveyed with a subtle but clever comedy.

Atomic cat

This brightly colored, unusual-looking creature is Doraemon, the atomic-powered cat, created by the Japanese cartoonist Hiroshi Fujimoto (1934–1996). Unsurprisingly, the cartoon's main fan base is in Japan, but Doraemon comics have sold an estimated 130 million copies worldwide.

For example, when he stole the moon, which was made of cheese, for the philanthropic purpose of giving it to a destitute grocer to sell, he was arrested because people were left in the dark. Eventually, Felix and Krazy Kat were animated, which led to a whole host of popular screen favorites such as *Tom and Jerry*, *Top Cat*, and *Sylvester and Tweetie Pie* (*see page 46*).

Other best-selling cat cartoons include the cleverly illustrated cat words, such as "cat alog" and "platy puss," of the French visual joker Siné (1928–), the signatory Kliban cat – a strongly striped and round-eyed feline – by American Bernard Kliban (1935–1990), the inimitable cat creations of Englishman Ronald Searle (1920–), and the blatantly sexual exploits of *Fritz the Cat*, created by the artist Robert Crumb (1943–).

But no cartoon cat has been as successful as the slovenly, lazy, cantankerous, self-centered, not to mention fat *Garfield* by Jim Davis (1945–). People the world over recognize both their cats and themselves in the character of Garfield, and love him all the more for it.

On the catwalk (right)
Louis Wain's highly sentimentalized, anthropomorphic cats can be seen taking part in a variety of typical Victorian pastimes. Here they are bedecked in their Sunday finery, enjoying a stroll around town.

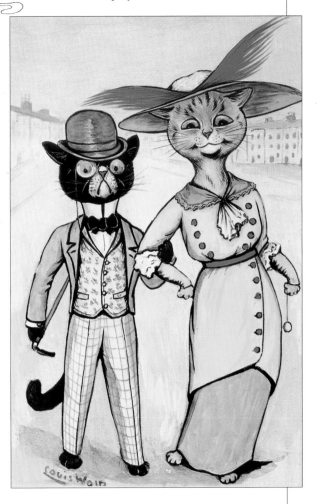

CATS IN ENTERTAINMENT

CATS RARELY MAKE HOLLYWOOD HEROES AND THEY CERTAINLY HAVE not yet climbed the pinnacles reached by dogs such as Beethoven, Benjie, and Lassie. This is simply because cats are a great deal more difficult to train than dogs, and their faces are not usually so expressive. Cats with successful careers in entertainment to their name have usually received many hours of painstaking training, which are only rewarded if the cat has any inclination to learn the tricks it is being taught. Those cats that do adapt to a life within the entertainment industry, as stars or in supporting roles, will always steal the show.

With very few exceptions, cats tend to play supporting roles in film and television, but in advertising, an area that is an important part of entertainment, cats are almost on a par with dogs. As human cultural changes continue to swing in favor of cats, and computer animation becomes more sophisticated, it is likely that their most "entertaining" years lie ahead.

EARLY ENTERTAINMENT
Historically, cats have only briefly appeared in circuses and other entertainment. In 1549, in Brussels, a "cat organ" was played for a visiting king, Phillip II. This cruel instrument prodded or pulled the tails of cats that were trapped in tiny cages in order to elicit mews and squeaks. In the early 19th century, in Italy, a troupe of cats were trained by Pietro Capelli and toured Europe. These cats balanced on high wires, performed trapeze acts, and juggled with their hind legs. Yuri Kouklachev of the Moscow State Circus continued the tradition in the 20th century. He said it took three years to teach a cat to do a "handstand" on its forelegs, and he found it easier to train his cats at night when they were more alert. However, the concept of performing animals is declining in popularity, and it is unlikely that cats will be trained for circus acts in the future. There are now more acceptable occupations for well-trained felines.

STAGE AND SCREEN CATS
Cats have long found employment in films, with walk-on roles that rarely demand acting ability. The 1958 film Bell, Book, and Candle has Kim Novak in the role of a witch who lives with a Siamese cat called Pyewacket. The cat won a PATSY (Picture Animal Top Star of the Year) award for its performance. Blake Edwards's Breakfast at Tiffany's (1961) features Audrey Hepburn's marmalade confidant "Cat," who is temporarily abandoned on New York's rain-swept streets. Sheila Burnford's novel The Incredible Journey was filmed in 1963, and this tale of a cat and two dogs who travel hundreds of miles to return to their home was believed by many filmgoers to be a true story. Paul Mazursky's touching film Harry and Tonto (1973) is the

Curtain call
The designer Alexander Benois painted cats on witches' broomsticks for the backdrop of the "St. Petersburg at Night" sequence in Igor Stravinsky's 1911 ballet Petrushka.

story of a widower, played by Art Carney, who is evicted from his New York home and travels to Chicago with his cat Tonto. Both stars won awards for their roles. In The War of the Roses (1989) the feuding couple, played by Kathleen Turner and Michael Douglas, have a cat and dog respectively. The film implies that "cat people" should not marry "dog people."

Not surprisingly, given their long association with evil, cats are popular in horror films. From Mexico, where an aristocrat keeps man-eating cats in The Night of the Thousand Cats (1972), through Hollywood B movies such as Cat People (1942) and The Shadow of the Cat (1961), to The Black Cat (1985), an Italian film about a killer cat, the medieval image of the cat is perpetuated.

Feline foe (left)
The comic strip Batman was made into a film in 1966. Batman's sidekick was Robin, and his opponents included The Joker and Catwoman. Despite the rivalry between Catwoman and Batman there were sexual undertones to the relationship that were made explicit in Tim Burton's 1992 film Batman Returns.

Best friends (right)
When Truman Capote's novel Breakfast at Tiffany's was filmed in 1961, the character of Holly Golightly was played by Audrey Hepburn. Her confidant was a ginger tom called Cat, who won a PATSY award for his acting prowess.

La Belle et la Bête (left)
In Jean Cocteau's 1945 film version of the fairy tale Beauty and the Beast, *the beast, played by Jeanne Marais, has strikingly feline features. The mask was actually based on the features of Cocteau's blue Persian cat.*

Curious cat (above right)
The animated film Felidae *is a far cry from Disney. The hero, Francis, investigating the death of a cat in his neighborhood, uncovers a world of mysterious sects and bestial murder.*

Cartoon cruelty (right)
Despite overtones of cruelty and sadism, the cartoon series Tom and Jerry *has been highly popular since 1939. Its success may lie in the fact that the victim, the mouse, is always the eventual victor over poor Tom.*

Cats fare better in science fiction films. In the 1978 film *Superman*, with Christopher Reeve in the starring role, the hero rescues a Devon Rex from a tree. In the same year, Disney made *The Cat from Outer Space*, featuring a cat called Jake (actually played by a female named Amber), who captains a spaceship, and in 1979 a red tabby accompanied Sigourney Weaver in *Alien*.

On stage and television, cats are more often played by people. The feline character Catwoman made her first screen appearance in the 1950s television version of *Batman*, and in the 1980s British space-comedy series *Red Dwarf*, the hip-cat character "Cat" evolves from the spaceship's ordinary feline. On stage, the relatively minor role played by real cats has been more than made up for by the huge success of the musical *Cats*, based on T.S. Eliot's poems (*see page 34*).

CARTOON CATS
The first animated cat was George Herriman's *Krazy Kat*, transferring from paper to screen in 1916. More successful was Pat Sullivan and Otto Messmer's *Felix*, who in his prime during the 1920s was as popular as Charlie Chaplin. *Felix* was succeeded by *Tom and Jerry*, created in the late 1930s by William Hanna and Joseph Barbera. This team's production company also made *Top Cat*, a popular 1960s television series.

The first full-length feature cartoon was Warner Brothers' *Gay Purree*, in the 1960s, with Judy Garland as the voice of Mewsette, the feline leading lady. This was followed in 1970 by Walt Disney's *Aristocats*, featuring the elegant Duchess, who was given voice by Eva Gabor, and the stouthearted drifter O'Malley, spoken and sung by Phil Harris. Robert Crumb's sexually explicit *Fritz the Cat* was transferred from a cartoon strip to screen in 1972.

Since then, with the exception of *Felidae* (1994), the animated film that director Michael Schaak adapted from the novel by Akif Pirinçci, felines have returned to peripheral roles such as the spiteful barnyard cat in the film *Babe* (1995).

CATS IN ADVERTISING
Advertising has brought fame to many cats. In Britain, the all-white Arthur is well known for eating his food from the can with his paw. In the United States, Arthur's equivalent was Morris, who won a PATSY in 1973 for advertising cat food. Another famous British cat was Solomon, a Chinchilla Longhair who started his career advertising carpets but went on to feature in the James Bond film *Diamonds Are Forever*.

Cats are featuring increasingly in advertising for two simple reasons. First, cat ownership is rising and now exceeds dog ownership in North America and many parts of Europe. The second reason is that market research has shown that people actually remember advertisements better when cats appear in them. One detergent company studied the effectiveness of their advertisements and discovered that more people remembered their product seven days after viewing a commercial with a cat in the starring role than when a dog, horse, chimpanzee, bird, "woman next door," or even a famous personality was featured.

Cats seem to suggest cleanliness and sensuality. Good advertisements appeal to our emotions and cats are ideal for representing what advertising experts classify as "female" values – warmth, beauty, capriciousness, and elegance. With these associations, the future is bright for cats in entertainment.

Glamour puss (below)
One of the most successful stage musicals of all time is Andrew Lloyd Webber's Cats, *based on a book of poems by T.S. Eliot. The musical includes the character Grizabella, excluded from the book because her life was judged too disreputable for children's ears.*

CAT EPHEMERA

HUMAN ATTITUDES TOWARD THE CAT ARE CONSTANTLY CHANGING.
Ideas and images that appeal to one generation pass rapidly out of
fashion as tastes change and we learn more about feline behavior.
In many early civilizations, big cats, especially the lion, were used
to symbolize power and royalty in official sculptures and royal
crests, much as they still are today. Meanwhile, the domestic cat
has been modeled in softer images such as religious amulets and
collectible ornaments. Examples of ancient, rare, and priceless
artifacts are now housed in museums and galleries throughout the
world, so that the cat's place in aesthetics is easily traced.

Since records began, people have used artistic
representations as part of folklore, customs,
and religious beliefs. Early civilizations, such as
those of the Egyptians, Aztecs, and Babylonians,
produced a range of feline-inspired artifacts,
some of which still survive. Many of these
primitive images represent members of the big
cat family – lions, tigers, leopards, and

Model cat
*Entrepreneur and
artist Emile Gallé
(1846–1904) was
well known for
decorative art of high
quality. This brightly
colored, green-eyed
cat is typical of the
faience (tin-glazed
earthenware) figurines
that were, and still are,
eagerly sought by collectors
of feline artifacts.*

cheetahs – that were prevalent at the
time. But a greater selection of cat
images were produced by later
societies, when the domestic cat
became a part of everyday lives.

EARLY FELINE ICONS
The most dramatic and enduring
legacy of the Egyptian and Greek
use of feline symbolism is the
sphinx – a mythical beast with the
head of a human and the body of
a lion. Some of the sphinxes that
flanked the entrances to important
funerary monuments can still be
viewed in their original settings. However,
many were removed by early archaeologists to
various museums, including the fine set now
adorning a staircase at the Louvre in Paris.

The lion, another enduring symbol, has been
associated with royalty since time immemorial
(*see page 26*). One of the most impressive finds
from the tomb of King Tutankhamen was his
stately, gold, lion throne (*c.* 1327 BC). Much
later, the great Cartier jewelry firm used the lion
and other big cats to create a selection of royal
gems for the Duchess of Windsor.

If big cats evoke masculine images of power,
strength, and royalty, then the domestic cat
embodies beauty, poise, and cleanliness,
which are all stereotypical feminine
traits. For example, statuettes of the cat
goddess Bastet (*see page 26*) wearing a
long, tight dress were commonplace
in early Egypt. A few of these are now
on permanent display in collections
housed at the Metropolitan Museum
of Art in New York, the British
Museum in London, and the
Egyptian Museum in Cairo.

THE POPULARIZED CAT
Ornamental representations of the cat
have always been popular. Fertility
amulets in feline form, dating from
c. 2300 BC, along with cosmetic pots
and gold jewelry, are all evidence of a
strong intimacy between cats and the
Egyptians. Relationships of a similar

Feline adornment
*Cats are central to the design of these
well-preserved pieces of Egyptian
jewelry. The gold spacer-bar was part
of a bracelet from the tomb of Queen
Sobekemsaf, dated around 1650 BC,
and the gold finger-ring
with seated carnelian
cat is of a similar date.
Sadly, it is now
impossible to
know whether
these cats were
employed for
decorative or
religious reasons.*

type can be traced to many parts of the world
through artistic relics. From Persia comes a
well-preserved bottle in the shape of a cat, from
Crete a fresco of a cat hunting scene, and from
Italy an intricately decorated vase (*see page 26*).
Much later, the Toby jug – originally a beer
mug shaped like a man – was produced in
feline form in many European countries.

From the 17th century onward, cat figures
became fashionable ornaments in both the East
and the West – they represented home values
and domestication. These figurines, sized for
the mantelpiece, were made in abundance, but
only a few are worthy of museum space. Cats
produced by Gallé and Fabergé inspired a host
of cheap imitations. Other fine examples of rare
and expensive collectors' items include German
Meissen cats, Dutch Delftware cats, Scottish
Wemyss cats, and Ch'ing cats from China.

Some cat forms are prized for sentimental or
superstitious reasons. The former is the case for
a bronze cat made by the French Art Deco
sculptor Chassagne. Since the mid-1920s the
cat has been a permanent fixture at Heal's, the
famous London department store, and is now
considered the company mascot. Superstitious
beliefs have kept Kaspar, a black cat, employed
by the Savoy Hotel in London. He is placed in
the 14th seat, with a napkin tied around his
neck, at dinner parties for groups of "unlucky
13," and the waiters are instructed to change
his place setting for each course of the meal.

Cat chorus (left)
This mid-19th century painting, Die Katzensymphonie *or* Cat Symphony *by Moritz von Schwind (1804–1871) is more of an artistic diversion than pure music. His cats get bolder in the crescendo and scamper off at the finale.*

Venerable playing card
This forgotten Rheinish card game Bird's Play *illustrates that games – like art, literature, and advertising – reflect the fashions and social values of their time.*

of Hoo-Hoo" adopted the black cat to promote the lumber and forest industry. There are now over 8,000 members, all of whom advertise their products using the cat.

CAT CURIOSITIES AND TRENDS
Although music cannot be put on display, it is nonetheless a part of cat history, as numerous composers have been stimulated by the beauty and movement of cats. Domenico Scarlatti (1685–1757) claimed that his cat, Pulcinella, helped in his compositions. Pulcinella had a habit of walking along the keys of Scarlatti's harpsichord, and on one occasion this inspired him to compose *Fugue in G Minor, L.499*, now generally known as *The Cat's Fugue.*

This musical association was taken to the extreme by Japanese makers of the samisen, an instrument similar to a guitar – cat skin was stretched across its soundbox, and its strings were made from cat intestines. In 17th-century Italy, violin makers advertised the use of catgut in their instruments, although in reality it was sheepgut. They did this to protect their design, but the term has stuck because of the din produced by inexpert violinists, which is often compared to the caterwauling of mating cats.

The preneutering days generated many unwanted cats, which led to a fashion during the 19th century for preserving these animals in the name of art. For example, taxidermist Walter Potter produced a number of works in which stuffed kittens were posed in human scenarios. Such a practice seems distasteful today, although the success of a recent cartoon book, *101 Uses for a Dead Cat*, suggests that modern tastes have barely changed.

HERALDRY AND EMBLEMS
The lion, known as "the king of the beasts," is the only feline to figure notably in heraldry. Early records show that cats were first used as heraldic emblems during the Roman Empire. A famous legion, the *Felices seniores*, bore the cat on its coat of arms, an early pun on the words *felis* (cat) and *felix* (fortunate or happy). This military pun was echoed by the popular cartoon character Felix the Cat (*see page 44*) that appeared on badges of U.S. Marine Corps pilots in World War II. Tomcat replaced Felix in the 1970s to celebrate the night-flying abilities of the Grumman F–14 Tomcat carrier-borne interceptor aircraft – comparisons were made with the cat's night vision.

In the 5th century AD, the king of Burgundy, Gundiracus, adopted the cat as a symbol of liberty and independence. In due course the cat came to be featured on more than a hundred European coats of arms, including the German Katzen family shield, with a silver cat holding a silver mouse on an azure background, and the Italian Della Gattas' cat *couchant*. In Scotland, a home of the wildcat (*see page 18*), various branches of the great Clan Chattan displayed the cat on their family crest with a variation on the motto "Touch not the cat but [without] a glove." These families were fierce warriors and the untamable, aggressive wildcat was an appropriate image for their coat of arms.

Images of the cat are not restricted to formal emblems. For example, in Germany the word "katz" is often found in the names of towns and villages, whereas in neighboring Austria it is incorporated in family names, such as Katzler.

In British pubs feline images are adopted in a similar way to heraldic signs. The Red Lion is a popular name, but establishments such as The Cat and Fiddle, or the Cat and Custard Pot are more memorable pub names. In France, shop signs incorporating the cat are common, as a result of the banning of coats of arms after the French Revolution. In fact, inns, clubs, cafes, and restaurants have all appropriated the domestic cat. In North America, a fraternal organization founded in 1892 as the "Concatonated Order

Heraldic cats (left)
Cat emblems abound. This 1970s badge features Tomcat, an American pilots' mascot, and the kilt pin is taken from a Scottish family's coat of arms.

Anthropomorphic ceremony (right)
The Jamaica Inn in Cornwall houses the exhibits of the British taxidermist Walter Potter. The Kittens' Wedding consists of the usual wedding party attended by a full congregation, and all are dressed in their wedding finery. This may have been popular with its original Victorian audience, but many people today find it macabre.

CAT COLLECTIBLES

MOST CAT LOVERS ARE TEMPTED AT ONE TIME OR ANOTHER TO BUY some picture or keepsake that reminds them of their feline friend, but for some ailurophiles collecting can become a major pastime. Due to the international surge in the cat's popularity during the mid-19th century, artists, manufacturers, and later advertisers recognized potential in exploiting the cat. This led to a variety of cat merchandise, ranging from postcards and stamps to toys and games, most of which is easily accessible and reasonably priced for the collector. If you would prefer to view, rather than collect, there are now many private collections open to the public.

Cultural artifacts that exemplify the role of cats in history are usually found in museums, art galleries, or in the sales of international auction houses. Whatever the case, they are inaccessible to most potential collectors. Perhaps this is why the "cat collectible" has become such big business. Modern manufacturing techniques have produced a plethora of collectible feline images that sell successfully worldwide.

MASS-PRODUCED CATS

Since the 17th century in Europe, and before that in Asia, ladies' fans have been variously decorated to make them more appealing to the user. Animals were always a popular choice of adornment, and the cat featured frequently in the early 1900s in the work of the great French fan-making firm Duvelleroy, among others, on cotton, silk, or paper fans.

It is likely that figurines in the shape of a cat were manufactured specifically with the collector in mind, perhaps as a direct result of the popularity of the cat fans.

Popular ornament
For those who cannot afford the fine porcelain cats of Meissen or Gallé, a 19th-century, mass-produced earthenware cat, such as this ginger and white, is an affordable alternative.

Spanish stamp
Lindbergh's cat is featured on this commemorative stamp (1930), although she remained behind.

During the 18th century, many manufacturers made cat figurines (*see page 48*). From that era only the mass-produced ones are still available, although there are plenty of cat figurines being produced today for the collector. However, a cat figurine may be pleasing to the eye, but it is uninspiring as a plaything. Luckily, Steiff, the German soft-toy maker, renowned for developing the Teddy Bear, rectified this with a line of black cats, which ran until the 1980s. The early ones, especially those that still display the company name with a button on the ear, are sought after today. The toy world went on to exploit the adulation surrounding cats with other items that now fetch high prices, including Victorian metal cats that nod their heads, key-wound plush cats from Europe, Japan, and China, and early American cat-based board games.

French fan
(above right)
With technical developments in the 1920s it was possible for the Duvelleroy firm to produce this popular fan shaped like a cat's head.

Folk art (left)
Rugs similar to this one were once a common sight in 18th-century American homes. Many artists prefer everyday subjects, which is why the family cat often appears on rugs.

Cat postcards are the ideal starting point for any novice collector. Most countries joined the international postal system in the late 1800s, and postcards became fashionable as a method for sending short communications. During this time, manufacturers produced a seemingly infinite variety of cat postcards, many of which included the caricature cats of German artist Arthur Thiele (1841–1919) and the delicate illustrations of Helena Maguire (1860–1909). Yet it is probably the anthropomorphic subjects of Louis Wain (*see page 44*) that are well known to collectors and noncollectors alike. This trend in the early postcards, to depict clothed cats participating in human events, was replaced later by black-and-white pictures of real, clothed cats. Often their eyes were artificially colored, sometimes with tinted glass, to emphasize this very appealing attribute. In the 1930s, the fashion was for cat breeds, which were replaced during the 1950s by brightly colored photographs of kittens, often held in the arms of young girls.

POSTAGE STAMPS

Naturally associated with the postcard is the postage stamp, which has proved to be another useful medium for displaying cats. The first stamp to feature a cat was issued in 1930 by Spain to commemorate the first, nonstop, transatlantic flight of Charles Lindbergh (1902–1974). Lindbergh's pet cat, Patsy, accompanied him on many flights, but not on this one, which is why she is portrayed gazing wistfully at the departing plane.

As with the postcard, stamps that feature cat breeds are immensely popular, especially complete cat stamp sets. The first "all-cats" set of stamps was issued in Poland in 1964, possibly because then, as now, it had one of Europe's highest cat populations per household.

In 1995, the West Indian island of St. Vincent issued a sheet of nine different $1 stamps depicting cats of the world. The sheet was designed in such a way that it formed a composite picture of a verandah, facing the ocean with mountains in the background, and a coterie of cats engaged in various activities – a real find for the dedicated ailurophile. In fact, most countries have capitalized on the collectible cat stamp, including Britain with a set of Elizabeth Blackadder's cat paintings (*see page 42*), Sweden with the Nordic goddess Freya, and France with a centenary stamp to celebrate the birth of their cat-loving novelist, Colette (*see page 36*). The cat stamp is now so popular that a specialized organization in North America is devoted purely to this subject.

Interestingly, the production of cat stamps is not exclusive to the country of the cat, so that the Russian Blue may be featured on a Danish stamp, or the Scottish Fold may be found on a stamp in China. However, the Isle of Man has capitalized on its unique feline, the Manx. This very important emblem appears not only on the island's stamps, but on its coins as well.

HALLOWEEN MEMORABILIA

Another large range of cat collectibles can be found in the merchandise for Halloween. The reason lies in the age-old association made between cats and witches (*see page 30*), as well as the naturally mysterious image of the black cat itself. Today, most superstitions about black cats and evil have been discarded, although their association with Halloween is as strong as ever. Sending special cards and decorating the house is still part of the fun: the difference now is that

Playing cards
These 20th-century playing cards penned by Austrian cartoonist Manfred Deix are now collectors' items. His humorous illustrations are very appealing, especially the chain-smoking King of Diamonds and cross-eyed Ace.

Halloween symbol
For many years, black cats have been associated with the Halloween festival. In some places, and especially in North America, people decorate their homes, and these cats are typical of Halloween decor.

designers depict the black cat as a benign creature and the Halloween cat is more decorative than frightening. For sure, Halloween merchandise will brighten up any cat collection.

CAT PROMOTIONS

Cats have figured prominently in advertising campaigns for over a century. Originally, the black cat was used, not because it was popular, but because the color lent itself to inexpensive mass production. One brand in particular became very successful, and advertisements for *Black Cat* label cigarettes, matches, stockings, shoe polish, whiskey, and even apples can now be bought at reasonable prices. Other manufacturers have seen the potential in collectible cat advertising and have designed different labels for the same product, such as the German wine *Zeller Schwarze Katz*. However, cat advertisements depict a variety of cats, not only black ones. Advanced reproductive technology and fluctuations in fashion for different breeds has left a huge range of collectible items.

It is easy to start collecting any of these curios as a hobby, but for some enthusiasts the collection takes over their lives, as well as their homes. Special museums for private collections can now be found in the United States, Great Britain, the Netherlands, Switzerland, and in Malaysia.

Advertising alcohol
Cats have been associated with gin for centuries in Europe, where Old Tom was once a well-known Victorian brand. In Germany a black cat has featured on the wine label for Zeller Schwarze Katz, or Black Cat wine, for many years. One such cat was once seen standing on their winning barrel at a local wine-making competition.

Feline greetings
Postcards were a popular form of correspondence throughout Europe during the early decades of the 20th century. The German card (above) shows an exaggerated, arch-backed tomcat ready to defend his turf, while the French postcard (left) depicts feline natural grace and beauty enhanced by Parisian haute couture.

WORKING AND COMPANION CATS

ORIGINALLY USED AS RATTERS AND MOUSERS AT HOME AND WORK, cats have proved highly effective at pest control all over the world. But it is the cat's endearing personality that has secured its continued usage now that there are other forms of rodent control. From Egyptian fowler and ship's mouser to parliamentary confidant, the domestic cat has fulfilled many roles in both work and play. In North America and many parts of Europe, cats are now the most popular pet, partly due to their predatory skills but more because they are easy to care for and excellent company.

From the time that people first stored grain, the cat has been a safe and very effective method of vermin control. Now, with the shift to urban living, there is less grain to protect, but there are just as many rats and mice to destroy.

INVETERATE HUNTERS

Theban tomb frescoes from the Twelfth Dynasty (c. 1980–1801 BC) indicate that cats may have assisted Egyptians during fishing and fowling expeditions. Whether or not these cats were domesticated is unclear, but they show that the family cat is an inveterate hunter.

Domestication was probably a symbiotic process; humans encouraged the cat to stay by providing meals and shelter, while in turn the cat purged the household of vermin. Over the years, cats have found work in all kinds of places, from offices to museums. Many of these cats have killed a prodigious quota of pests. For example, Towser (1963–1987), a Scottish distillery cat, was credited with

Egyptian hunting fresco
A few hunting scenes that include cats have been found in Theban tombs. In this one (c. 1450 BC), the sculptor Nebamun, and family, are employing the services of a cat to flush fowl out of their secluded, marshy hiding place.

catching a record-breaking 28,899 mice. There is even a convent in Cyprus – St. Nicholas of the Cats – named in honor of the cats that protected it, and the local population, from an infestation of venomous snakes. These cats were introduced to Cyprus from Egypt about AD 328, and they easily adapted to island life.

Cats have worked equally well indoors by protecting sacred scrolls in temples throughout Asia, rare books in libraries across Europe, and food stored in homes and farms the world over.

More recently in the United States, librarians have formed The Library Cat Society, in order to preserve the work of library cats that prevent rodents from damaging book bindings.

UNUSUAL MILITARY COMMISSIONS

Compared with dogs, cats have not only played a minor role in human warfare but also an unhappy one. Stories of their misuse start as early as 525 BC, when Cambyses of Persia took possession of Egypt. It is said that the Persian troops managed to take the city of Pelasium without a blow being struck. They went into battle with live cats secured to their shields, which rendered the Egyptians powerless to resist in case they harmed their sacred animals.

Other military cats have not been so lucky. Two thousand years later, in Germany, vessels were allegedly strapped to the backs of terrified cats, which were forced to run around enemy territory, spreading poisonous fumes.

A very recent tale concerns the US Army's attempt to employ the cat's excellent nocturnal vision by training cats as night scouts for their troops in Vietnam. As plausible as the story sounds, its origins lie with a writer for the satirical magazine *National Lampoon*.

Friends in high places (above)
Very few pictures exist of the president John F. Kennedy (1917–1963) with any of the family cats, although his wife Jacqueline and daughter Caroline look happy and relaxed here, photographed in 1960 with Tom Kitten. Past associations of untrustworthy, sly, or evil cats may have persuaded Kennedy not to appear with cats, even though he was known for liking them.

Public relations opportunity (below left)
Cats are loved regardless of the political beliefs of their owners. Vladimir Lenin (1870–1924), leader of the Communist Party and founder of the modern Russian state, is pictured here stroking a cat. It does appear to be an official pose rather than a casual moment, as Lenin pays more attention to the camera than to the cat.

Work, rest, and play (right)
The cats at the Nga Phe Cahung Monastery in Burma have shown a natural inclination for jumping through hoops. This was first discovered by the Buddhist monks when, during many long hours in meditation, the playful cats jumped through their outstretched arms, which were statically positioned in prayer.

We do know, however, that the British Army employed cats during World War I to act as gas detectors. When they were introduced to front-line trenches (much like canaries in coal mines), their sensitive olfactory system could detect unfamiliar smells well before humans could, therefore acting as an excellent alarm system.

At one time, before the introduction of quarantine laws, all ships carried a rodent-catching cat. Most are unsung heroes, but a few are remembered with honors. There is a bronze statue in Sydney, Australia, of Captain Flinders (1774–1814) and his feline companion, Trim. During the late 1700s they were among the first to chart the Australian coastline. Another ship's cat, Oscar, has been celebrated for his amazing survival rate after an extraordinary number of shipwrecks during World War II.

FAMOUS CAT LOVERS

A cat is the perfect confidant, which may be why so many leaders – American presidents in particular – have kept one. Abraham Lincoln (1809–1865) took back to Washington three bedraggled cats from the Civil War. Slippers, a cat of President Roosevelt (1858–1919), often attended glittering White House dinners. President Clinton (1946–) made "first cat" Socks off-limits to overeager photographers.

Grinding grain (left)
Attempts to train cats to work are usually unsuccessful. This crude 18th-century model of a mill driven by a cat trying to catch a mouse is fun but impractical. A horse or a donkey is certainly better suited to this type of work.

Pampered kittens (right)
The prominent French church leader Cardinal Richelieu (1585–1642) delighted in having kittens around him. Unfortunately, even though he made provision in his will for their continued care, Richelieu was an unpopular leader and his cats suffered when he died.

The official home of the British Prime Minister, 10 Downing Street, has had a succession of cats. Sir Winston Churchill (1874–1965) was known for his love of cats, and his last one, Jock, was provided for in his great owner's will.

The assembly of prestigious ailurophiles includes many other people from royalty and religious leaders to writers, poets, and artists. When a reporter asked the Swiss sculptor Alberto Giacometti (1901–1966) which of his masterpieces he would save from a fire, he replied, "It depends on what is in my house. If there was a cat, and my works, I would save the cat. A cat's life is more important than art." Remarks like this by influential people help to promote the cat's image.

IMPROVING HUMAN LIVES

In recent years, scientists have investigated our relationship with cats. An Australian study confirmed that cat owners visited the doctor less often than noncat owners. In the United States, fewer cat owners died during the year following a major heart attack than those in similar circumstances who did not own a cat.

What remains to be determined is whether an improved quality of life is created by living with cats, or whether living with cats is simply a manifestation of a good quality of life.

Gainfully employed (left)
In an attempt to reduce the risk of potentially dangerous microbes entering into Britain through smuggled food, customs officials commissioned a poster in 1935 showing cats sniffing at baggage, on the prowl for unusual scents. A small wage was even promised for these feline services.

Artistic calling (right)
There are many artists that paint cats but are there any cats that can paint? According to a recent publication, Why Cats Paint, *there are many artistically gifted cats, and Max – shown painting* Birdies *(1991) – is one of them. It is a brilliantly executed book that almost convinces us of innate feline artistic talent.*

CHAPTER THREE

FELINE
DESIGN

THE CAT IS AN ALMOST PERFECTLY DESIGNED predator. Its superb balance and flexibility enable it to catch small prey and escape from larger predators. Its brain, nerves, and hormones harmonize to avoid wasting energy, while still being capable of explosions of activity. The domestic cat's anatomy is almost identical to that of its close wild relatives; most medical problems are caused by injury or illness rather than poor design. Its internal organs and body functions have adapted for survival, its digestive and excretory systems allow it to cope without food for longer than other domesticated animals, and its unique reproductive system is adapted to ensure successful matings each year.

ABOVE MALE FAWN SIAMESE

LEFT ADULT CAT LEAPING THROUGH THE AIR

THE SKELETON

LIGHT YET MARVELOUSLY STURDY, THE FELINE SKELETON EVOLVED for a lifestyle that called for sudden bursts of speed combined with dexterous agility. This substructure is the basis of the extraordinary grace of the cat's movement. Cats have more bones than humans have, mostly because of their tails. All parts of the feline skeleton, from the skull to the tail vertebrae, are in proportion: the legs are slender but robust, supporting a narrow rib cage and a highly supple spine. The cat's shoulder blades are unattached to the main skeleton, permitting superb flexibility at any speed. The entire structure is held together by strong but elastic ligaments.

The hard, rigid structure of the cat's skeleton protects the internal organs, provides points of attachment for muscles, and acts as a system of levers and joints necessary for fluid movement. It is held together by fibrous ligaments, elastic tendons, and rapid-acting, powerful muscles.

THE STRUCTURE AND GROWTH OF BONE

Internally, a bone is a latticed structure of hard, calcified struts, called trabeculae, filled in its core with bone marrow. Bone is nourished by its own blood supply that enters each bone through a nutrient membrane, or foramen.

Bones grow continuously during kittenhood. The skull begins as separate bones, to permit birth, then fuses along suture lines. In some young kittens a small soft spot can be felt on top of the skull; this disappears rapidly.

The long bones of the limbs and rib cage begin as hollow tubes of cartilage, and calcify in infancy, replacing cartilage with bone. The outside of the tube, the periosteum, produces new cells, thickening the bone. Inside, the old bone is constantly remodeled to maintain uniform thickness.

Bones lengthen by constant production of new bone at the growth plates, or epiphyses, at their ends, which are fed by a rich supply of tiny arteries. The growth plates are prone to injury during skeletal development, and both growth hormones and sex hormones influence growth. Curiously, sex hormones inhibit activity; cats neutered very early tend to grow slightly longer leg bones.

If a bone breaks, cells on the periosteum are activated, producing new bone to bridge the gap. Usually, too much new bone is made, but the excess is gradually remodeled from the inside.

JOINTS AND LIGAMENTS

Cats have three very different kinds of joints: fibrous, cartilaginous, and synovial. Each of these has a different level of flexibility, and each of them performs a different function.

The joints at the suture lines between the fused bones that form the skull are made of hard fiber. These joints have no flexibility at all. The mandible or jawbone, for example, is really made up of two bones, with a fibrous joint at the midline between the incisor teeth. If a cat lands heavily on its jawbone in a fall, this hard fibrous joint may split: technically, the cat has not actually broken its jaw, although that is the apparent effect, but has torn this fibrous joint.

Other joints, like the thick discs between the spinal vertebrae, are made from tough cartilage. These cartilaginous joints are looser and more supple than similar joints in other species, such as humans and dogs, providing the cat with a far greater degree of flexibility in its torso.

During growth, the growth plates at the ends of the long bones are temporarily cartilaginous joints, and as such they are less sturdy and more prone to damage than in adulthood.

Synovial joints are found where the greatest degree of movement is needed. They are hinged or ball-and-socket joints, with pearly, smooth, articulating cartilage on their contact surfaces, and surrounded by a joint capsule filled with synovial fluid. This construction is found in the highly flexible joints of the legs and the jaw.

Skull
29 fused bones

7 CERVICAL VERTEBRAE

13 THORACIC VERTEBRAE

7 LUMBAR VERTEBRAE

Vertebrae
Cartilaginous discs sit between these

Scapula
Attached to the spine by muscles and ligaments

Thoracic spikes
These provide sites for muscle attachments

Acoustic meatus
Nerves from the ear enter here

Mandible
Shorter than that of the big cats

Clavicle
Held in position by muscles alone

HUMERUS

CARPALS

Metacarpals
Correspond to the bones in the palm of the hand

ULNA

RADIUS

Phalanges
In the forepaws, these correspond to fingers

Foreleg
Straight radius and ulna are long in cat

Sternum
Made up of 8 bones

Ribs
Usually 13 pairs

FLOATING RIB

Costal cartilage
Lower end of rib is cartilage

Costal arch
Formed by cartilage of last ribs

Wrists
Flexible carpals for dexterity

Tiptoe stance
Weight is carried on the fingers and toes

Synovial joints sometimes suffer from excess production of the lubricating synovial fluid or inflammation due to arthritis or synovitis through injury, disease, or allergic reaction.

Ligaments, the tough bands that hold bones together, are important in all joints, but vital in synovial joints, which inherently lack stability. The feline hip joint, in particular, is prone to dislocation; this is often, although not always, prevented by the ligament that holds the ball of the femur firmly in the socket of the pelvis.

SKELETAL VARIATIONS AND PROBLEMS
The cat's skeleton is one of evolution's superb achievements. In the natural cat, problems such as arthritis and decalcification are caused by disease or hormonal or dietary upsets, not poor design. Until recently, there was little skeletal variation in cat breeds: unlike the dog, which has been radically changed through selective breeding, the cat escaped extreme modification.

Environmental pressures do create natural variations. In hot climates, cats are naturally small; a small animal has a higher surface-area-to-weight ratio, which helps it to keep cool. Free-breeding cats in cold climates, such as Scandinavia, Russia, Canada, and the northern United States, have larger, heavier skeletons.

In natural circumstances, severe skeletal anomalies disappear, most often because lethal problems or survival drawbacks are associated with them. Some, such as taillessness or extra toes (polydactyly), may be perpetuated by their occurrence in a limited gene pool. The natural tailless breeds all developed on islands, and isolated gene pools also perpetuated the high proportion of seven-toed cats around Boston, Massachusetts, and Halifax, Nova Scotia.

Active selection for a breed standard has led to more dramatic changes recently. Siamese and Orientals today have much longer and thinner legs bones than their predecessors, while the British Shorthair's skeleton has become more compact, with heavier long bones. This kind of active intervention has perpetuated the most considerable and worrisome skeletal problems. Exaggerated shapes increase the risk of painful inherited arthritic problems.

EXTREME SKULL SHAPES
The cat has a short face compared with other domestic animals. Selective breeding has not compromised this natural shape as much as in the dog, but changes have occurred, and different breeds have more or less round or angular faces. The most dramatic alterations are those in the length of the head or muzzle.

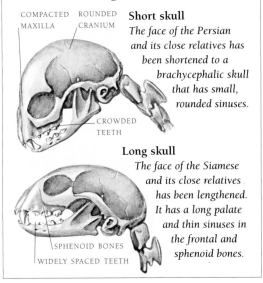

Short skull
The face of the Persian and its close relatives has been shortened to a brachycephalic skull that has small, rounded sinuses.

COMPACTED MAXILLA · ROUNDED CRANIUM · CROWDED TEETH

Long skull
The face of the Siamese and its close relatives has been lengthened. It has a long palate and thin sinuses in the frontal and sphenoid bones.

SPHENOID BONES · WIDELY SPACED TEETH

RETRACTABLE CLAWS
Claws grow from the last bone of the toe and are anchored by tendons. They are modified skin; an outer cuticle of hard protein, keratin, protects the dermis, or quick. Cats' claws are kept sheathed for protection on the move.

KERATIN CUTICLE · DORSAL ELASTIC LIGAMENT · EXTENSOR TENDONS · PROXIMAL PHALANX · LIVE DERMIS · MIDDLE PHALANX · RELAXED DIGITAL FLEXOR TENDON · DISTAL PHALANX · TAUT ELASTIC LIGAMENT · EXTENSOR PROCESS · PIVOT POINT · TAUT DIGITAL FLEXOR TENDON

Extending the claw
At rest, ligaments on the top of the paw naturally sheath the claws. A cat exposes its claws by contracting digital flexor muscles in its legs, pulling taut the flexor tendons under the paw.

ILIUM · 3 FUSED SACRAL VERTEBRAE

Pelvis
Ring made up of fused ilium, ischium, and pubis

PUBIS

Hip joint
Flexible ball-and-socket joint

ISCHIUM

Structure of the skeleton
The domestic cat's skeleton is almost identical to that of the big cats in both shape and proportion; the only real difference is in size. In all cats, the many vertebrae give superb mobility, but the forelegs also provide highly visible flexibility; when a cat walks, its shoulder blades rise above the spine, just as in the lion or tiger. Less apparent to the eye is the intricate bony structure of the wrists, which allows exceptional dexterity in actions such as retrieving prey from its hiding place or walking along narrow ledges.

Tail
Each vertebra of the supple tail articulates

18 TO 20 CAUDAL VERTEBRAE

FEMUR · TIBIA · FIBULA

Tarsus
Cat's foot starts here

PHALANGES · METATARSALS

BIOFEEDBACK AND THE BRAIN

ALL THE SENSES AND THE BODY'S HORMONE-PRODUCING GLANDS send information to the brain. This interprets the chemical signals, and uses the nervous system to tell the body how to respond. The brain also sends instructions to the master gland of the cat's hormonal system, the pituitary, which lies in the base of the brain.

Information from the brain stimulates the pituitary to produce the hormones that control functions and activities such as metabolic rate and sexual behavior. This demands a great deal of energy and, although the brain accounts for less than one percent of body weight, it receives 20 percent of the blood pumped by the heart.

All of the hormones that manage and maintain body functions or regulate feline behavior are under the direct or indirect control of the brain. In both cases, chemical messages are sent from the brain to the hypothalamus, which controls the pituitary. In turn, the pituitary produces hormones that stimulate events elsewhere.

BODY-FUNCTION CONTROLS
Hormones produced in the brain control most of the body's daily functions. Deep in the brain, the hypothalamus gland produces antidiuretic hormone (ADH), which controls the concentration of urine (see page 68), and oxytocin, which stimulates labor and milk release in female cats (see page 70). The pituitary, the "master gland" at the base of the brain, produces a number of hormones. Growth-hormone-releasing hormone (GHRH) and its opposite, growth-hormone-inhibiting hormone (GHIH), regulate the production of growth hormone·(GH) in the cat's brain. GH production continues after kittenhood, although its role in adult cats is not clear.

Thyroid-stimulating hormone (TSH) initiates activity in the thyroid, which controls metabolic rate (see page 68). Adrenocorticotrophic hormone (ACTH) stimulates the adrenal gland to produce cortisol in response to stress or danger. Production of sexual hormones, eggs, and sperm (see page 70) is controlled by follicle-stimulating hormone (FSH) in females and luteinizing hormone (LH) in males.

One of the more recently isolated hormonal controls is melanin. The pituitary produces melanocyte-stimulating hormone (MSH), stimulating melanin synthesis in the pineal gland. Melanin is involved in triggering sleep cycles and controls the body's internal clock, maintaining the day-and-night pattern known as circadian rhythm.

THE ADRENAL GLANDS
The adrenal glands lie adjacent to each kidney, and consist of an encapsulating cortex and a central core, or medulla. The adrenal cortex produces cortisol and other hormones, which are instrumental in controlling metabolic rate and determining the body's response to injury.

Early learning
A kitten's brain is almost fully developed at birth. By seven weeks of age, most areas have matured. Skills are acquired fastest during this development stage; learning before seven weeks of age is more important in cats than in dogs, whose brains continue to develop for another month, or humans, whose brain development takes years.

The adrenal medulla produces epinephrine and norepinephrine, better known as adrenaline and noradrenaline. These hormones control the heart rate and blood vessel dilation.

The adrenals are a vital component of the biofeedback circuit. This system controls the fight-or-flight response, and has the most direct effect on feline behavior. The biofeedback mechanism dictates the innate disposition, sociability, and tamability of the cat.

THE BIOLOGICAL COMPUTER
Sitting on top of all this activity is the brain. The brain is an almost incalculably intricate information storage system, which consists of billions of specialized cells called neurons, each with up to 10,000 connections with other cells.

The biofeedback mechanism
This mechanism is the cycle of response to any external stimulus: here, an unfamiliar scent. The balance of the cycle determines a cat's character. The African wildcat was willing to live close to humans because it had an innate ability to stay calm around them. It controlled its biofeedback mechanism, fine-tuning the interplay between its pituitary and adrenal hormones and resisting panic.

Adrenal gland
ACTH stimulates cortex to produce cortisol, while nervous stimuli make medulla produce epinephrine

KIDNEY

Cortisol released
Cortisol suppresses CRH production to bring the fight-or-flight reaction under control

Brain activity
CRH stimulates pituitary to release adrenocorticotrophic hormone (ACTH)

Hormone released
ACTH transmitted through blood to adrenal glands

Scent stimulus
Unknown scent is picked up and stimulates the hypothalamus to produce corticotrophin-releasing hormone (CRH)

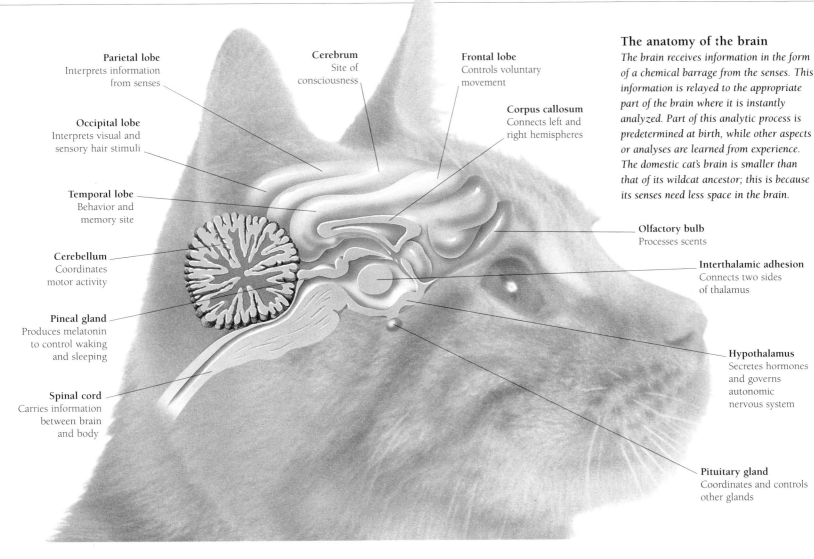

Parietal lobe
Interprets information
from senses

Cerebrum
Site of
consciousness

Frontal lobe
Controls voluntary
movement

Occipital lobe
Interprets visual and
sensory hair stimuli

Corpus callosum
Connects left and
right hemispheres

Temporal lobe
Behavior and
memory site

Cerebellum
Coordinates
motor activity

Olfactory bulb
Processes scents

Interthalamic adhesion
Connects two sides
of thalamus

Pineal gland
Produces melatonin
to control waking
and sleeping

Hypothalamus
Secretes hormones
and governs
autonomic
nervous system

Spinal cord
Carries information
between brain
and body

Pituitary gland
Coordinates and controls
other glands

The anatomy of the brain
The brain receives information in the form of a chemical barrage from the senses. This information is relayed to the appropriate part of the brain where it is instantly analyzed. Part of this analytic process is predetermined at birth, while other aspects or analyses are learned from experience. The domestic cat's brain is smaller than that of its wildcat ancestor; this is because its senses need less space in the brain.

Neurons communicate with each other through chemical substances called neurotransmitters. By seven weeks of age, messages move through the cat's brain at almost 240 mph (386 kph). This rate of transmission slows down with age, but recent studies have shown that this can be reversed. Elderly cats offered mental stimulation can actually grow heavier brains The increased weight is due not to new brain cells, but to more connections between existing ones.

The brain's capacity to store information is genetically predetermined. Some stored data is instinctive, or present at birth, and controls sexual behavior, territorial marking, aggression, and attachments made during kittenhood. But the feline brain can also absorb new data, such as how to use a cat flap or obtain food.

Anatomically, the cat's brain is similar to that of any other mammal. The cerebellum controls the muscles (*see* page 64),

Not idle dreams
Sleep is hormonally controlled. During sleep cats dream much as we do, probably sorting out memories of the day's events.

the cerebrum governs learning, emotion, and behavior, and the brain stem connects to the nervous system (*see page 62*). A network of cells called the limbic system is believed to integrate instinct and learning. Conflict between what a cat instinctively wants to do and what learning impels it to do probably takes place here.

FELINE INTELLIGENCE
Circuitry and hormones form the framework on which personality develops. This structure varies from cat to cat, and is genetically influenced. It is also only part of the picture; development also depends on learning. Just as humans have an instinct to communicate vocally at birth, but must learn how to use a language, cats are born with instincts to mark and defend territory, or hunt for sustenance, but must learn how to achieve these things. Cats that need not hunt to survive simply never

develop the "hunting" parts of their brains. Many still hunt, but do not succeed like those that have learned and practiced (*see page 84*). Feral cats develop a valid suspicion of other animals and people, because cats are small and relatively defenseless against such adversaries.

By raising kittens in our homes, we actively intervene in the development of their brains, biofeedback mechanisms, and behavior. A cat raised in a human home before seven weeks of age has modified biofeedback. It learns that humans are safe, knowledge that is fixed into its brain and hormonal responses to us.

Some people believe that cats cannot learn; they may appear unable to, because their brains are designed for solitary living, and respond poorly to the social learning that we, as pack animals, naturally use. Cats do not usually obey for praise, because esteem holds no survival advantage to a solo hunter, but for a food reward, they may comply with human wishes. The clearest example of feline thought is the cat that fights against entering its carrier to go to the veterinarian, but walks straight in for the return trip. Faced with two evils, the cat is quite capable of deciding which is the lesser.

THE SENSES

FROM THE MOMENT IT IS BORN, A CAT NEEDS SENSES TO SURVIVE. At birth, heat and smell receptors in its nose help it to seek out its mother. Over the next three months, all of the senses develop to maturity. Information from the cat's environment is picked up by sensory organs, which convert the information into chemical or electrical signals that are transmitted through specialized nerves to the brain. Feline senses are similar to ours, but they have developed along different lines. In addition to the classic five senses, cats have refined balance, the sex-scenting sense of the vomeronasal organ, and possibly, even an electromagnetic "homing" sense.

The cat is the most sophisticated and perhaps the most successful of all the land-based predators. Its small size, however, means that it is also prey to larger animals. The cat's senses have evolved to equip it for hunting prey, but also for sensing and avoiding danger.

TOUCH-SENSITIVE WHISKERS

Touch receptors are found all over a cat's body, but mostly in the paw pads and whiskers. Kittens grow their touch-sensitive whiskers, or vibrissae, while still in the womb, before they grow any other hair, and newborn kittens, although blind and virtually deaf, have fully functional whiskers. Later in life, the specialized sensory ability of the whiskers helps the cat in its nocturnal hunting, providing information about the environment and movement of prey. The mandibular and mystacial vibrissae, sited on the chin and upper lip, are the longest and most abundant. These whiskers can be angled forward in greeting or backward out of harm's way when fighting or feeding. The top rows can move independently of the bottom rows. Superciliary facial whiskers above the eyes and genal whiskers on the cheeks warn of dangers to the eyes as a cat explores, and a sixth set of whiskers extends from the back of each foreleg.

HEARING AND BALANCE

Evolution has equipped the cat with excellent hearing, well adapted for hunting small rodents. It can detect the faintest high-pitched squeaks of a mouse or the rustle of tiny movements. Noise consists of pressure waves traveling in the air. These are channeled through the ear, converted to electrical impulses, and carried to the brain, which interprets them. Pressure in the inner ear is regulated by its connection to the back of the throat via the Eustachian tube.

The other function of the ear is to help the cat to balance. While most domestic animals live on the ground, the cat is a natural climber, and has a sensitive sense of balance. In the inner ear is the organ of balance, the vestibular apparatus. Changes in direction or velocity register instantly in this organ, allowing the cat to compensate by changing its orientation.

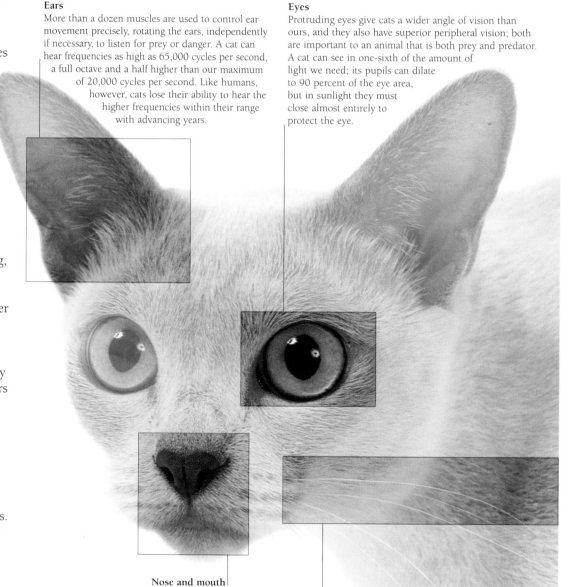

Ears
More than a dozen muscles are used to control ear movement precisely, rotating the ears, independently if necessary, to listen for prey or danger. A cat can hear frequencies as high as 65,000 cycles per second, a full octave and a half higher than our maximum of 20,000 cycles per second. Like humans, however, cats lose their ability to hear the higher frequencies within their range with advancing years.

Eyes
Protruding eyes give cats a wider angle of vision than ours, and they also have superior peripheral vision; both are important to an animal that is both prey and predator. A cat can see in one-sixth of the amount of light we need; its pupils can dilate to 90 percent of the eye area, but in sunlight they must close almost entirely to protect the eye.

Nose and mouth
Cats have twice as many smell-sensitive cells, or olfactory receptors, in their noses as we do, allowing them to register scents we are not even aware of. Their taste buds are specialized to detect the amino acids of meat, and are less able than ours to detect the carbohydrate constituents of vegetable matter.

Whiskers
Whiskers are highly mobile and incredibly sensitive, capable of detecting anything that displaces them by a distance 2,000 times less than the width of a human hair. Tip to tip, the facial whiskers indicate the smallest gap a cat can comfortably pass though.

Senses for survival

Although many pet cats hunt nothing more than fluffy toys or their owner's ankles, they retain virtually all of the sensory abilities of a wild hunter. Selective breeding and a protected life have not diminished the cat's sensory capacity, although this could happen in the future.

Breeding certain cats perpetuates sensory defects that would be limited under natural circumstances. Deafness, for example, is not life-threatening for the indoor cat, and some breeders deliberately breed deaf blue-eyed cats, knowing they will live safely indoors. Rexed cats may have whiskers more brittle than those of other breeds.

FELINE VISION

Most experts believe that cats are color-blind. Tests have shown that the color-sensitive cone cells on their retinas are sensitive to blue and green, but not to red. In trials, cats differentiate between green, blue, and yellow, but do not recognize red. In normal life, color appears meaningless to cats. Cats' eyes are more sensitive to movement than ours, with more motion-detecting rod cells in the retina. The cat's world is seen in soft focus, however; it cannot resolve detail sharply because the lens in its eye is large, to gather as much light as possible.

But by far the most spectacular modification in the cat's eye is the tapetum lucidum, a layer of reflective cells behind the retina. This bounces light back through the retina to give rods and cones a heightened ability to extract information.

THE CHEMICAL SENSES

Smell and taste are chemical senses. Cats have a good sense of smell, better than ours but not as refined as a dog's. A newborn kitten's nose is sensitive enough to smell differences between its mother's individual nipples. Later, the nose is used to scent prey or food, to detect potential danger, and to identify friend from foe and read the chemical messages left in urine or feces. Unlike us, but like many other mammals, cats have a vomeronasal, or Jacobson's, organ in the hard palate that forms the roof of the mouth. When a cat uses this organ, its mouth opens in something between grimacing and gaping, called flehmen. Assisted by the tongue, odors are "lapped" into the vomeronasal organ, and sent to the hypothalamus area of the brain (see page 58); odors from the nose take another route.

The cat's mouth is exquisitely equipped for discriminating eating. The tip, sides, and back of the tongue, and part of the throat, contain mounds of tissue called papillae. An adult cat has about 250 mushroom-shaped fungiform papillae, each holding anything from 40 to 40,000 taste buds. Cone-shaped vallate papillae at the back of the tongue contain more taste buds. Taste tests indicate that cats can detect sour, bitter, and salty tastes, but not sweet ones.

A SENSE OF PLACE

Scientific studies suggest that cats are equipped to find their way home. Research from Germany and the United States implies that older cats in particular show a homing ability if released within 7½ miles (12 km) of home. Researchers conclude that cats are probably aware of electromagnetic fields: magnets attached to cats disrupted the homing ability. This could explain why there are minute traces of iron in the cat's brain cells.

THE ANATOMY OF THE SENSES

The cat's senses work in a similar way to ours. Sights, sounds, physical contact, or chemicals in the cat's environment affect one or more of its sensory organs. These external stimuli are captured by the sensory organ, which then converts the information into either electrical or neurochemical messages. These travel at lightning speed to the brain. Some messages are analyzed instantly; others may take a fraction longer to interpret. The brain produces a physical, mental, or hormonal response. For example, a cat's left ear captures the squeak of a mouse and passes it to the brain. At the same time, its nose picks up scent and passes it to the pituitary gland. The cat instantly turns its head to capture sounds in both ears and look for any movement, and its pituitary secretes hormones as the cat prepares to pounce.

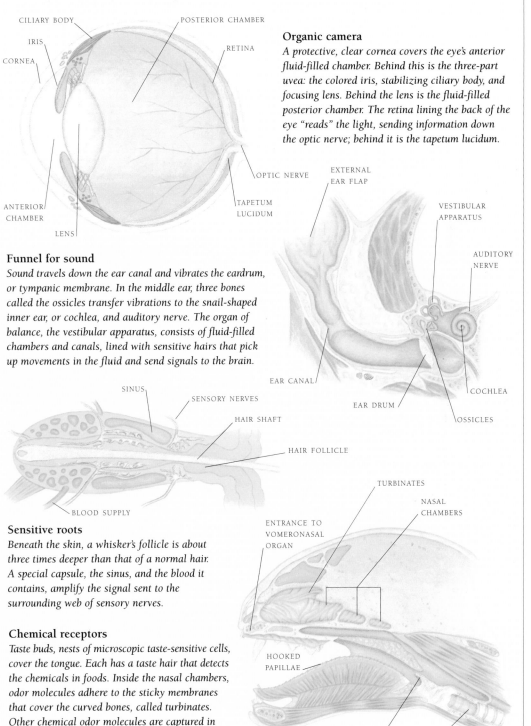

Organic camera
A protective, clear cornea covers the eye's anterior fluid-filled chamber. Behind this is the three-part uvea: the colored iris, stabilizing ciliary body, and focusing lens. Behind the lens is the fluid-filled posterior chamber. The retina lining the back of the eye "reads" the light, sending information down the optic nerve; behind it is the tapetum lucidum.

CILIARY BODY
POSTERIOR CHAMBER
IRIS
RETINA
CORNEA
OPTIC NERVE
ANTERIOR CHAMBER
TAPETUM LUCIDUM
LENS

Funnel for sound
Sound travels down the ear canal and vibrates the eardrum, or tympanic membrane. In the middle ear, three bones called the ossicles transfer vibrations to the snail-shaped inner ear, or cochlea, and auditory nerve. The organ of balance, the vestibular apparatus, consists of fluid-filled chambers and canals, lined with sensitive hairs that pick up movements in the fluid and send signals to the brain.

EXTERNAL EAR FLAP
VESTIBULAR APPARATUS
AUDITORY NERVE
EAR CANAL
COCHLEA
EAR DRUM
OSSICLES

SINUS
SENSORY NERVES
HAIR SHAFT
HAIR FOLLICLE
BLOOD SUPPLY

Sensitive roots
Beneath the skin, a whisker's follicle is about three times deeper than that of a normal hair. A special capsule, the sinus, and the blood it contains, amplify the signal sent to the surrounding web of sensory nerves.

Chemical receptors
Taste buds, nests of microscopic taste-sensitive cells, cover the tongue. Each has a taste hair that detects the chemicals in foods. Inside the nasal chambers, odor molecules adhere to the sticky membranes that cover the curved bones, called turbinates. Other chemical odor molecules are captured in the vomeronasal organ in the roof of the mouth.

TURBINATES
NASAL CHAMBERS
ENTRANCE TO VOMERONASAL ORGAN
HOOKED PAPILLAE
EPIGLOTTIS
WINDPIPE

THE NERVOUS SYSTEM

THE NERVOUS SYSTEM COORDINATES EVERY ASPECT OF A CAT'S LIFE. It works in close conjunction with the hormonal system, to which it is linked through the brain and pituitary gland, to coordinate all of the cat's natural functions second by second, day by day, even season by season. While hormones have slow but lasting effects, the nervous system, with its amazingly intricate circuitry, responds swiftly, accurately, and directly to both internal and external events. Some areas of the nervous system are under the cat's voluntary control; others function apparently on their own, but in reality they are controlled at deeper, unconscious levels.

Information travels through the nervous system in two directions: sensory nerves inform the brain about how a cat feels, and motor nerves carry information away from the brain, telling the cat's body what to do about how it feels.

CENTRAL AND PERIPHERAL

The nervous system is divided into two parts, central and peripheral. The central nervous system consists of the brain (*see page 58*) and spinal cord – the body's command center and the superhighway for two-way transmission of nerve impulses. The peripheral nervous system receives information about temperature, touch, pressure, and pain, and delivers instructions to muscles (*see page 64*). It consists of the cranial nerves and the spinal or peripheral nerves.

The cranial nerves are responsible for facial muscles and the transmission of information from the senses (*see page 60*). They spread out from under the brain in a region called the brain stem. The spinal nerves branch out from the spinal cord along its length, linking the body's extremities and central nervous system.

This division of the nervous system is for ease of understanding; it is not a physical split. Many nerve cells are partly in the central nervous system and partly in the peripheral nervous system.

CHEMICAL MESSENGERS

The nervous system consists of nerve cells, called neurons, and support cells that provide structure and produce myelin (*see page 63*).

A neuron's body is covered with branchlike structures, called dendrites, which receive messages from other cells. Each cell also has a long, tail-like structure, called an axon, which sends messages to other nerve cells or directly to organs. All of these messages are carried by neurotransmitters, chemicals produced in axons, which navigate the tiny gap between nerve cells, known as the synaptic cleft. Neurons never touch each other.

At any moment, even in deep sleep, a cat's nervous system is sending and receiving vast numbers of messages. Any cell commonly sends messages to thousands of other cells.

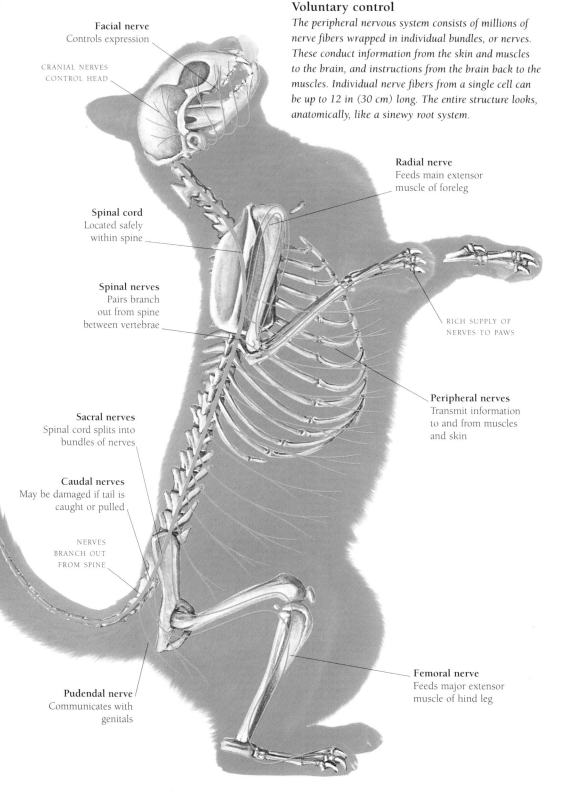

Facial nerve
Controls expression

CRANIAL NERVES
CONTROL HEAD

Spinal cord
Located safely
within spine

Spinal nerves
Pairs branch
out from spine
between vertebrae

Sacral nerves
Spinal cord splits into
bundles of nerves

Caudal nerves
May be damaged if tail is
caught or pulled

NERVES
BRANCH OUT
FROM SPINE

Pudendal nerve
Communicates with
genitals

Voluntary control
The peripheral nervous system consists of millions of nerve fibers wrapped in individual bundles, or nerves. These conduct information from the skin and muscles to the brain, and instructions from the brain back to the muscles. Individual nerve fibers from a single cell can be up to 12 in (30 cm) long. The entire structure looks, anatomically, like a sinewy root system.

Radial nerve
Feeds main extensor
muscle of foreleg

RICH SUPPLY OF
NERVES TO PAWS

Peripheral nerves
Transmit information
to and from muscles
and skin

Femoral nerve
Feeds major extensor
muscle of hind leg

THE MYELIN SHEATH

Myelin is a fatty, protective membrane found around the largest axons that increases the speed of communication along the nerves. Technically, a nerve fiber consists of an axon, its myelin sheathing, and the cell that makes the myelin. Myelin is produced by cells called oligodendrocytes inside the central nervous system, and neurolemmocytes in the peripheral system. Few nerves have myelin sheathing at birth, but the cat's nerves are myelinated quickly, and very effectively.

Protective layers
Myelin layers, seen here as colored lines, sheathe axons. The cat's well-myelinated system is one of the reasons why its physical responses are so good.

UNCONSCIOUS CONTROL

Many functions of the nervous system are under conscious, or voluntary, control. When a cat sees prey, it voluntarily controls its muscles so that it can pounce on its prey. Sensory nerves carry messages to the brain, and motor nerves carry messages back to the muscles, stimulating them to work in the controlled way necessary to pounce accurately.

But other activities are involuntary. These usually involve the internal organs, regulating heartbeat and breathing (*see page 66*) and the many digestive processes (*see page 68*). Such involuntary activities are controlled by the autonomic nervous system.

The autonomic system consists of two parts: sympathetic and parasympathetic. The former stimulates activity; the latter damps it down. When a cat is relaxed, the parasympathetic part controls involuntary activity: the pupils are relaxed, and the heart rate and breathing are slow and regular. When a cat becomes stressed, the sympathetic system takes over, triggering the hypothalamus and the pituitary in the brain to stimulate the adrenal glands (*see page 58*) into the "fight-or-flight" response. This chain of response, although complex, is instantaneous. Blood flows from internal organs into muscles, tiny subcutaneous muscles cause body hair to stand on end (*see page 72*), the heart speeds up, and pupils dilate for better vision (*see page 60*).

Inherent problems
Manx cats often suffer from a congenital neurological disorder called spina bifida, which interferes with normal nerve operation. Completely tailless Manx cats may have malformed sacral and caudal nerves and be incontinent as a result.

Even a perceived threat will trigger this cascade of activities in the autonomic nervous system. If the alarm is false, the sympathetic system is deactivated, and the parasympathetic system takes charge of involuntary activity once more.

NEUROLOGICAL PROBLEMS

Neurological disorders are remarkably rare in cats, a tribute to their evolutionary credentials. Viral infections like rabies, panleucopenia virus, and feline infectious peritonitis (FIP), as well as poisons and a variety of parasites, such as toxoplasma, damage nerves. However, traffic accidents are the most common causes of nerve damage: almost half of all cats hit by cars have head injuries. Also, broken backs, almost inevitably with severed spinal cords, are not uncommon. Unlike other body cells, nerve cells cannot regenerate; there is no repair possible.

Skin and coat
Blood vessels, surface nerves, and sweat glands are fed from ganglia

Combined control
Liver and digestive tract are controlled from same ganglion

Kidneys
These receive only parasympathetic signals

Central nervous system
Controls parasympathetic impulses

Control from brain stem
One parasympathetic locus controls most bodily functions

Esophagus and windpipe
Both of these receive only sympathetic signals

Ganglia
These nerve junctions beneath spinal cord control sympathetic impulses

Anal sphincter
Defecation is under conscious control

Automatic control
The autonomic nervous system controls involuntary functions and activities. While a cat is relaxed and not stressed, its parasympathetic nervous system is in charge. Under stress, its sympathetic nervous system instantly takes charge, increasing the heart rate, dilating the pupils, and diverting blood to the muscles for immediate action.

Lungs
There is limited conscious control of breathing

Bladder
Release of urine is under conscious control

Intestines
Digestive tract is not under conscious control

MUSCLES AND MOVEMENT

THE FELINE BODY RESPONDS SWIFTLY AND SUPERBLY TO MESSAGES sent by the brain via the nervous system. The cat's extraordinary balletic grace is partly attributable to its highly specialized skeleton, but its fast-acting muscles are also responsible. The strong, flexible musculoskeletal framework has evolved to fulfill two purposes: it makes the cat an efficient hunter, and enables it to escape from dangerous situations. This combination of power, flexibility, and balance has enabled the cat to survive in its ecological niche of small predator. Its speed and grace in movement depend upon its muscles or, more accurately, the types of cells within its muscles.

All muscles are divided into three basic types. One is cardiac muscle, found only in the heart (*see page 66*). The muscle controlling the other internal organs is "involuntary," or outside the cat's control, and is called smooth or non-striated, because this is how it appears under the microscope. The rest of the body's muscles are called striated or striped. They are controlled at will and used in all conscious or instinctive movement. Cats have fewer striated muscles than humans, in part because they use less facial expression for communication.

Each muscle has a Latin name according to its shape, attachments, function, location, or number of parts. Feline muscles are inherently more flexible than those of other mammals, giving a great range of movement. Most muscles are attached to bones (*see page 56*) on either side of a joint, and act to operate the joint itself.

Muscles can only contract – they cannot extend – so opposing muscles perform opposing actions; the gastrocnemius and quadriceps extend the hind leg, and the biceps femoris and tibialis bend or flex it. If the extensors, or their tendons or ligaments, are torn in an accident, the leg will be permanently retracted; if the retractors are torn, it will be permanently extended.

MUSCLE CELLS

Each individual muscle consists of many muscle fibers, which are held together as a group by connective tissue. The muscle tissue consists of three different types of muscle cells, all named after their actions. "Fast-twitch fatiguing" cells work quickly, but they tire equally quickly. "Fast-twitch fatigue-resistant" cells work quickly but tire more slowly. "Slow-twitch" cells work comparatively slowly and also tire slowly.

A FLOATING SHOULDER

The cat's shoulder is a feat of muscle, in that the forelimb is connected to the rest of the body only by muscle. Unlike our collarbone, which connects the shoulder and breastbone, the cat's vestigial clavicle "floats," anchored in place by muscle. The shoulder's freedom of movement effectively lengthens the cat's stride and enhances its range of motion.

Floating bone
The collarbone, seen in the top left corner of this X ray, is a mere sliver of bone held in place by the muscles.

The striated muscles
The striated muscles are symmetrical across the body and under the control of the central and peripheral nervous system (see page 62). These muscles act on joints, rather than individual bones. Generally, they are arranged in opposing groups with opposite actions.

Gluteal muscles
Extend hip

Sartorius
Raises knee or rotates thigh outward

Dorsals
Twist and curl torso

Trapezius
Draws shoulder up

Facial muscles
These are thin, and facial expression is limited

Jaw muscles
Capable of exerting enormous pressure

Deltoid
Pulls shoulder forward

Biceps femoris
Flexes or bends leg

Oblique abdominals
Layers of muscle hold in internal organs

Triceps
Straightens elbow, drawing back lower leg

Tail muscles
Sacrocaudals and intertransversarials raise, lower, and curl tail

Gastrocnemius
Extends lower leg and points toes

Pectorals
Draws back shoulder and foreleg

Digital extensor muscles
Extend toes and claws

Muscles in motion
The powerful hindquarters are used for leaps. In a well-timed jump, a cat might spring six times its own length.

The cat's muscles mostly consist of fast-twitch fatiguing cells: they give the cat its speed and permit it to leap several times its own length in a single bound, but they use up all their energy in an instant. They make cats superb sprinters, capable of reaching 30 mph (48 kph) in a few seconds, but this speed has a price. Because it has relatively few fast-twitch fatigue-resistant cells, the cat is a poor endurance athlete. Even when just trotting, a cat uses more energy than a dog of similar weight and size. If this exertion continues, a cat's muscles will generate so much power that it overheats. Its body temperature rises after less than a minute of sprinting, and it must stop and pant.

The third type of cell, slow-twitch, produces slow, sustainable contractions. These cells are called into play during hunting activities; they enable the cat to move almost imperceptibly slowly and stealthily, or wait for prolonged periods in a crouched, ready-to-spring position.

THE FELINE GAIT
When a cat walks, almost all of its forward movement is generated by the hind legs; the forelegs act like brakes when they hit the ground, almost negating the slight forward push they give on leaving it again. The same is true when a cat trots. In this gait the legs move in what is called contralateral fashion: the right front moves forward together with the left hind and vice versa. When a cat bounds or gallops, its body is propelled forward by the power of both the hind legs pushing off at the same time, and the whole body becomes airborne until the forelegs touch down.

POUNCES AND JUMPS
The cat's pliant muscles and flexible spine allow it to curl in a circle to sleep, or to rotate its body through 180º in midair. This snakelike flexibility also gives the cat a wide repertoire of graceful leaping movements suitable for different circumstances. When pouncing, a cat springs with its hind legs, arches its back, and lands with its forepaws on its prize. A refined arrangement of wrist muscles allows it to rotate its wrists, just as humans can, to grasp prey and to climb efficiently.

The vertical jump is carefully executed. A cat judges the distance to be covered and calculates how much propulsive power from its hind leg muscles is needed. This movement is different from the impromptu jumps made when chasing or being chased, and these are different again from the startle jump. In this, extensor muscles in all four legs activate simultaneously, and all the feet leave the ground at once, as if on springs.

HIGH-RISE SYNDROME
The excellent righting reflex, which allows the cat to flip right side up, and the soft paws and flexible joints that absorb the impact of landing, give the cat its legendary ability to survive falls. As more and more cats live in high-rise buildings, vets have observed a strange phenomenon. Cats that fall fewer than four floors usually survive their mishaps, but falls from five to ten floors are usually fatal. Computer modeling trials show that cats reach 60 mph (97 kph) after falling five floors, and the force of impact is too great to absorb. Curiously, falls from even greater heights sometimes cause little injury. This is because, once the righting reflex has served its purpose, the cat assumes the skydiver's free fall position: limbs outstretched and relaxed, and head held high. This muscular relaxation, taken together with the deceleration effected by outstretched limbs, lessens the impact and injury. These reflexes did not evolve to save cats in falls from windows, but natural abilities often have unexpected new uses.

Vertical climbing
Powerful leg muscles, flexible joints, extendable claws, and a sophisticated sense of balance allow the cat to live in a vertical as well as horizontal world.

The righting reflex depends upon keen sight, an efficient vestibular apparatus (*see page 160*), a flexible spine, and resilient musculature. This entire flip can be accomplished in just 2 ft (60 cm). Soft paw pads and flexible joints act as shock absorbers when the cat lands.

Instant response
The cat levels its head, and then rotates its upper chest and forelegs. The hindquarters follow, and the back arches. The forelegs come down first, and the flexible shoulders absorb the impact of landing.

THE HEART AND LUNGS

THE CAT'S LUNGS, HEART, AND CIRCULATORY SYSTEM ARE DESIGNED for an animal whose actions are usually controlled and planned, but occasionally demand sudden, rapid bursts of great energy. Instructions from the nervous and hormonal systems can rapidly increase the pumping action of the heart and divert circulating blood from the brain and internal organs to muscles. Blood carries oxygen from the lungs and nutrients from the intestines through the body. It collects waste to be expelled from the lungs, detoxified in the liver, or excreted through the kidneys. It is made primarily in the bone marrow; an emergency reservoir is held in the spleen.

Each time a cat takes a breath, it draws in vital oxygen and exhales waste carbon dioxide. Every beat of its heart pumps these and other substances through the circulatory system to and from the farthest reaches of the body.

THE RESPIRATORY SYSTEM

Inhaled air first passes through the scenting apparatus of the nose (see page 60), surrounded by the frontal sinuses, where it is is warmed, humidified, and filtered. It is then drawn down the trachea, or windpipe, and into the lungs through two bronchi. Each bronchus splits into many smaller bronchioles that end in tiny pockets called alveoli.

THE CIRCULATORY SYSTEM

The body of a typical 12-lb (5-kg) cat contains about 12 fl oz (330 ml) of blood, about the same amount as in a soft-drink can. Pressure is highest in the arteries, which carry blood from the heart, and lowest in the veins returning it to the heart. The muscular, elastic walls of arteries expand and contract as the heart pushes blood through them: this is the pulse. The thinner walls of the veins are more easily damaged; they have no pulse, and contain valves to ensure that the blood in them moves only one way.

Different parts of the body need different amounts of blood. The brain is a small part of the body's weight, but takes 15 to 20 percent of its blood. Resting muscles get about twice this, but during pursuits or in escape situations, up to 90 percent of the blood can be diverted into the muscles from the internal organs and even from the brain. The amount of blood that each part of the body receives is controlled by nerves and hormones that cause arterioles to dilate in response to local activity, dramatically increasing the blood supply to that region.

THE COMPOSITION OF BLOOD

The bulk of blood volume is pale yellow plasma. Another 30 to 45 percent is red blood cells, and the remainder is white cells and platelets. In kittens, the liver and spleen make blood cells; in adults bone marrow produces them.

The heart and lungs

The heart and lungs occupy the thoracic cavity, separated from the abdominal cavity by the diaphragm, which keeps the lungs fully inflated by maintaining negative pressure within the thoracic cavity. Arteries carry bright red blood, rich in oxygen from the lungs and nutrients from the digestive system, from the heart to the body. Veins bring darker blood laden with carbon dioxide and waste matter back to the lungs, liver, and kidneys. The exceptions to this are the pulmonary artery, which carries used blood to the lungs, and the pulmonary vein, which carries fresh blood to the heart.

Frontal sinuses
Vulnerable to inflammation in asthma

WINDPIPE

Axillary artery
Supplies forelimb

Anterior vena cava
Brings blood from head to heart

Aorta
Main artery supplying body with blood

Caudal vena cava
Brings blood from body to heart

Diaphragm
Separates heart and lungs from viscera

Lungs
Absorb oxygen and expel carbon dioxide

Spleen
Stores reserve blood

Pulmonary artery
Carries used blood to lungs

Kidneys
Filter toxins from blood

Pulmonary vein
Carries refreshed blood to heart

A BLOOD CLOT HERE MAY CAUSE PARALYSIS

Liver
Passes nutrients into veins

Intestines
Water and nutrients absorbed from here

Iliac artery
Supplies hind limb

Plasma in the blood provides transportation, carrying nutrients from the digestive system (*see page 68*), and transporting waste. Levels of plasma are maintained by liquid absorbed along the length of the large intestine.

Red cells carry oxygen through the arteries to the cells of the body. Oxygen attaches to a red-pigmented protein called hemoglobin in the cells to create oxyhemoglobin, which is bright red in color. The oxygen diffuses through capillary walls into cell tissue. In return, carbon dioxide diffuses into the veins and attaches to hemoglobin to make blue-red methemoglobin.

White blood cells defend the body against microbes and parasites, clear waste from injuries, detoxify substances released in allergic reactions, and help the body to acquire immunity against infections by producing antibodies. Disk-shaped platelets help to clot blood around wounds.

BLOOD TYPES

Cats have three blood types: A, B, and AB. Most cats are type A, but the incidence of types varies geographically. In the United States, almost 100 percent of cats are type A in New England, but this falls to 95 percent on the West Coast. Virtually all random-bred cats in Switzerland are type A, but this drops to 97 percent in Britain, Austria, and Holland, 94 percent in Germany, 89 percent in Italy, and 85 percent in France.

Many pedigreed breeds are almost exclusively type A, but others show varying levels of type B, most notably the Exotic Shorthair (*see page 150*) and Cornish Rex (*see page 198*) with up to 25 percent, and the British Shorthair (*see page 152*) and Devon Rex (*see page 200*) at nearly 50 percent. Type AB is extremely rare and not linked to breed.

BLOOD PROBLEMS

Some problems with circulation have external causes. If a cat does not eat, there is little water in the large intestines to be absorbed to maintain plasma levels, so water is drawn from elsewhere in the body, causing dehydration.

In anemia, the level of red blood cells falls, to be corrected by the bone marrow producing new cells. Heavy flea infestation, injury, stomach ulcers, or tumors can cause temporary anemia. Illness can inhibit the production of new cells.

The cat's meow
The ability to meow that sets the small cats aside from the big cats is due to a difference in the throat structure. Less certain is how a cat purrs. Some anatomists feel that it is the sound of turbulence in the anterior vena cava, creating vibrations that are transferred up the windpipe.

Such nonregenerative anemia is often caused by feline leukemia virus (FeLV), kidney failure, nutritional deficiency, or poisoning. Hemolytic anemias, resulting from the destruction of red blood cells, may be caused by the blood parasite *Hemobartonella felis*, or by acetaminophen, the active ingredient in many nonaspirin painkillers. Aspirin in excess can cause fatal bleeding. The bleeding disorder hemophilia is rare in cats.

Cats do not develop hardening of the arteries but may develop diseases of the heart muscle (cardiomyopathy) or valves (valvular disease), or disruption of the heart's rate (arrhythmias). They can suffer blood clots (thromboembolisms), causing pain and paralysis to the hind limbs.

INSIDE THE HEART AND LUNGS

Pulmonary arteries and their capillaries carry oxygen-depleted blood through the lungs to the alveoli, where oxygen is absorbed from inhaled air. Pulmonary veins return the refreshed blood to the heart, which pumps it out through arteries to the body. The oxygen diffuses into cells in exchange for carbon dioxide, and veins bring the depleted blood to the heart to be pumped to the lungs again.

In the lungs
Carbon dioxide from used blood is exchanged for fresh oxygen inside the microscopic alveoli of the lungs. In a typical domestic cat, the total surface area of the alveoli is about 215 sq ft (20 sq m).

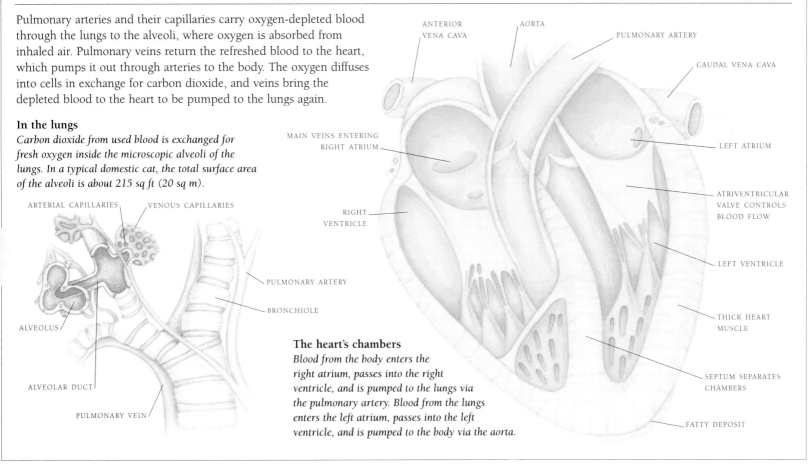

ARTERIAL CAPILLARIES

VENOUS CAPILLARIES

ALVEOLUS

ALVEOLAR DUCT

PULMONARY VEIN

PULMONARY ARTERY

BRONCHIOLE

ANTERIOR VENA CAVA

AORTA

PULMONARY ARTERY

CAUDAL VENA CAVA

MAIN VEINS ENTERING RIGHT ATRIUM

LEFT ATRIUM

RIGHT VENTRICLE

ATRIVENTRICULAR VALVE CONTROLS BLOOD FLOW

LEFT VENTRICLE

THICK HEART MUSCLE

SEPTUM SEPARATES CHAMBERS

FATTY DEPOSIT

The heart's chambers
Blood from the body enters the right atrium, passes into the right ventricle, and is pumped to the lungs via the pulmonary artery. Blood from the lungs enters the left atrium, passes into the left ventricle, and is pumped to the body via the aorta.

DIGESTION AND EXCRETION

THE DIGESTIVE SYSTEM IS RESPONSIBLE FOR BREAKING DOWN FOOD from its complex forms of proteins, carbohydrates, and fats into simple molecules that can easily be absorbed into the bloodstream through the wall of the small intestine. Its other equally important role is to act as a protective barrier against any harmful bacteria or other disease-causing agents that a cat may inadvertently ingest. Food is usually consumed, digested, utilized, dehydrated, and excreted within 24 hours. The cat's digestive system is similar to the dog's or ours, but because it is an obligate carnivore, which must eat meat to survive, there are some important adaptations.

The cat's digestive system is in essence like our own, but simpler. As a carnivore, it does not need a cecum to digest fiber, and its intestines are short relative to those of herbivores, such as sheep, or omnivores, such as humans.

INGESTION AND DIGESTION

The cat's teeth tear meat like serrated blades, and the barbed tongue scrapes it from bones. Saliva lubricates and binds food for swallowing. Food passes down the esophagus and into the stomach. The top of the stomach, the fundus, produces acid to break down fibers, and an enzyme to break down protein. The secretion of these digestive "juices" is hormonally controlled. The stomach also secretes mucus to protect it and the intestines against damage from the juices. Muscle contractions mix food, which then passes into the duodenum. The duodenum receives fat-dissolving bile from the gallbladder in the liver and enzymes from the pancreas. Along the length of the small intestine, which is made up of the duodenum and ileum, digestion continues and nutrients are absorbed through the intestinal wall (*see page 66*).

The blood carries these products to the liver, the largest internal organ. The liver processes them into essential fatty acids and amino acids, the "building blocks of life." Unlike the human or canine liver, the feline liver needs animal protein to manufacture the full complement of acids, so a cat will die if it does not eat meat. The liver also breaks down toxic substances.

Calculated bite

The cat's canine teeth sit in beds of sensitive tissue. A cat adjusts its grip on prey until it feels a tiny depression in its neck, just behind its skull. The shape of a cat's canine teeth has evolved to fit perfectly into this depression and deliver a spine-severing bite and instant death.

WASTE DISPOSAL

After the nutrients are absorbed, waste enters the large intestine, or colon. Benign bacteria here break down the waste and neutralize any hostile bacteria in it. Water is absorbed through the colon wall, and mucus is secreted to lubricate the dry waste. When waste accumulates in the rectum, nerves signal that discharge is needed.

The blood carries waste from the liver to the kidneys, where tubules, called nephrons, filter it out and excrete it in urine, of which cats daily produce 2 fl oz (60 ml). Nephrons die with age and disease, but only when 75 percent are lost does a cat obviously drink and urinate more. Failing kidneys have difficulty clearing urea and creatinine, by-products of protein metabolism and muscle exertion. The blood levels of these chemicals indicate the state of the kidneys, and treatment includes reducing both protein in the diet and the amount of exercise. The kidneys also regulate the blood pressure, maintain the chemical balance of the blood, activate vitamin D, and produce erythropoietin, a hormone that stimulates the production of red blood cells.

DIGESTIVE HORMONES

Behind the mechanics of digestion lie hormones produced by the thyroids and parathyroids and the pancreas. The thyroids, two glands on either side of the windpipe, control the metabolic rate. Pedigreed cats tend to have higher thyroid activity than random-bred cats. Overactive thyroids, almost unknown until 1978, but now common in older cats, cause dramatically increased heart rate, a voracious appetite, and weight loss. Underactive thyroids are extremely rare.

THE CAT'S DENTITION

When kittens are born, 26 needle-sharp milk teeth are already in place. The milk teeth are replaced by 30 permanent teeth during the first six months of life. The upper and lower incisors are used to grasp the prey or food, the canines grip and kill, and the premolars and molars shear, cut, and chew meat. The cat has few molars, and the upper ones are almost vestigial because they are not vital in its mainly carnivorous natural diet.

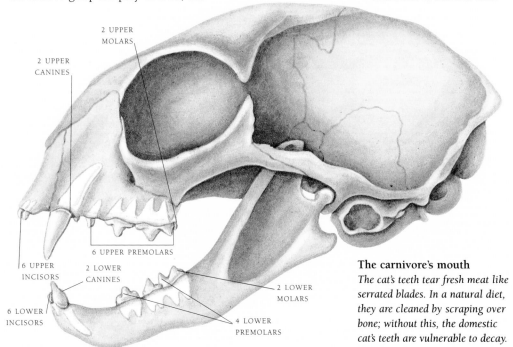

2 UPPER MOLARS

2 UPPER CANINES

6 UPPER PREMOLARS

6 UPPER INCISORS

2 LOWER CANINES

6 LOWER INCISORS

4 LOWER PREMOLARS

2 LOWER MOLARS

The carnivore's mouth
The cat's teeth tear fresh meat like serrated blades. In a natural diet, they are cleaned by scraping over bone; without this, the domestic cat's teeth are vulnerable to decay.

Saliva glands
Saliva lubricates
food for easy passage
to stomach

STOMACH MUSCLES
CHURN FOOD

THYROID AND
PARATHYROID
GLANDS

Stomach
Produces acids and enzymes
that begin digesting food

Kidneys
Cleanse waste
products from
blood

Esophagus
Peristaltic muscle
contractions push food
to stomach

From consumption to disposal
*Feline digestion and excretion are adapted to eating little
and often. Food passes down the esophagus and into the
stomach, where digestion begins. Small amounts leave
the stomach at intervals, entering the small intestine,
where nutrients are absorbed. Water is absorbed from
solid waste in the large intestine. The kidneys filter
liquid waste from the blood and pass it to the bladder.*

ELASTIC WALL
STRETCHES EASILY

Ureters
Pass liquid waste
to bladder

Large intestine
Absorbs water from
solid waste

Cardiac sphincter
Ring of muscle closing
entrance to stomach

Rectum
Solid waste discharged
through anus

Anal sphincter
Triggered by brain
to relax and allow
excretion

Liver
Processes
nutrients and
produces bile

Pyloric sphincter
Ring of muscle that
releases food into
duodenum

URETHRA

Pancreas
Secretes digestive
enzymes and the
hormone insulin

Duodenum
Nutrients absorbed
from first part of
small intestine

Bladder
Feline bladder
can hold 3½ fl oz
(100 ml) of liquid

Next to each thyroid is a tiny parathyroid gland,
which produces a hormone needed to extract
calcium, important in muscle contraction, from
bone. Insulin, secreted in the pancreas, allows
cells to absorb vital glucose from the blood.
Many hormones counteract insulin; diabetes in
cats can be caused by overactive pituitary,
thyroid, or adrenal glands (*see page 58*).

DIGESTIVE DISORDERS
Cats regurgitate for a variety of reasons, some
not at all serious: eating too quickly, swallowing
hair when grooming, a tight cardiac sphincter,
or a dilated esophagus. In vomiting, stomach
and abdominal wall contractions force back up
the stomach contents, which have a distinctive
acidic smell. This is usually more serious than
regurgitation. Vomiting and diarrhea are fairly
common in cats, and may result from changes
in diet, food intolerances or allergies, poisons,
ingested foreign bodies, infections, or parasites.
Older cats may develop liver, kidney, or pancreas
conditions, hyperthyroidism, inflammatory
bowel disease or colitis, and intestinal cancers.

One common feline food intolerance is to milk.
Kittens produce the enzyme lactase to digest
milk sugar, lactose, but adult cats often lack
this enzyme, and milk may cause diarrhea.
Other intolerances are less easily isolated.

The cat's liver is very slow at processing some
drugs; for example, it takes about 72 hours to
break down aspirin, so even small amounts are
dangerous if given more than twice weekly. Other
medications are lethal in even smaller amounts.
The kidneys can be irreversibly damaged by
some ingested poisons, most notably antifreeze.

Ingested objects, such as string, can loop
around the tongue or anchor in the intestines.
Never pull out such ingested objects, because
you can cause damage; seek veterinary help.

Feline immunodeficiency virus (FIV), feline
leukemia virus (FeLV), and the preventable feline
panleukopenia virus (FIP) all cause vomiting
and diarrhea. The parasite giardia is difficult to
confirm, and may be more common than is
realized; vomiting is often the only sign of
heartworm. Vomiting caused by inflammation to
the stomach may be stress-induced in some cats.

URINARY PROBLEMS

The kidneys filter the blood of unwanted or
toxic substances and pass them to the bladder.
The lower urinary tract, comprising the bladder
and urethra, may suffer feline lower urinary
tract disorder (FLUTD), caused by diet or
infection. Another problem is cystitis, typified
by inflammation and a burning sensation that
causes the cat to urinate frequently. In some
cats, this can be caused by emotional upsets.

Feline lower urinary tract disorder
*In FLUTD, crystals or stones form in the bladder.
These can be so large that they block the urethra;
they usually cause the cat pain during urination.*

THE REPRODUCTIVE SYSTEM

THE CAT HAS EVOLVED A VERY EFFICIENT REPRODUCTION STRATEGY, ideally suited to the lone hunter. Males are eternal opportunists, always ready to mate. Females come into season as daylight hours increase in spring, ensuring births during the spring and summer, when food is most plentiful. She signals her sexual receptivity to males by leaving hormone-laden urine markings and by "calling," emitting a unique, sonorous tone, which can be heard by any males nearby. Because each cat has its own hunting territory, there may be no males in the vicinity at the time. Rather than waste her eggs, females release them from the ovaries only after mating.

Puberty in cats usually occurs between six and nine months, although some breeds, such as the Oriental types, are sexually precocious, reaching puberty in just four months.

THE MALE SYSTEM

As with many other mammals, the male cat's reproductive system is on permanent standby from puberty, ready for use if the chance arises. Luteinizing hormone (LH) from the pituitary gland (see page 58) stimulates the testes to make both sperm and the male hormone testosterone. Sperm production begins in coiled tubes in the testes, and it continues throughout life. Because sperm production is best at slightly less than body heat, testes are held in the scrotal sac outside the body.

Sperm is stored in the epididymis at the base of the testes until needed, when it travels through the two spermatic cords to the prostate and bulbourethral glands. Here semen, a sugar-rich transportation medium, is added.

The male shows sex-related behavior, such as roaming, fighting, and spraying, all year round. His reproductive system is placed on high alert by scent. If his vomeronasal organ (see page 60) captures female scent, he will disregard all else to seek out the female giving off the scent, and fight over her if necessary.

FEMALE HORMONES

Like most other domestic animals, the female cat is polyestrous, meaning she has many estrous periods, or seasons, throughout the year. But, unlike many other animal species that have estrous cycles all year round, cats are seasonally polyestrous; the female's reproductive cycle is most active as daylight hours increase, and then winds down as daylight hours decrease.

At the end of winter, increasing daylight hours stimulate her pituitary gland to produce follicle-stimulating hormone (FSH). The FSH induces her ovaries to manufacture eggs and the female hormone estrogen. The estrogen is released in the female's urine, acting as a calling card to any available males. Her two ovaries are suspended from the roof of the abdomen, just behind the kidneys. At puberty, which occurs at the same time as male puberty, the necessary eggs are waiting in the ovaries. In contrast to the reproductive systems of virtually all other mammals, however, the ovaries will not release these eggs until after mating has taken place.

Male reproductive system

The reproductive organs of the male cat are kept on permanent standby from the onset of puberty at a few months of age. When a male picks up the scent or hears the distinctive call of a female in heat, the brain analyzes the sensory information and sends a hormonal signal to the reproductive organs. This stimulates him into a state of immediate readiness to mate.

SPERMATIC CORDS

BLADDER

SPERM IS STORED IN EPIDIDYMIS

Testes
Respond to LH by producing sperm

PENIS

Penile barbs
Abrade the vulva on withdrawal

Bulbourethral gland
Absolute function is poorly understood in cats

Prostate gland
Produces semen to carry sperm

LH CARRIED IN BLOOD TO TESTES

Scent stimulus
Male picks up female's scent

NEUTERING

Neutering a male is a minor operation. Under general anesthesia, the testicles are removed through a small incision in the scrotum. The spermatic cords and associated blood vessels are tied. This is usually done at about six months. Neutering a female, or spaying, is more major abdominal surgery. The ovaries and uterus down to the cervix are removed. Spaying can be done before sexual maturity.

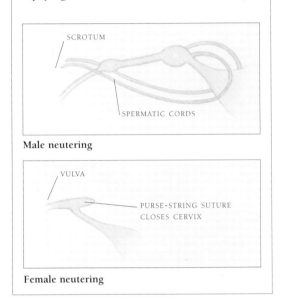

SCROTUM

SPERMATIC CORDS

Male neutering

VULVA

PURSE-STRING SUTURE
CLOSES CERVIX

Female neutering

FELINE MATING

Feline sexual activity is flagrant and noisy. It is also curiously dignified. In the wild, cats are lone hunters. The female overcomes her natural solitude by vocally advertising her sexual state. She urinates more frequently, leaving as many scent markers as possible, to attract male cats from a wide area. Other behavior also changes; she rolls on the ground, stretches out her body, raises her hindquarters, or drags herself on the ground by her forepaws, as if her hind legs no longer work. She may utter plaintive noises, which some owners misread as pain. She does not permit a male to mate with her until she is completely ready. When she is finally receptive, the male is permitted to mount her. He grasps the skin on her neck and mates immediately.

The male's penis is covered by hooklike barbs. As he withdraws, these barbs abrade the vulva. The female "screams" and turns to bite, but an experienced male will maintain his hold on the skin on her neck. He releases her and draws away when he feels it is safe to do so.

The abrasion of the vulva stimulates the release of eggs. Cats are induced ovulators, only releasing eggs under the stimulation of mating. One mating is often not enough to induce this egg release: two or more are usually necessary.

The pair mate repetitively, the male tiring first. The female retains her receptivity; other males are often then permitted to mate. When enough matings have occurred, production of FSH in the female's brain stimulates eggs to leave the ovaries and travel through the fallopian tubes to each horn of the uterus. If no matings occur when a female is in heat, no eggs are released. A period of calm ensues, lasting from two days to two weeks, followed by another heat cycle. Under the influence of artificial indoor light, unspayed females can eventually come to be in permanent, yowling season.

PREGNANCY AND BIRTH

Fertilization takes place in the pencil-like uterine horns, and the fetuses are positioned in rows in each horn of the uterus. Pregnancy lasts about 63 days, during which progesterone, the hormone of pregnancy, brings behavior changes and the swelling of the mammary glands.

Birth is usually uncomplicated, although some kittens may not live. Milk let-down occurs shortly after the birth, stimulated by suckling. The mother often leaves the birth nest a few days after the delivery, carrying her kittens one by one to a new, more odor-free and thus, to her mind, much safer den.

Female reproductive system

Females conserve their eggs, concentrating their reproductive activity into intense and well-advertised estrous "heat" periods, during which they seek out potential mates almost tirelessly. Sensory information from the vagina during mating triggers the production of FSH in the brain and the subsequent release of eggs, which occurs between 24 and 48 hours after mating has finished.

Multiple fathers

Although females frequently mate with several male cats, veterinarians and geneticists still do not know how many fathers can be involved in a litter: the possible combinations of coat colors in cats that are not bred specifically for color are too diverse. Only by intentionally permitting controlled group matings within a variety of color-restricted purebreds could information be gathered.

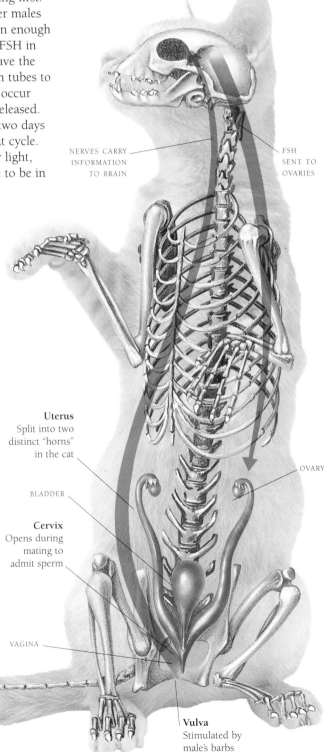

NERVES CARRY
INFORMATION
TO BRAIN

FSH
SENT TO
OVARIES

Uterus
Split into two
distinct "horns"
in the cat

OVARY

BLADDER

Cervix
Opens during
mating to
admit sperm

VAGINA

Vulva
Stimulated by
male's barbs

THE SKIN AND COAT

THE SOPHISTICATION AND IMPORTANCE OF THE FELINE'S SKIN AND coat is sometimes underestimated, because it seems inert to the naked eye. The skin is the body's largest organ. The cells within it constantly carry out surveillance duty, warning of potential dangers, acting as waste managers, and even producing nutrients to maintain a variety of beneficial skin microbes and keep them healthy. Regions of the skin are modified for specific purposes: paw pads for durability, claws for traction, and glands in the chin, lips, and anal area for scent marking. Hair growth is under a variety of external and internal controls.

The skin and hair have prosaic but significant, even life-preserving, responsibilities. The skin contains cells vital to the immune system; it is the cat's first and most important line of defense, keeping harmful microorganisms or chemicals from entering the body. Sensory functions are carried out by millions of nerve endings that detect heat, cold, pain, itches, and pressure. A profusion of microscopic blood vessels, a far greater blood supply than is necessary simply to nourish the skin, forms a sophisticated thermodynamic system that helps a cat to regulate its body temperature when moving from a warm area to a cold one. Skin secretes glandular substances that help rid the body of waste and help to protect against the harsh world outside, and also produces vitamin D, necessary for building sturdy bones.

COAT STRUCTURE

Hair consists mostly of keratin, the same tough protein that makes up the skin's outer layer (epidermis) and the claws (see page 57), which are technically skin. Because hair is made mostly of protein, normal hair growth consumes a good percentage of daily protein intake.

The surface of a hair consists of overlapping cuticle cells, which point away from the body. A hair stroked from root to tip feels smooth, while one stroked from tip to root feels rough because of the "lay" of the cells. The cuticle reflects light and helps to give the coat its sheen; a dull coat may signify cuticle damage. Hair grows in cycles that are controlled by hormones, length of daylight hours, and the surrounding temperature.

Cold-weather coat
The longhaired cat's coat has a protracted growth stage. Hair grows for a longer time, rather than faster, than in shorthairs.

Curled cat
In rexed cats, long- or shorthaired, the growth of hair is genetically retarded. The Cornish Rex has no guard hairs, while the Devon Rex, seen here, has soft guard hairs virtually identical to down hairs.

Humans have simple follicles: a single, large hair grows from each hair follicle. Cats have more efficient insulation, in the form of compound hair follicles: up to six primary (guard) hairs grow from each follicle, each surrounded by finer secondary (down and awn) hairs. Each follicle has its own arrector muscle, which can make the primary hairs stand on end. Cats "raise their hackles" like this when alarmed or angry, but also to increase insulation and cut heat loss.

Cats have two types of hair specialized for sensation. The whiskers, or vibrissae, are thick, stiff hairs found on the head, the throat, and the forelegs (see page 60). Other large, single hairs, called tylotrichs, each surrounded by a complex net of blood vessels and nerves, are scattered over the skin and act like short whiskers.

COATS FOR CLIMATES

Evolution has equipped the cat with excellent defenses against heat and cold. Breeds that have adapted to northern climates, such as the British Shorthair, Maine Coon, and Norwegian Forest Cat, are densely coated with insulating down. In cold weather, the hair erects, trapping a layer of air, much as double glazing traps a wall of air between the cold outside and the warmth indoors. A layer of fat under the skin insulates the body; heat is lost through fat one third as fast as it is through muscle. In extreme cold, a cat curls up and covers its face with its tail to protect it from freezing air.

Breeds adapted to hot climates radiate heat more efficiently. Siamese lack down hair; cats that have this insulating coat shed it in hot climates. If still too warm, they shed primary hairs. Blood vessels in the skin dilate, speeding the loss of body heat. Cats do not sweat to lose heat as we do. Instead, they lick their fur, and the evaporating saliva carries away body heat.

THE FELINE HAIR GROWTH CYCLE

Feline hair grows to a genetically predetermined length during a 60-to-90-day growth period (anagen). After a short transitional stage (catagen) and 40 to 60 days of rest (telogen), it falls out, giving way to a new hair. Because hairs are at different stages at any time, shedding is gradual. The main external influence on growth is light: increased light stimulates a heavy spring molt. Under artificial light, indoor cats often shed all year. There is no such thing as a nonshedding cat.

ANAGEN   CATAGEN   TELOGEN   ANAGEN   ANAGEN

Awn hair
Fine secondary hair

Down hair
Soft, wavy
secondary hair

SMOOTH
SURFACE

Nerve
Carries
signals
from skin
and hair

Follicle
Sheath
containing
multiple
hairs

Sebaceous gland
Secretes skin oil

Tylotrich hair
Single sensory
hair

Primary hair
Carries the
coat's coloring

Cornified layer
Dead cells form
protective barrier

Basal layer
Supplies cells to
cornified layer

Dermis
Strong
elastic tissue

Blood supply
Dermis is rich
in capillaries

SUBCUTANEOUS FAT

Sweat gland
Responds to
nerve signals

The structure of the skin

Hairs grouped on the skin's surface provide insulation and sensory input. The cornified and basal layers of the epidermis provide protection. Beneath them lies the dermis, rich in nerves and blood vessels, containing the hair follicles and their glands, and held together by tough elastic tissue.

NATURAL FLORA AND FAUNA

As on all animals, the surface of the cat's skin is naturally colonized by a variety of microbes. These flora and fauna survive and proliferate without causing skin disease – in fact, they are vital to the health of the skin. Different regions of the skin have different "microclimates," some of them more attractive to microbes than others. Regions that are frequently moist or wet, and areas with dense hair and concentrated sweat glands, are most attractive to microbes. Relatively hairless regions are least attractive.

SKIN AND HAIR PROBLEMS

As a cat's first line of defense, coat and skin are prone to a variety of problems, from allergic or hormonal disorders to parasites, infections, or tumors. Coat problems are obvious because the hair becomes brittle, dry, lusterless, or falls out. Hormonal influences on the skin and coat are not well understood, but hormone-related disorders are usually not itchy.

Many cats carry the spores of the fungal infection ringworm without suffering infections. When it occurs in a cattery, other cats may be symptomless carriers. Ringworm can also infect people; in Paris it is estimated that 90 percent of human ringworm infections are from cats.

A more common problem is a crusty, itchy condition called miliary dermatitis. This has many possible causes, but an allergy to fleas is overwhelmingly the most common one.

While these control mechanisms are efficient, cats are still prone to both heat prostration and frostbite. Sensible cats avoid high temperatures and humidity but, like dogs, they die quickly if trapped inside a hot car in sunshine. Cats are prone to frostbite, because their fur loses its insulating capacity when wet; cats are most at risk from hypothermia in freezing, wet weather.

SKIN STRUCTURE

Cat skin has two distinct strata. The surface, or epidermis, consists of about 40 layers of dead, flattened cells, embedded in fat-rich sebum, an oily skin secretion. Beneath this "cornified" layer is the living epidermis, or "basal" area, about four cells thick. The epidermis is not very strong, but plays an important role in the body's immune system. In normal circumstances, it takes about three weeks for cells to migrate from the basal layer to the cornified layer, but this process speeds up when the skin is injured, reducing the replacement time to two weeks. Beneath the epidermis is the dermis, the major structural component of the skin. It consists of strong elastic connective tissue, and contains glands, blood vessels, nerves, and receptors.

Each hair follicle has an associated sweat gland and sebaceous gland, buried in the dermis. The sebaceous glands produce fatty sebum, which controls bacteria and helps to give hair its sheen. They are concentrated on the neck and rump, and especially around the lips and on the chin. Specialized sebaceous glands line the eyelids and produce an oily protective film for the eyes. Other specialized sebaceous glands around the anus and between the toes may produce pheromones, or sex scents.

Unlike humans, cats do not sweat to control their body temperature; they pant inefficiently or lick themselves. Sweat-gland secretions maintain the skin's pliability, excrete waste, provide nutrients for the skin's microflora, and contain substances that protect the body from chemicals and dangerous microbes. They probably also secrete pheromones. Sweat glands associated with hair follicles are called epitrichial (formerly apocrine). Atrichial (formerly eccrine) glands, such as those on the footpads, open onto the skin, rather than into hair follicles.

Sweat glands

Scent-producing glands in cats are concentrated in the areas they use to mark territory: the face, the neck and shoulders, the rump, and between the toes, where they scent paw prints. Specialized anal sacs under the tail also produce scent.

FELINE GENETICS

ALTHOUGH THE DETAILS OF GENETICS ARE COMPLEX, THE BASIS OF these inherited characteristics is quite simple. All the information needed for life is carried in the genes contained in each body cell. Most of that information is common to all mammals. The rest makes cats what they are, and us what we are. The science of genetics began with Gregor Mendel (1822–1884), who showed that some traits are not diluted when crossed, but masked. In 1953, Crick and Watson's modeling of DNA, the genetic storage system that is the basis of life, led to a new understanding of the influence of genetics on physical characteristics, emotional behavior, and disease.

Genetics follows simple, mathematical laws. Every cell in a cat's body contains a nucleus at some stage in its development. Each nucleus contains 38 chromosomes, arranged in 19 pairs, which are just large enough to be seen with a powerful optical microscope. Each chromosome is formed from a tightly wound double helix of deoxyribonucleic acid (DNA), which in turn is made up of thousands of units called genes, strung together like beads. Each gene is made from four different proteins – A, T, C, and G – and the combinations of these proteins provide the information for all aspects of a cat's life.

COPYING AND MUTATIONS

Each time a cell, such as a skin cell, is replaced, its chromosomes are copied. The DNA unwinds and unzips down the middle. Ribonucleic acid (RNA) is generated to match each half-strand, and then used as a template on which new DNA forms from proteins within the cell. The copying process is so accurate that there may be only one mistake, or mutation, in one gene, for every million copies: this would be like retyping these two pages five million times before typing one wrong letter. These rare mistakes can create cancers, and may contribute to aging.

Information is passed down the generations in a different way. Egg and sperm cells contain only 19 chromosomes, each one half of a pair. At conception, the 19 chromosomes in the egg unite with the 19 in the sperm, creating a new, unique set of 19 pairs. Each kitten inherits half of its genetic material from each parent. When chromosomes pair up, the genes for each characteristic also pair up, side by side. Mistakes, or mutations, sometimes occur in egg or sperm cells, creating new traits.

DOMINANT AND RECESSIVE TRAITS

Genetic variations in characteristics, for example coat length, are called dominant if one copy of them is needed to show its effect, and recessive if two copies, one on each chromosome in a pair, are needed. Original traits tend to be dominant, and new mutations recessive: cats originally had short coats, and the gene for it is notated L, but a mutation occurred long ago, producing a recessive gene for long hair, which is notated l.

A cat showing a dominant trait may be heterozygous, carrying the recessive alternative "masked" beneath the dominant one: a cat with a recessive trait must be homozygous for it, carrying no alternatives. Two heterozygous shorthaired cats – both Ll, carrying the recessive gene for long hair –

produce, if mated, an average of two Ll kittens, one LL kitten, and one longhaired ll kitten. Appearance gives no clue as to which of the three shorthaired kittens carry the l gene that enables them to produce longhaired kittens.

Unfortunately, not all genetics is this simple. Many traits are polygenetic, governed by an unknown combination of genes. Also, not all genes are simply dominant or recessive; some mutations show partial dominance over others, or even over the original form.

CHROMOSOME

X-shape
All chromosomes except for one have this shape

Gene
DNA can be "snipped" into individual genes

DNA
Tightly coiled DNA forms chromosomes

NUCLEUS

Chromosomes
Half come from each parent

CELL

Nucleus
Carries all information needed for replicating cell

The basis of life

Every living cell contains a nucleus, in which 19 pairs of chromosomes are stored. The sex chromosomes are referred to as X and Y chromosomes; the others are autosomes. Each chromosome, when unfurled, is a complex helix of four nucleotides. Called DNA, it forms the basis of life and all inherited characteristics.

ALLELES

Specific information about a trait is always carried at the same site on each chromosome: in a pair of chromosomes, this pair of sites is called a locus. Varient forms of a gene are called alleles. If two alleles at a locus are the same, the individual is homozygous for the trait.

Matching pair
A genetic trait is determined by the genes from both parents, located at matching sites on the paired chromosomes.

ALLELES OF A GENE

THE FOUNDER EFFECT

For hundreds of millennia, the African ancestors of today's domestic cats were almost uniformly shorthaired, striped tabbies. Yet after only a few millennia of migration out of Africa, hundreds of coat colors, patterns, and lengths exist.

In the large population of cats in North Africa, any random gene mutation had little chance of spreading widely unless it offered a substantial advantage to the cat. Most genetic mutations simply vanished within a few generations. In an isolated feline population, mutations have more chance of surviving. The orange-and-white cats of Scandinavia (*see page 94*) or the polydactyls of Boston and Halifax (*see page 99*) are both mutations from the genetic "norm." When these cats were taken to regions with few or no cats, they represented a large percentage of a small gene pool. The long-term genetic influence of early members of a cat population is called the "founder effect." The founders have a potent influence on a new population. This is why certain patterns or colors are prevalent in some countries; it is also the basis for the development of new breeds. This leads to the question of just what makes a breed.

From a purely genetic perspective, there is no such thing, because the potential genetic differences within a breed, particularly those with large numbers, outweigh the average genetic differences between two different breeds. For example, the DNA profiles of two Siamese can differ far more than those of a Siamese and a Persian. The definition of a breed is decided on a few obvious effects, such as coat color or length and body type: from a genetic perspective, these differences are slight.

Spine
Sugar-phosphate spine holds nucleotides in sequence

Nucleotide pairs
These split, unzipping DNA, when cells are renewed

Nucleotides
Each gene combines four nucleotides in a unique pattern

Polydactylous cat
The gene for polydactyly, or extra toes, is the result of a dominant mutation. Polydactyl cats were among the early populations of Boston and Halifax; this trait is now more common in these places than anywhere else in the world.

BREEDS AND GENETIC DISEASES

Breeders use the laws of genetics to select for specific features such as color or body type. Unfortunately, they may also unwittingly select for other hidden, dangerous genes. This is how genetic diseases gain ground in purebred lines. To name only a few of these: several breeds are prone to the lethal disease amyloidosis; certain lines of Persians suffer from polycystic kidney disease; Himalayan Persians have a marked incidence of cataracts; Abyssinians can develop retinal degeneration; the Devon Rex carries a spastic muscular disorder; and some Burmese suffer from flat-chested syndrome, episodic weakness syndrome, and a lethal head malformation.

In natural selection for survival of the fittest, such dangerous genes are removed from the gene pool or persist at a very low level; selective breeding has allowed them to survive and be passed on. This is the greatest genetic problem facing cats; responsible breeders now investigate genetics as part of their breeding programs. Scientists are learning more about cats' genetics. The National Cancer Institute in the United States has a gene-mapping project investigating feline genetics in detail. In England, Alex Jeffreys developed "genetic fingerprinting," which can identify an individual from a sample of DNA from any body tissue. This can be used in cats, as in humans, to investigate paternity. Because pedigreed cats often have similar DNA, however, especially in the rarer breeds, genetic profiling can only exclude a sire, not identify one.

In reality, the vast majority of cat matings remain random, and selection for survival of the fittest remains the most powerful influence on the genetic future of the domestic cat. Increasingly, however, advances in genetics will be used to monitor exactly what is happening.

MENDELIAN INHERITANCE PATTERNS

Several major traits in feline appearance have been identified (*see list, right*). Dominant traits are notated in capitals, recessive traits in lower case. A shorthaired cat is notated L unless test matings show it to be LL, because L needs to appear only once in an allele to show an effect, and the nature of the second gene in the pair usually remains unknown.

Inheritance patterns
This diagram shows how long- and shorthaired traits are passed on, giving the average results over many matings.

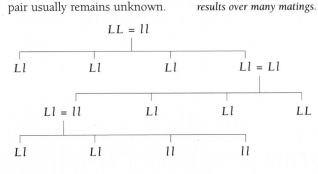

$LL = ll$

Ll	Ll	Ll	$Ll = Ll$
$Ll = ll$	Ll	Ll	LL
Ll	Ll	ll	ll

A	agouti, or tabby
a	non-agouti, or self
B	black
b	brown, or chocolate
b^l	light brown, or cinnamon
C	full color, or solid
c^b	Burmese pattern, or sepia
c^s	Siamese pattern, or pointed
D	dense, dark color
d	dilute, light color
I	inhibitor, or silvering
i	pigmentation sound to roots
L	short hair
l	long hair
O	orange, or sex-linked red
o	melanistic, non-red color
S	white spotting, or bicolor
s	solid color over whole body
T	striped, or mackerel, tabby
T^a	Abyssinian, or ticked, tabby
t^b	blotched, or classic, tabby
W	white, masking all other colors
w	normal color

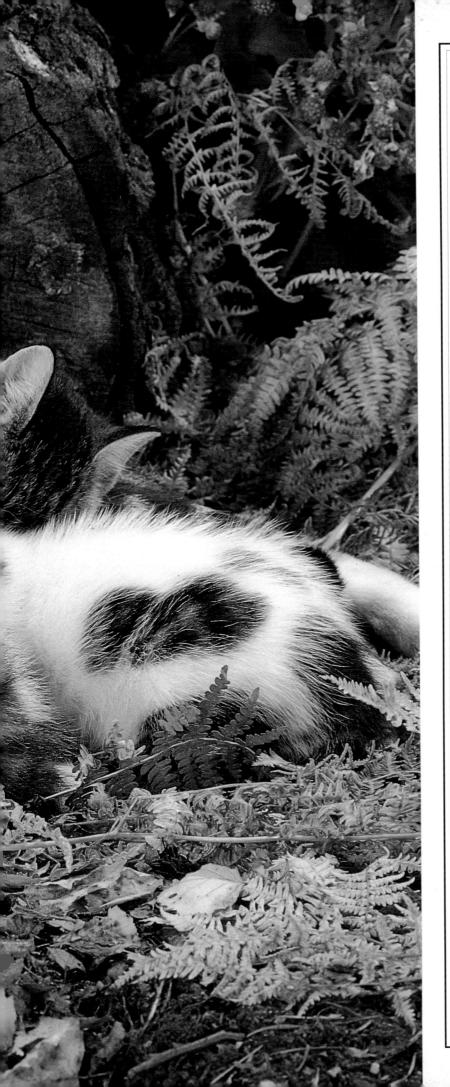

CHAPTER FOUR

CAT BEHAVIOR

ALTHOUGH THE CAT IS A SOLITARY HUNTER, content to live on its own in the absence of other cats or people, it is now in the process of evolving from total independence to more willing dependence. Its behavior toward other cats and people reflects this evolutionary development. Our intervention in the domestic cat's living environment has modified its natural behavior. We have encouraged the kitten in cats, making adults more reliant on us, and more sociable, in the process. However, regardless of how much we intervene, the cat's inherent need to hunt, and its ways of conceiving and mothering its kittens, are unlikely to change.

ABOVE A CAT FOLDS ITS EARS BACK AS A SIGN OF FEAR

LEFT FERAL MOTHER AND KITTENS

THE FELINE MIND

PROGRESSIVELY INCREASING IN POPULARITY, CATS OUTNUMBER DOGS across the United States, Canada, Britain, the Netherlands, Austria, and Switzerland. In Sweden, Denmark, and Norway, the number of pet cats is expected to exceed that of dogs before the end of the century.

As cats replace dogs as our favorite companions, it becomes more important to realize that they are not dogs in disguise. The cat is unique among all the animals that have become domesticated – the only species that first, foremost, and forever follows its own mind.

Like all species, including humans, the cat instinctively strives to survive and leave descendents. Unlike people or dogs, it does this in an independent manner; the cat is not naturally a pack animal.

ALONE IN THE CROWD
Although we are countering its natural independence through selective breeding and early learning, the cat remains a far more "freelance" creature than any other domestic animal. The ways in which cats socialize, hunt, court, and mate differ from those of more communal species.

To us, the cat's behavior, caring only for its own comfort and security, can appear selfish. Such moral judgments ignore biological reality; the cat behaves like number one because it is number one. In their natural state, cats see other cats only as competition for territory. Even mating (see page 86) can create conflicts; it may be the only time after kittenhood that a cat makes physical contact with another cat.

Reliable food supply
Although their coats differ widely, a sign that they are not closely related, these cats are showing no aggression; this is because food from fishing boats is plentiful.

The cat's mind is flexible enough to allow it to change its behavior, in part according to how much food is available. The most sociable time in a cat's life is kittenhood, when, together with its mother and siblings, it is a part of a group. This pattern can be extended into adulthood, with cats living in groups usually consisting of mothers and their female kittens; males are tolerated rather than welcomed. Although they do not hunt together, their group behavior, including looking after each other's young, is not unlike that of the all-female pride of lions.

ABILITY TO LEARN
The cat's mental adaptability has allowed it to enter our lives successfully. Through selective breeding we increase our cats' sociability, and by raising kittens in our homes and exposing them to a variety of experiences during the period from three to seven weeks of age we perpetuate their kittenlike dependency on us for food, warmth, comfort, and security.

Early experiences radically influence the adult cat. Kittens that are raised without human contact will always be fearful of strange humans, but kittens raised with people or other animals will accept and enjoy their company throughout life.

LEAVING A MARK
Cats communicate face to face through voice and body language (see page 80). They also leave signs on their territories that can be read in their absence. Boundaries are marked with urine, feces, and scented chemicals, rubbed against upright objects. These are not warnings, but simply mark the territory as occupied. When a cat rubs against its owner's leg, we interpret it as affection. In part it is, but it is also a territorial marking.

Visual markers, such as scratches on trees, are also important. This visual aspect of cat's language means that urban cats often use the same markers that we recognize – such as hedges or walls – as their boundaries.

DOMESTIC PREDATOR
While all cats show hunting behavior, each cat's hunting skills are learned (see page 84). Learning by observation is most effective; ethologist Paul Leyhausen found that the most important factor in a cat's preferences and success as a hunter is its mother. Some mothers teach their kittens to hunt birds, while others teach them to hunt rodents.

The cat's natural diet consists of small rodents and birds, usually only big enough to feed one small stomach. This one factor, more than any other, is the most potent reason for the cat to be independent, to be a lone hunter. In spite of this evolution as a solitary hunter, cats can live in close proximity if food is plentiful. This is clearly seen in some city parks, where cat lovers provide daily food for feral cats, in fishing ports, where cats will gather to eat the unwanted part of the catch, and in our homes (see page 82). Free of the need to defend a hunting territory, cats are able to socialize.

Scent marking
Glands on the cat's lips, face, ears, feet, and body all contain distinct chemicals that act as scent markers. This cat is leaving its scent on a tree trunk – not to frighten other cats but simply to proclaim its presence.

Instinctive hunter
All young kittens naturally play in ways that mimic an adult cat's predatory behavior. This kitten uses instinctive stealth to creep silently closer to its victim, which may be a small rodent but is much more likely to be a leaf or a littermate. Its ears are turned forward to pick up the faintest sounds most efficiently.

GROUP ACTIVITY

Lions live and hunt as a group, preying on large mammals. A pride, made up of blood-related females, is similar in many ways to a feral cat colony. They eat and sleep together, groom each other, and care for each other's kittens, sometimes even suckling them when the natural mother is otherwise occupied. These rulers of the African savanna are also capable of forming emotional bonds with people if raised with humans during early kittenhood. Big cats, however, lack the innate tractability of the domestic cat, and remain dangerous.

The family that naps together
Lions can sleep as a group, knowing that other predators would not risk attacking an entire pride. Mothers with young cubs remain vigilant.

Catnapping
Sleep seems to be the natural state for a cat with a full stomach. No one knows why cats sleep more than other species. The benefit for us is that the sight of a sleeping cat relaxes us.

THE NEED FOR SLEEP

A unique and curiously appealing aspect of the cat's behavior is its ability to relax into deep sleep apparently at will. As in all other animals, the cat's natural rhythms are controlled by an internal biological clock, a complex interaction between the body and the mind.

The most common rhythm in animals is a 24-hour cycle called circadian rhythm. This dictates when animals are most and least active. The cat is most alert at dawn and dusk, when hunting is best, and sleepiest around midday and the middle of the night. The cat's need to be active when humans want to sleep, and to sleep when humans are most active, is difficult to change, because its origins are so deeply embedded in feline behavior.

French research has shown that sleep is induced by a chemical, melatonin, released in the brain (*see page 58*), and that this release is probably under the control of the gene that determines circadian rhythm. Melatonin is thought to be responsible for the cat's habit of

sleeping for 16 hours a day on average. Just why cats sleep so much is not yet properly understood, although in kittenhood, growth hormone is released only during sleep. Sleep is certainly necessary for all animals to maintain general health, and feline dreams, like ours, may act as periods during which the cat's mind can reorganize and reclassify information.

LEARNED BEHAVIOR

Because cats cannot be trained like dogs, it is sometimes thought that they cannot learn at all. It is possible, however, to train cats to press a button for a food reward. The key to all cat training is the use of reward; discipline, which works in pack species, such as dogs, does not work with cats, who either hide or leave.

The cat's mind is at its most receptive when it is very young; it loses its ability to absorb new experience earlier than most other species. Experiments from over a century ago show that

cats can learn by watching what other cats do, and learn best of all by watching their mothers. Other work from the same time showed that cats are not good at solving puzzles, and escaping from mazes was due more to luck than to logic.

There are some things, however, that a cat may never learn or unlearn. Pet cats must adapt to a sometimes alien lifestyle, especially if kept indoors. Some use their hunting instincts to stalk and destroy household objects. Others try to remain nocturnal and demand nighttime activity from their diurnal human companions.

Less certain are the cat's reputed "psychic" abilities. Most of the evidence for these is anecdotal, but there is scientific confirmation that cats have a sense of direction and can foresee earthquakes. Tests in Germany and the United States suggest that cats may have a superior sense of direction (*see page 60*), and Professor Benjamin Hart in California recorded increased unusual behavior before earthquakes.

Unaware of danger (right)
This kitten (safe on a sheet of glass) has blithely crawled over the apparent edge of the step although it could see it; in a few weeks it will stop and investigate first.

Performing cat (right)
Natural dexterity develops when a kitten plays with its littermates and practices hunting. Even adult cats can still be actively trained, using food rewards, to complete "assault courses" that include jumps and even tunnels.

COMMUNICATION

CATS COMMUNICATE SUBTLY AND SUCCESSFULLY WITH OTHER CATS, but less so with us. Social relationships are of little importance to them, so the nuances of facial expression and "distance-reducing" body language are not highly defined: the human smile or a dog's wagging tail do not have overt equivalents in cat communication. Other methods by which cats exchange information are refined. These include the voice (our favored medium), touch, scent, and visual displays or markers. With our tendency to rely on speech, we often fail to understand what is meant by scratches on the sofa or feces left unburied.

Our cats greet us, demand food, complain, and protest vocally, and with experience we know exactly what they are saying. Different breeds have different verbal habits; some "chirp" more than others, some breeds are almost silent, and Oriental breeds are notoriously loud. In the 1930s, psychologist Dr. Mildred Moelk defined 16 different cat sounds; Dr. Patricia McKinley more recently split sounds into 23 categories. In general, however, feline sounds fall into three types: murmurs, vowels, and high-intensity sounds.

Vocal request
Cats' questions and commands all include vowels. The associated body language is alert and confident, as with this relaxed and plaintive young Persian.

Murmurs include purring and the soft, happy chirp of greeting. The source of the cat's purr remains a mystery (*see page 67*). However it is done, it is not always a sign of happiness. Stressed or traumatized cats also purr, a phenomenon familiar to vets who treat injured or ill cats. The chirp, like the purr, does not involve vowels. It sounds like a "brrrp" or "brrrm," and is uniquely used to show pleasure.

Vowels, the classic "meows," vary according to what is meant. Domestic cats talk with meows because we have extended their kittenhood (*see* Family communication, *opposite*). Requests, demands, commands, complaints, and bewilderment have subtle variations that are easy to understand, and with which owners become familiar.

High-intensity sounds are natural adult cat language, and as such they are usually reserved for communicating with other cats, although some are familiar to owners and veterinarians.

Assertiveness
It is easy to interpret shows of confidence or aggression. This cat's fur bristles to enhance its size, and it stares down its opponent, leaning forward and rotating its ears.

Changing the shape of the mouth creates many sounds, from a grumbling, irritated growl to a threatening snarl, a hiss, or a defensive spit. Shrieks of fear or pain and the wail of females in heat are made in the same way.

BODY LANGUAGE
Vocalizing conveys information over distance, while body language remains the logical and favorite communication method face to face. Feline body language is most refined in sending "go away" signals, and aggressive and defensive displays are overt and simple. The whole body is used to send "loud" signals, while the ears and tail are more subtly expressive.

A safe and secure cat moves with fluid ease and a raised tail. It settles in total relaxation, and on waking it loosens its muscles with a whole body stretch. Nervous cats quietly avert their eyes from others and tend to yawn.

An offensive display involves direct eye contact, often with constricted pupils, and a posture permitting instant attack. Head and whiskers lean forward.

Communicating contentment
Movements are relaxed when a cat is content and secure. Safe in its territory, this feral cat wakes on a warm, sunny windowsill and stretches to prepare for activity – or further inactivity. A yawn and a stretch communicate an absence of tension to other cats, and may also be used to defuse tense situations.

Ears are held up and out so that the opponent sees the backs of them. Fearful aggression is seen in the typical Halloween cat, with its arched back, dilated pupils, and bristling hair.

Apprehension is seen in the crouch assumed by a cat when it feels insecure. As apprehension increases, the crouch becomes lower, the pupils dilate, and the ears flatten against the head. When a cat feels threatened, it rolls over into a defensive position that reveals its claws and teeth. Hair may bristle all over the body.

FELINE GRAFFITI

Cats leave visual markers on their territory to communicate either their presence or their ownership of the domain. While scratching is a method of maintaining sharp claws, it is also used to leave a visible sign of a cat's presence. This is why domestic cats prefer to scratch something highly visible, like the arm of a sofa, and why scratching posts should be placed in a prominent position in a room, rather than tucked away in a corner (*see page 226*).

Feces are also used by a dominant cat to mark its territorial boundaries visibly. This is why some cats leave their feces unburied in neighbors' yards, but not in their own; the cat feels that its territory extends beyond its own yard and its feces are a visible sign of the extent of its jurisdiction.

SCENT MARKING

Feces also serve as a territorial marker through their powerful scent, an important part of the feline communication repertoire (*see page 82*). Each time a cat empties its bowels, it squeezes a smelly secretion out of the adjacent anal sacs, anointing its deposit with an "identification tag." French research has identified at least 17 different chemicals in anal discharge, which suggests that this malodorous substance transmits a wide variety of information.

The same purpose is fulfilled by feline urine, which is either deposited on the earth as body waste, or used solely as a scent marker when spraying upright objects. Both male and female cats are able to scent-mark in this way, and both may sometimes continue to do so even after they have been neutered (*see page 70*).

Marking the territory
This Siamese scratches a tree in the heart of its territory to leave a high and visible marker, not as a threat, but simply to indicate that the territory is occupied.

Males, in particular, leave a sour, pungent odor, which is sufficiently potent to inform the relatively insensitive human nose that a male has claimed the territory.

Scent from the sweat glands on the paws also leaves an aromatic trail anywhere that a cat has visited. Further glands on the face produce substances that cats use as scent markers. Cats rub their heads against objects, leaving a scent marker that is often sniffed when the cat returns to the area. This most subtle form of scent marking is used by many domestic cats as part of their basic greeting ritual when their human family returns home.

TOUCH-SENSITIVE

While a cat announces its presence by leaving scent markers, its ability to communicate its needs or demands using touch is exquisite. Cats use a nose-to-nose touch, in part to smell each other but also to make physical contact.

Many cat owners know the featherlight touch of their cat's paw on the face early in the morning, a gentle reminder of a new day and impending mealtime. Those who disregard the light touch know that it becomes an urgent tap. If this is ignored, some cats will turn the tap into a veritable punch. They need no words.

FAMILY COMMUNICATION

All of the domestic cat's wild kin use similar methods of communication. In adults, vocal noises are mostly murmurs and high-pitched sounds; vowels are restricted to kittenhood. Territorial body language is highly refined, as is the use of both scent markers and touch. Because territory is so important, most large cats leave obvious scratch marks: in some regions where few trees grow, specimens are densely and deeply marked with generations of scratching. Markers may also be sprayed, to act as scent posts as well as visible signs.

Traditional practice
The heavy scratch marks on this fallen tree indicate that this ocelot and many others before it have used the tree as a scratching post for a considerable time.

While feral cats may abhor physical contact with people, cats raised from kittenhood with humans usually enjoy physical comfort given by people. Stroking is analogous to the comfort of being groomed as a kitten, and the contact communicates security. Socialized cats seek out people and demand to be touched and stroked.

Taboos, however, remain in the gentlest cat. Touching the abdomen often provokes a mock, or even genuine, aggressive response, because the abdomen is the least defended part of the body. Ordinary stroking may also provoke a sudden aggressive response. This is because, while cats enjoy stroking, it remains a learned rather than a natural adult behavior. A mental conflict arises, and the cat instinctively bites, then often apologizes, coming back to ask for more "maternal" care.

Universal submission
All mammals try to "shrink" when indicating submission. This fearful Abyssinian tightens itself into a low crouch, both to appease another cat and to prepare for explosive activity if it should be needed.

Show of weapons
Subtle body language usually averts conflict, but sometimes it is not enough. This kitten is in full defensive posture, baring all its weapons in a last-second attempt to either dissuade attack or protect itself.

SOCIAL BEHAVIOR

WE OFTEN EQUATE FELINE SOCIAL BEHAVIOR WITH OUR OWN OR with that of our other most popular companion animal, the dog: this is misguided. Cats live together on their own terms and for their own reasons, which are quite unlike ours. The cat's social behavior is governed by territory and food; relationships with other cats are possible, but less important than control of property. Almost any cat feels overwhelmingly threatened when another cat, even a kitten, appears on its territory. From a human perspective, such behavior appears antisocial, but this is not strictly true. Cats are far less solitary and more sociable than was once thought.

Feline social behavior is enormously varied. In some circumstances, cats show great intimacy: females may groom each other and even feed each other's kittens. In other circumstances, females fiercely protect their dens and feeding territory from others who happen into them. Some females accept males on their home turf; others drive them off. Males are equally elastic. Young cats may be tolerated or viciously attacked, sometimes even by their mothers.

POPULATION DENSITY

This vastly adaptable range of social behaviors depends upon a variety of environmental factors, but by far the most important of these are the size and proximity of the food source. Sociable behavior increases when food is plentiful, and decreases when food is scarce. Studies that have been carried out on feral cats to learn how many cats will occupy an area of 250 acres (100 ha) in different circumstances clearly illustrate this. When the only food available to the cats is prey, such an area will not support more than five cats. When both prey and garbage can be exploited for food, the same area may support as many as 50 cats. But when there is unlimited food, as there is from the cat lovers who feed the feline colonies in Rome's

Peaceful coexistence
Kittens that routinely meet dogs before seven weeks of age seldom develop fear of this potential adversary.

The family that eats together
If food is plentiful, as in this Greek fishing village, cats live in familial groups, often identifiable by their similar appearance. An outsider, such as the ginger tabby here, may be met with reserve or hostility.

public gardens, or around fish-processing plants in Japan, the area can contain over 2,000 felines. In these circumstances there will be an overlapping of many smaller cat colonies, each of them consisting of up to 50 related feline members.

Social interactions naturally increase with population density. Thinly scattered hunting cats will restrict their social gestures mostly to defensive postures. Well-fed cats in colonies are spontaneously and surprisingly sociable, resting together, greeting each other, and sometimes grooming each other. When they sleep, half of the time they are in contact with one or more other cats, although males make only half as many bodily contacts as do females. In one extensive study of a feral cat colony, 64 percent of interactions involved licking, 29 percent involved rubbing, and only seven percent involved forms of aggression. Contacts were initiated by kittens and females, seldom by males.

Feral cats are also flexible enough to change their social behavior regularly according to the prevailing conditions. On the Hebridean Islands, off Scotland,

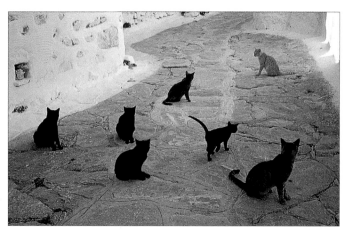

each cat has its own rabbit-hunting territory in summer, and defends it from others. But when the winter sets in, these cats move close to the security of local cottages, live on handouts, and accept the presence of other cats.

THE COHABITING CAT

Pet cats modify their social activities according to circumstances, just like ferals. A pet cat still needs its own territory, but this may be simply a favorite sleeping place. It may be friendly and sociable to other house cats in all other areas, but defend its chosen spot passionately.

The level of sociability of pet cats depends to a large extent on their early experiences, but is affected even more by their sexual status. Most pet cats are neutered, often before reaching sexual maturity, influencing their social activities in a marked manner. While feral tomcats make fewer social bodily contacts than females,

Quiet life
Both related and unrelated cats can cohabit. Plentiful food reduces potential conflict, but neutering is the most powerful behavior modifier.

neutered toms make as many body contacts with other cats as do neutered females, who make more body contacts than entire females. Although we neuter our cats as a method of population control, the effect on their sociability is both dramatic and very positive.

In a household of several mature pet cats, disputes seldom occur because rank has been established. If two cats do meet unexpectedly, whoever arrives first or holds the higher ground is the social superior, but this ranking is fluid. Rank is of social importance to cats, but it is more variable than in other species, and is often forgotten when all gather for their meal.

In some instances, however, a group of cats treats one in particular as a "pariah," viciously attacking it when it nears, and denying it any social contact. Paul Leyhausen has observed one colony in which the pariah cat was forced to live trapped on water pipes near the ceiling, even toileting from its perch.

ESTABLISHING SOCIAL RELATIONSHIPS
Observations of cats in catteries show that it takes a cat from two to five weeks to adapt to its new territory. It is likely that it takes as long or longer for a cat to adapt to a new cat on its home territory. Early learning has great impact; kittens under seven weeks old bond to new companions better than do older individuals. Forging social bonds is more difficult later in life, and depends in part upon natural characteristics: one study reported that Persians adjusted to a new cat in their home more easily than Siamese.

Even a short break in social bonds, such as when one cat is hospitalized for a few days, may affect social structures, with the returning cat being viciously attacked by its fellow cats.

Group dynamics
Social relationships are dynamic, responding to changing conditions. During this two-month study of favored resting places, Kaspar, the dominant cat, died. This did not alter Maurice and Tom's patterns, but Willow ventured downstairs, and Si, previously confined to the top of the refrigerator, soon became a dominant cat. The kitten Am, at first allowed everywhere, found his territory restricted as he matured. Disputes were settled by eye contact.

SI FEMALE
SIAMESE ADULT

KASPAR MALE
RANDOM-BRED ADULT

AM MALE
SIAMESE KITTEN

MAURICE MALE
RANDOM-BRED ADULT

TOM MALE
RUSSIAN BLUE ADULT

WILLOW FEMALE
INVALID ADULT

In most circumstances, however, social bonds remain strong once established, and anxiety occurs if they are broken. An American study of pet cats living together in indoor households found that when one died, its survivor showed "mourning" behavior: over half the survivors ate less than before, they became more vocal, and they demanded more affection from people in the household. Over 40 percent of surviving cats sought out the deceased cat's favorite spot and spent more time there for a period of up to six months after the death of the other cat.

Conversely, although it has not been formally studied, veterinarians are frequently told by cat owners how much "happier" the survivor is now that it has the house to itself. When these cats are medically examined, they appear to be both more robust and more relaxed than they were previously. Author Rudyard Kipling was lucid and eloquently observant in his creation of "the cat who walks by himself" (*see page 36*). While feline social behavior may sometimes mimic ours, cats often remain social loners through to the depths of their being.

Walking the boundaries
Cats often use human territorial markers, such as fences, as their demarcation lines. Social groups remain within the boundaries, making no social contact with outsiders.

DEMARCATION DISPUTE

All the domestic cat's wild relatives create and defend their own distinct hunting and breeding territories. When cats from adjacent territories meet at a demarcation point, potential injuries are avoided through displays of intent. During the ritualized stage of a demarcation dispute, cats will arch their backs and bare their teeth, and their fur will bristle. They also stare each other down, until one cat turns its head and breaks eye contact. It signals that it will withdraw, but any abrupt movement now provokes a lashing response from the victor. In domestic cat disputes, this is when the vanquished cat is bitten on its tail as it leaves the scene.

Facing off
These jaguars are using body language and voice to intimidate each other, just as domestic cats hiss, spit, and stare each other down, before actually fighting.

HUNTING AND PLAY

HUNTING IS AN INSTINCTIVE ACTIVITY, CENTRAL TO FELINE NATURE. Indeed, the cat is one of the most successful land-based predators in the world. All cats hunt. Rural feral cats refine their techniques to suit the available prey, while urban feral cats scavenge more than they hunt. Pet cats hunt for the thrill of stalk-and-pounce, rather than to fill their stomachs, and indoor cats may hunt toys. While most cats prey on land-based mammals, some become specialized at catching birds. This may have a profound effect on the population of small birds in regions where, historically, there has been an absence of land-based predators similar to the cat.

There is a tendency among urban cat owners to deny the cat's place as nature's best-packaged small, land-based predator. Quite simply, cats hunt, and this has little to do with hunger. Biologist Robert Adamec has found that hunger and hunting are controlled by different parts of the brain. He allowed cats to see a rat while eating a favorite meal: they stopped eating to kill the rat, but returned to the meal. Because of this split, hunting is more common than many owners realize. In one German survey of the stomach contents of pet cats killed in road accidents, 40–60 percent of home-fed cats also had the remains of prey in their stomachs.

When driven by hunger, a cat is more likely to scavenge than to hunt: it is far easier to slash through plastic bags to find a cooked chicken carcass than it is to hunt patiently for a mouse. On a full stomach, however, the most carefully bred, expensive, lovable pet cat will still be a hobby hunter, impelled to stalk and pounce.

Instinctive pounce
Pouncing is biologically built into the feline nervous system. It is an instinctive behavior, present from the moment a kitten begins to play. This kitten is in the classic pounce pose, with ears forward and tail high.

PREFERRED PREY
Cats are opportunist hunters, taking what is available. Most prey upon land mammals and reptiles, but some, learning from their mothers and their experiences, become adept at catching birds.

There are local variations in cats' prey; in the German study of cats' stomach contents, the rural cats had eaten 14 different species of animals, while the urban cats had eaten only cat food and a single grasshopper. Prey also varies on a larger scale. North American cats eat mice, ground squirrels, flying squirrels, chipmunks, gophers, and robins. European cats take mice, voles, sparrows, and fledgling birds, taking shrews only when they are very hungry. In southern Sweden, males catch more rabbits than do the smaller females. Kittens around the world, and adults in the tropics, eat spiders and insects. On subantarctic islands, noddies, terns, and penguins are taken. In Australia, where cats were imported in order to control the introduced European rabbit, they will eat opossums, reptiles, and ground-nesting birds.

Some cats take unusual or inedible prey in the absence of appropriate prey, or because they lack hunting experience. Cats may hunt frogs, but this is done for the thrill of the chase,

Tense anticipation
As it crouches ready to pounce, this Tonkinese treads its hind legs in excitement or to keep the muscles ready for action.

and few cats will actually eat their catch. Poisonous toads are occasionally killed by cats, with painful or fatal consequences.

HUNTING METHODS
Feline senses suggest cats should hunt at dawn and dusk, and in full moonlight (*see page 60*), but this varies. In hot summers, cats hunt through the night, and in cold winters, they hunt at noon. These changes also reflect prey activity. The cat's favorite hunting strategy is to sit and wait. It locates a good hunting ground, such as a small mammal's pathway, and sits by it patiently, staring intently. When prey appears, the cat pounces. It may throw itself on its side and, pinning the prey with its forepaws, rake it with its hind claws. When hunting birds, the cat uses ground cover to stalk, slinking forward close to the ground, freezing if it thinks it is detected, until it finally leaps, sprints, springs, or pounces.

Well-fed cats are more patient than hungry cats. Ferals are better hunters than pets, and nursing mothers are best. Studies of Swiss farm cats found that mothers took on average just over an hour and a half to capture a rodent, catching something every third or fourth pounce, while nonmothers took almost three times as long and caught every twelfth pounce.

Practiced pounce (left)
All cats, young or old, need to find a release for their hunting instinct and their energy. Rural, free-ranging cats satisfy this inclination naturally. Urban or other housebound cats need other outlets, such as small balls, feathers, and other toys, which they will "capture" and "kill" exactly like real prey.

Stealth tactics (right)
A cat crouches low and uses long grass as cover when it stalks prey. On surfaces such as manicured lawns or smooth paving, hunting is seldom productive.

Specialized hunting skills
Few cats can catch birds. This cat, playing with a bird it has killed, may not eat it, as even fewer cats can pluck feathers. Bird kills seem high because they are made in the yard during daylight, and because few birds are eaten, most being left in a visible larder. It is thought that up to six percent of backyard birds are killed by cats each year. The simple way to reduce this is by belling the cat.

TRANSPORTING AND STORING KILLS

The domestic cat's hunting instinct is similar to that of most other members of the cat family. In the wild, cats use similar strategies to stalk, capture, and kill, according to their abilities. Just as the domestic cat often returns to its home territory to eat its kill, many wild cats drag their prey back home, and even up a tree, where it can be consumed in safety. Wild cats consume only what they need to satisfy their hunger, saving excess food to consume later. Like the larders of corpses often built up in yards by domestic cats, wild cats that prey on large herbivores will keep a larder of meat until it is finished, as a guaranteed food source. But while house-fed domestic cats accumulate an overflowing larder of excess meat, wild cats always consume what they kill unless there is a sudden and overwhelming supply of game.

Spoils of a successful hunt
Hunger satisfied, this leopard keeps the rest of a gazelle to eat over the following days, until it hunts again.

Whether prey is promptly eaten, or even killed, depends on the cat and the context of the hunt. If it is hungry, a cat kills its prey with a swift bite – a cat's canine teeth are perfectly formed to slip between the neck vertebrae of a small rodent, killing it instantly (*see page 68*). Many cats bring live prey back to their home territory, and may even seem to offer it to their owners. Mothers bring back prey for their young to kill, teaching them hunting skills, and these cats may regard their owners as helpless kittens.

Live prey that is carried some distance is disoriented, and easier to recapture or play with. Hunting play is a curious phenomenon; after the hunt, many pet cats literally dance with delight, taking high, curving, pantomime leaps. This is most common after dangerous prey, such as a rat, has been killed. Ethologist Paul Leyhausen termed this "overflow play," a cathartic release from the tension of the hunt.

It is a common behavior in pet cats, perhaps a perpetuation of juvenile behavior, but is rarely seen in feral cats. Tormenting of prey, such as batting and throwing, may also serve some as yet unknown function.

PREVENTION OF HUNTING

Cats can have devastating effects on wildlife in isolated environments. Most dramatically, the single pet cat taken in 1894 to Stephen's Island off the coast of New Zealand killed the entire world population of the Stephen's Island Wren. Domestic cats also aided the extinction of other island birds. In the Galápagos Islands, off the coast of South America, feral cats also consume vast numbers of freshly hatched baby turtles as they scrabble across the sand to the sea.

Wildlife protection agencies and legislators have been concerned about feline predation of wildlife for a long time. The legislature of Illinois passed a law in the 1940s restricting cats to homes, but it was vetoed by the governor. In the 1990s many states are seeking to control feral cats. In Switzerland, cats must return to their homes every night. But the debate over whether cats should be prevented from hunting has been most heated in Australia,

Experimenting with prey
The cat's hunting instinct provokes it into a response to anything that moves, animate or inanimate. This cat is fascinated by a frog, and is about to bat it. If the cat were hungry, it would quickly consume the frog, rather than playing with it in this way.

which has few natural, land-based predators. In 1989, a suburb of Melbourne imposed a dusk-to-dawn curfew on pet cats. By 1995, the state of South Australia had laws permitting the destruction of any unidentified domestic cat.

Although we can prevent hunting, we have not removed the instinct. Increasing numbers of cats live permanently indoors. When these cats see prey through a closed window, their teeth may chatter – this is not fully understood, but does not occur in any other circumstances. Owners should play with their indoor cats and provide plenty of toys, or in the absence of live prey they may find their ankles being stalked.

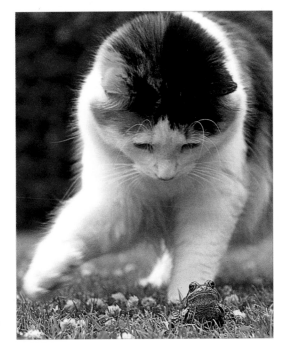

COURTSHIP AND MATING

CATS ARE NOISY, PROMISCUOUS, AND ENTHUSIASTIC ABOUT SEX. There are sound biological reasons for such torrid behavior, all of which derive from the cat's natural ecological niche of lone hunter. Sociable species, such as humans, dogs, or domesticated livestock, have ideal mating circumstances: males are constantly available.

Cats, however, evolved as lone hunters with individual territories, and when a female comes into season it is possible that no males will be in the vicinity. Because a female must take advantage of any and every male available, she appears to be overwhelmingly promiscuous when compared with other mammals.

Feline courtship is usually rather perfunctory, with a dominant tom invoking his rights over other males, and a receptive queen eventually accepting his advances. The female controls the timing of mating activity, only permitting the male to mate when she is ready (see page 70). Repeat matings occur over one or more days, and may involve several toms.

CALLING FOR A MATE

Out of season, an unspayed female will behave much as neutered males or females, but at the onset of estrus, dramatic changes occur. The first signs of heat are increased restlessness and a heightened desire to rub against objects or other animals. If allowed out, she will urinate more frequently and in new places, and she may also spray to announce her condition to local toms (see page 81). At this stage, however, she will not permit a tom to mate with her.

Pushing ahead
In uncontrolled or feral matings, many males vie for the right to mate. Toms may fight before mating, and occasionally, as here, one may refuse to wait patiently, but this is unusual.

Soon after, she begins to make a plaintive and distinctive sexual call, a vocal signal to all toms that she is receptive. The call carries further than scent, alerting the widest possible area. Inexperienced owners often mistake it for pain.

At this stage in her cycle, a queen frequently rolls over on her back, and, if touched at the base of her tail, she will crouch with her hindquarters raised and her tail held to the side, ready to mate. Often she purrs, treads with her front paws, and stretches her body. Even normally withdrawn females may become lasciviously affectionate during estrus.

First overtures
The female (left) sets the pace in all sexual encounters. This male waits cautiously. If he is too forthright he risks a rebuff and a vicious attack.

All this advertising is done because the female cat is an induced ovulator: her ovaries will not release eggs until after mating (see page 70). This is sensible given the cat's independent nature, ensuring that eggs are not wastefully shed when there are no males in the area.

ANSWERING THE CALL

The male cat is an opportunist. If unneutered, he patrols his territory regularly, spraying and responding to any scent markers and calls that tell him that a female in the area is receptive. When he scents a receptive female, his spraying activity increases dramatically. Often, however, he is not the only male who has been alerted. Dominant males will fight for the right to mate. When several toms gather, one will dominate the others, most often through intimidation or strength. After this, there is usually no further fighting among the toms; other males wait for a turn. Releasing eggs after a single mating would reward the most dominant male, but he may not be the best father. Queens only release eggs after repeated matings, so any male who mates with the female has a chance to father a kitten.

Rejected advances
Inexperienced males can be impetuous. This male has made an approach to the female, but is rejected. She will mate with the male of her choice when she is ready.

MATING PROCEDURE

Courtship is usually perfunctory. The female allows the male to sniff her, which he does repeatedly, drawing scent into his vomeronasal organ (*see page 60*); any attempts to do more may be viciously rebuffed. British ethologist Roger Tabor has observed low-ranking males assiduously courting queens in early season; Queens often accept the low-ranking male, rather than the dominant male, as the first mate.

Mating itself is brief and tense. When she is ready, the queen assumes a crouching position with her hindquarters raised (called lordosis) and permits the male to proceed with mating. As the male mounts, he grasps the scruff of the female's neck between his jaws. This stimulates the dependent "scruff response" seen in kittens (*see page 88*), and subdues the queen.

The tom ejaculates almost at once. As he withdraws, his penis abrades the queen's vagina (*see page 70*). She cries out, and may even turn on the tom, hissing, spitting, and trying to bite. Experienced toms, who are familiar with this behavior, will relax and groom themselves nearby until the female is receptive once more.

Swedish researcher Olaf Liberg has observed that cats will mate between 10 and 20 times each day, and that mating sessions can continue for as long as four to six days.

The first male often becomes exhausted, and may be replaced by other toms waiting in the line. These multiple matings stimulate the cascade of hormones that induces egg release. For many cats, mating is the only time that they make physical contact with others; after mating, the male rarely has any parental role.

SURVIVAL VALUES

Feline mating rewards those males who subdue other toms, assiduously court the queen, or patiently wait for their turn. Each has excellent qualities: strength, intelligence, or persistence. Multiple matings also help to ensure a varied genetic mix. In lions, a new male claiming the breeding position in a pride often kills the cubs of the last dominant male. The frequency of infanticide in our domestic cats is unknown, but zoologist David Macdonald has observed a newly arrived male cat enter the communal nest of three queens in their absence and kill six kittens. A male believing he had kittens in the litters would have a strong disincentive for such behavior. Maternal infanticide in cats is extremely rare, and mostly due to inexperience or stress from real or imagined threats.

Stimulating ovulation

As the male withdraws, his penile barbs scratch the female's vagina, provoking a yowl from her. Although it sounds painful, the sensation does not impede her desire to repeat the mating, often within 20 minutes.

Post-coital grooming

After each mating, both the individuals groom themselves. Grooming has a calming effect. It begins with cleansing the genitals but then extends to the whole body before mating resumes. Serial matings will often continue all day.

Perseverance brings success

The female accepts the male and assumes a crouch. To secure his grip, subdue her, and prevent her from biting him, he grasps the skin of her neck in his jaws. He will not let go until he has completed mating – almost instantaneously – and withdrawn.

SURVIVAL IN THE WILD

Mating in wild cats is very similar to that of domestic cats. A significant difference is that wild cats seldom have the luxury of a surplus of readily available mates. The female gathers males from as wide a territory as possible, by leaving increasingly frequent scent markers and vocally proclaiming her impending heat. This is a sensible solution to the problem of being a solo hunter in a large hunting range. All of the cat family are induced ovulators. To find the best genes for her young, a female must hold on to her eggs as long as possible, then mate with the male she considers the most suitable. The onset of estrus in wild cats varies according to location: increasing daylight hours are a major stimulus, leading to summer kittens. Once begun, estrus cycles succeed each other until a series of successful matings produces a pregnancy.

Call of the wild

In the vastness of her range, this female bobcat seeks out a high rock; her vocal call to inform all potential mates that she is in heat can best be heard from here.

MOTHERS AND KITTENS

THE PREGNANT QUEEN BECOMES WITHDRAWN AND SEEMINGLY SERENE. As the two-month pregnancy progresses, she seeks out a safe place in which to give birth, and becomes restless as birth approaches. Mothers move their kittens frequently during their first days and, in communities, will care for each other's kittens.

A young kitten is extraordinarily precocious in its development. By three weeks its senses have matured and by seven weeks it has developed its full repertoire of behavior. A kitten develops social bonds to other cats, to us, to dogs, or to almost any companions, if it meets them frequently between these ages.

There are few visible signs of early pregnancy. At around three weeks of gestation the nipples become firmer and "pink up." The belly grows more rotund, and progesterone (*see page 71*) induces a serene disposition.

Pregnancy takes anywhere from 57 to 70 days, but a few days before the birth the female grows restless and seeks a nest. She rearranges her bedding and paces until the contractions begin. Litter sizes vary, but three to six is average, and labor can take an hour or a whole day. Kittens are delivered enclosed in fluid-filled sacs. The mother licks these away, stimulating the kitten's first breath, and chews through the umbilical cord. More contractions expel the placenta, which the mother eats: she consumes all birth wastes to prevent predators from scenting the litter. At birth, production of the hormone prolactin stimulates milk production and release.

GOOD MOTHERING

Mothering ability depends in part upon genes, but also upon emotional maturity and the early experiences a cat had with her mother. Fathers as a rule play no part in kitten care, although some breeders report "mothering" toms.

Instinctive care
This Tonkinese queen instinctively curls around her young, offering comfort and protection as well as nourishment. Her abilities depend on her maturity, her own upbringing, and her innate qualities.

On the other hand, Italian scientist Dr. Eugenia Natoli has observed that all females within a cat community may act as midwives, licking the newborns and severing umbilical cords.

There is no more fearsome aggression than that of a mother cat. Dropping the usual feline subtleties, she defends her kittens ferociously. Her other behavior is as noble. In the first few weeks of life a kitten depends upon its mother to stimulate all body functions: her licking prompts the release of bladder and bowels.

Just as she tidied her nest at birth, she also consumes all of each kitten's body waste products, to hide her litter's presence from predators. Although she keeps her birthing den immaculately neat in this way, she may move her kittens shortly after birth and then again when they are about four days old. Her first instinct is to keep her litter together and safe, picking up each kitten by the scruff of its neck and carrying it to a new, safer nest. Feral cats carrying their kittens over long distances outside may move them in stages to avoid leaving any for too long.

Many behaviorists believe that mothers frequently move their newborns in this way to protect them from predators, yet some studies show that new mothers will quickly move their kittens into the just-vacated dens.

Personal care
As a lone hunter, a cat cannot depend on others for grooming. This kitten began self-grooming at three weeks.

By the scruff of its neck
Kittens are always carried by the scruff of the neck. When "scruffed" and carried, the kitten instinctively stops wriggling and draws its legs close to its body to prevent them from being injured during transport. The scruff response remains throughout the cat's adult life.

Superior mothers
In natural conditions, only the fittest kittens of the best mothers survive, going on to become excellent mothers themselves later.

Displaced hunting behavior
The hunting instinct is buried deeply in the mind of even the youngest kitten. Rather than just eat its food, this kitten prods it, as it would an animal brought back from the hunt, to check whether it is safe to approach. During their early learning period, kittens may pounce on food to "capture" or "kill" it before sniffing or eating it. Adult cats will rarely play with their food in this way.

Instinctive cleanliness
The cat is a naturally hygienic animal. A kitten's instinct to use a specific site for elimination is profound and fully developed by three weeks of age, when it starts to explore. These kittens, provided with a litter box, investigate it and, because the texture is more natural underfoot than the hard surface of a household floor, they are inclined to use it as their toilet. Dry food and litter are sometimes confused, however.

EARLY LEARNERS
At birth, a kitten is totally helpless, unable even to regulate its own temperature. But within four days it can find its mother and crawl to her from over 2 ft (0.5 m) away. Ten days later, its coordination is sufficiently developed for it to use its front legs. By three weeks of age, it is tentatively standing, scenting, hearing, seeing, and responding. By seven weeks of age, it is running and leaping and somehow seems to have developed near-perfect balance.

Early actions are instinctive, but learning begins soon after birth. At one week, a kitten knows the smell of its nest and returns to it if separated. At only 18 days, it shows some signs of independence, leaving its mother to explore. It can now control urination and defecation, and it will use a litter box if one is offered. While it still depends upon its mother for most of its grooming, it is capable of fully grooming itself by five weeks. Relationships with its mother and littermates remain close but even now the seeds of separation are being sown.

Numerous studies have shown that kittens learn from their mothers how to negotiate obstacle courses and open door latches; without an example they cannot perform the task, or do so only by chance.

SUCKLING AND WEANING
A kitten uses heat receptors in its nose to find a teat; it will return to this teat throughout its suckling period. Milk release is stimulated by "treading" the breast with the forepaws, a behavior some cats continue into adulthood.

Cat milk is highly concentrated in fat and protein. The kittens must compete for the most productive teats; a kitten already knows which teat is best at two days. Kittens that latch onto the most productive teats grow fastest, unless displaced by more dominant littermates. Suckling is needed for nourishment for five to six weeks, but continues beyond this age for emotional benefits. In a cat community, kittens may be suckled by half-sisters or aunts.

For the first few weeks the mother induces her kittens to suckle, but then they begin to pester her for meals. At three weeks a kitten starts to eat solid food; by five weeks it has a full set of pin-sharp teeth (*see page 68*) and is ready to eat solid food. Those sharp teeth play a role in weaning; continued suckling becomes annoying. When kittens try to suckle, a mother may hiss and spit at them, even bat them away.

Feral mothers bring prey back to the nest and tear it up for their young. As they mature, the kittens have to do more of the tearing up for themselves. Soon live prey is brought, an invigorating learning experience. As a mother's kittens stop suckling her and move on to meat, the mother's milk dries up, and her hormonally induced urge to mother diminishes.

FULL INDEPENDENCE
In a natural situation, large litters disband by the time the kittens are six months old, while smaller litters remain together longer; their suckling seems to be less annoying, and they are allowed to continue to suckle for longer.

At the same time, play between littermates becomes increasingly rough; between males and females it is even vicious. By six months, the mother and her daughters are seemingly so exasperated with the rough play of the male kittens that these are permanently expelled from the nest. The females form the blood-related colony that is the basic feline social group (*see page 82*). The outcast males join a "brotherhood," willing to spend time together sunning themselves, but each with its own independent territory, and each waiting its chance to father another generation.

PROLONGED DEVELOPMENT

Kittens of big cats are proportionally small at birth; although adult male Siberian tigers can weigh 770 lb (350 kg), their cubs weigh about 2 lb (1 kg) at birth. They take longer to mature; born as helpless as domestic kittens, tiger cubs remain in the den until about eight weeks of age, when they emerge and start following their mother around. Unlike domestic kittens, which become independent early, tiger cubs depend on their mothers for food for a full 18 months. Even when mature enough to hunt on its own, a young tiger continues to hunt on its mother's territory for another year before moving on to set up its own home range of 8–39 sq miles (20–100 sq km). As with the domestic cat, males play no parental role.

Staying in the nest
Although it has considerable strength and size, this tiger cub will remain dependent on its mother for safety, security, and food for at least another year.

CHAPTER FIVE

DOMESTIC CAT BREEDS

UNTIL RECENTLY THERE WERE VERY FEW breeds of cat. Those that did exist were the result of environmental pressures – heavier coats in cold climates and sparse coats in hot climates, larger size where cats preyed on large game such as jackrabbits, smaller size where prey consisted of small rodents and birds. In the last century, cat fanciers have created many new breeds. Some were developed by selectively breeding cats that evolved to survive in a specific environment, others by breeding for coat color and density. Recently, breeders have perpetuated mutations such as curly coats or short legs to produce new breeds with unusual features.

ABOVE FEMALE CHOCOLATE TORTIE TONKINESE

LEFT CATS' EYES CAN BE ROUND, SLANTED, OR ALMOND-SHAPED

THE HISTORY OF SELECTIVE BREEDING

CATS HAVE BEEN KEPT IN OUR HOMES FOR MILLENNIA, BUT ONLY IN the last century or so has selective breeding been actively pursued. The first cat shows, at the end of the last century, stimulated the creation of breed clubs throughout Europe and North America. The first breeds were those that had developed naturally, but soon breeders were using their new knowledge of inheritance patterns to create a palette of coat colors and patterns in both short and long coats. This recent human intervention in feline evolution has produced some remarkable results.

Possibly the first cat show was held in the time of Shakespeare, at St. Giles' Fair in Winchester, England, in 1598. Shakespeare called the cat a "harmless, necessary creature," and this show was probably about mousing abilities as much as personality and looks. On the other side of the world, in Thailand, the *Cat Book Poems*, possibly written at the same time, recorded cats of varying colors and types. Readings of the original old Thai script imply that this is not quite the world's oldest breed register; while it identifies different types, there is no suggestion that the Thais actively bred for these types.

THE START OF BREED REGISTRIES

The first formal cat show was held in 1871 at the Crystal Palace in Hyde Park, London. It was organized by Harrison Weir, who wrote the standards for all the breeds shown and acted as one of the three judges; a Persian kitten stole the show. Most exhibitors were British gentry, so as well as breed classes, there was a special class for "Cats Belonging to Working Men."

The first cat show to attract wide attention in North America was organized by James T. Hyde in 1895 at Madison Square Garden, New York; a Maine Coon was champion. These shows, and others in mainland Europe, proved an enormous success and were the main impetus for modern selective breeding, stimulating a vogue in "purebred" cats.

Lucky cats
All the cats described in the Cat Book Poems *bring different kinds of luck to their owners; they seem to have been regarded as simple varieties, not special breeds.*

Associations formed to create rules for shows; in 1887 the National Cat Club was started in Britain, with Harrison Weir as its president, and in 1896 the American Cat Club became North America's first registry to verify pedigrees. Within 11 years of Harrison Weir forming the National Cat Club, a challenger, the Cat Club, was founded. Feline politics entered the world of cat breeding and remain there today.

The role of breed registries in governing breeds is fraught with inconsistencies. It is very hard to say, for example, what exactly a breed is. Not all breeds are recognized by all registries; a cat might be recognized as one breed in one registry but another breed in a different registry, and several breeds do not even breed true to their standards. All breeders agree on the importance of their cats' health and welfare, but the finer points of breed etiquette remain a matter of constant (and lively) debate.

MODERN REGISTRIES

Just as fashions change with time, the cat fancy, like the breeds themselves, is constantly evolving. Those who favor experimentation pursue as many new developments and traits as possible. Purists want to keep breeds as distinct, and often as limited, as possible. Each registry has a range of opinions between these two extremes.

Founding father
Harrison Weir is often described as "the father of the modern cat fancy." He raised the cat to a new status.

CAT SHOW
R[ ]E
PR[ ]

The world's largest registry of pedigree cats is the Cat Fanciers' Association (CFA), founded in 1906, which has clubs in the United States and Canada, South America, Europe, and Japan. CFA's registering philosophy is purist, allowing, for example, only four Burmese colors and four Siamese colors. Perhaps the most liberal or experimental of registries is The International Cat Association (TICA), founded in 1979 and based in North America. This registry accepts new breeds more rapidly than any other major association, even if only provisionally, and by doing so it encourages experimentation. Britain's Governing Council of the Cat Fancy (GCCF) was formed in 1910. Its policies are staid, but less so than CFA's, and its influence is worldwide: registering bodies in countries such as South Africa, New Zealand, and Australia base their decisions on GCCF rules.

Ancient or modern
The Birman has a pattern that might naturally evolve in an isolated area, but it might also be a man-made breed, the product of more recent selective breeding .

Island breed
Cats with bobbed or kinked tails occur with a high frequency on the Malay Peninsula. Such cats may become especially prevalent in isolated locations.

Character cats
There is a new tendency to breed for temperament; the famously placid Ragdoll is the most obvious example of this, but it is not alone.

Most European countries have several registries, but at least one from each country belongs to the Fédération Internationale Féline (FIFé), established in 1949. FIFé claims to be the largest feline organization in the world, and has affiliated clubs outside Europe. In policy, it is similar to Britain's GCCF: neither organization will recognize breeds like the Munchkin (*see page 123*) or the Scottish Fold (*see page 124*) and frown upon breeding for type associated with known defects, such as blue-eyed white cats, which have a high incidence of associated deafness.

OLD AND NEW BREEDS

Cat breeds can be broken down into two groups, which emerged chronologically. The first are the breeds that appeared naturally in free-breeding, although possibly isolated, feline populations. Many of these are characterized by coat color or pattern, and genetically these are almost always homozygotes that breed true (*see page 75*). For example, the Abyssinian is recessive for the ticked tabby pattern, emphasized through selective breeding. Some other breeds are characterized by distinctive mutations: the Japanese Bobtail (*see page 144*) and tailless Manx (*see page 156*) are examples. Some breeds developed naturally into types that were then formally recognized as breeds; the British, American, and European Shorthairs (*see pages 152, 160, and 166*), Norwegian Forest Cats and Siberians (*see pages 118 and 120*), and Maine Coons (*see page 114*) are in this category. A final major feature defining these early breeds is coat length. The longhairs, going under the various names of Persian, Angora, French, or Chinese cats, predate registries, but type and standards were very loose in those times.

More recently, breeds have been developed actively and sometimes very scientifically. Oriental Shorthairs (*see page 192*), Tonkinese (*see page 186*), Ocicats (*see page 206*), Angoras (*see page 140*), and Asians (*see page 178*) in Britain, and many others, have been created from scratch. This is the "growth" area in the cat world, with more new breeds appearing this century than in the entire history of domestic cats preceding it. Some new breeds, like the Somali (*see page 132*) or Balinese (*see page 136*), are simply longhaired versions of older shorthaired breeds. Others are coat mutations. A trait such as a rex coat may disappear but through careful nurturing, this genetic "fault" has been perpetuated to create a range of breeds. Other mutations die out or are limited because they are potentially lethal: Manx and Fold genes are harmful when homozygous, and breeders take utmost care in their breeding programs; free-breeding cats never exercise such caution. Controversy over breeds such as the hairless Sphynx (*see page 202*) and the short-legged Munchkin has led some to question certain modern breeding practices and to reexamine breeding toward potentially unhealthy extremes such as may be seen in some Persians (*see page 104*) and Siamese. Most breeds have closed registries, with no outcrossing.

Future directions
Africa remains an untapped source of types and genes. The type, blue eyes, and mitted bicolor pattern of this Cameroon cat are prevalent among the street cats in its town.

Breeders argue that if they select for outward good health, they can produce healthy cats even in a small gene pool. This is not always true: genetic health problems and lowered disease resistance take time to show.

WIDER EFFECTS

Selective breeding has only a peripheral effect on the species as a whole. Pedigreed cats make up less than 10 percent of the domestic cat population, even where they are most popular; in most countries, they account for less than two percent. However, the existence of breed registries is of value for all cats, raising the profile of cats as desirable, worthwhile animals. Indirectly, these associations improve the welfare of all cats, not just pedigreed breeds.

Questionable status

In most associations, the pointed kittens born in this Oriental Shorthair litter would be registered as Siamese. Some, such as CFA, refuse to grant such kittens champion status.

COAT COLORS

THE CAT'S ORIGINAL COAT WAS OF COLOR-BANDED AGOUTI HAIR, designed for camouflage in the natural environment. The first mutation away from hair with bands of color to a single color, or non-agouti hair, was probably to black; this mutation is often seen in other cats, such as the "black leopard" or "black panther."

Other mutations occurred for red, white, and dilution of the solid colors, and all were perpetuated because the domestic cat no longer needed its wild, hunting camouflage to survive. These few, simple genetic variations created the framework for the seemingly endless variety of coat colors that exist in cats today.

All colored hairs contain varying amounts of the two forms of melanin pigment, eumelanin and phaeomelanin. Eumelanin produces black and brown, while phaeomelanin produces red and yellow. All colors are based on the absence or presence of these pigment granules in the shafts of each hair. Pigment is made in skin cells called melanocytes, and the distribution of these cells is genetically determined. Most knowledge about coat colors is based upon observation and informed guesswork rather than microscopic investigation of genes, so there are still many questions to be answered.

Cats with single-colored "non-agouti" hair are called self or solid. Self coats are recessive: the cat must carry two copies of the non-agouti gene (see page 75) in order to conceal its "true" original tabby pattern (see page 96).

Under wraps
Black is the most dominant eumelanistic color. It may be masked by white, but itself masks the genetic potential for other coat colors.

DENSITY OF COLOR
Some cats have vibrant, deeply colored coats. These come in the colors black, chocolate, cinnamon, and sex-linked red. Cats with these coats have at least one copy of the "dense" gene (D), which is dominant and ensures that each hair is packed tightly with numerous pigment globules to give the richest color. Other cats have lighter, "dilute" coats in blue, lilac, fawn, and sex-linked cream. These cats have two copies of the dilute gene (d), which is recessive and results in clumping and scatterering of the pigment globules in each hair: the effect is to create a paler shade of any of the dense colors. Some breeders think that there is also a "dilute modifier" gene, provisionally called D^m, which modifies action of the dilute gene d, but is located at a different site on the chromosome, and so is able to "interact" with d. If a cat carries both the dd dilute trait and the D^m modifier gene it will have a "modified" color:

Natural distinction
Dilute self colors always breed true, and so have become a defining characteristic of several naturally developed breeds, including the Russian Blue.

blue and lilac modify to different shades of caramel, and cream modifies to apricot. Other cat breeders dispute this, and claim that these colors are just bad blues, lilacs, or creams.

SEX-LINKED RED
There is firm evidence that the gene for red or orange color in cats is located at a specific site on the sex-determining X chromosome. In its dominant form (O), it makes the cat red; in its recessive form (o), it lets whatever other color the cat is carrying show through. A male cat, with an XY chromosome combination, can only ever have one copy of the gene, so if he carries one O he is red and if he has one o he will be any other color. The female cat, because she has an XX combination, can carry two copies. She will be red if she carries two copies of O, or another color if she carries two copies of o,

Red Burmese
Although sex-linked red existed in the East, the first Burmese in the West were brown. Red was re-created, and it is still not widely recognized.

CAT COLORS

DENSE	DILUTE	DILUTE MODIFIER
Black B– D–	Blue B– dd	Caramel B– $d^m d^m$
Chocolate bb D–	Lilac or Lavender bb dd	Caramel bb $d^m d^m$
Cinnamon $b^l b^l$ D–	Fawn $b^l b^l$ dd	Undefined brown $b^l b^l$ $d^m d^m$
Red D– $O/O(O)$	Cream dd O–$/O(O)$	Apricot $d^m d^m$ O–$/O(O)$
Chocolate tortie bb D– Oo	Lilac tortie or Lilac-Cream bb dd Oo	Caramel tortie bb $d^m d^m$ Oo
Cinnamon tortie $b^l b^l$ D– Oo	Fawn tortie $b^l b^l$ dd Oo	Undefined tortie $b^l b^l$ $d^m d^m$ Oo
Tortoiseshell B– D– Oo	Blue tortie or Blue-Cream B– dd Oo	Caramel tortie B– $d^m d^m$ Oo

but unlike the male cat, a female can also be heterozygous (*Oo*). This combination makes her tortoiseshell, a mosaic pattern of both red and black, with some melanocytes obeying the *O* gene and others obeying the *o* gene. This mosaic combination interacts with all of the other color-controlling genes, producing torties in all the solid and dilute colors.

The distribution of mosaic colors cannot be controlled through selective breeding, so whether your tortie fulfills American preferences (distinctly patched) or the British standards (softly mottled) is purely a matter of luck. Tortoiseshell mosaicism can be so slight as to be virtually nonexistent. At least one tortie was classified as black at birth, won prizes as a black, then produced red and tortie kittens and had to be reregistered as a (very poor) tortoiseshell.

EASTERN AND WESTERN COLORS

The traditional Western cat-coat colors are black and its dilute blue, and red and its dilute cream, together with their bicolor versions and solid white. Western breeds, such as British, American, and European Shorthairs (*see pages 152, 160, and 166*), Maine Coons (*see page 114*), and Norwegian Forest Cats (*see page 118*), began in these colors only, and some still exist in these colors only. Some breeds have even more exclusive colors, such as the Turkish Van (*see page 126*), which originated in red and cream bicolors only. (However, other colors are now being bred, and have been accepted by many registries, both here and abroad.)

The traditional Eastern colors are chocolate and its dilute lilac, and cinnamon and its dilute fawn, although many historical works of art confirm that Western colors also coexisted in Oriental feline populations. Cat-coat colors have now been "transposed" from one group of breeds to another. In Britain, British Shorthairs are accepted in Eastern colors and, similarly, Burmese (*see page 182*) are now often bred in "Western" reds and creams. Conservative cat associations, most notably CFA, do not accept these transposed colors in all breeds.

WHITES AND BICOLORS

White is dominant over all other color genes, whether as all-over white (*W*), or as the white spotting gene (*S*) that gives us the bicolors. White hair, unlike all other hairs, contains no color-producing pigment at all.

Behind its snow white exterior, the white cat is genetically colored, and it passes on this color potential to its offspring. White cats carry the dominant *W* gene, which masks the expression of all other color genes. Often, a hint of a cat's underlying color breaks through

in a "kitten cap" in the hair on the head of newborn kittens. As the kitten grows, the cap disappears to leave pure white. Deafness is sometimes associated with the *W* and *S* genes, although it is more common in white cats with blue eyes than in those with yellow or orange eyes. These white cats are different from albino white cats that have no pigment in their pink eyes: albino white is uncommon.

Bicolored cats are white-coated with patches of color – tortie-and-whites are variously classified as bicolor or tricolor – and come in two types. The standard bicolor has a pigmented saddle over its back, with the white principally concentrated on the underparts and legs. The Van pattern, originally associated solely with the Turkish Van, but now also seen in other longhair and shorthair cats, consists of predominant white with solid or tortoiseshell patches restricted to the head and tail. One theory is that these cats carry two copies of the white spotting gene *S*, giving them a superabundance of white.

STANDARDS FOR COLORS

Although there are only a few genes responsible for solid colors, breed associations complicate matters by giving the same genetic color different names, depending on the cat it appears in. This tendency is most prevalent in the patterned coats (*see page 96*) but also happens in the self colors. Lilac is also called lavender or frost in some associations, black Oriental Shorthairs (*see page 192*) are also called ebony, genetically chocolate Oriental Shorthairs are called havana in Britain and chestnut in North America, and chocolate Havana Brown (*see page 171*) looks closer to

cinnamon and is called chestnut.

Reds are often specified to be red selfs, perhaps because the distinction between red selfs and red tabbies is subtle (*see page 96*), and in the Turkish Van red-and-white may be called auburn-and-white. Tortie-and-white cats are called calicos in some North American associations, notably CFA, because someone, at some time, perceived a resemblance to brightly printed calico cloth.

According to breed standards, the color of the nose, lips, and paw pads (the leather) should be in harmony with the coat color: pink in white cats, black in black cats, blue in blue cats, pink to brick red in reds. This can vary; in some cases, the color of the leather depends on the particular breed, or even the association.

Maturing color
Many self cats show vestigial tabby markings, known as "ghost markings" in kittenhood, especially reds, such as this young Angora. These marks often fade as the cat matures, although they may have a tendency to persist in dilute coat colors.

Van pattern
Found naturally in cat populations in the Mediterranean areas of Europe, this pattern is now widespread in carefully bred pedigreed cats. First identified in cats from the Lake Van region of Turkey, it takes its name from the Turkish Van breed.

Mosaic color
The spotting gene S seems to have a predictable effect on tortoiseshell mosaicism. Solid tortoiseshells may have subtly mixed colors, but tortie-and-whites almost always show large, crisply distinct patches of black and red.

COAT PATTERNS

BENEATH THEIR EXTRAVAGANT VARIETY OF SHIMMERING SHADES and patterns, all cats remain tabbies in disguise. Just as the most pampered of pet cats retains the abilities of its predatory ancestors, the hidden tabby pattern is a reminder of the cat's roots under the sophisticated exterior, an origin to which it can return at any time.

Through selective breeding, spotted, tipped, and pointed patterns are nurtured, or even created, by breeders. These are made possible by mutations in the genetics of feline coat patterns, mutations that would have reduced natural camouflage in the wild, but were no longer dangerous once the cat chose to live with us.

The domestic cat's ancestor, the African wildcat, is a striped tabby, camouflaged for hiding and hunting in the wild. The original, genetically dominant (see page 74) tabby pattern is inherited by all domestic cats. The hair between the tabby stripes or spots contains bands of color, almost always light at the base and dark at the tip, which act as a camouflage. This pattern is found in other animals, including squirrels, mice, and the agouti, the rodent after which the pattern is named. The bands of color give a "salt-and-pepper" appearance, which combines with tabby stripes to help a cat blend into its environment.

Cat in disguise
All selfs are tabbies in disguise; if a self cat is bred to a tabby, at least some of the kittens should be tabbies.

DOMINANT PATTERN

All cats inherit some form of the tabby gene, even those with solid, or "self" coats (see page 94). Geneticists call the dominant agouti gene A. Any cat that inherits A from at least one parent will have a patterned coat, and is notated as $A-$.

Two tabbies
The mackerel (below left) tabby pattern is genetically dominant over the classic (below right), but classic tabbies are still common in European, North American, and Australian cats.

Solid colors exist because there is a genetically recessive alternative to agouti, called non-agouti or a. In cats that inherit this from both parents, which are notated aa, the coat appears to be a single, even color, but careful examination may reveal disguised tabby markings. This "ghosting" is most apparent in young kittens, often disappearing with age.

There are four basic types of tabby markings in felines: mackerel or striped, classic or blotched, ticked or Abyssinian, and spotted. Although these four patterns look distinctively different they are in fact all mutated variations of the same basic tabby gene.

New spots
The patterns of some breeds, such as the Ocicat, have been created to emulate those of wild feline species. The genetics behind these newer spotted patterns are undefined.

Mackerel tabby stripes are narrow, parallel, and run from the spine down the flanks to the belly. This pattern was predominant in Europe until a few centuries ago. It was superseded by the classic tabby pattern. Classic tabbies have wide stripes that form "oyster" swirls on the flanks, centered on a blotch. The distribution of this pattern in the North American and Australian cats shows that it was a popular, if accidental, export from 18th- and 19th-century Britain. Ticked tabbies are more subtle: clear markings are restricted to the head, legs, and tail, and the body is softly flecked. The African wildcat often carries overall ticking. Ticked coats appear to have spread eastward into Asia, rather than northward into Europe. Naturally ticked cats, often with striped legs, are found in Sri Lanka and Malaysia, down to Singapore. The Abyssinian (see page 172) was the first breed to sport this pattern. Spotted tabbies have spotted bodies, often combined with striped legs and tails. Spotted patterns are formed when tabby stripes are broken up. The spots of many older European and American breeds follow mackerel tabby lines, but there are other patterns. Spots of the Ocicat (see page 206) fall in a blotched tabby configuration, while those of the Egyptian Mau (see page 204) appear random. The Spotted Mist (see page 174) has perhaps the most complicated combination in the newer breeds, including seemingly random spots interspersed by ticking. All of these characteristics suggest that patterning may be more complex than breeders realize.

Pattern on pattern
Tabby markings over tortoiseshell mosaicism creates possibly the most complex of all coat patterns.

Shaded Persian
Multiple genes appear to be involved in the creation of show-quality silver, shaded, and tipped cats. The genetics behind Shaded Goldens such as this young Persian (see page 106) have not yet been defined.

Strange smoke
The inhibitor gene usually produces a white undercoat, but extraordinary effects may be seen in long coats, such as this Persian (see page 104).

Fascinating new patterns, such as the rosetted and "King Spangle" coats under development in the California Spangled (*see page 203*), often lead to heated debate among geneticists and breeders over the possible factors at work.

Subtle shading

Hair color is produced by skin cells that feed pigment into the hair. The inhibitor gene, or *I*, allows pigment to fill only the first part of the hair to grow. This produces a variety of subtle patterns that appear to change as a cat moves. In self cats, it creates a "smoke," with a white undercoat. In agouti coats, the color is more restricted. Different degrees of shading give us shaded and silver colors and silver tabbies, which have appreciable colors, and tipped coats, which are merely "frosted" with color. The names for these colors are inconsistent. Tipped coats are often, but not always, called "chinchillas," while shaded or tipped reds may be called shaded or tipped "cameos." In some breeds, there is a distinction between shaded cats, with warm-toned undercoats, and silver shadeds, with clear silver undercoats.

Colorpoint patterns

The *I* gene is not the only gene to restrict color. Limitation of color to the extremities is called pointing. Pointed cats are light on their bodies and darker on their "points," namely their ears, feet, tail, and nose. In male cats, hair is also darker on the scrotum.

A heat-sensitive enzyme in the melanocytes, the pigmenting cells in the cat's skin, controls this pattern. Normal body temperature inhibits pigment production over most of the cat's body, but the enzyme is activated and hair pigmented at the points where skin temperature is lower. Pointing can occur in any color or pattern. Because it is temperature-sensitive, kittens are born white, cats in cool countries have darker coats than those in warm parts of the world, and all cats' bodies darken markedly with age.

The clearest form is the Siamese (*see page 188*) pattern: an almost-white body and dark points, called "pointed" in this chapter. The Burmese (*see page 182*) pattern, usually called "sepia," shows so little difference between body and points that some do not regard it as pointed. Tonkinese (*see page 186*) or "mink" pointing is a hybrid of Siamese and Burmese pointing. Neither gene dominates, and Tonkinese can produce mink, sepia, and pointed kittens.

Pointed patterns
Pointing genes interact with all other color and pattern genes. The Birman's mittens (see page 110) have a charming myth attached to them, but the story may simply be a breeder's inspired creation.

True colors

The variety of feline coat colors and patterns may be more than cosmetic. Research in other animals has suggested a relationship between "tamability" and non-agouti coats. Population geneticist Dr. Neil Todd studied the distribution of feline coat colors and found ever-increasing percentages of non-agouti coats along old trade routes out of Africa and up the rivers of Europe. In Britain, the end of the routes, he found the highest percentages of non-agouti cats. Todd holds that, along these routes, human selection favored the tamest cats. Long before the registries began, owners may already have been picking their cats by color.

COAT PATTERNS

SELF (*aa*, non-agouti)
TABBY (*A–*, agouti)

SMOKE (*aa I–*, shaded non-agouti)
SILVER TABBY, SHADED, TIPPED
(*A– I–*, shaded agouti)

SIAMESE (*cˢcˢ*, pointed)
BURMESE (*cᵇcᵇ*, sepia)
TONKINESE (*cᵇcˢ*, mink)

All cats carry a tabby pattern, either striped (*T–*), ticked (*Tᵃ–*), blotched (*tᵇtᵇ*), or some other, as yet undefined pattern. The *aa* allele masks tabby markings: melanic pigment (*see page 94*) fills the entire hair and cats appear self or tortie. The *A–* allele shows the tabby markings. Whether a cat is *aa* or *A–* has less effect on sex-linked red colors. The difference between selfs and tabbies in these colors is one of subtle polygenic effects that determine whether the markings are faint or strong.

The inhibitor gene *I* blocks color production. In non-agouti cats, only the roots are white, while in agouti cats, more of the hair shaft is affected. The difference between shaded silvers and silver tabbies is polygenic, affecting not only pattern but also depth of color. Polygenic effects may also differentiate shaded from tipped coats, although some claim there is a "wide-band" inhibitor gene. In the sex-linked red colors, the differences between the smoke, shaded, silver tabby, and tipped cats are all polygenic.

Technically, all of these patterns are pointed. All are heat-sensitive, with virtually all the color (in the Siamese) or the very deepest color (in the Burmese) concentrated in the cooler extremities, or points of the body. Color is also slightly degraded or lightened; for example, black becomes Seal in the Siamese and Sable in the Burmese. The Tonkinese does not have its own gene, but it is a softly pointed hybrid of pointed and sepia alleles. It will always produce variants in these patterns, as well as its own mink pattern.

FACE SHAPE AND BODY FORM

MOST CAT BREEDS ARE NOT DEFINED BY COAT COLOR OR PATTERN: many breeds share these attributes with each other. Breeds are more often differentiated by the characteristic shapes of their bodies and faces, and sometimes by distinctive physical characteristics such as taillessness or folded ears. Cat breeds show personality differences that are consistent to a considerable extent with these different body shapes: lean, long breeds are generally more lively and demonstrative than more compact, densely muscled breeds. These differences in breed type, from compact and cobby to sleek and sinuous, follow a general Europe/North America-to-Asia path.

The breed differences that we see today have been developed – sometimes to extremes – from natural variations found in free-breeding cat populations. To a great extent, these original variations in type were molded by the environments in which they evolved, and a breed's type is often a good indication of its geographical origin.

COLD-WEATHER CATS

The heaviest and most compact of domestic cats evolved through natural selection in cold climates. Many of these "natural breeds" have fairly large, rounded heads, moderately short, broad muzzles, solid bodies with broad chests, sturdy legs and round paws, and short to medium-length, thick tails. They are, in essence, built to retain as much body heat as possible.

Shorthair examples of these cobby cats are the British Shorthair (*see page 152*) and American Shorthair (*see page 160*), as well as the chunky-looking Chartreux (*see page 168*). Other breeds that derive from these may differ at first in just a single aspect of their body type. The Scottish Fold (*see page 159*) was developed through the use of British Shorthairs, and is distinguished primarily by its abnormal ears. American Shorthairs were used in the American Wirehair (*see page 162*), although this breed has now diverged in its looks,

Persian looks
Over the decades, the face of the Persian (below) has become more flattened. The degree to which this has been taken varies between registries; the popularity of extreme "peke-faces" has waned.

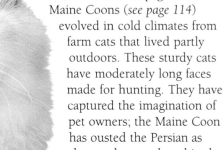

Old-fashioned face
The Chinchilla is the one longhair coat color that has generally avoided the breed's radical facial shortening; in South Africa it even has its own standard within the breed, allowing it to have a longer nose.

Norwegian Forest Cats (*see page 118*), Siberians (*see page 120*), and Maine Coons (*see page 114*) evolved in cold climates from farm cats that lived partly outdoors. These sturdy cats have moderately long faces made for hunting. They have captured the imagination of pet owners; the Maine Coon has ousted the Persian as the number one breed in the United States, and is Britain's second most popular breed just 20 years after it arrived.

SEMIFOREIGN BREEDS

A second group of cats has physical characteristics that are somewhere between the muscular cats of northern Europe and the more sinuous cats that developed in the warmer climates of Africa and Asia. These lean but muscular cats are often called "semiforeign." Breeds such as the Turkish Angora (*see page 130*), Russian Blue (*see page 170*), and Abyssinian (*see page 172*) have slightly oval, slanted eyes set in moderately wedge-shaped heads, slender but muscular legs, oval paws, and long, gently tapering tails.

A number of new breeds have been derived from the natural semiforeigns, and tend to have similar conformation. Some are simply new colors or coat lengths of their parent breeds, including the Nebelung (*see page 129*), Somali (*see page 132*), and the more controversial Russian Blacks and Russian Whites (*see page 170*).

Humble origins
The ancestors of the British Shorthair worked hard as mousers or fended for themselves in city alleyways. The result was a robust, solid build and a coat designed for warmth in cold, wet winters, characteristics of the breed to this day.

becoming increasingly "oriental" or "foreign" in appearance. The development of the Manx (*see page 156*) was parallel to that of the British Shorthair, rather than as an offshoot; it now looks even heavier than its close relative.

The original longhaired cats, the Persians or Longhairs (*see page 104*), were also thickset and muscular – physical features that enabled them to withstand the harsh winters in the high mountains of Turkey, Iran, and Caucasia. The breed still retains its original powerful body; other distinguishing features, such as the flattened face, have been introduced and exaggerated through decades of selective breeding. This has often led to facial-hair staining from overflowing tears from the eyes, because the more compressed and flattened the face is, the more difficult it is for tears to drain from the eyes into the nose. Extreme flattening of the face now seems to be waning in general popularity. Other solid and robustly built longhaired cats developed naturally in northern climes.

Unique departure
The Scottish Fold, like many recently developed breeds, is distinguished by a single unique, striking characteristic. Registries are strict about breed identity being unmistakable, so this trend is likely only to increase.

Some of the more recent efforts to create wild-looking cats, such as the Ocicat (*see page 206*), used semiforeign parent breeds and reflect this in their type. Some newer breeds also fit into this type of build; American Curls (*see page 122*) have modified-wedge heads and svelte bodies, and are distinguished primarily by the ear tips. Fashion seems to favor the semiforeign look just now; for example, a Somali could be a very popular cat in advertising, since it is perceived as elegant and striking without being extreme or odd-looking.

ORIENTAL BREEDS

The most dramatically slender cats are the Oriental breeds, most of which evolved in warm climates where losing excess body heat was much more important than retaining it. With their large-eared, wedge-shaped heads, fine legs, slender bodies, and long, thin tails, these cats have developed maximum body surface area for their size, in order to rid themselves of excess heat. This conformation traditionally has oval, slanted eyes, and its most classic example is the Siamese (*see page 188*). Some claim, with good evidence, that it did not always look like this, and that a stereotyped Western image of Oriental delicacy has refined a cat that never was. Others claim that the cat was always meant to look like this, and cite old breed standards, which do seem to bear this out but are open to interpretation. One breed that seems to lend support to the theory of Western "refinement" is the Japanese Bobtail (*see page 145*), which is distinctly chunkier in Japan than it now is in North America, where it is being bred to look more typically "Oriental" and delicate. Curiously, however, the North American breed standard for the undeniably Eastern Burmese (*see page 182*), imported from Rangoon, has increasingly emphasized solidity.

Newer breeds have been created in the West to mimic Oriental style. The Oriental Shorthair (*see page 192*), the solid-colored version of the Siamese, was created in the West, as non-pointed shorthairs that were among the original Southeast Asian imports were not preserved as a distinct breed. In Britain this new breed was originally called Foreign, and recently became Oriental, a name change that may have been made to ease international confusion, but which also reflects the way the has breed evolved. Other distinctly Western breeds like the Cornish Rex (*see page 198*)

Heading eastward
The Devon Rex originated in Britain and is popular in North America, but its look is Oriental. Large ears and fine boning are not common in cats from Devon.

Warm-weather cat
Oriental breeds like the Siamese were always lightly built, but their modern type is far finer than that of free-breeding cats in Thailand.

and Devon Rex (*see page 200*) have been bred to resemble Eastern breeds, with the Cornish Rex having become one of the most extreme in North America. The Devon Rex has contributed significantly to the Sphynx (*see page 202*).

Among the Oriental breeds, the Siamese remains the most popular, but less than it was in the past. It may be that, as possibly with the Persian, some people are now repelled by the extreme look. By contrast, the Siamese-Burmese hybrids, the moderate-looking Tonkinese (*see page 186*), are soaring in popularity.

NEW DEPARTURES IN BUILD

The possibility of breeding bigger or smaller cats, either naturally or through outcrossing to other species, intrigues many. When this has been attempted, the large or small cats tend to revert back to normal domestic-cat size in the next generation.

Nonpedigreed pedigree
The American Curl is most notable for its extraordinary and unique ears. Its build is semiforeign. It differentiates itself further from many older breeds by using nonpedigreed cats as outcrosses.

Unlike dogs, the domestic cat seems to have a genetically predetermined, limited size range. Only outcrossing to another species, which is a controversial move, is likely to change this.

A few breeds are classified according to a single anatomical feature, often arguably a malformation. For example, the taillessness of the Manx is associated with potentially lethal medical conditions. Other cats have extra toes, which is another malformation. These cats exist in abnormally large numbers in the New England states of Boston in Massachusetts and in Halifax, Nova Scotia. While it might seem absurd to breed these cats selectively to create a new breed, there has been at least one, albeit short-lived, attempt. In a way, this is no different than breeding selectively for any other body malformation. The single most striking change in the build of cats is the Munchkin. Taking its undeniably cute name for a term of endearment used in *The Wizard of Oz*, this is a unique breed in that most of the bones in the body are normal, but the long bones of the legs are dramatically shortened. The domestic cat evolved to its virtual perfection through hundreds of thousands of years of natural trial and error. Interventions in its breeding that may threaten such inherent flawlessness are of deep concern to a number of cat lovers.

Transatlantic fashions
In North America, Burmese have a rounded look, most noticeable in the head shape (left). The European counterparts of this breed (above) have developed a typically foreign, angular look.

EYE SHAPE AND COLOR

BEAUTY IS IN THE EYE OF THE BEHOLDER, BUT IN THE CASE OF CATS it is often in the vivid, unblinking eyes of the beheld. Cats have unusually large eyes for the size of their head. This relationship of eye size to head size mirrors the proportions seen in most animals, including humans, during infancy; it is without doubt one of the subliminal factors that triggers our willingness to care for young animals, and cats benefit from this. Because cats' eyes are among their most appealing attributes, many breeders take great pains to breed for specific eye color, creating a range of intense shades. Even the best photographs are unlikely to do their efforts justice.

Kittens are born with blue eyes, and their eyes change color as they mature. Adult cats have eyes of coppery brown, orange, yellow, or green; a few remain blue due to coat-color genes. Some cats are shown only during their early years when color is most vivid, while others may not begin to show their best eye color until they are over two years old.

EYE COLORS

Wildcats have hazel or copper eyes, sometimes tending toward yellow or green. Breeding has produced a range of colors in domestic cats from sparkling blue through green to orange.

Most eye colors are not governed by coat color, although some breed standards do link the two: silver tabbies, for example, are often required to have green eyes, but genetically they can have copper or gold eyes. The only color that is linked to the coat color is blue. Blue eyes are caused by forms of albinism that lead to a lack of pigmentation in both the coat and the iris, and occur in

BROWN

Green-toned eyes

Green eyes have become common in random-bred cats, and pure greens of varying shades define several breeds. The Chinchilla Longhair's sea green eyes may be another route for breeders to blue eyes.

PURE GREEN

SEA GREEN

cats with a high degree of white in their coats. Blue-eyed white cats are often deaf, because the gene causing the lack of pigment unfortunately also causes fluid to dry up in the organ of Corti, the receptor for hearing in the cochlea, leading to deafness.

Siamese (*see page 188*) blue eyes – found by the 19th-century naturalist Peter Pallas in the Caucasus – have a different source. They are not linked to deafness, but may be associated with poor three-dimensional vision. Early Siamese often squinted to compensate; breeding has removed the squint, with no apparent loss of visual acuity.

There is at least one other rare blue-eyed gene in cats, appearing in any coat color. It was noted in Britain in the

HAZEL

1960s, New Zealand in the 1970s, and in the United States, in New Mexico, in the 1980s. The genetics of these rare cats, now called Ojos Azules, are still under investigation.

EYE SHAPE

Wildcats' eyes are oval and slightly slanted. Breeds considered close to the "natural" cat, such as the Maine Coon (*see page 114*), have these "wild" eyes, although some North American standards are tending toward rounder eyes. Natural shape has been altered in two ways: eyes may be rounder, or may be more slanted. Generally speaking, old Western breeds, such as the Chartreux (*see page 168*), have round, prominent eyes. Some Eastern cats, such as the Burmese (*see page 182*), also have rounded eyes, but almond-shaped, slanted eyes are most common in foreign or Oriental breeds. This has been taken to its extreme in the Siamese and Oriental (*see page 192*) breeds.

Extremes of shape can cause problems. Prominent eyes in flat faces are prone to tear overflow and infection, while extremely slanted eyes tend to retain mucus, increasing infections.

SIAMESE BLUE

BABY BLUE

BIRMAN BLUE

Yellow-toned eyes

These eye colors are closest to those of wildcats. Many green eyes go through an early brown or yellow stage before they mature to their adult color. Copper eyes may "fade" with age, while yellow-gold eyes can vary greatly in appearance, depending on the ambient light.

COPPER

GOLD

Blue eyes

The lack of pigment in blue eyes allows higher absorption of sunlight, used by the body to produce vitamin D. This is why blue eyes are usually found in light-starved regions; the Siamese mutation may have occurred in northern Asia and spread south with human help. Blue eyes vary considerably in depth.

BREED PROFILES EXPLAINED

ALTHOUGH THE OVERWHELMING MAJORITY OF PET CATS ARE STILL random-bred, pedigreed cat breeds are popular even with those who neither breed them nor own them. Many of the people who attend cat shows each year have never owned a pedigreed cat and never will. An overview of the pedigreed breeds can provide an intriguing insight into the makeup of even our random-bred cats. Pedigreed cats originally came from random-bred populations and sometimes have an influence on them in return through accidental breedings – as in the case of the pointed pattern introduced to the West in one breed and now found in many household cats.

A few decades ago, there were just a handful of recognized breeds. Today, there are dozens. New mutations have been adopted by some registries, new breeds have been created from existing breeds through the introduction of new colors or another coat length, and breeds from one country have been recognized in others.

BREED DESCRIPTIONS

Each breed profile includes a description of the breed's appearance and character. While the appearance of pedigreed cats is highly consistent, the personality traits can vary. Much depends on an individual's experiences; cats from the most genial of breeds can be rendered nervous and even intractable by poor early socialization.

Breed histories outline the breed's ancestry and its route to acceptance by the registries. Some histories are easy to trace, but others are less distinct; older breeds may be wrapped in romantic myths, and even the exact origins of some of the newer breeds, such as the Ragdoll (see page 112), have been a matter of debate.

Salient facts are summarized in the Key Facts box found in each profile, which provides an overview of the history, names, breeding policy, personality, and colors of the breed.

INTERNATIONAL DIFFERENCES

Not all registries will recognize the same breeds, or the same colors and patterns in each breed. The same breed may even develop different looks in different countries, depending on the "fashions" prevalent. For example, in the Siamese (see page 188), colors recognized as part of the breed in Britain and Europe are recognized as a wholly separate breed by CFA, the main registry in North America.

This chapter has been made as international as possible, using cats from different countries to illustrate differences. Information on colors for each breed lists (in roman text) the colors accepted by most of the registries for North America and Britain that recognize the breed – CFA and TICA for North America, GCCF for Britian – and (in italic text) additional colors that occur but are either not accepted, or may be accepted in other major registries. Note that TICA recognizes wider ranges in most breeds.

Introductory text
Outlines physical and psychological traits of breed

Secondary pictures
Show additional colors or kittens

Key facts
Summarize information on history, names, breeds allowed as outcrosses, and traits

Symbols
Indicate aspects of personality and level of grooming required

Breed colors
Gives generally accepted colors in roman text and indicates less universal colors in italic text

Swatches
Where relevant, illustrate further colors or variants

Labels
Highlight additional characteristics

Main picture
Illustrates physical characteristics, wherever possible in breed's most notable or popular color

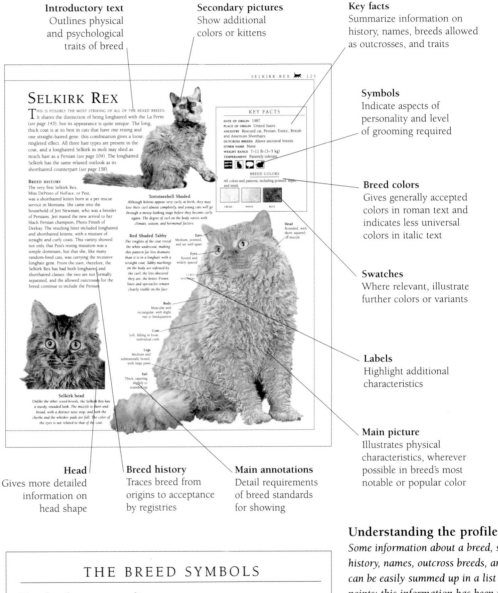

Head
Gives more detailed information on head shape

Breed history
Traces breed from origins to acceptance by registries

Main annotations
Detail requirements of breed standards for showing

THE BREED SYMBOLS

The details on personality given in these profiles were gathered via questionnaires sent to breeders and breed clubs. They provide a guide to the tendencies across the breed, but an individual cat may not match some of these traits: one may even find some silent Siamese.

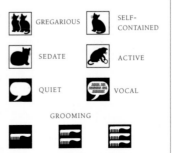

GREGARIOUS   SELF-CONTAINED

SEDATE   ACTIVE

QUIET   VOCAL

GROOMING

LITTLE   MODERATE   DAILY

Understanding the profiles
Some information about a breed, such as history, names, outcross breeds, and traits can be easily summed up in a list of brief points: this information has been placed into a Key Facts box for instant reference. But such a list of points can never give a full and fair impression of a whole breed, so greater detail is given in the breed description and history. Any additional information about build or particular colors is contained in the captions to the main and secondary photographs. Details of the exact standards that are expected of show-quality cats are contained in the annotations to the main picture.

INTRODUCTION TO LONGHAIRS

GENETICALLY, ALL LONGHAIRED CATS SHARE THE recessive allele that causes their coats to grow longer than those of their wildcat ancestors (*see page 75*). The difference between full-coated longhairs and silky semilonghairs is one of polygenetic factors. Some sources still state that the gene for long hair was introduced into these domestic cats from the wild Pallas' cat of Tibet (*see page 17*), but there is no evidence that this is so: a simple genetic mutation is almost certainly the cause. Although their exact origins are unknown, longhairs occurred naturally centuries ago in Central Asia. Some of these cats reached Europe; the French authority Dr. Fernand Mery reported that specimens were brought to Italy around 1550 and to France shortly after. Early longhairs in Europe were called Russian, French, or Chinese; almost three centuries passed before these cats acquired the classifications we know today.

Balinese
Like its shorthaired cousin the Siamese, the Balinese has no insulating undercoat, and its semilong hair is more decorative than functional. In summer, these cats may shed so much of their long hair that they look like shorthairs.

La Perm
Among the newest breeds, the La Perm is descended from a mutation that occurred in an ordinary farm cat. Most rex mutations lessen the effectiveness of the coat as insulation, but cats living as pets are not unduly disadvantaged by this.

Persian kittens
Among the first longhair breeds was the Persian, or Longhair. Over the years, the coat of this breed has been bred to ever greater length, and many breeders clip their cats when not showing, since they must otherwise groom the cats several times a day.

Turkish Van
The coat of the Turkish Van is extremely fine and, because it lacks an undercoat, it is easy to groom. Although the coat pattern and general type were known for centuries in Turkey, the breed was a relatively late arrival in the West.

Norwegian Forest Cat
Breeds that developed in harsh climates, such as the Norwegian Forest Cat, or the Maine Coon, show their origins in their coats. They tend to have water-repellent topcoats and thick, insulating undercoats.

After the Crystal Palace Cat Show in London in 1871, standards were published for Longhairs, called Persians in North America (*see page 104*), and Angoras, revived in the Angora (*see page 140*) in Britain, and Turkish Angoras (*see page 130*) elsewhere. The most popular longhair in early American shows was the Maine Coon (*see page 114*). This breed's coat may have come from Central Asia via Britain, but some early settlers' cats may have carried the longhair gene from another mutation. Certainly New England's harsh climate favored the survival of big cats with long, insulating coats. Other longhaired breeds are the result of introducing the longhair gene into shorthaired breeds. New breeds, such as the Tiffanie (*see page 135*) and the Nebelung (*see page 129*) have been developed on both sides of the Atlantic. Perhaps the most extraordinary and striking of the longhaired breeds are the rexed longhairs, with a curly or rippled coat, such as the La Perm (*see page 143*), the Maine "Waves" (*see page 116*), and the obscure Bohemian Rex – a rexed Persian – (*see page 143*).

Somali
Longhaired kittens occurred in Abyssinian litters for a number of years before an attempt was made to develop them into a separate breed. The resulting Somali is now one of the more popular cats in North America.

PERSIAN

THIS BREED, USUALLY AN INDOOR DWELLER, IS A LOUNGE LIZARD. The Persian, known as the Longhair in Britain, is a relaxed observer. In surveys of veterinarians, it is cited as the quietest and least active of cat breeds, and the one most likely to accept other cats into its home. This does not mean that the breed is entirely passive: in Britain and mainland Europe, pedigreed cats have more access to the outdoors than they do elsewhere, and the Persian will guard its territory and catch and kill prey with surprising ease, given its shortened face. The coat needs daily care; veterinarians are frequently called on to clip densely matted coats. Breed problems include polycystic kidney disease, which can be screened for, and a high incidence of fertility problems.

BREED HISTORY

The first documented ancestors of the Persian were imported from Persia into Italy in 1620 by Pietro della Valle, and from Turkey into France by Nicholas-Claude Fabri de Peiresc at about the same time. For the next two centuries their descendents, known by a variety of names, were status symbol pets. In the late 1800s, the Persian was developed within the guidelines of Harrison Weir's first written breed standards. The original stocky build is still an essential mark of today's Persian breed, although other characteristics have been dramatically altered. The breed was recognized by all registries by the turn of the century.

Brown Classic Tabby
The blotched, or classic, tabby is the traditional pattern for the British Longhair, although some North American associations now allow others. The Persian is recognized in multiple tabby colors, including brown tabbies.

Body
Large and cobby, with good muscling

Coat
Long and thick, but not woolly

Tail
Full and short, but not disproportionate

LONG, BUSHY HAIR

COAT IS SOFT

Shaded Silver
Once classified together with the tipped Chinchilla, the darker Shaded Silver is now judged separately. Like almost all silvered Persians, it has green eyes. A copper-eyed version of the Shaded Silver is recognized in Europe under the name Pewter.

Blue Self

The shortened face can lead to health problems, but it gives the Persian the infant look that has kept it high in the popularity stakes. In Britain, only the self colors are also called Persians. The Blue is one of the oldest colors, seen at the first cat show in London, in 1871, and has remained popular. Medium to pale blue is required, with deep orange or copper eyes. Any shading, white hairs, or tabby markings are penalized.

Ears
Small, round-tipped, and set low on head

FULL EAR FURNISHINGS

Head
Round, massive, and broad

FULL CHEEKS

Neck
Short, thick, and sturdy

Nose
Short and broad with definite stop

Eyes
Large, round, and widely spaced

POWERFUL JAW

BROAD CHEST

Legs
Short and thick

Paws
Large and round, preferably tufted

KEY FACTS

DATE OF ORIGIN 1800s
PLACE OF ORIGIN Great Britain
ANCESTRY Middle Eastern Longhairs
OUTCROSS BREEDS None
OTHER NAME Called Longhairs in Great Britain; some colors briefly called Kashmirs
WEIGHT RANGE 8–15 lb (3.5–7 kg)
TEMPERAMENT Interested observer

BREED COLORS

SELF AND TORTIE COLORS
Black, Chocolate, Red, Blue, Lilac, Cream, Tortoiseshell, Chocolate Tortie, Blue-Cream, Lilac-Cream, White (Blue-, Orange-, Odd-Eyed)

TABBY COLORS (CLASSIC, MACKEREL)
Tabby equivalent of recognized colors
Other tabby patterns

SMOKE COLORS
Colors are as for self and tortie, excepting White

SHADED COLORS
Shaded Silver (green-eyed), Blue Shaded Silver, Red Shaded Cameo, Golden Shaded Tortie, Cream Shaded Cameo, Shaded Blue-Cream
Other self and tortie colors

TIPPED COLORS
Chinchilla, Red Shell Cameo, Cream Shell Cameo, Shell Tortie, Shell Blue-Cream
Other self and tortie colors

SILVER TABBY COLORS (CLASSIC, MACKEREL)
Silver, Blue Silver
Any other tabby colors, other tabby patterns

BICOLORS (STANDARD AND VAN)
All allowed self, tortie, smoke, and tabby colors with white
Shaded and tipped colors, with white

Red and White

Originally, only Black, Blue, Red, and Cream bicolors were allowed. This Red and White has symmetrical markings, but these are no longer required by the standard.

NEWER PERSIAN COLORS

ORIGINALLY RECOGNIZED ONLY IN A LIMITED COLOR RANGE, the Persian is now bred in an abundance of new shades. But the color range seen here is not the only development; the coat, build, and, most dramatically, the face have all changed in this century. The coat is now so long that many breeders keep their cats clipped when not showing, rather than groom them several times a day. Early Persians were less compact, with short, but not flat, faces. Breeders in Europe still select Persians for their moderate noses, but American breeders and, more importantly, American show judges, have tended to prefer a flatter, or "ultra-type" face. This reached its most extreme in the "Peke-faced" Persian. Narrowed nostrils and tear ducts make the look undesirable. Breeding for large heads has also increased the need for Caesarean deliveries of the Persian's small litters.

Golden Persian
This color, with deep tipping on an apricot base, looks like a golden version of the Shaded Silver. There are two versions in the US, the Shaded and the Chinchilla; only the first is recognized in Britain. The genetics of the color are still disputed.

Blue-Cream
Although this color has existed from the early days of the breed, it was not recognized until 1930; this was mostly because the genetics of coat colors were not understood, and Blue-Creams were only produced by accident.

PASTEL-TONED COAT

Cream Shell Cameo
Chinchillas and Shaded Silvers were recognized early in the Persian's history, but other tipped Persians were not developed until after World War II. This Cream Shell Cameo is essentially a Cream Chinchilla, with warm-toned tipping to the hairs and deep, brilliant, copper-colored eyes.

COLORS WELL DISTRIBUTED

Chocolate Tortie
The Chocolate came from a Persian-Havana cross in the 1950s, and it is now accepted in all the major registries. Chocolate Tabbies and Torties inevitably followed. As in many breeds, the British standard calls for mingled colors, while the North American registries prefer patches.

Lilac Tabby

Together with the Chocolate colors, Lilac colors were once categorized in North America as a separate breed, known as the Kashmir. Coat and type are now typically Persian: this example is a young cat, in less heavy coat.

COPPER EYES

BEIGE GROUND

SPOTTED UNDERPARTS

FADED LILAC PAW PADS

Chocolate and White

Tortie-and-Whites were recognized in the 1950s, and other colors in the 1960s. The recognition of bicolors in 1971 greatly boosted popularity. Today, most colors are allowed together with white spotting, and these colors may occur in both traditional and Van patterns.

TAIL MOSTLY COLORED

EVEN SHADING

Red Shaded Cameo

The inhibitor gene was present in Persians from the start, but Cameos came to the scene relatively late. They were developed in a breeding program in the United States during the 1950s, and were accepted by CFA in 1960. There was subsequent worldwide interest; breeding began in Europe in 1962.

Cream Shaded Cameo

This dilute version of the Red Shaded Cameo is a cooler, lighter color. Only Red, Cream, Tortie, and Blue-Cream Shaded Cameos are accepted in Britain, because the original breeding was done with Tortoiseshells. The Shaded Silvers and Pewters have different origins.

HIMALAYAN PERSIAN

POSSIBLY THE FIRST DELIBERATE HYBRIDIZATION OF TWO BREEDS, this version of the Persian (*see page 106*) was also the first recognized "export" to another breed of the Siamese pointed pattern (*see page 188*). The resulting cat has the luxurious, thick, long coat of the Persian, and the exotic color pattern of the Siamese. Eye color is less intense than in the Siamese, and the pointing, being heat-related, is softer in the longer coat; masks are generally less dense and body color is paler. Himalayan Persians also moderate the diverse characters of their parent breeds: while the average Persian is content to watch the world go by, and the Siamese is always at the heart of the action, the Himalayan Persian is an outgoing but relaxed companion. Owners should attend to neutering, however – the sexual precocity of their Siamese forebears may also manifest itself in these cats.

Chocolate Point
An ivory-white body combines with brown points, which should be even in tone and depth.

BREED HISTORY

The first experiments in crossbreeding Siamese and Persians were made in the 1920s in Europe. A breed known as the Khmer existed in mainland Europe until the 1950s, and some say that the Birman (*see page 110*) is also a result of these experiments. In the 1930s, American geneticists investigating inherited traits bred a black longhair with a Siamese. The first generation were all black longhaired cats, but produced a pointed longhair cat when back-crossed. This was later called the Himalayan, after the pointed pattern seen in many Himalayan rabbits, but there was little interest in pursuing it as a breed. In Britain, parallel efforts at creating a pointed cat with good longhair type progressed through the 1930s and 1940s. The breed was accepted as the Colorpoint Longhair in 1955; in mainland Europe, the name Khmer was changed to match. Resurgent interest in Himalayans during the 1950s in North America led to recognition by all major registries by 1961. The status of the type varies internationally: the GCCF and some North American registries classify them as colors of the Persian, while others regard them as a separate breed.

Cream Point kitten
The points of all colors take a longer time to develop than in shorthairs, and the points of the dilute colors, such as the Cream Point, take longer to develop fully than those of the darker shades.

KEY FACTS

DATE OF ORIGIN 1950s
PLACE OF ORIGIN Britain and United States
ANCESTRY Persian/Siamese crosses
OUTCROSS BREEDS Persian
OTHER NAMES Sometimes called Colorpoint Longhair in Britain
WEIGHT RANGE 8–15 lb (3.5–7 kg)
TEMPERAMENT Calm and friendly

BREED COLORS

SELF AND TORTIE POINT COLORS
Blue, Chocolate, Cream, Lilac, Red, Seal, Blue-Cream, Chocolate Tortie, Lilac-Cream, Seal Tortie

TABBY POINT COLORS
Colors are as for self and tortie points

CREAM LYNX POINT | RED POINT | BLUE POINT | SEAL LYNX POINT

SHADING DEVELOPS ON OLDER CATS

Seal Point
A mature Himalayan's mask covers the face, but should not extend over the rest of the head. Some cats may have more extensive masks than others.

Tail
Short, but in proportion
to body, and bushy

Head
Round and massive,
with full cheeks

Ears
Small and round-tipped,
not unduly open at base

Eyes
Large, full, round,
and brilliant blue

Body
Large to medium-sized,
cobby, set low on legs

Coat
·Long, thick, and silky,
with no woolliness

Pattern
Evenly colored points
and minimal shading
on body

FRILL ON
SHOULDERS
AND CHEST

Legs
Short, thick, and
strong

Paws
Large, round,
and tufted

Lilac Point

*This color has warm-toned lilac points and a
magnolia white body. Himalayans are interbred with
other types of Persians. Because the pointing gene is
recessive, all offspring from these matings may carry
the hidden potential for producing Colorpoint kittens,
and this potential will be noted in their pedigrees.
Carriers of the pointing gene will not differ in type
from other Persians.*

BIRMAN

THIS STRIKINGLY MARKED BREED, WITH ITS MYSTERIOUS HISTORY, is a well-built cat with highlighted paws and large, blue eyes. Its silky hair is not as thick as that of the Persian (*see page 104*), and is less prone to matting, but daily grooming is still necessary. Breeders say that neutered males demand most attention, while neutered females can be rather bossy. The breed was almost extinct in the West at the end of World War II, when only two individuals remained in France. These were outcrossed with other cats to perpetuate the breed, increasing the genetic base and introducing the potential for a variety of point colors. As with all breeds with a small genetic base, inbreeding may concentrate and increase hereditary problems, but, fortunately, only rare skin and nerve disorders are hereditary in this breed.

BREED HISTORY

According to tradition, the Birman descends from the temple cats of Burma, specifically from Sita, a pregnant female, brought to France in 1919 by August Pavie. Legend links Birmans to a white cat called Sinh who lived in a temple dedicated to Tsun-Kyan-Kse, a golden goddess with sapphire eyes. When the temple was attacked, Sinh took on the goddess's colors and inspired the monks to fight the attackers. The breed may be a distant relative of the similarly patterned Siamese (*see page 188*). It originates in Burma, but a less romantic version holds that Birmans were created by French breeders at the same time as the Himalayan (*see page 108*) was developed.

Profile
The Birman profile is characterized by a Roman nose, giving a distinctive look unlike any other breed. The chin tapers slightly from the nose, but it should not be receding.

Face
The Blue Point shows a full mask from nose to forehead, connected to the ears by "tracings." In self colors, the mask should be even and dense, and the nose leather should match the coat.

Lilac Point
Together with the Chocolate, this was one of the first "new" colors to be accepted. The points must be pinkish gray, with nose leather to match, and the body a warm magnolia color.

Blue Lynx Point
The tabby pattern was one of the earlier additions to the range of Birman points, and now comes in a full range of colors. Tabby Points should show clear frown marks and lighter "spectacles," spotted cheek pads, striped legs, and a ringed tail.

YOUNG CAT HAS INCOMPLETE MASK

Tail
Full and evenly colored

Point color
Dense and uniform in self points

KEY FACTS

DATE OF ORIGIN Unknown
PLACE OF ORIGIN Burma (now Myanmar) or France
ANCESTRY Disputed
OUTCROSS BREEDS None
OTHER NAME Sacred Cat of Burma
WEIGHT RANGE 10–18 lb (4.5–8 kg)
TEMPERAMENT Friendly and reserved

BREED COLORS

SELF AND TORTIE POINT COLORS
Seal, Chocolate, Red, Blue, Lilac
*Red, Cream, Seal Tortie, Chocolate Tortie, Blue Tortie,
Lilac Tortie*

TABBY POINT COLORS
Colors are as for self and tortie points

LYNX TORTIE
POINT

CHOCOLATE

Cream Point
*Together with the Red Point, this is one of the most recent
additions to the Birman range. This is a young cat; with maturity
the mask extends to cover all of the face, and tabby markings fade.
Faint tabby markings are not a serious fault in these two colors.*

FRECKLES ON
SKIN ACCEPTED

Head
Broad and rounded,
with full cheeks and
strong chin

Ears
Medium-sized
and well-spaced

Ruff
Less apparent in summer
and on young cats

Eyes
Deep blue color
and almost round

Body
Long and
strongly built

Mask
Covers entire face
of mature cat

Body color
Paler shade of
point color

Seal Point
*The "classic" Birman, this cat exemplifies the colors
described in the legendary version of the breed's
origins: white mittens and gauntlets on the paws,
dark brown points, a slightly golden body, and deep
blue eyes. For a long time, only the Seal and its
dilute form, the Blue, were accepted.*

UNDERPARTS
PALER

Seal Tortie Point
*A good Tortie Point can be difficult to
produce because although the patterning
need not be entirely even, and a facial blaze
is not necessary, each of the points must
show an intermingling of the colors.
The lighter shading over the body
must also be slightly uneven.*

Legs
Thickset and
medium-length

Forepaws
Mittens end
below ankle

RAGDOLL

Mostly known for its famously placid disposition, the Ragdoll is a big and surprisingly heavy cat. Its medium-long coat has a soft texture and does not mat as readily as that of the Persian (*see page 104*). Ragdolls are essentially pointed cats, born white and slowly developing color and pattern over two years. Although well-muscled and with a weight advantage over most other cats, this breed has a gentle disposition. The Ragdoll is open to training with rewards and can easily be induced to use a scratching post. In Australia it is preferred as a breed that shows little enthusiasm for hunting, ensuring popularity in the face of the continent's wildlife problems (*see page 84*). Tales of a high pain threshold have been comprehensively disproved.

BREED HISTORY

Although the Ragdoll is a relatively new breed, its history is confused. In the 1960s, Californian breeder Ann Baker bred the first Ragdolls from Josephine, a white, probably nonpedigreed, longhair, and Daddy Warbucks, a Birman or a Birman-type tom. She claimed that Ragdolls went limp when handled. She formed a breed association, but its Ragdolls were not accepted by other associations. Other individuals later bred her Ragdolls to produce the breed accepted by the major registries today. The Ragdoll's success resulted from the demand for placid, indoor-dwelling cats. Similar breeds are now being developed, all with equally cozy names, and some with more bizarre claims about their history and traits than were made for the Ragdoll.

Blue Mitted
There is certainly a mitted colorpoint in the Ragdoll's ancestry, and it has been passed on in this coat pattern. Some resistance to the mitted cats, and indeed the whole breed, comes from those who feel this is a Birman "look-alike." However, there is one difference in pattern: the Ragdoll's gauntlets extend over the hock.

Seal Point
This color and its dilute, blue, are the most common colors found in Ragdolls; it has proved difficult to produce excellent chocolate and lilac colors, and some breeders believe there may be other unidentified colors in the gene pool. The body color on Ragdolls is allowed to be deeper than on many other pointed breeds.

Paws
Large and round, tufted

Legs
Medium-length, with shorter fur than on body

Neck
Short and heavyset

KEY FACTS

DATE OF ORIGIN 1960s
PLACE OF ORIGIN United States
ANCESTRY Unclear
OUTCROSS BREEDS None
OTHER NAME None
WEIGHT RANGE 10–20 lb (4.5–9 kg)
TEMPERAMENT Genial and relaxed

BREED COLORS

POINTED COLORS
Seal, Chocolate, Blue, Lilac

MITTED COLORS
Pointed colors with White

BICOLORS
Pointed colors with White

CHOCOLATE BICOLOR   LILAC POINT   CHOCOLATE POINT

Seal Bicolor

The standard requires the white area to begin in an inverted "V" on the face and cover the entirety of the underparts from the chin to the base of the tail. The forelegs should be entirely white, the hind legs white on the lower part. White spots are accepted elsewhere on the body, but not on the head, ears, or tail.

Ragdoll head

In profile, the face should have a very gentle break for the nose, which is of medium length. This Seal Mitted has a narrow white blaze on the nose, which is allowed in this coat pattern.

Head
Medium to large, with full cheeks and rounded muzzle

Ears
Medium-sized, wide at the base with rounded tips

Body
Long and muscular, with broad chest

COAT FLOWS ON BODY

Tail
Long and bushy, slightly tapered

Coat
Medium-length, dense and silky

Eyes
Large and oval, slightly slanted

MAINE COON

STRONG, TRANQUIL, AND LUXURIOUS TO BOTH LOOK AT AND TOUCH, the Maine Coon has recently become an outstandingly popular companion. Maines look their best in winter when the heavy, glossy coat is at its most luxurious. A distinctive characteristic that sets this breed apart from others is its frequent and enchantingly happy chirping trill, which it uses as a greeting to its human or feline family. While the Maine enjoys the company of people, it is not a dependent breed, but is content to pursue its own activities; some owners report that these include swimming. Females retain their dignity more than males, who tend to be slightly goofy, but no Maines are lap cats. These are easygoing buddies or companionable pals, not dependent babies. Because of this, many men find the large Maine Coon appealing.

BREED HISTORY
The distant history of the Maine is unknown. Its probable ancestors include British cats that came with early settlers, and longhaired Russian or Scandinavian cats on ships in Maine's ports. The harsh New England winters require dense coats and a size sufficient for hunting jackrabbits. The black-and-white Captain Jenks of the Horse Marines was the "first" Maine, noted at Boston and New York shows in 1861, when the breed first became popular. At the turn of the 20th century, the Maine lost ground to the luxuriously coated Persians. It survived as a breed because farmers recognized its excellent hunting ability. Interest rekindled in the 1950s, and became extensive by the 1980s; it is now one of the world's top breeds.

Brown Mackerel Tabby and White
Originally, only brown tabbies were given the name Maine Coons: the coat, together with the massive build and huge tail, made these cats resemble raccoons. Other colors and patterns were generally called Maine Shags in the early years of the breed.

Red Classic Tabby
The classic and mackerel tabby patterns are the most popular, in keeping with the Maine's traditional image. Reds should show excellent rufousing, setting them apart from the more usual ginger coloring seen on random-bred cats.

Maine face
The preferred look of the Maine Coon, in particular the size and set of the ears, varies between different breed associations. In all, however, the eyes are to be green, gold, or copper, with blue or odd eyes allowed in whites.

Black
The Maine Coon is traditionally associated with tabby colors and patterns in most people's minds, but selfs are widely bred. Dark colors, in particular, show the glossy quality of the coat well; the Maine coat is hard, with a unique texture.

POINTED EAR TIPS

Head
Slightly longer
than it is wide

Ears
Large, upright,
and set high
on head

SQUARE MUZZLE

Eyes
Full, round, and
slightly oblique in set

Neck
Thick in males

LONG BACK

Body
Medium to large,
with solid
musculature

Coat
Long and glossy

Tail
Long, with
flowing fur

Tortie Tabby

*The image of the Maine Coon as a big, shaggy, tabby cat
is so ingrained into public consciousness that any cat
answering to this description is liable to be tagged as a
Maine by the unscrupulous. True Maines conform to a
rigorous standard, and careful breeding is needed to
consistently produce rich colors such as this example.
The size of the Maine Coon has also become a matter of
some myth: claims of breeding lines that tip the scales at
weights of 33 lb (15 kg) remain unsubstantiated.*

KEY FACTS

DATE OF ORIGIN 1860s
PLACE OF ORIGIN United States
ANCESTRY Farm cats
OUTCROSS BREEDS None
OTHER NAME Maine Shag (now obsolete)
WEIGHT RANGE 9–22 lb (4–10 kg)
TEMPERAMENT Gentle giant

BREED COLORS

SELF AND TORTIE COLORS
Black, Blue, Cream, Red, White, Tortie,
Blue Tortie

SMOKE AND SHADED COLORS
Colors are as for self and tortie colors with the
exception of White

TABBY COLORS
Brown, Red, Blue, Cream, Tortie, Blue Tortie
Other tabby patterns

SILVER TABBY COLORS
Colors are as for standard tabbies

BICOLORS
All self, tortie, and tabby colors with white

CREAM
SHADED

BLACK SMOKE

BROWN
CLASSIC TABBY

BLUE SILVER
TABBY

MAINE COON VARIATIONS

THE STRUCTURE OF THIS BREED'S COAT IS UNDOUBTEDLY THAT OF A FARM CAT. Despite being long and thick, it requires surprisingly little maintenance, and it is water-repellent, so it is fortunate that washing is rarely necessary. Some of the colors, however, have raised questions among breeders; it has been suggested that Persians were used to introduce the smoke and silver colors. This seems unlikely, because many cats in the random-bred cat population of North America, which had nothing to do with Persians, carry the inhibitor gene that causes these colors. In Britain, the same color range is allowed in self, smoke, shaded, tabby, and silver tabby coats. In North America a more complex situation exists.

Blue and White kitten
The sturdy build of this breed is apparent from the earliest age. The Maine Coon can be unpredictable in its maturing, with some excellent breed examples only emerging as such in full adulthood.

Red Shaded Tabby
A good Red Tabby is a rich red tone in both the background color and the darker markings. The inhibitor gene removes the color of the background, but the markings should show the same pronounced rufousing as a full-colored coat.

Maine Wave
These controversial cats are fully pedigreed Maine Coons, with a rex mutation; however, once thought to be lethal different lines now seem to be breeding healthily. The coat lacks guard hairs, and so is completely unlike the typical Maine Coon coat – these cats are unlikely ever to be accepted as part of the Maine Coon breed. Since the mutation is recessive, they are also unlikely to disappear.

Black Smoke
The heavy topcoat of the Maine conceals the white undercoat over most of the body. Only where the coat breaks – around the legs and neck – does the silvering shine through. The undercoat is much more apparent when the winter coat is shed in the warmer months.

Odd-Eyed White
As in all breeds, Whites can suffer from deafness. This applies mostly, but not entirely, to Blue-Eyed and Odd-Eyed Whites. Some breeders claim that kittens that have large "kitten caps" of darker hair are less prone to this deafness, and are seeking to breed hearing Whites consistently by breeding for larger caps.

North American look
This Silver Tabby shows the Maine Coon style preferred by TICA, a primarily North American registry. The face is slightly more angular than the preferred British look, with larger ears set higher on the head, and rounder eyes.

British look
This Silver Tabby is an example of the look that is preferred by the GCCF for the Maine Coon. A broad face with oval eyes is topped by moderate-sized ears, angled out from the corners of the head. The body and legs are correspondingly stocky, giving an impresssion of a cat that could hold its own anywhere.

NORWEGIAN FOREST CAT

SOMEWHAT RESERVED WITH STRANGERS BUT CALMLY CONFIDENT WITH people it knows, the Norwegian Forest Cat shares attributes with the Maine Coon (*see page 114*) and Siberian (*see page 120*). Large size and long hind legs give the "Wegie" a commanding presence. Norwegian breeders like to think of this "natural cat" as their little lynx. While it makes a gentle household cat, it defends its territory vigorously. It is a superb climber and hunter, and owners who live near streams report that their Wegies fish. The breed is generally sound, although breeding for longer bodies and noses must be guarded against to avoid spinal and dental problems.

BREED HISTORY

Cats arrived in Norway by around AD 1000, at which time Vikings maintained trade routes with the Byzantine East. Proof that cats were traded directly from Byzantium to Norway comes from Norwegian cat populations with coat colors common in Turkey but rare across Europe. It is possible that the Norwegian Forest Cat traces its ancestry back to longhaired Turkish cats. The harsh Scandinavian winter favored large, longhaired cats, which became popular with farmers. The Wegie was not regarded as a singular breed until the 1930s, and planned breeding did not begin until the 1970s. The first Wegies arrived in the United States in 1979 and in Britain in the 1980s.

Ears
Open, wide at base, and continuing lines of face

Head
Triangular, with long, straight profile and strong chin

MEDIUM FURNISHINGS PREFERRED

Eyes
Large and open but not round, and slightly oblique in set

Body
Large, with solid bone structure and good musculature

Black Smoke and White
The Norwegian type should always remain elegant. While large and robust, the build should not appear stocky, and the facial features should be angular and give an impression of alertness, rather than be rounded or "sweet."

FULL RUFF DESIRABLE

Coat
Smooth, glossy, water-repellent topcoat and woolly undercoat

Legs
Long but not delicate

Paws
Large and round, with tufts between toes

Blue Tabby and White

Tabbies and bicolors are both common in the random-breeding cat populations from which the Norwegian is drawn. The predominance of tabbies and bicolors reflects the population from which the breed is descended.

Silver Tabby and White

In almost all cats, coats will sometimes appear slightly yellowed or "tarnished" due to rufous genes; the effect is most obvious in silver tabbies. Although regarded as a flaw in many breeds, and vigorously selected against, it is less a fault in Wegies.

KEY FACTS

DATE OF ORIGIN 1930s

PLACE OF ORIGIN Norway

ANCESTRY Farm cats

OUTCROSS BREEDS None

OTHER NAME Skogkatt or Skaukatt, Wegie

WEIGHT RANGE 7–20 lb (3–9 kg)

TEMPERAMENT Reserved and contained

BREED COLORS

SELF AND TORTIE COLORS
Black, Red, Blue, Cream, White, Tortoiseshell, Blue-Cream

SMOKE COLORS
Colors are as for self and tortie colors, except White

SHADED AND TIPPED COLORS
Colors are as for self and tortie colors, except White

TABBY COLORS (ALL PATTERNS)
Brown, Red, Blue, Cream, Tortie, Blue Tortie

SILVER TABBY COLORS
Colors and patterns are as for standard tabbies

BICOLORS
All allowed colors and patterns with white

| BROWN TABBY | BLUE AND WHITE | RED TABBY |

Black

Swathed in a thick, black coat for winter, the Norwegian could pass for one of the fierce cats of Nordic legend. Eye color is unrelated to coat color, so Black selfs may come with eyes of glowing gold or witch's-cat green. Black coats tend to show a degree of "rusting," unless the cat is rigorously kept out of sunlight.

Tail
Long and bushy, equal in length to body

Silver Tabby

The breed standard for the Norwegian Forest requires that its appearance reflect its natural heritage as a farm cat. The most important features are type and coat quality: there are no points specifically allocated to coat color in the scoring system. Tabbies are popular, reinforcing the "natural" image.

SIBERIAN

FAMED FOR ITS HARSH WINTER, THE HOMELAND OF THIS BREED favored large, sturdily built cats with thick, protective coats. It is impossible to be sure of this cat's most ancient ancestry, but what is certain is that the Siberian has been perfected by its environment, just like the Norwegian Forest (*see page 118*). Every aspect of this cat is honed for survival in tough conditions: its topcoat is strong, plentiful, and oily, its undercoat is dense enough to keep out the most piercing winds, and its build is large. Sturdy does not mean staid, however; these are active and highly agile cats. The Siberian character is also a product of its past; while sociable, it is disinclined to play the passive lap cat.

BREED HISTORY

Longhaired cats are found across the northern wastes of Russia. Like many natural breeds, the Siberian was not regarded as noteworthy until recently. Serious breeding to standardize the type began in the 1980s, and the breed is recognized by many registries in its homeland. The Neva Mascarade, a native Russian pointed cat, is also becoming popular. Siberians came to the United States in 1990, through the efforts of Elizabeth Terrell. Her cattery name, Starpoint, exists in the pedigrees of most top American Siberians. Among major registries, only TICA recognizes the Siberian. Some Russian clubs fear that the cats exported to the West are not always the best. The "TICA face" is different, and the Siberian may develop two distinct looks internationally.

Brown Classic Tabby
The appearance of the Siberian is more reminiscent of a wildcat than any other breed. The face is also unique: great breadth, and oval, slightly tilted eyes, give a distinctly wild and decidedly Asiatic cast. Russian cat clubs wish to see this wild appearance preserved.

Red Shaded Tabby and White
While the accepted list of colors is more limited in the Siberian's homeland, a wider range is recognized in North America. The inhibitor gene, which produces shaded colors, is naturally present, although not prevalent.

Ears
Medium in size, with rounded tips, and angled out

Head
Broad, and flat between ears

ABUNDANT FURNISHINGS

Eyes
Large, oval, and slightly slanted in set

Body
Long, well-muscled, and powerful

Neck
Short and sturdy

BROAD CHEST

Coat
Long, with slightly oily topcoat

Legs
Medium to long, with substantial boning and muscle

Paws
Large, round, and tufted

FEMALES FINER-BONED
THAN MALES

ROUNDED EYES
PREFERRED IN
NORTH AMERICA

Tortie Tabby and White

*Siberian females are, as in many
breeds, slightly smaller and
lighter than the males.
In both sexes, the hind
legs are slightly longer
than the forelegs
when straight, and
the body is carried
with a slightly
arched spine.*

KEY FACTS

DATE OF ORIGIN 1980s
PLACE OF ORIGIN Eastern Russia
ANCESTRY Household and farm cats
OUTCROSS BREEDS None
OTHER NAMES None
WEIGHT RANGE 10–20 lb (4.5–9 kg)
TEMPERAMENT Sensible and resourceful

BREED COLORS

SELF AND TORTIE COLORS
Black, Red, Blue, Cream, White, Tortie, Blue Tortie
All other self and tortie colors

SMOKE, SHADED, AND TIPPED COLORS
Colors are as for self and tortie

TABBY, SILVER TABBY COLORS (CLASSIC, MACKEREL, SPOTTED)
Brown, Red, Blue, Cream, Tortie, Blue Tortie
Ticked pattern, all other self and tortie colors

BICOLORS
All allowed self, tortie, and tabby colors with white
All self, tortie, and tabby colors with white

| CREAM AND WHITE | TORTIE AND WHITE | BLUE | SILVER TABBY |

Brown Mackerel Tabby

*The TICA standard for the Siberian
head is less "wild" than that preferred
by Russian clubs. Although the head
should be broad, the impression should be
of "roundness and circles," with a sweet
expression and eyes that are almost round
in shape. North American Siberians have
medium to large ears.*

Tail
Medium-length
and thick, with
rounded tip

Brown Spotted Tabby and White

*Originally, there was a great predominance of tabby coats in the Siberian, as is to be
expected of a breed that developed outdoors, where natural enemies abound.
Breeders are almost certain to wish to develop a wider range of self and
shaded colors, but tabbies of all patterns still
make up a fairly high
proportion of the
breed.*

AMERICAN CURL

THIS QUIET AND GENTLE BREED IS SIMPLY THE HOUSEHOLD CAT OF the United States with a single, striking mutation: its ears curl back away from the face toward the back and center of the head. This distinctive feature gives the Curl a dramatic, pixielike face, full of astonishment. The trait is dominant, so a Curl bred to any cat should give at least 50 percent Curls. The rest, called American Curl Straight Ears, are used for breeding programs or sold as pets. Outcrossing, which has created a shorthaired Curl (*see page 163*), ensures that genetic diversity continues to flourish within the breed. Spontaneous mutations such as this can carry crippling side effects; none are yet apparent in Curls, but some registries fear that problems may emerge.

Eyes
Walnut-shaped and slightly tilted

Head
Rounded, modified wedge

Ears
Point at back of head

KEY FACTS

DATE OF ORIGIN 1981
PLACE OF ORIGIN United States
ANCESTRY American household cat
OUTCROSS BREEDS Nonpedigreed domestic cats
OTHER NAME None
WEIGHT RANGE 7–11 lb (3–5 kg)
TEMPERAMENT Quietly affable

BREED COLORS

SELF AND TORTIE COLORS
Black, Chocolate, Red, Blue, Lilac, Cream, White, Tortoiseshell, Chocolate Tortie, Lilac Tortie, Blue Tortie
All other self and tortie colors

SMOKE COLORS
Colors as for self and tortie
All other self and tortie colors

SHADED AND TIPPED COLORS
Shaded Silver, Shaded Golden, Shaded Cameo, Shaded Tortoiseshell, Chinchilla Silver, Chinchilla Golden, Shell Cameo, Shell Tortoiseshell
All other self and tortie colors

TABBY COLORS (ALL PATTERNS)
Colors as for self and tortie
All other self and tortie colors

SILVER TABBY COLORS
Silver, Chocolate Silver, Red Silver (Cameo), Blue Silver, Lavender Silver, Cream Cameo, Tabby Torties, Silver Patched
All other standard tabby colors

BICOLORS (CLASSIC AND VAN)
Colors as for self and tortie with white
All tabby colors with white
All other colors with white

SELF AND TORTIE POINT COLORS
Seal, Chocolate, Red, Blue, Lilac, Cream, Tortie, Chocolate Tortie, Blue-Cream, Lilac-Cream
All other colors, sepia and mink patterns

LYNX (TABBY) POINT COLORS
As for self and tortie points
All other colors, sepia and mink patterns

Seal Point
The pointed pattern, once confined to a single breed, is now found in a vast range of cats. Newer breeds, such as the Curl, often have this pattern. Longer coats generally soften and lighten the pointing.

Tortoiseshell and White
This pattern, also called Calico in North America, is almost exclusively female. The Curl's moderate breed standard favors females; in heavier breeds they can lose awards to sturdier males.

Body
Moderately muscled and semiforeign in build

Coat
Silky and flowing, with minimal undercoat

BREED HISTORY

People most often acquire cats by adopting strays; this is the origin of the Curl. In 1981, a stray kitten appeared at Grace and Joe Ruga's home in Lakeland, California. Cats are adept at targeting nurturing individuals; Grace Ruga left food on her porch for the stray kitten, who ate it, liked the ambience of the household, and made it her new home. An affectionate black female, she had a long, silky coat and unusual ears. Joe Ruga named her Shulamith, after the shepherdess in the *Song of Songs*. All Curls trace their origins to Shulamith. That December, Shulamith had a litter of four kittens, two of which had the same curly ears. These cats were shown in California in 1983 and the breed is fully recognized in North America. Although the first Curls to reach Europe arrived in 1995 they probably will not be accepted by the GCCF or FIFé.

Legs
Medium length and boning

Tail
Full plume equal to length of body

MUNCHKIN

WITHOUT DOUBT THE MOST CONTROVERSIAL AND extraordinary breed to emerge in years, the Munchkin is defined by a single, dominant factor: the long bones in its legs are simply not long. There is no direct effect on other bones, and breeders claim that the short legs have no detrimental side effects; only time will tell. The flexible feline spine may save the breed from the back and hip problems of dwarfed dog breeds, but in all other species dwarfs are prone to arthritis, and dwarfed cats, including the Munchkin, might not escape this. (Dwarfed cats are not minature cats, in which all body parts are smaller.) In cats who live indoors, short legs may not seem a handicap, but this breed, endearing and comical as it is, seems unlikely to become popular outside the United States.

BREED HISTORY

Dwarfed individuals occur in many species; the cat is no exception. Many Munchkins trace their ancestry to a cat found in Louisiana in 1983. As breeders began to work with the mutation, outcrossing to nonpedigreed cats, controversy grew along with popularity. TICA granted the Munchkin "new breed" status in 1995; as yet, it is the only major registry to recognize the breed, and the standard is still very general. Breeders of other pedigreed breeds have expressed fears that dwarfed "editions" of their breeds will emerge. Although the lure of novelty cannot be denied, and some breeders may choose to pursue such a course, the TICA standard specifically bars any other pedigreed breeds as outcrosses, and no registry would be likely to accept dwarfed versions of established breeds.

Munchkin head
The shape is between an almost equilateral triangle and a modified wedge: "medium" and "moderate" are the words most used in the standard because the breed is derived from the typical domestic cat. Eye and coat colors are not related to each other.

Tail
Medium thickness, tapering to rounded tip

Body
Medium-sized, with level spine or slight rise from shoulder to rump

Head
Medium-sized, neither round nor wedge-shaped

Ears
Triangular, moderately large in size

Eyes
Large and walnut-shaped, with open expression

Legs
Short, straight; paws should point straight ahead

Red and White
The Munchkin is recognized in all possible colors and patterns; it would also be almost impossible to limit the range in a breed that is outcrossed to random-bred cats. Tabbies and bicolors are common, and pointed colors are quite popular.

Black and White kitten
It is apparent at birth which kittens in a litter are Munchkins and which are not. Proponents of the breed claim that one of the breed's most attractive traits is not in its physique, but its personality; Munchkins are said to keep their kittenish curiosity and comical behavior into adulthood.

KEY FACTS

DATE OF ORIGIN Unknown
PLACE OF ORIGIN United States
ANCESTRY Household cats
OUTCROSS BREEDS Nonpedigreed cats
OTHER NAME None
WEIGHT RANGE 5–9 lb (2.25–4 kg)
TEMPERAMENT Appealing and inquisitive

BREED COLORS

All colors and patterns, including pointed, mink, and sepia

SCOTTISH FOLD

WITH THE SAME DISTINCTIVE EARS AS ITS SHORTHAIRED COUSINS (*see page 159*), the longhaired Scottish Fold has a coat with a lush, warm look. Like all longhairs, the breed is best seen in winter, when it sports an imposing ruff, elegant breeches, and a huge, fluffy tail. All kittens are born with straight ears, which begin to fold at about three weeks of age. The joint problems that result from breeding Fold to Fold appear at four to six months: a short, thickened tail is a sign that might be missed in a longhaired kitten, so tails should be checked carefully – and always gently.

Head
Well-rounded, with prominent cheeks and whisker pads

Ears
Small, with rounded tips, tightly folded to head

Body
Medium, rounded, and firm

Eyes
Large, rounded, and sweet in expression

Coat
Medium to long, soft, and standing away from body

Legs
Medium-length, sturdy, but not coarse

BREED HISTORY

Cats with folded or pendulous ears have been recorded for over two centuries. All Scottish Folds, however, can be traced back to Susie, a white farm cat born in 1961 in Scotland. Two geneticists, Pat Turner and Peter Dyte, oversaw the early development of the breed, and found that Susie carried the longhair gene, which could be carried in shorthaired offspring and appear in later generations. The Fold is still rare: the absence of any longhaired outcross breed makes the longhaired version even rarer.

Tortie Tabby and White

This combination of tortoiseshell and tabby is also called "patched tabby" in CFA or "torbie" in TICA. The tabby pattern should show clearly in both brown and red patches, which are larger and more defined in bicolors such as this one. The required eye color, which should be as brilliant as possible, is gold.

Blue Smoke and White

This individual falls short of the show standards for the Fold in two respects: the ears are not pressed tightly to the head, and the face shows slight tabby markings rather than the perfectly even blue that the standard requires. Such cosmetic quirks, however, make no difference to the cat's character or qualities as a pet.

KEY FACTS

DATE OF ORIGIN 1961
PLACE OF ORIGIN Scotland
ANCESTRY Farm cat, British and American Shorthairs
OUTCROSS BREEDS British and American Shorthairs
OTHER NAME Highland Fold
WEIGHT RANGE 6–13 lb (2.4–6 kg)
TEMPERAMENT Quietly confident

BREED COLORS

All colors and patterns, including pointed, sepia, and mink occur

BROWN TABBY   RED TABBY   LILAC   WHITE

SELKIRK REX

THIS IS POSSIBLY THE MOST STRIKING OF ALL OF THE REXED BREEDS. It shares the distinction of being longhaired with the La Perm (*see page 143*), but its appearance is quite unique. The long, thick coat is at its best in cats that have one rexing and one straight-haired gene: this combination gives a loose, ringleted effect. All three hair types are present in the coat, and a longhaired Selkirk in molt may shed as much hair as a Persian (*see page 104*). The longhaired Selkirk has the same relaxed outlook as its shorthaired counterpart (*see page 158*).

BREED HISTORY
The very first Selkirk Rex, Miss DePesto of NoFace, or Pest, was a shorthaired kitten born at a pet rescue service in Montana. She came into the household of Jeri Newman, who was a breeder of Persians. Jeri mated the new arrival to her black Persian champion, Photo Finish of Deekay. The resulting litter included longhaired and shorthaired kittens, with a mixture of straight and curly coats. This variety showed not only that Pest's rexing mutation was a simple dominant, but that she, like many random-bred cats, was carrying the recessive longhair gene. From the start, therefore, the Selkirk Rex has had both longhaired and shorthaired classes: the two are not formally separated, and the allowed outcrosses for the breed continue to include the Persian.

Tortoiseshell Shaded
Although kittens appear very curly at birth, they may lose their curl almost completely, and young cats will go through a messy-looking stage before they become curly again. The degree of curl on the body varies with climate, season, and hormonal factors.

Red Shaded Tabby
The ringlets of the coat reveal the white undercoat, making this pattern far less dramatic than it is in a longhair with a straight coat. Tabby markings on the body are softened by the curl; the less obscured they are, the better. Frown lines and spectacles remain clearly visible on the face.

KEY FACTS

DATE OF ORIGIN 1987
PLACE OF ORIGIN United States
ANCESTRY Rescued cat, Persian, Exotic, British and American Shorthairs
OUTCROSS BREEDS Above ancestral breeds
OTHER NAME None
WEIGHT RANGE 7–11 lb (3–5 kg)
TEMPERAMENT Patiently tolerant

BREED COLORS

All colors and patterns, including pointed, sepia, and mink

CREAM   WHITE   BLUE

Head
Rounded, with short, squared-off muzzle

Ears
Medium, pointed, and set well apart

Eyes
Round and widely spaced

CURLY WHISKERS

Body
Muscular and rectangular, with slight rise to hindquarters

Coat
Soft, falling in loose, individual curls

Legs
Medium and substantially boned, with large paws

Tail
Thick, tapering slightly to rounded tip

Selkirk head
Unlike the other rexed breeds, the Selkirk Rex has a sturdy, rounded look. The muzzle is short and broad, with a distinct nose stop, and both the cheeks and the whisker pads are full. The color of the eyes is not related to that of the coat.

TURKISH VAN

With its incredibly soft coat, and large, rounded eyes, this breed might appear to be the ideal, soft-centered lap cat. Turkish Vans descended, however, from rural cats in an area where life was far from easy, and retain minds and spirits of their own. This is a cat to be respected and won over, not taken for granted. The breed is distinguished for two reasons: the restricted color of its coat, so distinctive that the pattern is called Van even in other breeds, and its reputation for enjoying a dip in hot summer weather, which has earned it the alternative name of "Swimming Cat" in its homeland.

BREED HISTORY

The modern history of this breed began when two cats were brought to Britain in 1955. The breed spread across Europe, but acceptance by registries took some time. In 1982, Turkish Vans reached the United States, where they are accepted by CFA and TICA. In GCCF, only the original red and the more recently accepted cream are allowed. Other registries allow black-based colors in the breed; most recently, FIFé altered its rules to include these colors.

Tortie and White

Tortie Vans appeared when black was introduced to the breed. The "thumbprints" of color above this cat's tail make it less than perfect according to the breed standard; the difficulty of meeting the standard means that although the Van is scarce, there are relatively high numbers of pet kittens available.

Ears
Large and set high on head, fairly close together

Red
The color of this Van, called red in North America, is more poetically called auburn in Europe. This coat pattern, accompanied by amber eyes, was the original appearance of the Van when it arrived in the West. The coat should be chalk white, the markings ideally confined to the top of the head and the tail, and the leather pink.

Eyes
Large and oval

Head
Short wedge with long, straight profile

Body
Long and sturdy, with males particularly muscular

Coat
Long and silky, with no undercoat

Tail
Full brush as long as body

Legs
Medium-length, with neat, rounded paws

Van face

The color markings on a Van's head should not extend below the level of the eyes, or beyond the base of the ears at the back. Ideally, there should be a white blaze on the forehead, dividing the color into two separate areas, and the ears should be colored.

Local detail

The Van pattern occurs in naturally high numbers in the cat population of the Near East, but is rare elsewhere. Its unusualness impressed visiting artists in the 19th century, and in many paintings of bazaar and camp scenes a Van-patterned cat is to be seen tucked in a corner between the silks and the rugs. This cat is in The Arab Scribe, Cairo, by John Frederic Lewis (1805–1876).

Blue

Blue can vary widely in depth, and this cat, an early Blue, is darker than most breed standards allow. Introducing new colors into the Van inevitably also brought in some undesirable traits. The rich, golden eye color is a difficult quality to fix, and some green eyes have appeared.

COAT "BREAKS" READILY

Cream

The dilute of the Red and White, this color resembles it in all aspects of pattern and eye color. The Van's soft coat is water resistant, and tends to "break" open over any curves, rearranging itself with every move.

KEY FACTS

DATE OF ORIGIN Pre-18th century
PLACE OF ORIGIN Lake Van region, Turkey
ANCESTRY Household cats
OUTCROSS BREEDS None
OTHER NAME Turkish Swimming Cat
WEIGHT RANGE 7–19 lb (3–8.5 kg)
TEMPERAMENT Self-possessed

BREED COLORS

BICOLORS (AMBER-, BLUE-, ODD-EYED)
Red, Cream, Black, Blue, Tortie, Blue-Cream with White
Corresponding tabbies, silvers, and smokes with White

CYMRIC

Solid, and with a bunny-hop gait, this breed matches the original shorthaired Manx (*see page 156*) in all but coat, which is semilong and double. Like its shorthaired cousin, it produces variant "stumpies" and "longies" with some degree of tail, as well as the showable, tailless "rumpies." Although the Cymric originated in North America, the name comes from "Cymru," the Welsh name for Wales; there is a belief that Wales had its own strains of tailless cats. The breed is also known as the Longhaired Manx, but it is the more poetic name that has gained the wider currency.

BREED HISTORY

Although its name suggests a Welsh ancestry, this is an exclusively North American breed. Manx cats have always produced the occasional longhaired kittens and, in the 1960s, breeders, including Blair Wright in Canada and Leslie Falteisek in the United States, worked to gain these longhaired variants recognition. By the 1980s, CFA and TICA both recognized the cats as a separate breed with the name Cymric, but CFA has now reclassified them as Longhaired Manx. The breed is not recognized in Britain.

Orange-Eyed White
White Cymrics' eyes may be deep blue, brilliant copper, or one of each color. The coat should be pure white, with no hint of any yellowing, and no stray colored hairs should be present.

Brown Mackerel Tabby and White
The coat color and markings are relatively unimportant in the Cymric's points system. Most important are complete taillessness, a cobby appearance, and a rounded head with prominent cheeks and whisker pads. Cymrics can take two years to develop the required deep flanks and rounded body.

Rump
Should feel completely rounded, with no hint of tail

Body
Medium-sized, sturdy, and well-muscled

Ears
Medium-sized and wide at base, with rounded tips

Head
Rounded, with gentle dip from forehead to nose

Eyes
Large, round, and set at slight angle

Neck
Short and thick

Legs
Sturdy, with forelegs much shorter than hind legs

KEY FACTS

DATE OF ORIGIN 1960s
PLACE OF ORIGIN North America
ANCESTRY Manx
OUTCROSS BREEDS Manx
OTHER NAME Longhaired Manx
WEIGHT RANGE 8–12 lb (3.5–5.5 kg)
TEMPERAMENT Friendly and even-tempered

BREED COLORS

SELF AND TORTIE COLORS
Black, Red, Blue, Cream, White, Tortoiseshell, Blue-Cream
All other self and tortie colors

SMOKE COLORS
Black, Blue
All other self and tortie colors

SHADED AND TIPPED COLORS
Shaded Silver, Chinchilla Silver
All other self and tortie colors

TABBY COLORS (CLASSIC, MACKEREL)
Colors as for above selfs and torties
Spotted and ticked patterns, all self and tortie colors

SILVER TABBY COLORS
Silver, Silver Tabby Tortie
All other standard tabby colors

BICOLORS (STANDARD AND VAN)
All self, tabby, and tortie colors with white
All colors and patterns with white

POINTED COLORS
All colors and patterns in pointed, sepia, and mink

BLACK AND WHITE   CHOCOLATE (NOT CFA)   RED TABBY   BLUE

NEBELUNG

THE SILVER-TIPPED BLUE HAIR GIVES THIS BREED A LUMINOUS elegance. Light reflects off the Nebelung's guard hairs, creating a misty incandescence. Only when you stroke the semilong hair against the grain do you notice the solid blue ground color to the shafts of both the guard hair and the down. This new breed, the name of which is German for "mist-creature," is based upon a "lost" longhaired strain of the Russian Blue (*see page 170*).

Nebelung head
A modified wedge of seven flat planes, the face has a slight smile. The green eyes take time to develop, being yellow in kittens and younger cats. A green ring should appear around the pupil by four months, and the eyes should turn green with maturity.

BREED HISTORY

Blue shorthairs and longhairs from Russia were exhibited over 100 years ago. Shorthairs became known as the Russian Blue, but the longhairs lost their separate identity. In 1986, Siegfried, the founding father of this revived breed, was mated to his longhaired sister, who produced longhaired blue kittens. The breed was first shown in TICA in 1987, and it was also recognized by TCA in 1993, but other major registries have not accepted it.

Blue
The Nebelung standard is very similar to that of the Russian Blue, calling for the same lithe appearance, the same silver tipping, and a semilong version of the characteristic double coat. Whether this breed will develop to be identical to the Russian in all but coat length, or diverge in other ways, remains to be seen.

KEY FACTS

DATE OF ORIGIN 1986
PLACE OF ORIGIN United States
ANCESTRY Russian Blue
OUTCROSS BREEDS Russian Blue
OTHER NAME None
WEIGHT RANGE 6–11 lb (2.5–5 kg)
TEMPERAMENT Retiring

BREED COLORS

SELF COLORS
Blue

Eyes
Very slightly oval, green, and widely spaced

Ears
Wide at base, with slightly rounded tips

Neck
Long and slender under ruff

Body
Lithe and slender, but not tubular

Coat
Fine, double, and medium-length, with silver-tipped guard hairs

Head
Modified wedge, with flat forehead and straight profile

Paws
Small and round, with an impression of being on tiptoes

Tail
Long and fluffy, tapering from thick base to fine tip

TURKISH ANGORA

RACEFUL AND ATHLETIC, WITH FINE BONES AND A SILKY COAT, this is a breed that fits the fashions of the late 20th century. It is a small to medium-sized cat with a muscular body, covered by a single coat that shimmers when it moves. Turkish Angoras come in all colors other than the Oriental shades. They are vivacious cats, considered quick-witted and quick-moving by breeders. Some published information on the breed still repeats the theory that it is descended from the wild Pallas' cat (*see page 17*). The story goes that Tartars domesticated the Pallas' cat and took it into Turkey, but this is very unlikely. The Turkish Angora's medium-long coat is probably the result of a mutation that occurred centuries ago in an isolated population of domestic cats in central Asia.

National cat
Turkish Angoras often appear on stamps; this Odd-Eyed White commemorates 25 years of the Turkish veterinary service.

BREED HISTORY

Angoras from Turkey first reached France and Britain in the 17th century, but it was not until the mid-1800s that breeders chronicled the differences between this breed and longhairs from Persia and Russia. By the beginning of this century, crossbreeding with other longhaired cats had led to the virtual extinction of the breed outside Turkey. The breed is said to have been saved through a breeding program at Ankara Zoo, although this may be a rather romanticized tale. Certainly, breeders in Sweden, Britain, and the United States imported Angoras after World War II from Turkey, where the breed is now protected, and established a successful breed revival program. Turkish Angoras are not recognized in Britain, where there is an unrelated breed called the Angora (*see page 140*).

Ears
Large and high-set, slightly pointed

Eyes
Large and oval, slightly slanted

Head
Modified wedge of small to medium size

Neck
Slim and graceful

Body
Long and slender, but muscular

Coat
Fine and silky with negligible undercoat

Legs
Long, with hind legs longer than forelegs

Tail
Tapering from wide base to fine tip

FULL PLUME OF HAIR

Red Shaded
The inhibitor gene has been present in the Turkish Angora for centuries. Combined with the agouti gene, it gives silvered, or shaded, colors; these are not recognized by CFA, but are by TICA and FIFé. When the coat is shed in the summer, the silver becomes more apparent, especially on the face, as here.

Tortie and White

The predominantly white Van bicolor pattern is prevalent in Turkish cats. In the Turkish Angora bicolors, the underparts should be uniformly white, and the black and red patches should be solid and even in color.

RUMP HIGHER
THAN SHOULDERS

Black

The coat of a Black Turkish Angora must be coal black, and solid from the roots to the tip. As in all cats, the color tends to take on a rusty tinge with prolonged exposure to sunlight, recovering its solid tone when the summer coat is shed and the fuller winter coat comes in. All longhairs are at their best in winter, but especially black cats.

Tortoiseshell Smoke

Smoke Angoras were first documented in Britain in the latter part of the 19th century. Smoke Turkish Angoras should appear to be full-colored cats in repose, the undercoat only apparent with movement. The loss of the long coat in summer decreases the effect.

Turkish Angora head

The head is a smooth wedge, with the narrow muzzle continuing the lines without a pronounced pinch at the whisker pads. The eyes, odd or not, may be any color – copper to gold or green to blue.

KEY FACTS

DATE OF ORIGIN 1400s
PLACE OF ORIGIN Turkey
ANCESTRY Household cats
OTHER NAME None
OUTCROSS BREEDS None
WEIGHT RANGE 6–11 lb (2.5–5 kg)
TEMPERAMENT Energetic exhibitionist

BREED COLORS

SELF AND TORTIE COLORS
Black, Red, Blue, Cream, Tortie, Blue-Cream, White
Chocolate, Lilac
All other self and tortie colors

SMOKE COLORS
As for self and tortie colors, except White

SHADED COLORS
As for self and tortie colors, except White

TABBY COLORS (CLASSIC, MACKEREL)
Brown, Red, Blue, Cream
Spotted and ticked patterns, all other self and tortie colors

SILVER TABBY COLORS (CLASSIC, MACKEREL)
Silver
Spotted and ticked patterns, all other self and tortie colors

BICOLORS
All self and tortie colors with white
All other colors and patterns with white

RED   BLUE TABBY   BLUE-CREAM   SHADED SILVER

SOMALI

WITH ITS BUSHY TAIL, ARCHED BACK, AND APPEARANCE OF walking on tiptoes, this striking cat is one of the world's most popular newer breeds. Like its shorthaired Abyssinian forebear (*see page 172*), the Somali has a ticked coat: each hair on its body has three to twelve bands of color. The bands are darker than the ground color and produce a glossy, vibrant shimmer when the cat is in full coat. The facial markings are very striking, resembling theatrical eyeliner. This is an active breed: living up to its slightly wild looks, it is a natural hunter and thrives on outdoor activities. The Somali will only accept confinement if introduced to this lifestyle at an early age.

BREED HISTORY

The genetic roots of this breed go back to founder stock in Britain. Longhaired kittens appeared occasionally in Abyssinian litters, and in the 1940s, breeder Janet Robertson exported Abys to North America, Australia, and New Zealand. Descendents of these Abys sometimes produced fuzzy, dark kittens and in 1963, Canadian breeder Mary Mailing entered one of her longhaired cats in a local show. The judge, Ken McGill, asked her for one to breed from, and the official first Somali was McGill's May-Ling Tutsuta. Evelyn Mague, an American Aby breeder, was also developing longhairs, which she named Somalis. Using McGill's stock, Don Richings, a Canadian breeder, began working with Mague, and by the late 1970s the breed was fully accepted in North America. Somalis appeared in Europe in the 1980s, and by 1991 had worldwide recognition. More colors are accepted in Europe than in North America.

Fawn

In summer, the Somali loses much of its coat and may appear almost shorthaired, but for the plumed tail. The Fawn is the dilute of the Sorrel, and has a pale mushroom or oatmeal undercoat and fawn ticking. In the pale colors, good contrast between base color and ticking is hard to achieve.

KEY FACTS

DATE OF ORIGIN 1963
PLACE OF ORIGIN Canada and United States
ANCESTRY Abyssinian
OUTCROSS BREEDS Abyssinian
OTHER NAME Longhaired Abyssinian
WEIGHT RANGE 8–12 lb (3.5–5.5 kg)
TEMPERAMENT Quiet voice, active behavior

BREED COLORS

TABBY COLORS (TICKED)
Ruddy, Sorrel, Blue, Fawn
Chocolate, Red, Cream, Lilac
Corresponding torties

SILVER TABBY COLORS (TICKED)
Colors are as for self and tortie

BLUE   SORREL   CREAM

Ticking
At least three dark bands on each hair

Tail
Long, with full brush of hair

DARK TIP

Lilac

The Lilac's warm-toned coat has an oatmeal base with lilac-toned ticking; the paw pads and nose leather should be a matching mauvish pink. Like all self and tortie Somali colors, it may be white only around the lips and chin.

Somali face
All Somalis have dark-rimmed eyes surrounded by "spectacles" of lighter hair, and show clear tabby markings on cheeks and forehead. This young Silver shows slight tarnishing, which should fade. Silver Somalis have white chests and underparts.

Eyes
Large and almond-shaped, amber, hazel, or green in color

Ears
Wide-set, large, cupped, and tufted

Body
Medium-sized, lithe, and muscular

Head
Moderate wedge, with smooth lines and slight nose break in profile

Coat
Soft and fine, medium-length

FULL RUFF PREFERRED

LIGHTER UNDERPARTS

Ruddy or Usual
This color, which is called Usual in Great Britain, was one of the first colors to be accepted for showing; the other was Sorrel. The base coat is a deep red-brown shade of apricot, while the ticking is jet black. The lithe and slightly angular body type of the Somali, together with the full coat and possibly this reddish color, have earned the breed the nickname of "fox cats."

Legs
Long, with oval, tufted paws

CHANTILLY/TIFFANY

STILL EXTREMELY RARE, THIS BREED HAS A MODERATE DISPOSITION, neither as quiet as a Persian nor as active as Oriental-type longhairs. The Chantilly will communicate happiness with an endearing "chirp" that sounds like a pigeon cooing; once you have been chirped at, you become addicted to this pleasurable sound. Although the first examples of the breed were deep chocolate in color, the Chantilly comes in the whole range of Oriental colors, as well as tabby patterns. This is a late bloomer: the medium length, single coat is not fully mature until two to three years of age.

Chocolate Tabby kitten
Although this breed is usually thought of in terms of self colors, tabbies are also bred. Kittens can take some time to show their potential: eye color in particular can take years to reach its full intensity.

BREED HISTORY

This companionable and undemanding breed is not as new as its recent fame suggests, but its history is beset by confusion. In 1967, in New York, Jennie Robinson purchased a pair of chocolate-colored, gold-eyed, longhaired cats of unknown background, although the color implied a Burmese parentage. Signe Lund, a Florida breeder, bought the cats, and coined the name Tiffany. As she also bred Burmese, the association with that breed was inadvertently perpetuated. In the 1980s, confusion led to the breed almost vanishing. In 1988, in Alberta, Canada, Tracy Oraas reestablished the breed and researched their history, concluding that they were probably an offshoot of the breeding program that created the Angora (*see page 140*). The name Tiffanie was now being used by British breeders for the longhaired variety of the shaded Asian or Burmilla (*see opposite*), causing yet more confusion, so the Canadian breeders have altered the name to Chantilly/Tiffany.

KEY FACTS

DATE OF ORIGIN 1970s
PLACE OF ORIGIN Canada and United States
ANCESTRY Uncertain
OUTCROSS BREEDS Angora, Havana Brown, Nebelung, Somali
OTHER NAME Tiffany, Foreign Longhair
WEIGHT RANGE 6–12 lb (2.5–5.5 kg)
TEMPERAMENT Gentle and conservative

BREED COLORS

SELF COLORS
Chocolate, Cinnamon, Blue, Lilac, Fawn

TABBY COLORS (MACKEREL, SPOTTED, AND TICKED)
Colors are as for self colors

Chocolate

This is the original color, which has led to the breed being tagged "the chocoholic's delight." Deep golden eyes appear to glow against the coat's even shade of warm, rich brown. Nose leather and paw pads match, and chocolate brown whiskers complete the look.

Ears
Medium-sized, wide at base, with rounded tips

Head
Triangular, with gently curved profile, slightly indented at eye level

Eyes
Golden or copper, oval, and slightly slanted

Legs
Medium-length, well-muscled but not stocky

Body
Medium-length, slender, and elegant

Tail
Plumed, equal in length to body

TIFFANIE

ALTHOUGH SOMETIMES CONFUSED WITH THE CHANTILLY/TIFFANY
(*see opposite*), a longhaired version of the American Burmese
which has been referred to by the name Tiffany in TICA, British
Tiffanies have nothing to do with that breed. Essentially longhaired
Asians (*see page 178*), they are descended from Chinchilla Persians
(*see page 104*) and European Burmese (*see page 184*). Tiffanies take
after their longhaired forbears only in coat; the conformation is
Burmese. In temperament, they combine the traits of their parent
breeds to great advantage, with more liveliness than the average
Persian and more restraint than the Burmese. An easygoing, easy-
to-care-for longhair, the Tiffanie deserves wider popularity.

BREED HISTORY

The Tiffanie, essentially a longhaired Burmese,
is the only longhaired cat in the Asian breed
group. This group's origins can be traced to an
accidental mating, in London in 1981, of a
Chinchilla Longhair (Persian) and a Lilac
Burmese belonging to Baroness Miranda von
Kirchberg. The first-generation offspring were
shorthaired, shaded Burmillas, but subsequent
breedings inevitably brought the recessive
longhair and sepia pointing genes back to the
surface. The breed group was developed with
the help and support of Burmese breeders,
and remains quite distinct from this breed.
There are two distinct threads in the Asian
group, however: FIFé cats come from some
of the same lines as GCCF cats, but more
diverse lines are now used in Britain.

Brown
*This color is one of those often confused with the
Chantilly/Tiffany. Although it looks like a very
dark chocolate, the color is in fact black, slightly
degraded by the sepia pointing pattern; it is
called sable in the Burmese. Sepia pointing is
allowed in self Tiffanies; the long coat prevents
them from being mistaken for Burmese.*

Blue Silver Shaded
*Shaded Tiffanies are the longhaired equivalent of
the Burmilla, the original Asian coat pattern. All
members of the Asian group aim for the same
physical conformation, differing in coat colors,
patterns, or length. The semilong coat of the
Tiffanie is longest in the ruff and on the tail.*

Ears
Medium to
large, continuing
lines of face

Head
Short wedge, with
distinct nose
break in profile

SHADES FROM
YELLOW TO
GREEN ALLOWED

Eyes
Neither almond-
shaped nor round,
slightly oblique
in set

Body
Medium build, with
straight back and
good musculature

Coat
Semilong,
fine and silky

Tail
Medium to long,
elegantly plumed

Legs
Medium-length,
with round paws

KEY FACTS

DATE OF ORIGIN 1970s
PLACE OF ORIGIN Great Britain
ANCESTRY Burmese/Chinchilla crosses
OUTCROSS BREEDS Burmese/Chinchilla
OTHER NAME None
WEIGHT RANGE 8–14 lb (3.5–6.5 kg)
TEMPERAMENT Lively and affectionate

BREED COLORS

SELF COLORS (SOLID, SEPIA)
Black, Chocolate, Red, Blue, Lilac, Cream, Caramel,
Apricot, Black Tortie, Chocolate Tortie, Blue Tortie,
Lilac Tortie, Caramel Tortie

SHADED COLORS (SOLID, SEPIA)
Colors are as for self colors

TABBY COLORS (SOLID, SEPIA, ALL PATTERNS)
Brown, Chocolate, Red, Blue, Lilac, Cream, Caramel,
Apricot, Black Tortie, Chocolate Tortie, Blue Tortie,
Lilac Tortie, Caramel Tortie

BALINESE

SLENDER, FINE-BONED, AND REFINED AS ROYALTY IN APPEARANCE, the Balinese is in fact an intensely social breed, happiest when it is underfoot or at the center of activity. Highly inquisitive, it is indefatigable in its investigation of vacuum cleaners, cupboards, and shopping bags. Its tubular body permits it to accomplish Houdini-like acts of contortion; veterinarians know that, like the Siamese (*see page 188*), this is a superb escape artist, seemingly able to pick locks. It is a talkative cat, sometimes appearing, like its shorthaired cousin, to talk to itself. The Balinese is an energy burner, and needs both mental and physical stimulation. A typical pointed cat, it does not have dramatically long hair, and from a distance some individuals look Siamese except for the graceful plume of a tail.

Striking namesake
Delicate movements, unshakable poise, and a lithe physique are all prerequisites for the Balinese temple dancers who were the inspiration for this breed's name.

BREED HISTORY

Siamese have produced semilonghaired kittens for a long time: whether they historically carried the longhair gene or were outcrossed is not clear. A longhaired Siamese was actually registered with the CFA in Britain, in 1928. Breeders often passed these mutants on as pets, until after World War II, when Marion Dorsey, in California, began to breed to produce longhairs. Longhair Siamese were exhibited in 1955, and were recognized in 1961. Breeders of Siamese protested at the use of the name, and an early breeder suggested Balinese because the cats reminded her of Balinese temple dancers. In the mid-1970s, the breed arrived in Europe. Most registries call all colors Balinese. In CFA, the original colors are Balinese; the rest are called Javanese (*see page 138*).

Chocolate Point
As in all pointed cats, the coat darkens with age; a cat's show "career" may be quite short. This cat's shading is too heavy to show now, but he was a winner in younger days.

Lilac Point
The dilute version of the Chocolate, this color is a study in delicacy. The warm, magnolia coat may bear soft lilac shading, while the nose leather and paw pads are pinkish or faded lilac to match the points. As in all the colors, the eyes should be a clear, vivid, and brilliant blue. This color is also generally called Lilac Point in the various North American associations, although it has also been called Lavender Point and Frost Point.

Body
Medium-sized, lithe and graceful

Coat
Medium-long, fine and silky, lying flat

NO WOOLLY UNDERCOAT

Blue Point
The standard for the Blue calls for a body of glacial white, with points and any shading on the back to be a cold blue. The nose leather must also be blue. It should not be possible to mistake a Blue Point for a Lilac Point in any respect.

Seal Point

Points of an even, deep brown and a soft shading of fawn on the body characterize this color. The Seal is less warm than the Chocolate, just as in the dilutes of these two colors the Blue is cooler than the Lilac.

Balinese head

Seen full face (left), the Balinese face is wide between the ears, narrowing in straight lines to a fine muzzle. This Blue Tabby Point also shows clear facial markings in the mask. Seen in profile (above), the nose should be straight and the chin strong. This Seal Tortie Point has a fully developed mask.

Ears
Large, wide at base, and pricked

Mask
Connected to ears by faint tracings

DILUTE COLORS
SHOW VESTIGIAL
FROWN LINES

Head
Long and wedge-shaped, with elegant lines

Eyes
Widely spaced, and Oriental in shape and set

Tail
Long and plumed

ABSENCE OF FRILL
PREFERRED

Points
Clearly contrasting with pale body

Paws
Small and oval, with pads to match points

KEY FACTS

DATE OF ORIGIN 1950s

PLACE OF ORIGIN United States

ANCESTRY Longhaired Siamese

OUTCROSS BREEDS Siamese in the United States, Angora in Britain

OTHER NAME Some colors called Javanese in U.S.

WEIGHT RANGE 6–11 lb (2.5–5 kg)

TEMPERAMENT Energetic and exhibitionist

BREED COLORS

BALINESE POINT COLORS
Seal, Chocolate, Blue, Lilac

OTHER POINT COLORS (JAVANESE IN CFA)
Red, Cream, tortie and tabby versions in all colors
Cinnamon, Fawn, Smoke, Silver and particolor versions

RED TABBY   BLUE TORTIE

NEWER BALINESE

ORIGINALLY, ONLY SEAL, BLUE, CHOCOLATE, AND LILAC POINTS WERE recognized in the Balinese and Siamese; breeders have worked to create the other colors and patterned points we know today. In Britain and Australasia, the name Balinese encompasses all colors and patterns, just as the name Siamese covers all of their shorthaired cousins. However, CFA in North America and some smaller associations in other countries still recognize only the four "traditional" colors in these breeds. Other colors, such as red and cream, and the tabby and tortie patterns, are classed as separate breeds. The longhairs are called Javanese, while the shorthairs are known as Colorpoint Shorthairs. To complicate matters further, many European cat organizations use the name Javanese for the Angora (see page 140), a different breed entirely, but one to which the Siamese did contribute. The Balinese can be thought of as a longhaired Siamese, although its fine coat is not as long as that of most Persians, and does not form a ruff.

Seal Lynx Point
As with all pointed breeds, kittens are born white, and young cats are paler than older individuals. However, some shading is inevitable on all lynx points, and the Seal Lynx Point in particular is noticeably shaded, with a cream body shading to a warm fawn color over the back. There should be no vestige of tabby markings on the body. The legs, tail, and face should show clear tabby markings; the whisker pads in particular should be heavily spotted.

BRIGHT, INTENSE
BLUE EYES

FACIAL BLAZES
DESIRABLE

Chocolate Tortie Point
Tortie Point Balinese must show some mingling of colors on each point, no matter how small or uneven, and any shading on the ivory body color should be uneven. Chocolate Tortie Point patches are a mixture of light chocolate and varying shades of red; larger red areas may show faint tabby marks. The nose leather and paw pads are a mixture of chocolate and pink.

MOTTLED SHADING
ON BODY

BODY FREE OF
MARKINGS

Chocolate Lynx Point
Lynx points must show clear facial markings, with distinctly spotted whisker pads and dark-rimmed eyes. The legs and tail should also be barred or ringed, but it is not possible to distinguish which tabby pattern is present on a pointed cat. Lynx points are called tabby points in Britain.

Seal Tortie Point

With points of deep, seal brown mixed with shades of red, this is the darkest of the tortie points. As in all other tortie colors, each point must show a mixture of colors. European and North American standards for mottling differ. In North America, an even mottling is desirable, but often one color or the other will predominate. This applies to the ears, feet, and tail, as well as the mask.

Blue Lynx Point

Unlike self-pointed Balinese, lynx points may have noses that do not match their points. A Blue Point must have a blue nose, but a Blue Lynx Point may have a pink nose outlined in blue. The eyes, however, must follow the same standard as self points. The "thumb" marks on the backs of the ears may be less apparent in a Blue Lynx Point than in other lynx points.

SPOTTED WHISKER PADS

Seal Tortie Lynx Point

All points of a Tortie Lynx Point must show both tabby marks and mingled colors, and body shading should be uneven, as in lynx points. In lynx points and tortie lynx points, the color is not judged quite as strictly as it is in the self points; variances in the exact tone are allowed, since some body shading is also to be expected in these patterns.

ANGORA (BRITISH)

THIS BREED IS SIMILAR IN BOTH TEMPERAMENT AND TYPE TO THE Oriental breeds – lively and inquisitive, and long and lean, with a tail that forms a delightfully elegant plume. The fine, silky, medium-length coat has no woolly undercoat, so this cat is fairly easy to groom. Balinese (*see page 136*), Siamese (*see page 188*), and Oriental Shorthairs (*see page 192*) are all permitted outcrosses in Angora pedigrees. The Angora breed suffers from a profusion of confusing names. Not related to the Turkish Angora (*see page 130*), in mainland Europe it is called the Javanese to avoid confusion with it, but some North American associations use Javanese for some colors of Balinese. In North America, the British Angora has been called the Oriental Longhair, with the misleading implication that it is directly descended from the Oriental Shorthair. There is now an Oriental Longhair (*see page 142*) with that descent, and it is to be hoped that Angoras can simply remain Angoras from now on.

BREED HISTORY

The Angora was developed in Britain by Maureen Silson, who mated a Sorrel Abyssinian (*see page 172*) to a Seal Point Siamese in the mid-1960s, attempting to produce a Siamese with ticked points. The descendents inherited both the cinnamon trait, producing cinnamon Oriental Shorthairs, and also the gene for long hair, which eventually led to the creation of the Angora. Descendents of this mating are behind the majority of today's British Angoras. The breed is not related to the 19th-century Angora, or to the revived Turkish Angora, or to the recently created Oriental Longhair.

Blue-Eyed White
To many people, this is the classic color of the historical Angora, or French cat. The blue eyes are bright and vivid, similar to those of the Siamese, rather than the paler baby blue of Western breeds.

KEY FACTS

DATE OF ORIGIN 1970s
PLACE OF ORIGIN Britain
ANCESTRY Siamese/Abyssinian crosses
OTHER NAMES Javanese (Europe), previously Oriental Longhair (United States), Mandarin
OUTCROSS BREEDS Siamese, Balinese, Oriental Shorthair
WEIGHT RANGE 5–11 lb (2.25–5 kg)
TEMPERAMENT Energetic exhibitionist

BREED COLORS

SELF AND TORTIE COLORS
Black, Chocolate, Cinnamon, Red, Blue, Lilac, Fawn, Cream, Caramel, Apricot, White (Blue-, Green-, Odd-Eyed), Tortoiseshell, Chocolate Tortoiseshell, Cinnamon Tortoiseshell, Blue Tortoiseshell, Lilac Tortoiseshell, Fawn Tortoiseshell, Caramel Tortoiseshell

SMOKE, SHADED, SILVER SHADED, AND TIPPED COLORS
Colors are as for self and tortie colors, with the exception of White

TABBY COLORS (ALL PATTERNS)
Brown, Chocolate, Cinnamon, Red, Blue, Lilac, Fawn, Cream, Caramel, Tortie, Chocolate Tortie, Cinnamon Tortie, Blue Tortie, Lilac Tortie, Fawn Tortie, Caramel Tortie

SILVER TABBY COLORS (ALL PATTERNS)
Colors are as for standard tabbies

CHOCOLATE TORTIE TABBY   CINNAMON TORTIE TABBY   CARAMEL TORTIE

Coat
Fine and silky, with no woolly undercoat

COAT LIES FLAT ON BODY

Chocolate
The rich, warm tones of this color create a truly luxurious-looking cat. The color should be even all over, but all hair tends to lighten in the sun, so longer areas of the coat, such as the tail, may become paler than the rest.

Tail
Long, tapering to fine end

PLUMELIKE TAIL

Red Shaded Silver

In shaded Angoras, the undercoat is a very pale, but warm, shade. The shaded silver colors, like this Red, have a pure silvery white undercoat, which provides a more dramatic contrast to the tipping. The Angora coat is slow to mature: this young cat has a short coat.

Historical model

The Angora was bred to recreate the elegant longhairs recorded in paintings such as this (1813) portrait by Louis Léopold Boilly (1761–1845).

Ears
Large and following lines of wedge

WIDE BASE

Head
Moderate, triangular wedge

Body
Medium-sized, svelte, and muscular

Neck
Long and slender

Eyes
Green in all colors of Angora except white

SLANTED EYES

FINE MUZZLE

Paws
Small and oval

HIND LEGS LONGER THAN FORELEGS

Legs
Long, slim, and well-muscled

Cinnamon

The first Angora, Cuckoo, was a Cinnamon. The gene for this color came from the Abyssinian parentage, where it is known as Sorrel. The tone should be warm, and eye rims and nose leather should match the coat.

ORIENTAL LONGHAIR

THIS BEAUTIFUL, FULLY COLORED, SEMILONGHAIRED VERSION of the Oriental Shorthair completes the quartet of Oriental breeds. Just as the Siamese (*see page 188*) has a semilonghair counterpart in the Balinese (*see page 136*), the Oriental Shorthair (*see page 192*) has its own silky alternative in the Oriental Longhair. The coat of the Oriental Longhair lacks an undercoat and tends to lie flat against the body. In summer, except for the plumed tail, it may resemble shorthairs. This breed reflects its family in all respects; it bears the colors of the Oriental, and the soft coat and plumed tail of the Balinese.

BREED HISTORY
In spite of the efforts of breeders to control matings, cats still manage to spring some surprises. In 1985, an Oriental Shorthair and a Balinese at Sheryl Ann Boyle's Sholine cattery conspired to produce a litter of silky, semilonghaired Orientals. These kittens were much too attractive to be ignored; the breed was then developed, and is now recognized by both TICA and CFA. As with Oriental Shorthairs, the breed associations differ as to the status of pointed kittens. There may occasionally be some confusion in name between this cat and the British Angora (*see page 140*), which has in the past been called an Oriental Longhair in North America; visually and historically, the two are quite distinct.

Ears
Large, pointed, and continuing lines of face

Head
Tapering wedge, no whisker pinch

Eyes
Medium-sized, almond-shaped, and slanted

Neck
Long and slender

Body
Long and sleek, tubular

Chestnut Silver-Ticked Tabby
The ticked pattern should show clear tabby markings on the face, legs, and tail, and at least one necklace. Silvering reduces the amount of color, and the contrast between the topcoat and undercoat may outshine the ticking's shimmer.

Legs
Long and slim

Chestnut
In North America, the colors in the Oriental Longhair breed follow the naming conventions of the Oriental Shorthair. In Britain, Orientals of this color are called Havanas, while in other breeds the color is called chocolate. The coats of Chestnut cats should be a rich, warm brown, somewhat redder than is usual for chocolate.

Tail
Long and tapering, softly plumed

KEY FACTS

DATE OF ORIGIN 1985
PLACE OF ORIGIN North America
ANCESTRY Oriental Shorthair, Balinese
OUTCROSS BREEDS Siamese, Balinese, Oriental Shorthair
OTHER NAME None
WEIGHT RANGE 10–13 lb (4.5–6 kg)
TEMPERAMENT Friendly and inquisitive

BREED COLORS

All colors/patterns, except pointed, sepia, and mink
All colors/patterns, including pointed, sepia, and mink

| BLUE TORTIE TABBY | FAWN AND WHITE | WHITE | BLACK |

LA PERM

CURLY HAIR AT EAR BASE

MOST OF THE REXED BREEDS IN EXISTENCE HAVE ORIGINATED, AND therefore been developed in, shorthairs. The longhaired La Perm and the Selkirk Rex (*see page 125*) are the only longhaired curly cats accepted by major registries. The Bohemian Rex, which is a proposed rexed longhair, has never achieved recognition, and the rexed Maine Coon (*see page 117*) is also highly controversial. Although La Perms are descended from random-bred American stock, they have a foreign appearance, with a wedge-shaped head and lean build. They are very active, inquisitive cats, and the breed description reflects their farm-cat ancestry, noting that they are "excellent hunters."

Eyes
Large and expressive, slightly slanted in set

Ears
Wide-set and continuing lines of face

Head
Medium-sized, modified wedge, with rounded contours

BREED HISTORY

In 1982, a farm cat in The Dalles, Oregon, produced a litter of six kittens that included a single bald kitten. In spite of this disadvantage, the kitten survived, and she eventually grew a coat. Unexpectedly, her coat, unlike that of her littermates, was curly and soft to the touch. Linda Koehl, the owner and founder of the breed, named this kitten Curly. Over the next five years, Koehl bred a number of curly-coated kittens, which were to become the basis of the La Perm breed. The gene is dominant, so wide outcrossing to increase the gene pool can be done while still producing reasonable numbers of rexed kittens. Of the major registries, only TICA has recognized the La Perm.

KEY FACTS

DATE OF ORIGIN 1982
PLACE OF ORIGIN United States
ANCESTRY Farm cats
OUTCROSS BREEDS Nonpedigreed cats
OTHER NAME Also called Dalles La Perm
WEIGHT RANGE 8–12 lb (3.5–5.5 kg)
TEMPERAMENT Affectionate and inquisitive

BREED COLORS

All colors and patterns, including sepia, pointed, and mink

WHITE

Body
Medium size and build, with good musculature

Red Tabby

The proportion of red cats in the random-bred population varies geographically. However, it is predictable that there are few red selfs because dedicated breeding is usually needed to eliminate tabby markings from this color. In any new breed, especially one outcrossing to nonpedigreed cats, this work has to begin from scratch.

Blue Mackerel Tabby kitten

The first La Perm was born bald and then grew a rexed coat, but most La Perms are born with a slightly curly coat. This curl becomes more pronounced as the cat matures.

Legs
Hind legs longer than forelegs

Coat
Medium-length and ringleted, with heavy undercoat

Tail
Long, tapering plume

KURILE ISLAND BOBTAIL

BOTH THIS BREED AND ITS HOMELAND ARE OF UNCERTAIN ownership. The Kurile Island chain, running from the easternmost point of Russia to the tip of Japan's Hokkaido Island, is disputed between the two nations. The Kurile Island Bobtail is of quite a different type from the Japanese Bobtail (*see opposite*), although it has the same short tail. Its coat, conditioned by the harsh winters of its northern home, is longer and thicker than that of its more southerly relative, and its build is sturdier. A relatively small range of colors is recognized by the breed standard. A friendly breed, it nonetheless retains its independence.

Red Self
Sex-linked red is common in cats from this area, and is ideally accompanied by copper-colored eyes. The coat is longest over the throat and in "breeches" on the hind legs. Males often develop a full face, with clear jowls.

BREED HISTORY

Until recently, there was only one widely known bobtailed breed, the Japanese. With the advent of a more open attitude in the countries of the former Soviet Union, new breeds are emerging, among them some surprises such as this hitherto obscure breed. The Kurile Island Bobtail represents the same mutation as the Japanese Bobtail, and has almost certainly been present on the Kurile Islands for centuries. While this genetic similarity causes no problems to the Russian bodies that register the Kurile, the shared mutation that causes its bobtail might be a barrier to the breed's acceptance in Europe.

Tortie and White
Even female Kuriles like this one develop an impressive build by maturity, with strong legs and broad shoulders. The hind legs are longer than the forelegs, and the spine is carried with a slight rise from shoulders to rump. The tail should be a soft ball of longer hair, carried high.

Ears
Medium-sized and set upright

Head
Broad, with gentle nose break at eye level, and slight whisker pinch

Body
Medium-sized, strong, and muscular

Tail
Short, curled, and carried high

Eyes
Oval, slightly tilted, wide range of colors

KEY FACTS

DATE OF ORIGIN Pre-18th century
PLACE OF ORIGIN Kurile Islands
ANCESTRY Domestic cats
OUTCROSS BREEDS None
OTHER NAME None
WEIGHT RANGE 7–10 lb (3–4.5 kg)
TEMPERAMENT Busy and friendly

BREED COLORS

SELF AND TORTIE COLORS
Black, Red, Blue, Cream, Tortoiseshell, Blue-Cream, White

SMOKE, SHADED, AND TIPPED COLORS
Colors are as for self and tortie, except White

TABBY COLORS (CLASSIC, MACKEREL, SPOTTED)
Brown, Red, Blue, Cream, Brown Tortie, Blue Tortie

SILVER TABBY COLORS
Colors are as for standard tabbies

BICOLORS
Any allowed color with white

Legs
Sturdy, but not heavy for build, with round paws

Coat
Semilong, with discernable undercoat

JAPANESE BOBTAIL

SOCIABLE AND INQUISITIVE, THIS LONGHAIRED BREED STILL EXISTS only in small numbers. The Japanese Bobtail is bred by very few breeders worldwide. This is in part because the longhair gene is masked in longhair-to-shorthair breedings, and the low numbers of longhairs means that mating only longhair to longhair could lead to serious inbreeding. In this semilonghaired version of the Bobtail, the short tail makes a full, fluffy pom-pom: this trait does not carry spinal or bone deformities with it. The Bobtail is highly gregarious but easily bored and, when bored, can be mischievously destructive.

BREED HISTORY

Although it has only recently received much publicity, this cat is a natural variant of the shorthaired Bobtail (*see page 196*). Examples of both types can be found in Japanese prints and paintings going back over the last three centuries (*see page 38*), and the longhaired cats would have had an advantage in the cold climate of Japan's northernmost areas. The documented breeding history, however, only dates from 1968, when shorthaired Bobtails were brought to the United States, carrying with them the longhair gene, which was noticed in the early 1970s. Now that the shorthaired version is firmly established in North America, the less common longhaired cat is gaining some ground there. It has yet to gain recognition in Britain.

Bobtail face
An almost equilateral triangle, the face has gentle curves and high cheekbones. Odd eyes are prized in Japanese Bobtails, especially in the tortie-and-white coat pattern, known as Mi-ke.

KEY FACTS

DATE OF ORIGIN 700s
PLACE OF ORIGIN Japan
ANCESTRY Household cats
OUTCROSS BREEDS None
OTHER NAME None
WEIGHT RANGE 6–9 lb (2.5–4 kg)
TEMPERAMENT Vibrantly alert

BREED COLORS

SELF AND TORTIE COLORS
Black, Red, Blue, Cream, White, Tortie, Blue Tortie
All other self and tortie colors, pointed, mink, and sepia

TABBY COLORS (ALL PATTERNS)
Colors as for self and tortie

BICOLORS
Above accepted colors with White
All other colors and patterns with white

Head
Broad, with noticeable whisker break and gentle dip at eye level in profile

Ears
Large, set wide apart and upright

Eyes
Large and oval, with definite slant when viewed in profile

Body
Long, straight, and slender, but well muscled

Tail
Short pom-pom, either straight or curled

Legs
Long and slender but not dainty

Coat
Semilong, soft and silky

Red and White
The overall look of the Japanese Bobtail is one of long, clean lines. Although well muscled, it is athletic rather than massive in build. The legs, correspondingly, are slender but not fragile. The hindlegs are longer than the forelegs, but they are carried bent so that the torso is almost level when the cat is standing or walking.

RANDOM-BREEDS

BY FAR THE MOST COMMONLY OWNED DOMESTIC CAT IS THE HUMBLE, random-bred household pet. Even in countries with high populations of pedigreed cats, these self-selected pets outnumber them four to one. While some people are set on the looks and personality traits of a certain breed, random-bred cats usually satisfy those of us with less definite requirements. A cat's personality depends on its early experiences, so a random-bred cat is as friendly as one makes it, although it may not achieve the chattiness of Oriental breeds or the extreme placidity of some longhaired breeds. Only a few of these "alley cats" have long hair, because it is a recessive trait, but cats in the style of the Angora (*see page 140*) or the Maine Coon (*see page 114*) do turn up: after all, these breeds sprang from such nonpedigreed cats.

Blue
Blue, the defining color of several naturally developed breeds, is often found in the feline populations of the Western world. The semiforeign build of a cat like this indicates a heritage in common with southern European breeds, such as the Turkish Angora (see page 130); cats like this are often seen on Greek islands.

Green-Eyed White
This cat, which has often been mistaken for an Angora, has a white coat as pure as that of any pedigreed cat. The eyes may not be the brilliant green achieved by careful selective breeding of top show cats, but many pet-quality pedigrees also fail to meet such rigorous standards.

Black

Many longhairs with northern origins, such as the Maine Coon (see page 114) or the Norwegian Forest Cat (see page 118), have broad faces, a sturdy build, and thick, almost shaggy coats. These breeds were developed from random-breeding farm cats, which still produce beautiful individuals.

Cream and White

Creams are less common than reds among random-bred cat populations. In both colors, even selfs almost always show some ghost tabby markings. Breeders of pedigreed cats select carefully to minimize these markings and produce consistently clear self coats, but even in random-bred cats the occasional individual shows a suprisingly solid color.

Shaded Silver

The shaded and tipped Persians (see page 104) epitomize elegance. The extraordinarily long coat of that breed is the result of a century of breeding, and is highly unlikely to turn up in nonpedigreed domestic cats. However, the shading, the dramatic black eyeliner, and the outlined nose all appear, and many pet cats have coats that would not have disgraced the breed in its earlier days.

INTRODUCTION TO SHORTHAIRS

Black Bombay
The Bombay was the first of the breeds to emulate a wild cat, being bred to resemble a black panther in miniature. Several more breeds of similar character have since been created.

THOUSANDS OF YEARS AGO, DOMESTIC CATS spread from Egypt to varying environments. The early African wildcat type – moderate-sized, lean, with a fine coat – was not naturally suited to all the new conditions. The new varieties that evolved now form the basis of today's breeds. Survival of the fittest in the north favored stocky individuals, with dense, insulating undercoats of weatherproof down hair to protect them in winter. In northern climates, cats developed "cobby" bodies, a type later developed into the British Shorthair (*see page 152*) and exported as the foundation stock for many of the world's cats, including the American Shorthair (*see page 160*). At the same time, the cat was also spreading east across Asia. In warm climates, natural selection favored thinner, sparser coats and a smaller body to increase the surface-area-to-weight ratio and help to lose excess heat. These cats grew longer and leaner than their antecedents, and their smoother, thinner coats often lacked any down hair. Such cats are now called foreign or, if extremely slender, Oriental types.

Colorpoint Exotic
Some breeds are the unexpected results of breed programs: this shorthaired Persian was the result of an attempt to create a longhaired American Shorthair.

Ocicat
At first an accident, this breed brought a new spotting pattern into the spectrum, and is a fine example of the recent trend for breeding wild-looking cats. It requires a charitable eye to see the supposed resemblance to the ocelot.

Mutations in coat type have always occurred, but have died out without human intervention. Some shorthaired breeds have wavy or curled "rex" coats, first bred in the Cornish Rex (*see page 198*). The extreme mutation of hairlessness may be selected against in the natural population, but with selective breeding it has formed the basis of the Sphynx's extraordinary appearance (*see page 202*).

Siamese
This breed was once defined for most people solely by its pointed pattern. Today, many breeds include this pattern, and the Siamese is recognized more by its extremely fine, elongated type, which has helped to make it one of the more distinctive breeds.

A new trend in breeding is that of creating a new look rather than refining what nature has already achieved. Many of these breeds emulate wild cats: the Ocicat (*see page 206*) is a typical example. The Bengal (*see page 208*) was the first breed produced by mating the domestic cat with a wild cat, the Asian leopard cat (*see page 17*). It has been followed by the Pixiebob (*see page 211*), reputedly with bobcat (*see page 14*) ancestry, and Chausies, crossed to *Felis chaus* (*see page 16*).

Korat kitten
Some of the newer breeds have achieved huge popularity in a short time, while some of the older ones, such as the Korat, still retain a certain rarity value. Known in its native Thailand for centuries, the breed was not recognized for showing in the West until 1965.

European Shorthair
Like its British and American counterparts, this type developed naturally in random-bred cats over many hundreds of years. It has been preserved and perpetuated by breeders in the 20th century.

EXOTIC SHORTHAIR

GENUINELY EXOTIC IN LOOKS, THIS SHORTHAIRED Persian (*see page 104*) has the gentle personality and soft, squeaky voice of its parent breed. Exotics have the conformation of Persians, but a highly original coat: not quite short, but not semilong either. Outcrossing to bring in the short coat has given the Exotic a slightly livelier and more inquisitive disposition than its antecedents; it has not, however, eliminated the anatomical problems of the face inherited from the Persian. The dense, double coat of these cats benefits from combing twice weekly. Exotic Shorthair litters may include some longhaired kittens. In some associations, these longhaired Exotics may compete as Persians.

BREED HISTORY

In the early 1960s, breeders of the American Shorthair (*see page 160*) attempted to introduce the Persian's coat texture into their breed. Instead, they produced cats with the Shorthair's coat on the Persian's cobby, compact body. Unintentionally, the "shorthaired Persian" was born, complete with a flattened, "teddy bear" face and small, plaintive voice. To differentiate their cats from American Shorthairs, breeders called them Exotic Shorthairs, and used British Shorthairs (*see page 152*), Burmese (*see page 182*), and even Russian Blues (*see page 170*) in their breed programs. CFA recognized the breed in 1967. In North America only outcrosses with Persians and Himalayans are allowed; elsewhere other breeds are still used.

Black
With a coat of lustrous black hair and eyes of brilliant gold, this color might have been the model for many of the lucky black cats produced as promotional toys by companies over the years. Black kittens may show gray or rusty tinges in their coats, but these are not acceptable in adult show cats.

Seal Point
The pointed pattern is included under Exotic, rather than being named separately, like the Himalayans. All points should be evenly matched, and the mask should extend over the entire face. Point colors develop at different rates, the dense colors, such as the Seal, maturing first.

Coat
Dense, plush, standing out from body

Blue-Cream
The standard for all tortie Exotics calls for the colors to be balanced and softly intermingled, and for all four feet and the tail to contain both colors. Some distinct patches of color are allowable, and facial blazes are desired. Tortie patterning is inherently unpredictable.

Tail
Relatively short

Exotic head
The Exotic has inherited some of the Persian's flaws, such as overflowing tear ducts, constricted nostrils, and dental problems. The British standards for both breeds are less extreme than the American standards, calling for the upper edge of the nose leather to be below the level of the lower edge of the eye, penalizing drastically short faces. The head conformation is already apparent in kittenhood.

Brown Mackerel Tabby
Exotic Shorthairs may be seen in a variety of tabby patterns including the mackerel. The facial markings of each of these patterns are the same; only the body markings vary. The Mackerel Tabby should have numerous narrow vertical stripes covering the body and rings on the tail.

Blue
The color standard for the Blue Exotic is similar to that for the blue British Shorthair, a cat involved in its creation. Comparing the two breeds shows how distinct breed conformations are, even in two relatively stockily built cats. The Exotic is the roundest of all the shorthairs, with a breed standard that calls for rounded lines in every contour from the ears to the toes. The cuddly appearance can give a deceptive illusion of softness; beneath the plush fur, the curves should be all muscle.

Ears Small, with rounded tips, set wide and low

Eyes Large, round, and prominent

Body Medium to large and cobby, carried low on legs

Head Round and massive, with full cheeks

MASSIVE SHOULDERS

Paws Large, round, and firm

Legs Short, thick, and strong

KEY FACTS
DATE OF ORIGIN 1960s
PLACE OF ORIGIN United States
ANCESTRY Persians/American Shorthairs
OTHER NAME None
OUTCROSS BREEDS None
WEIGHT RANGE 7–14 lb (3–6.5 kg)
TEMPERAMENT Gently inquisitive

BREED COLORS
All colors and patterns, including pointed, sepia, and mink

BRITISH SHORTHAIR

THIS IMPRESSIVELY BUILT CAT IS SELF-POSSESSED AND SELF-RELIANT. Although undemanding and gentle, British Shorthairs are not overly tolerant of handling; judges and breeders describe them as "four-feet-on-the-ground" cats. Numerous firm guard hairs give the dense, bouncy coat a distinctive, crisp feel, and the protective undercoat insulates the cat on the frostiest day. Thick-legged and well-muscled, this breed is both compact and surprisingly heavy. Large, round eyes highlight its essentially gentle disposition, although, if prey appears, it is an inordinately successful hunter.

BREED HISTORY

British Shorthairs were developed in the 1800s from the farm, street, and household cats of Britain. Although it was the most-shown breed at the first British shows, and Harrison Weir, the "inventor" of the cat fancy, bred "British Blues," the breed was in decline by the turn of the century, and had almost died out by the 1950s. It was revived by dedicated breeders who exported stock to Ireland and throughout the British Commonwealth. By the 1970s, it had arrived in the United States where, as the British Blue, its calm, loyal, enduring, and reserved manner won it immediate admirers. A curious feature separates the British Shorthair from most shorthaired cats: about half of all British Shorthairs have Type B blood, a rare trait.

British Shorthair profile
Seen here in a red spotted tabby, the head is round and the neck sturdy. The standard calls for a rounded forehead, moderate nose break, and short, straight nose.

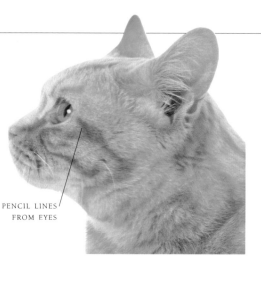

PENCIL LINES FROM EYES

FROWN LINES

NOSE LEATHER RED OR BLACK

Blue
This is the classic British Shorthair. It was one of the earliest colors, and has always remained the most popular. For a long time, the British Blue was the only British cat recognized in North America. When the breed population fell in World War II, breeders outcrossed first to other breeds, including Persians, which resembled the British Shorthair in type. This led to problems with fluffy coats and short noses, but the breed has long since regained form. It is still sometimes confused with the Chartreux (see page 168).

Ears
Medium in size, with round tips

Eyes
Large, round, and copper or gold in most colors

BROAD NOSE

Head
Round face with full cheeks

SHORT, STURDY NECK

Silver Spotted Tabby
This striking pattern was also one of the earliest, appearing in the 1880s. There are silver versions of all the tabby colors and patterns, but the black remains one of the most popular. Unlike other colors, the Silvers often have green or hazel eyes.

Red Classic Tabby
The original tabby was the brown, less often seen today, but reds also made an early appearance. Ginger reds are common in the nonpedigreed cats of the world, but a century of breeding has modified this color to deep mahogany shades.

UNBROKEN NECKLACES

SHORT, STRONG LEGS

Chest
Good width in shoulders and broad chest

Paws
Compact, firm, and round

NOSE LEATHER PINK

KEY FACTS

DATE OF ORIGIN 1880s
PLACE OF ORIGIN Great Britain
ANCESTRY Household, street, and farm cats
OTHER NAME Tipped colors once called
Chinchilla Shorthairs
WEIGHT RANGE 9–18 lb (4–8 kg)
TEMPERAMENT Genial and relaxed

BREED COLORS

SELF AND TORTIE COLORS
Black, Red, Blue, Cream, Tortoiseshell, Blue Tortie,
White, (Blue-, Odd-, Orange-Eyed)
Chocolate, Lilac, Chocolate Tortie, Lilac Tortie

SMOKE AND TIPPED COLORS
As for self and tortie colors except White
As for self and tortie colours except White

TABBY COLORS (CLASSIC, MACKEREL, SPOTTED)
Brown, Red, Blue, Cream, Tortie, Blue Tortie
Ticked, Chocolate, Lilac, Chocolate Tortie, Lilac Tortie

SILVER TABBY COLORS
Colors and patterns are as for standard tabbies
Colors and patterns are as for standard tabbies

BICOLORS
All self and tortie colors with White
All colors and patterns with White

RED SPOTTED   BLUE SPOTTED   BLACK SMOKE   BROWN
TABBY   TABBY   CLASSIC TABBY

PAW PADS
PINK

Orange-Eyed White
*This color was developed from the
Blue-Eyed White, which appeared at
the turn of the century. An increased
susceptibility to deafness occurs in white
cats, with an apparently greater risk in
Blue- rather than Orange-Eyed individuals.
Selection for deep blue Siamese-type eyes
may lessen the likelihood of blue due to the
action of the white gene, which causes deafness.*

FACIAL BLAZE
ACCEPTABLE

Tortoiseshell
*A difficult color to breed, this was nevertheless one of the very
first to be recognized. The standard for the Tortoiseshell pattern
in this breed allows an even mingling of colors without obvious
patches, in contrast to the Tortoiseshell standard in the
American Shorthair (see page 160). Brindling or tabby
markings are faults.*

Body
Cobby and strong,
carried low
on legs

Coat
Dense, with
crisp feel

PAW PADS MAY
BE MOTTLED

Tail
Short and thick,
with blunt tip

COAT DEVELOPS
RUSTY TINGE IN
SUNLIGHT

Black
*Superstitions about
black cats have cut both
ways (see page 30), but
in Britain a black cat has
been fully rehabilitated and is
treated as a lucky omen. Even so,
these cats fell into obscurity after
World War I. The clear golden eye
color is only rarely seen among
nonpedigreed cats, which are
usually green- or hazel-eyed.*

THICK COAT
"BREAKS" EASILY

NEWER BRITISH SHORTHAIR COLORS

SINCE THE BREED WAS FIRST DEVELOPED, OVER A CENTURY AGO, THE RANGE of British Shorthairs has increased enormously. Some of these appeared before World War II, but since then there has been an even greater development of colors and patterns. In the 1950s, numbers were low, and breeders outcrossed surviving British Shorthairs with Persians (*see page 104*) to ensure the survival of the blue coat. Although now rare, the Persian influence means British Shorthair matings still occasionally produce kittens with fluffy coats. The Persians also brought in the tipped coat, resulting in a new category of colors. More recently, adventurous matings have created delightful new coat colors, which indicate outcrossing to Oriental cats, although these cats are not universally accepted. The Siamese (*see page 188*) gene, however, brings not only its pattern but the possibility of a Blue-Eyed White without deafness.

Chocolate kitten
The gene for this rich brown color came originally from Oriental breeds. Crossbreeding brought the color into the Persians, from which it was introduced into the British Shorthair. Because of its outcross origins, this color is not universally recognized outside Britain.

Black-tipped
This was known until 1978 as the Chinchilla Shorthair because it was developed through matings with Chinchilla Persians. Persian heritage is still apparent in kittens before they acquire their adult coats.

Cream
Although creams, which are dilute red selfs, appeared from the turn of the century onward, they were not recognized until the 1920s. Breeders did not know how to produce them, and early creams were "hot," resembling reds. Good, "cool" creams, as far as possible from red, took a great deal of work.

Lilac kittens
The dilute version of the Chocolate, the Lilac, was introduced into the British Shorthair by outcrossing with Persians. Both blue and lilac are shades of gray, but they are quite distinct in good examples.

Black and White Bicolor
Although there have been bicolor British Shorthairs from the earliest days of the breed, the show standard originally specified that the markings should be symmetrical, a standard almost impossible to meet. A revision to allow less rigid distribution of color in the one-third to half-white coat brought more popularity. At first, only black, blue, red, and cream were allowed.

NOSE LEATHER SHOWS TWO COLORS

Blue-Cream

Although both the dilute blue and the tortoiseshell were among the earliest colors recognized, this dilute tortoiseshell did not achieve the same status until the 1950s; in part this was because the genetics behind it were not understood.

BALANCE OF
COLORS MUST
BE EVEN

Seal Colorpointed kitten

These colors have been fully accepted in Britain only during the 1990s, and they are still not allowed worldwide. The result of outcrossing to Siamese, they still resemble the traditional British Shorthair in all respects other than their exotic pattern.

PALE EYES DEEPEN
WITH MATURITY

Tortoiseshell and White

Unlike the solid tortoiseshell, this pattern has distinct patches of red and black. The bicolor gene decreases the number and increases the size of the pigment colonies, making mingled colors almost impossible to achieve in tortie-and-whites. The color balance of the coat should be one-third to half white, as in other bicolors.

THICK, CRISP COAT

Blue-Cream Colorpointed

As with the solid colors, pointed torties should show evenly mingled colors on their points. Ideally, each point shows a mix of colors. Despite the Oriental influence, these cats tend to have the placid nature of their British forebears.

MANX

THE LACK OF A TAIL IS THIS BREED'S MOST OBVIOUS VISIBLE CHARACTERISTIC, but its "bunny-hop" gait is just as unique. If there is any single word that encapsulates the Manx it is "round" – round-bodied, round-eyed, round-rumped, round-headed, even round-pawed. Slow-maturing Manx come in a huge range of colors and patterns, although pointed patterns are not accepted by all associations. Cats may be "rumpies" (with no tail, just a dimple at the base of the spine), "stumpies" (with short tails), and "tailies" (with almost natural, although perhaps kinked, tails). Stumpies and tailies make excellent pets, with retiring but friendly personalities, but show cats are all rumpies. Taillessness has consequences, since the gene can result in overly extreme kittens with spinal defects, gait abnormalities, and bowel and bladder problems. Using less extreme Manx (stumpies and longer tails) in the breeding program may help decrease the incidence. Manx do not breed true for taillessness – the homozygote fails to develop in the uterus. Thus all Manx also carry the gene for normal tails.

Local emblem
Manx appear on stamps in their homeland; this is one of the first.

Black and White
A common combination in random-bred British cats, this coat must show no blurring or speckling at all in a show cat. This "stumpy" has a vestigial tail, making it unsuitable for showing.

BREED HISTORY

The Manx originated on the Isle of Man in the Irish Sea. Taillessness occurs occasionally in feline populations as a spontaneous mutation; in large populations it will usually disappear, but in isolated groups, such as those on islands, it has a good chance of surviving. This is how the Manx, Japanese Bobtail (*see page 196*), and Kurile Island Bobtail (*see page 144*) developed. The dominant Manx mutation is not that of the Asian cats, belying myths that they are related. The traditional Manx was rangier than today; now it is bred for roundness, "like a hairy basketball with legs" as one breeder put it. Manx have been shown in Britain since the late 19th century; they reached North American shows in 1899, and were recognized by CFA in the 1920s.

Rump
No rise of bone or cartilage discernible when stroked

Coat
Thick and double, with quality more important than pattern

PADDED LOOK TO COAT

Manx head
The full-cheeked face of the Manx shows its roots in the typical random-bred British cat. The head should be broad and rounded, with a straight nose and a firm chin.

KEY FACTS

DATE OF ORIGIN Pre-1700s
PLACE OF ORIGIN Isle of Man
ANCESTRY Household cats
OTHER NAME None
OUTCROSS BREEDS None
WEIGHT RANGE 8–12 lb (3.5–5.5 kg)
TEMPERAMENT Mellow and even-tempered

BREED COLORS

Colors are as for British Shorthair
All colors and patterns

BLUE TABBY   WHITE   RED   SILVER TABBY

EARS ANGLED OUTWARD

Brown Classic Tabby and White

The Manx's hind legs are markedly longer than its forelegs, although they are often carried bent. This contributes to its rounded look and gives it its characteristic, bouncing gait. The deep flanks of the breed provide a broad canvas to display tabby markings, especially the bull's-eye motif of the classic or blotched pattern.

Ears
Widely spaced and set slightly outward

Eyes
Color in keeping with coat color

Head
Large and round, with medium-length nose

Brown Tortie Tabby

The Manx is one of the stoutest of all cat breeds. The CFA showing standard states that the proportion of the body to the legs should be such that, taken together, they describe a square, while the GCCF standard calls for the cat to have "good breadth of chest" and "flanks of great depth." The show standards of all breed registries call for a completely tailless individual, with a definitely rounded rump that is slightly higher than the shoulder when the cat stands squarely.

Body
Solid and compact, with short back

Tortoiseshell

As in all breeds, the British prefer a more softly mingled tortoiseshell pattern than the North American registries. This individual is a stumpy, with a short, stubby tail, and is therefore unsuitable for showing in any registry.

Legs
Relatively short and powerful

SELKIRK REX

REXING IS APPARENT IN THE SOFT, THICK, PLUSH COAT OF THIS breed from the minute a kitten is born, but it then disappears, to reappear at eight to ten months. While the coat, in which all hairs are curled, needs routine grooming, excessive combing and brushing, especially after bathing, straightens the hair. In body conformation, this patient and relaxed breed most closely resembles the British Shorthair, especially in its leg length. It also comes in two versions, the plush shorthair and the more dramatic longhair (*see page 125*). As with any other breed that is developed from a mutation, careful study is needed in order to make sure that there are no health problems associated with this trait. The Selkirk is unlike most other Rexes in that the trait is dominant, so outcrossing to broaden the gene pool still produces 50 percent rexed litters.

BREED HISTORY

Every year, many kittens are born at shelters. In 1987, a female calico kitten was born at For Pet's Sake, a pet rescue service run by Kitty Brown in Montana. This kitten, one of a litter of seven, was the only one to have curly hair and curly whiskers. Miss DePesto of NoFace, as she was called by the breeder who adopted her, Jeri Newman, was bred; three in her litter of six had curly coats, indicating that the rexed coat was genetically dominant. It is assumed that Pest herself was the source of this genetic mutation. Further breedings, including one back to her son, revealed that she carried the recessive genes for long hair and pointing. TICA recognized the breed first, but other associations have also demonstrated interest.

KEY FACTS

DATE OF ORIGIN 1987
PLACE OF ORIGIN United States
ANCESTRY Rescued domestic cat, Persian, Exotic, British and American Shorthair
OUTCROSS BREEDS Persian, Exotic, British and American Shorthairs
OTHER NAMES None
WEIGHT RANGE 7–11 lb (3–5 kg)
TEMPERAMENT Patiently tolerant

BREED COLORS

All colors and patterns, including pointed, sepia, and mink

RED TABBY AND WHITE

BLACK AND WHITE

SHADED SILVER

Head
Rounded, with distinct stop to nose

Ears
Medium and pointed, set well apart

Eyes
Round and widely spaced

CURL ON NECK PROMINENT

CURLY WHISKERS

Body
Medium in build, with good musculature

Coat
Thick, medium length, in loose curls

CURL ON BODY VARIABLE

Tail
Thick, tapering to rounded tip

Legs
Medium-length and substantially boned

Black Smoke
Like other rexed breeds, the Selkirk shows smoke and shaded colors to great advantage. Outcrossing to pedigreed breeds allows a new breed like the Selkirk to take advantage of the decades of breeding that have gone into producing traits such as deep copper eyes, achieving them in a shorter time itself.

Selkirk head
The Selkirk has a Western look, rather than the Oriental style favored for other rexes. The full-cheeked face has round eyes and a short muzzle.

SCOTTISH FOLD

FOLDED EARS ENSURE THAT THIS BREED IS IMMEDIATELY ARRESTING, but it also has a distinctive, rounded look, with a short neck, round head, and compact body. Those unique ears are due to a dominant gene that causes varying degrees of fold. The first Fold had what is now called a "single" fold, where the ears bend forward; today's show-quality cats have tight "triple" folds. Straight-eared cats are still essential for breeding healthy Folds. The breed has a placid personality, and its undemonstrative behavior suits its reserved appearance.

BREED HISTORY

Susie, the Fold's founding mother, was a farm cat born in Tayside, in Scotland. Local shepherd William Ross and his wife Mary were given one of Susie's kittens, named Snooks. Bred to a British Shorthair (see page 152), she produced Snowball, a white male who was shown locally. In 1971, Mary Ross sent some Folds to Neil Todd, a geneticist in Newtonville, Massachusetts. Development continued in the United States, using British and American Shorthairs (see page 160), and Folds were fully recognized by 1994. In Britain, the problems of crippled homozygous Folds prevent recognition.

KEY FACTS

DATE OF ORIGIN 1961
PLACE OF ORIGIN Scotland
ANCESTRY Farm cat, British and American Shorthairs
OUTCROSS BREEDS British and American Shorthairs
OTHER NAME None
WEIGHT RANGE 6–13 lb (2.5–6 kg)
TEMPERAMENT Quietly confident

BREED COLORS

All colors and patterns, including pointed, sepia, and mink occur

Brown Classic Tabby
The distinctive ears of the Fold are present from birth, although how folded they are may not be apparent until later. The skeletal problems associated with homozygosity for this gene are not apparent in kittens; the abnormal bone growth shows up with maturity.

Blue Tortie Tabby and White
The scoring system for Folds places most of the emphasis on body type. After the ears, the most important part of the body is the tail: any shortening or stiffness indicates skeletal problems. All aspects of the Fold standard call for a healthy, well-proportioned, supple cat.

Ears
Folded, with rounded tips

Eyes
Large and rounded

Head
Rounded, with broad, short nose

Body
Medium, sturdily built, and flexible along spine

Coat
Short and dense

Legs
Must not be short

Tail
Long, tapering tail preferred

Fold head
The ears of a Scottish Fold should be "set in a caplike fashion," flat against the head. Small, tightly folded ears are the ideal. The face should have a sweet expression.

AMERICAN SHORTHAIR

THIS EASY-GOING, SELF-SUFFICIENT, AND NO-NONSENSE CAT has won friends in both the home and the showring in the United States and Canada; elsewhere, it is uncommon. American Shorthairs can be quite large, and the full-cheeked face and robust, muscular body exude strength. The CFA standard specifies, as should all standards, that "Any feature so exaggerated as to foster weakness" brings disqualification in a show. American Shorthairs still share features with household cats, and the aim of breeding is to produce kittens that have the best of these qualities. Until relatively recently, any nonpedigreed cat that met the standard could be registered, and these cats widened the gene pool; this practice is no longer allowed.

Household origins
The ancestors of this breed were often recorded in naive scenes, such as this one by an unknown artist of the late 19th century.

BREED HISTORY

Domestic cats arrived in North America with the first settlers, whether in British settlements from Newfoundland to Virginia, the French possessions from Nova Scotia to Louisiana, or the Dutch colony in what is now New York. Many of these cats were brought on voyages to catch rats on ships, but some remained in the New World as pioneers for the world's largest domestic cat population. This new land brought new environmental pressures to bear; the descendents of surviving cats developed thick, hard coats, dense enough to protect them from moisture, cold, and superficial injuries. With more natural predators around, these cats evolved to be bigger than European felines. Early this century, some American breeders realized that their domestic cat's marvelous characteristics should be preserved in a breed. The first intentional litter, in 1904, was from a mating of American and British Shorthairs. The breed was called the Domestic Shorthair until 1965, when it acquired its present name.

Silver Tabby
The Silver Tabby is a popular color, with dense, inky black markings on a background of sterling silver. In 1965, a Silver Tabby won the United States Cat of the Year award, prompting the breed's name change from the original "Domestic Shorthair" to its present "American Shorthair."

Ears
Medium-sized and well-spaced, with rounded tips

GENTLY CONCAVE NOSE

Head
Large, slightly longer than it is wide

Eyes
Large, rounded, and very slightly tilted

Chin
Vertically in line with nose

Neck
Medium-length and muscular

Body
Solid, powerful, and muscular

Coat
Short, thick, and hard in texture

Legs
Medium-length and heavily muscled

Tail
Medium-length, thick at base

BROWN EYES
LATER TURN GOLD

Brown Classic Tabby kittens
In CFA, only the blotched and striped tabby patterns are accepted, while TICA accepts the spotted and ticked patterns as well. The blotched tabbies were prevalent among the breed's immigrant ancestors: blotched tabby populations show a high correlation with old trading routes.

BRILLIANT GOLD
EYES PREFERRED

Blue-Cream
Females, as tortoiseshells virtually always are, may be much lighter than males, and have a less "heavy" face. The standard for the American Shorthair, like most other North American standards, calls for clearly defined patches of unbrindled color.

TAIL TAPERS TO
BLUNT END

KEY FACTS

DATE OF ORIGIN 1900s
PLACE OF ORIGIN United States
ANCESTRY Domestic cats
OUTCROSS BREEDS None
OTHER NAME Once called Domestic Shorthair
WEIGHT RANGE 8–15 lb (3.5–7 kg)
TEMPERAMENT Easygoing

BREED COLORS

SELF AND TORTIE COLORS
Black, Red, Blue, Cream, White, Tortoiseshell, Blue-Cream
All other self and tortie colors

SMOKE COLORS
Black, Cameo, Blue, Tortoiseshell, Blue-Cream
All other self and tortie colors, except White

SHADED AND TIPPED COLORS
Colors are as for self and tortie colors
All other self and tortie colors

TABBY COLORS (CLASSIC, MACKEREL)
Brown, Red, Blue, Cream, Brown Patched, Blue Patched
Spotted and ticked patterns, all other self and tortie colors

SILVER TABBY COLORS
Colors and patterns are as for standard tabbies
All other self and tortie colors

BICOLORS (STANDARD AND VAN)
Colors are as for self and tortie colors
All other self and tortie colors

SMOKE, SHADED, AND TIPPED BICOLORS
Black Smoke, Cameo Smoke, Blue Smoke, Tortoiseshell Smoke, Shaded Cameo, Shell Cameo with White
All other smoke, shaded, and tipped colors with White

TABBY BICOLORS
All tabby colors with White

SILVER TABBY BICOLORS
Silver Tabby, Cameo Tabby, Silver Patched Tabby with White
All other silver tabby colors with White

Black Smoke
Buster Brown, the first all-American cat to be registered in the breed, in 1904, was a black smoke of street origins. In repose, the smoke coat colors look almost indistinguishable from those of the selfs, but in motion, the undercoat shimmers softly.

TABBY LINES ON
CREAM AREAS

Tortie and White
This coat pattern is sometimes called calico – or dilute calico if it is a blue tortie and white – in North America. This name has been in use since the earliest cat shows, and comes from the pattern's resemblance to the bold patterns once commonly printed on calico fabric.

AMERICAN WIREHAIR

THIS BREED'S MOST NOTABLE CHARACTERISTIC IS, OF COURSE, its coat. Distinctive to the touch, it feels like stroking a steel wool pad. Every hair is thinner than usual and crimped, hooked, or bent, giving the overall appearance of "wiring." The most prized coat is dense and coarse; a kitten born with a coat that appears to have ringlets may have only a wavy coat at maturity, while coats that are only lightly wired early in life may continue to develop throughout the cat's first year. A cat with curly whiskers is highly valued. The American Wirehair is a relaxed and friendly breed. Its advocates say it is rarely destructive and enjoys being handled.

BREED HISTORY
This breed descends from a kitten born in 1966 on a farm in Verona, in upstate New York. Local breeder Joan O'Shea obtained both this male kitten and his normal-coated sister. Through a careful breeding program, she determined that this was a dominant mutation. Successive crossings with American Shorthairs developed the breed, and for a while its standard, apart from the wired coat, was the same as that of the Shorthair. Distinctive qualities in the shape of the head, body, and tail consistently occurred in litters, however, and a breed standard was written for the Wirehair in 1967. Although there are now American Wirehairs throughout the United States and Canada, the breed remains unrecognized in most other regions of the world.

Ears
Medium-sized, with rounded tips

Head
Rounded, with prominent cheekbones

Eyes
Large and round, widely spaced, with a slight tilt

Body
Level back and rounded torso

Coat
Springy and tight, medium-length

Legs
Medium-length and sturdy, with compact, rounded paws

Tail
Tapering to rounded, but not blunt, tip

KEY FACTS

DATE OF ORIGIN 1966
PLACE OF ORIGIN United States
ANCESTRY Farm cat, American Shorthairs
OTHER NAME None
OUTCROSS BREEDS American Shorthair
WEIGHT RANGE 8–15 lb (3.5–7 kg)
TEMPERAMENT Busy, occasionally bossy

BREED COLORS

SELF AND TORTIE COLORS
Black, Red, Blue, Cream, White (Blue-Eyed, Gold-Eyed, Odd-Eyed), Tortoiseshell, Blue Tortie
All other self and tortie colors

SMOKE COLORS
Black, Red, Blue
All other self and tortie colors with the exception of White

SHADED AND TIPPED COLORS
Silver, Cameo
All other self and tortie colors

TABBY COLORS (CLASSIC, MACKEREL)
Brown, Red, Blue, Cream
Spotted and ticked patterns, all other self and tortie colors

SILVER TABBY COLORS
Silver, Cameo
All other tabby colors

BICOLORS
Self and tortie colors with white
All colors and patterns with white

WHITE   BLUE   BROWN TABBY

Black Smoke and White
Smoke bicolors are softer in contrast than solid bicolors. In most shorthairs, the undercoat is unseen except when the cat moves, but the Wirehair's coat ensures that a little white always shines through.

Red Classic Tabby and White
The original male kitten in which the wirehair trait began was red and white. In all colors except the silvers, CFA requires Wirehairs to have eyes of brilliant gold, while TICA recognizes no relationship between eye and coat color.

AMERICAN CURL

THIS ELEGANT AND SWEET-TEMPERED BREED COMES IN TWO COATS, long and short. The shorthaired American Curl has taken longer to develop, because the original Curls (*see page 122*) were all longhaired; the shorthair gene is dominant, so a great many shorthaired Curls carry a hidden longhair gene and produce longhaired kittens. The extent of curl to the ears is of profound importance to breeders. The curl is graded in three stages: cats with ears just turned back (first degree) become pets, those with more curl (second degree) are used for breeding, and those with full crescents (third degree) are shown. The curled ears should be handled with care; uncurling them risks damaging the cartilage.

EAR FURNISHINGS DESIRABLE

Curl development
All American Curls are born with straight ears. When they are two to ten days old the tips begin to curve; they then curl and uncurl until they "set" permanently at about four months.

BREED HISTORY
For over a decade, the cat has been America's most popular pet, and California is where the most active breeding programs exist. This new breed is the result of a genetic mutation that occurred in a black, longhaired, stray kitten who was named Shulamith. Half of her kittens also showed this unusual feature, a genetically dominant characteristic, and were distributed to form a breeding program. All members of this shorthaired breed descend, like their longhaired cousins, from this mother and her kittens, and are accepted on a show standard that differs from the Shorthair only in coat.

Silver-Ticked Tabby
The Curl standard calls for distinct striping on the face, legs, and tail, as in several other breeds with this pattern. TICA recognizes this pattern in the silvered colors, while CFA does not.

Head
Modified wedge with gentle curves

Ears
Curving at least 90° in smooth arc

Eyes
Upper rim oval, lower rim rounded

Body
Semiforeign shape, moderately muscled

Coat
Soft and close-lying, with minimal undercoat

Tail
Equal to length of body, wide at base, tapering to tip

Legs
Medium length and build

KEY FACTS

DATE OF ORIGIN 1981
PLACE OF ORIGIN United States
ANCESTRY American household cat
OTHER NAME None
OUTCROSS BREEDS Nonpedigreed domestic cats
WEIGHT RANGE 7–11 lb (3–5 kg)
TEMPERAMENT Quietly affable

BREED COLORS

SELF AND TORTIE COLORS
Black, Chocolate, Red, Blue, Lilac, Cream, White, Tortoiseshell, Blue-Cream
All other self and tortie colors

SMOKE COLORS
Colors as for self and tortie, except White and with the addition of Chocolate Tortie
All other self and tortie colors

SHADED AND TIPPED COLORS
Shaded Silver, Shaded Golden, Shaded Cameo, Shaded Tortoiseshell, Chinchilla Silver, Chinchilla Golden, Shell Cameo, Shell Tortoiseshell
All other self and tortie colors

TABBY COLORS (ALL PATTERNS)
Brown, Red, Blue, Cream, Brown Patched, Blue Patched
All other colors

SILVER TABBY COLORS (CLASSIC, MACKEREL)
Silver, Chocolate Silver, Cameo, Blue Silver, Lavender Silver, Cream Silver, Silver Patched
All other standard tabby colors, spotted and ticked patterns

BICOLORS (CLASSIC AND VAN)
All other self and tortie colors with white
All other colors with white

TABBY BICOLORS
Colors are as for standard tabbies

SELF AND TORTIE POINT COLORS
Seal, Chocolate, Flame, Blue, Lilac, Cream, Tortie, Chocolate Tortie, Blue-Cream, Lilac-Cream
All other colors, sepia and mink patterns

LYNX (TABBY) POINT COLORS
As for self and tortie points, excepting Red
All other colors, sepia and mink patterns

MUNCHKIN

ALTHOUGH BREEDERS CLAIM THAT THE DWARFISM OF THESE CATS causes no problems, the Munchkin, a short-legged cat in longhair (*see page 123*) and shorthair versions, has stirred up unprecedented controversy. The breed has had to undergo rigorous health investigations to gain the level of acceptance it has, but many breeders still feel that Munchkins are "uncatlike." While their playful personalities are unmistakably feline, it cannot be denied that the breed represents a radical departure from normal feline anatomy. Those who see the cat as a lovable pet may well be drawn to this breed; those attracted to the cat's self-sufficient image are unlikely to approve of it.

KEY FACTS

DATE OF ORIGIN Unknown
PLACE OF ORIGIN United States
ANCESTRY Household cats
OUTCROSS BREEDS Nonpedigreed domestic cats
OTHER NAME None
WEIGHT RANGE 5–9 lb (2.25–4 kg)
TEMPERAMENT Appealing and inquisitive

BREED COLORS

All colors and patterns, including pointed, sepia, and mink

RED CLASSIC TABBY	TORTIE AND WHITE	BLACK

Munchkin head
The breed standard is for a cat of moderation. The head should be neither rounded and jowly nor angular and foreign. All colors and patterns are allowed.

Red Spotted Tabby
In some ways, the Munchkin resembles a squirrel, both in its gait and in its tendency to sit up on its haunches with its forepaws held in front of it. This characteristic pose contributes to the image of the breed as curious and comical.

BREED HISTORY

The Munchkin has been bred for a little over a decade in North America, and from the start attracted a high level of attention. After health investigations, the breed was recognized by TICA in 1995. Some breeders are working with pedigreed breeds, producing rexed and curled-ear Munchkins, but these programs are not widely approved and none of the results have been recognized.

Brown Spotted Tabby
Color and pattern are relatively unimportant in the breed standard. Build alone accounts for half the points. Part of the Munchkin's appeal may be that an adult cat's proportions resemble those of a kitten, whose legs are usually fairly short in relation to the body.

Ears
Moderately large, wide at base, and upright

Head
Almost triangular, with nose of medium length

Eyes
Walnut-shaped, large, and slightly tilted

Neck
Thick and firmly muscled

Body
Medium-sized, substantially muscled, neither svelte nor cobby

Tail
Set high, medium-thick, tapering to rounded tip

Legs
Short but not misshapen, well-muscled

Paws
Round, compact, and pointing forward

SNOWSHOE

NAMED FOR ITS CHARACTERISTIC WHITE MITTENS, THIS breed combines the pointing of the Siamese (*see page 188*) with white spotting, giving it crisp white paws. Two patterns exist: the mitted, with limited white, and the bicolor, with more white on the face and body. The white mittens may be inherited from the breed's American Shorthair (*see page 161*) ancestry, or they may come from its Siamese side; white toes were a known fault in early Siamese. Snowshoes are gregarious and affectionate, and although they are talkative, they have soft voices.

BREED HISTORY

In the 1960s, Philadelphia breeder Dorothy Hinds-Daugherty began to cross her Siamese with American Shorthairs. The resulting hybrid faced some opposition from Siamese breeders at first, partly due to fears that the spotting might find its way into Siamese bloodlines after decades of breeding to eradicate this early fault. The dramatic pointing pattern was also almost a trademark of the Siamese breed at that time, although it is recognized in many breeds today. The Snowshoe remained little known until the 1980s, when it was recognized by TICA. It has since gained wider popularity, but remains rare. It is not recognized by other major registries.

Snowshoe face

The facial pattern decides if a Snowshoe is mitted or bicolor. An inverted "V" of white makes the cat a bicolor; anything less makes it a mitted. The amount of white on the body determines whether it is a good or bad example of either pattern.

Seal Bicolor kitten
The white areas must not exceed two-thirds of the total body area. The body should be colored, showing subtle shading to lighter underparts; there should be no isolated white spots.

Ears
Medium to medium-large, continuing lines of face

Head
Broad modified wedge, with slight stop in profile

Eyes
Medium-sized, oval, and blue

Coat
Short, smooth, and close-lying, with no noticeable undercoat

Legs
Length in proportion to body, with medium musculature

Paws
Medium-sized, oval, and white in both patterns

Body
Moderate size and musculature, semiforeign build

Tail
Medium thickness, tapering slightly

KEY FACTS

DATE OF ORIGIN 1960s
PLACE OF ORIGIN United States
ANCESTRY Siamese, American Shorthair
OUTCROSS BREEDS Solid eumelanistic Siamese, traditional eumelanistic solid, and bicolor American Shorthairs
OTHER NAME None
WEIGHT RANGE 6–12 lb (2.5–5.5 kg)
TEMPERAMENT Active and friendly

BREED COLORS

MITTED COLORS
Seal, Chocolate, Blue, Lilac

BICOLORS
All mitted colors with white

Mitted Blue

The mitted pattern is the "classic" Snowshoe. White paws ideally stop at the ankles on the forelegs and below the hocks on the hind legs, and the amount of white must not exceed one-third of the body. There may be some white on the face. Sex-linked red colors and cinnamon colors do not occur in the Snowshoe.

EUROPEAN SHORTHAIR

A CAT WITH A WHOLE CONTINENT TO CALL HOME MIGHT EASILY BE assumed to have wide popularity, but the European Shorthair is less known than either its British Shorthair (*see page 152*) or American Shorthair (*see page 160*) counterparts. Over the years since the breed was established, it has become less cobby than the British type, with a slightly longer and less heavily jowled face, perhaps reflecting the typical feline type of warmer mainland European countries more than it did in the past. It has many of the same basic traits as the British cats, however, being strong and hardy with an all-weather coat. Its personality tends to be calm and affectionate, and it is a relatively quiet breed.

BREED HISTORY
Until 1982, European Shorthairs were classified with British Shorthairs. FIFé then gave the breed its own category, and it began effectively as a "ready-made" breed, with a full range of colors, established type, and breeding stock with known histories. Despite this advantage, or maybe because it is so similar to the British and American Shorthairs, the European Shorthair does not seem to have caught the imagination of breeders, and remains rare. The breed is now being selectively bred, with no British Shorthair crosses permitted in the pedigree. It is not recognized by GCCF or major breed registries outside Europe.

Ears
Medium-sized and upright, with rounded tips

Head
Triangular to rounded, with well-defined muzzle

Eyes
Large, round, and well-spaced, with colors to match coat

MUSCULAR NECK

Body
Medium to large, well-muscled, but not cobby

Legs
Medium-length and well-muscled

Coat
Short and dense, standing away from body

Silver Mackerel Tabby
The European Shorthair is bred in the three "traditional" tabby patterns of classic, mackerel, and spotted. The ticked pattern, not historically present in Europe, is not recognized. The silver tabby is popular because of the vibrantly contrasting colors in its coat. The markings should be symmetrical on both sides of the body.

Tail
Medium-length, thick at base, tapering to rounded tip

Tortoiseshell Smoke

In the European Shorthair, the patches of black, red, and cream in the tortoiseshell pattern should be broken into clearly defined patches, rather than subtly intermingled. Because the coat does not lie flat, the white undercoat of a Smoke can be seen and has the effect of "watering down" the colors slightly.

KEY FACTS

DATE OF ORIGIN 1982
PLACE OF ORIGIN European mainland
ANCESTRY Household cats, British Shorthairs
OUTCROSS BREEDS None
OTHER NAME None
WEIGHT RANGE 8–15 lb (3.5–7 kg)
TEMPERAMENT Intelligent and reserved

BREED COLORS

SELF AND TORTIE COLORS
Black, Blue, Red, Cream, Tortie, Blue Tortie, White (Blue-, Odd-, Orange-Eyed)

SMOKE COLORS
Colors are as for self and tortie, except White

TABBY COLORS (CLASSIC, MACKEREL, SPOTTED)
Brown, Blue, Red, Cream, Tortie, Blue Tortie

SILVER TABBY COLORS (CLASSIC, MACKEREL, SPOTTED)
Colors are as for standard tabbies

BICOLORS (STANDARD AND VAN)
All self and tortie colors with white
Smoke, tipped, and tabby colors with white

BROWN TABBY   BLUE-CREAM AND WHITE   SEAL POINT

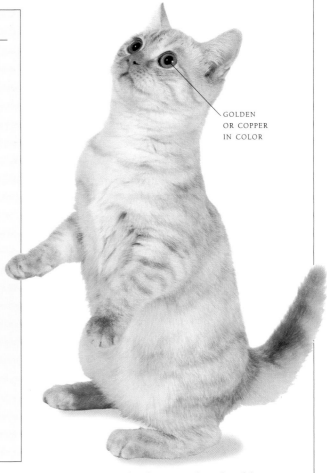

GOLDEN OR COPPER IN COLOR

Red Silver Mackerel Tabby

In the silver tabby colors, the undercoat is a pure, glistening white, giving a cool tone to the color. The markings retain their full intensity over this, giving a striking contrast. This cat is heavily silvered, with color restricted to the ends of the hairs.

Blue Point

The European Shorthair, just like the British Shorthair, has "imported" the pointing pattern of the Siamese breed (see page 188). The body tends to show more shading than that of the flat-coated Siamese, and darkens markedly with age.

Cream Shaded Cameo Tabby

The inhibitor gene does not always produce a silvery white color. Sometimes the undercoat retains a creamy tone, and these tabbies are called "shaded" rather than "silver." Although creams are bred to look "cooler" than reds, a cream shaded may look warmer than a red silver.

CHARTREUX

A KEEN OBSERVER OF LIFE, RATHER THAN AN IMPULSIVE PARTICIPANT, the Chartreux is a tolerant breed, less talkative than most, with a rather high-pitched meow and an infrequently used chirp. Its short legs, stockiness, and dense, close coat mask its true size. This is a big, powerful, late-maturing cat. Although a good hunter, it is not a fighter: individuals tend to withdraw from conflicts rather than become aggressive. There is an intriguing naming system for Chartreux: each year is designated by a letter (omitting K, Q, W, X, Y, and Z), and cats' names begin with the letter determined by the year of birth. For example, cats born in 1997 have names beginning with N.

BREED HISTORY

Possibly originating in Syria, the Chartreux's ancestors would have arrived in France by ship. By the 1700s, the breed was described by the naturalist Buffon as the "cat of France" and given a Latin name, *Felis catus coeruleus*. After World War II it effectively became extinct and was reestablished by outcrossing survivors with blue Persians (*see page 104*) and British Blues (*see page 152*). The Chartreux reached North America in the 1970s, but is not bred in many European countries. FIFé assimilated the Chartreux and British Blue under the name Chartreux during the 1970s, and all British and European Blues were described as Chartreux for a time; these breeds are now distinct again.

Blue male
Male Chartreux are much larger than females, with a heavier build, although they should never become cobby. They also develop pronounced jowls with age, which adds to the broadness of the head.

COAT "BREAKS" OVER CURVES

Color
Even, bright blue-gray, from ash to slate in tone

Coat
Short- to medium-length, with dense undercoat

SLIGHT IRIDESCENT SHEEN

Tail
Thick at base, tapering to rounded tip

Chartreux head
The Chartreux head is broad but stops just short of becoming a sphere. The muzzle is relatively narrow, but the rounded whisker pads and heavy jowls prevent it from looking too pointed. The expression should be sweet, with a slight smile.

WARM-TONED PADS

The patriotic pet

The Chartreux was the chosen companion of both French president Charles de Gaulle and author Colette, seen here with two of her pets. Colette's choice of the Chartreux was as much a part of national pride as her continued presence in Paris throughout the German occupation.

Chartreux kitten

Chartreux can take up to two years to mature fully; below this age, allowance is made for a coat that is finer and silkier than the ideal. In very young cats the eye color may also be less brilliant; it brightens as the cat matures, and then fades again with age.

Ears
Medium-sized, set high on head

Head
Broad but not round, with high forehead

Eyes
Large and round, gold or copper in color

SLATE GRAY NOSE

Neck
Short and heavy

Chartreux build

The Chartreux build is neither cobby nor slender: it has been termed "primitive." Other descriptions include a "potato on matchsticks" because of the relatively fine-boned legs. In fact, the Chartreux today looks much the same as its forebears, because the breed standard is kept close to historical descriptions of the breed.

BROAD CHEST

Body
Robust and densely muscled

KEY FACTS

DATE OF ORIGIN Pre-18th century
PLACE OF ORIGIN France
ANCESTRY Household cats
OUTCROSS BREEDS None
OTHER NAME None
WEIGHT RANGE 7–17 lb (3–7.5 kg)
TEMPERAMENT Calmly attentive

BREED COLORS

SELF COLORS
Blue

Paws
Small relative to body, round in shape

Legs
Short and sturdy, rather slender

RUSSIAN SHORTHAIR

THE ORIGINAL OF THIS GROUP IS THE SLIGHTLY RESERVED AND immensely dignified Russian Blue. A cautious cat, it is sensitive to changes in its environment and controlled in its activities with strangers. Its most vivid features are its thick, lustrous coat and its emerald green eyes. The soft, dense, insulating, double coat is unique in feel, and described in the British breed standard as "the truest criterion of the Russian." The Russian's trademark eye color is of more recent origins; the first Russian Blues exhibited in the West, at the Crystal Palace show in England in 1871, had yellow eyes. It was not until 1933 that breed standards called for eye color to be as vividly green as possible. This is a gentle breed, among the least destructive of all cats, and an ideal indoor companion.

Lucky Blue
The Blue is considered lucky in Russia, and images, such as this 19th-century engraving, are given to brides.

BREED HISTORY

Legend says that the Russian Blue descends from ships' cats brought from the Russian port of Archangel to Britain in the 19th century. Russian Blues are mentioned by name in Harrison Weir's 1893 book *Our Cats*, but from the Russian Revolution in 1917 until 1948, they became known as Foreign Blues. The modern Russian Blue contains bloodlines from British Blues (*see page 152*), and even from Blue Point Siamese (*see page 188*), consequences of Swedish and British efforts to revive the breed in the 1950s. Black and white versions have been developed in New Zealand and Europe; these are accepted in Britain, but not by FIFé or North American fancies.

Ears
Large, pointed, and set vertically

Eyes
Large, almond-shaped, and widely spaced

LONG, GRACEFUL OUTLINE

Head
Longer from ears to eyes than from eyes to nose

Body
Well-muscled, but never cobby or heavy

Coat
Double, with very dense undercoat

Russian Blue

The original, and to some the only, Russian, this color is an even blue with a silvery sheen. This sheen gives the coat a luminous appearance, and many breeders say that the less the cat is brushed, the more radiant the coat becomes.

Legs
Long, but not delicate

BLACK NOSE LEATHER

Tail
Moderate length and thickness, tapering to rounded tip

KEY FACTS

DATE OF ORIGIN Pre-1800s
PLACE OF ORIGIN Possibly Russian port of Archangel
ANCESTRY Domestic cats
OTHER NAME Archangel Cat, Foreign Blue, Maltese Cat, Spanish Blue, Russian Shorthair
OUTCROSS BREEDS None
WEIGHT RANGE 7–12 lb (3–5.5 kg)
TEMPERAMENT Reserved and wary

BREED COLORS

SOLID COLORS
Black, Blue, White

Russian Black

The Russian Blue bred true for centuries because the dilute color is recessive, never masking other colors. Black and White Russians are a recent development, and regarded by many as controversial. Least welcome of all are the blue-pointed "Russians," a result of past Siamese outcrosses, and being worked on by a very few breeders.

HAVANA BROWN

ELEGANT AND GRACEFUL AS ITS OUTWARD APPEARANCE IS, the Havana Brown is a very physical breed. The indoor Havana plays hide-and-seek to Olympic standards, treats leaping out from behind furniture to surprise people as an excellent game, and is a superb climber. Although its origins are the same as those of the Oriental Shorthair (*see page 192*), it has developed to resemble the Russian Blue more (*see opposite*). The Havana Brown stands high on its legs for such a moderate-sized animal, and is heavy for its size. Kittens and young adults have ghost tabby marks that disappear with age, leaving an even, rich shade of brown, tending toward mahogany.

BREED HISTORY

During the 1950s, British cat breeders developed a solid chocolate of Siamese type. The color was called Havana, but the breed was registered in Britain as Chestnut Brown Foreign. Havana Browns were exported to the United States, where breed development produced Quinn's Brown Satin of Sidlo, which is now found in the background of all North American Havana Browns. Chestnut Brown Foreigns continued to be imported into America and registered as Havana Browns until 1973, when CFA accepted the Oriental Shorthair breed; from then on these imports were registered as Chestnut Oriental Shorthairs. Ironically, the Oriental Shorthair color called chestnut in North America is now called havana in Britain, leading to some confusion.

KEY FACTS

DATE OF ORIGIN 1950s
PLACE OF ORIGIN Great Britain and United States
ANCESTRY Chocolate Point Siamese, black household cat, Russian Blue
OTHER NAME None
OUTCROSS BREEDS None
WEIGHT RANGE 6–10 lb (2.5–4.5 kg)
TEMPERAMENT Sweet and sociable

BREED COLORS

SOLID COLORS
Chocolate
Lilac

Havana head
The long head narrows to a slim muzzle with a pinch just behind the whisker pads. In profile, the chin is strong, giving the muzzle an almost squared appearance.

Lilac
Use of Russian Blues introduced the dilution trait, which resulted in occasional lilac kittens. They are recognized by TICA, in which the breed name is now simply Havana, but not by CFA. The color is warmer than that in other breeds.

Eyes
Oval in shape, green in color

Ears
Large, wide-set but upright

Head
Long and slender, with narrow muzzle

Body
Medium-length, carried level

Color
Even shade of warm mahogany

Tail
Medium length and thickness

TAPERED TIP

Chocolate
The standard for this shade of brown varies considerably across the different breeds in which it is found. In the Havana Brown, it is defined as a warm brown, tending toward red-brown; to some eyes, it comes close to cinnamon. A dark, sable-type coat is a serious fault.

Paws
Oval and compact

ABYSSINIAN

THE ALMOST TRANSLUCENT COAT PATTERN OF THIS BREED IS due to a single gene, first noted in the Abyssinian. This gene gives each hair several dark bands, evenly dispersed on a lighter background, resulting in a striking "ticked" coat pattern. Abyssinians' ears sometimes have caracal-like tufts, which add to their striking appearance. Although often almost silent, Abyssinians are active cats; they become attached to their owners, and demand attention and play. They are natural athletes, climbing and investigating anything available: curtains, people, or, if allowed out, fences and trees. They can suffer inherited forms of retinal atrophy, a blindness more common in dogs.

Lilac kitten
One of the newer colors not yet recognized in North America, lilac is the dilute shade of chocolate. Both colors were introduced through outcrosses to Orientals in the 1970s, and they are still not accepted by the more traditional registries.

CLEAR FROWN LINES

BREED HISTORY

The Abyssinian's ticking is a perfect camouflage in the dry, sunburned habitat of North Africa. The founding cats, including one called Zula, were brought to Britain from Abyssinia (now Ethiopia) after the Abyssinian War in 1868. There is a strong similarity between these cats and some ancient Egyptian images, and it is likely that the ticked mutation occurred thousands of years ago. Accepted in 1882, the breed was almost extinct in Britain earlier in this century, but by the 1930s it was established in the United States and France. Today it is most popular in North America. Standards differ internationally; Europeans have a more extreme shape and a wider range of colors.

Blue male
This dilute form of the ruddy has underparts of pale oatmeal, which stands out well against the warm, blue-gray ticking of the coat on the rest of the body. Like the ruddy, the blue has dark paw pads.

Abyssinian head
The face (below left) is a wedge; the profile has a slight nose break (below right). Almond-shaped eyes are gold or green, deep shades preferred.

DARK TIPS

"MASCARA" LINES

Ears
Large and cupped, ideally with tufted tips

SLIGHT NOSE BREAK

Eyes
Dark rims set in spectacles of lighter hair

Muzzle
Nose and chin align vertically

Chin
Should be cream but may be white

Neck
Only faint necklaces are acceptable

Legs
Slender, elegant, and moderately long

UNDERPARTS LACK TICKING

SMALL FEET

CHOCOLATE
TICKING

APRICOT BASE
COAT

KEY FACTS

DATE OF ORIGIN 1860s
PLACE OF ORIGIN Ethiopia
ANCESTRY Ethiopian household and street cats
OUTCROSS BREEDS None
OTHER NAME Color names vary internationally
WEIGHT RANGE 9–17 lb (4–7.5 kg)
TEMPERAMENT Attention-demanding

BREED COLORS

TABBY COLORS (TICKED)
Ruddy, Sorrel, Blue, Fawn
*Chocolate, Red, Lilac, Cream Tortie, Chocolate Tortie,
Cinnamon Tortie, Blue Tortie, Lilac Tortie, Fawn Tortie*
SILVER TABBY COLORS (TICKED)
All standard ticked tabby colors

CREAM   CHOCOLATE

Red or Sorrel

*Once called red in all registries, this color is now
often called sorrel to avoid confusion. It is not,
however, the true sex-linked Red, but the recessive
light brown that is more commonly known as
cinnamon in other breeds.*

EARS ARE
TICKING COLOR

Body
Medium-sized and
muscular

PINK PADS

Coat
Close-lying, fine but
not soft

Ticking
At least four bands of
darker color required

TICKING LINE ON TAIL

Fawn kitten

*This color is the dilute
version of sorrel and was once
called cream, but it is generally
less bright in appearance than a
true sex-linked Cream. In some
associations only these colors are accepted,
but in Britain true reds and creams have also
been bred and are accepted for showing.*

Ruddy

*The historical Abyssinian color, ruddy is genetically black agouti, the
color most commonly called "brown" in other tabby patterns. In the
early days, it was similar to the coat of the wild rabbit, and earned
the cat the name of "hare cat" or "rabbit cat" for a while. The
color is still called lièvre, or hare, in French, but selection for
rufism has led to a warmer, reddish base color today. In
Britain, ruddy was known as Normal or Usual until the
1970s; now it is simply called Usual.*

Ruddy Silver

*With the warm base coat lightened to white, ruddy
becomes a sparkling silver. The inhibitor gene, which
produces this effect, seems to have been present in the
early Abyssinians, naturally or through early crossing.
These colors have now been reestablished in Britain, but
are not yet universally accepted in North America.*

Tail
Gently tapering, and
the same length as
the body

TIP IS TICKING
COLOR

BLACK RUNS
UP TO HOCK

SPOTTED MIST

THIS IS THE FIRST BREED THAT HAS BEEN DEVELOPED ENTIRELY IN Australia. The Spotted Mist has been bred to have a playful and home-loving nature. Gentleness of spirit is prized, and the standard penalizes any aggression on the show bench. Similar in some ways to the Asian Spotted Tabby (*see page 181*), its appearance is moderate in all ways: medium in size, foreign in build but not extremely so, with a short, but not close-lying coat. The rather delicate markings create a misty appearance and account for the breed's name; the background ticking is essential to this effect. The breed is recognized in six colors, some of them unique in appearance. Full color takes a year to develop, and in some colors the delicate spots can be hard to see.

BREED HISTORY

Dr. Truda Staede in New South Wales developed a program to produce an indoor-loving, people-oriented breed, with the Burmese shape and a spotted tabby coat. The Burmese contributed conformation, companionability, and four of the six Spotted Mist colors. The Abyssinian added two more colors, the essential ticking, and a lively disposition. Domestic tabbies gave the spots and offset the tendency toward early sexual maturity. In January 1980, the first half-Burmese, quarter-Abby, quarter-domestic tabby kittens were born. A recognized breed throughout Australia, the Spotted Mist is still very rare and remains unknown elsewhere.

Ears
Medium-sized, upright or slightly flared in set, with rounded tips

Head
Rounded wedge, with smooth, flowing lines

Body
Medium-sized, with moderate muscling

Eyes
Deep gold in color, almond-shaped, and slightly tilted

Coat
Short, stands out softly from body

WHITISH UNDERPARTS

Legs
Medium-length, neither stocky nor slender

Paws
Small and round

WHITE LIPS AND CHIN

LEGS ARE STRIPED

Tail
Medium-length, tapering slightly to rounded tip

Peach
Salmon-toned markings on a warm, pinkish cream ground make this the closest thing yet to a pink cat. Underneath, it is a dilute cinnamon, but this coat shows the effect that different combinations and polygenic influences can have.

Gold
One of the colors brought in from the Abyssinian ancestry, this is genetically a cinnamon. The mixture of genetic influences in the Spotted Mist has transmuted the coat to gold and bronze markings on a cream ground.

KEY FACTS

DATE OF ORIGIN 1975
PLACE OF ORIGIN Australia
ANCESTRY Abyssinian, Burmese, Nonpedigreed shorthairs
OUTCROSS BREEDS None
OTHER NAME None
WEIGHT RANGE 8–13 lb (3.5–6 kg)
TEMPERAMENT Lively and harmonious

BREED COLORS

TABBY (SPOTTED AND TICKED TOGETHER)
Blue, Brown, Chocolate, Gold, Lilac, Peach

SINGAPURA

Peaceful, even retiring, by temperament, these cats are at the smaller end of the feline scale. Singapuras are distinctive in their one recognized coat, a ticked tabby in a color called sepia. The Singapura's temperament and physical attributes are widely reputed to be a natural result of selective pressures. In Singapore, most cats are feral and nocturnal. Cats that attract the least attention are more likely to breed successfully, leading to small size, a quiet voice, and a retiring disposition. Western cats are larger than Singapore's "drain cats," either because of genetic differences or better diet. On the basis of this and other factors, some people believe that Singapore's feral stock was the inspiration for the breed, rather than its sole genetic founders.

BREED HISTORY

This new breed's name is Malaysian for Singapore, from where Hal and Tommy Meadows brought cats to the United States in 1975; all registered Singapuras today originate from their breeding program. Within seven years of embarking on planned breeding, the Singapura was recognized, and it received its first formal championship recognition in 1988. The breed has reached Europe, but neither FIFé nor the GCCF recognize it, and there is controversy about its origins. Tommy Meadows also bred Burmese (*see page 182*) and Abyssinians (*see page 172*), and there are claims that these were used to create the Singapura. Others maintain that this is untrue, and allows unscrupulous breeders to sell fake Singapuras. Because there are still less than 2,000 Singapuras, some believe that the closed registry could work to its detriment, while allowing outcrosses to other breeds could help the Singapura.

Singapura kittens
The coats of Singapura kittens seldom meet the breed standard for adults: they are longer in relation to the small bodies, and also show less developed ticking. Even quite young kittens, however, show the "cheetah lines" that run from the inner corner of the eye to the whisker pads.

Sepia Agouti
This is the only color in which the Singapura is bred. Genetically a sable ticked tabby, it combines the Burmese color allele with the tabby pattern first known in the Abyssinian. The ticking is brown on an ivory ground, with tabby markings showing on the face and inner legs.

Ears
Wide and deeply cupped, set at a slightly outward angle

Head
Rounded, with straight nose and broad, blunt muzzle

Coat
Short and close-lying, with at least two bands of ticking

Eyes
Hazel, green, or yellow outlined in black, almond-shaped and slightly tilted

Body
Medium length and build

Tail
Slightly shorter than body, slender, with blunt tip

UNDERPARTS PALE

Legs
Strong but not stocky, slight barring on insides allowed

Paws
Small and oval, with brown pads, dark hair between toes

KEY FACTS

DATE OF ORIGIN 1975
PLACE OF ORIGIN Singapore and United States
ANCESTRY Disputed
OUTCROSS BREEDS None
OTHER NAME None
WEIGHT RANGE 4–9 lb (2–4 kg)
TEMPERAMENT Affectionately introspective

BREED COLORS

TABBY (TICKED)
Sepia Agouti

KORAT

Medium-sized, with a semicobby body and a silver-blue coat, the Korat is similar to the Russian Blue (*see page 170*) in size and color. Korats, however, are a densely muscled and rounded breed, with a single rather than double coat and peridot green rather than emerald green eyes. The large, prominent eyes give it an innocent expression, but this is a strong-willed, even pushy, cat. While gregariousness makes Korats playful and trainable, they do thrive on having their own way. They have an excellent capacity to grumble and, without attention, can become demanding, stubborn, and territorial. Very rarely, individuals may carry neuromuscular disorders, called GM1 and GM2; blood tests exist for these.

Korat kitten
Young Korats lack both the silver tipping and the brilliant eye color of adults, both of which may take two years to reach their full intensity.

BREED HISTORY

The *Cat Book Poems* of the Ayutthaya Kingdom (AD 1350–1767) describe the silver-blue Si-Sawat from Korat, a remote, high plateau in northeast Thailand. The first Korat in the West may have been entered in English cat shows in the 1880s as a solid blue Siamese (*see page 188*). Modern Korats were introduced into the United States by Mrs. Jean Johnson in 1959; they were recognized in the United States in 1965. The first pair was imported into Britain in 1972, and the breed was recognized in 1975. It remains rare everywhere.

Ancient breed
The Thai Cat Book Poems *distinguish the Si-Sawat and its luck-bringing properties from those of other blue cats recorded in it.*

Ears
Large, wide at base, with rounded tips

Head
Large, flat forehead and firm, rounded muzzle

Eyes
Luminous, prominent, and rounded

Body
Strong and semi-cobby build

Coat
Glossy, fine, and close-lying

Korat head
Oversized eyes and a heart-shaped face described by gentle curves give the Korat a much softer appearance than its compatriot breeds, but it has every bit as much personality.

Blues only allowed
As is to be expected from a breed that developed in a warm climate, the Korat has dispensed with the unnecessary insulation of an undercoat, and the single, silver-blue coat is short. Some lilacs have been bred in mainland Europe, but they are unlikely ever to be accepted.

COAT "BREAKS" OVER SPINE

KEY FACTS

DATE OF ORIGIN Pre-1700s
PLACE OF ORIGIN Thailand
ANCESTRY Household cats
OTHER NAME Si–Sawat
OUTCROSS BREEDS None
WEIGHT RANGE 6–10 lb (2.5–4.5 kg)
TEMPERAMENT Demanding and opinionated

BREED COLORS

SELF COLORS
Blue

Tail
Heavy at base, tapering to rounded tip

MEDIUM LENGTH

Paws
Oval and compact

BOMBAY

THIS MAJESTIC BREED HAS A COAT LIKE JET BLACK PATENT LEATHER, a pleasant and distinctive voice, and a gregarious personality. Like its Burmese forebear (*see page 182*), the Bombay thrives on human company. It is a real heat-seeker, most often found in the lap of a heat-emitting human. The coat is almost maintenance-free: an occasional rubdown with a chamois, or even your hand, is all that is needed to keep its sheen and texture. The breed standards can be difficult to meet: the brilliant copper eye color is thought to be the result of two genes, one for color and the other for intensity, and can fade or turn slightly green with age. Litters are large, but the Bombay remains rare, especially outside North America: it is sometimes confused with the British Bombay (*see page 180*).

Bombay kitten
The full depth of color and texture of the Bombay coat can take up to two years to develop, and allowance is made for this in the breed standards.

KEY FACTS

DATE OF ORIGIN 1960s
PLACE OF ORIGIN United States
ANCESTRY Black American Shorthairs and Sable Burmese
OTHER NAME None
OUTCROSS BREEDS None
WEIGHT RANGE 6–11 lb (2.5–5 kg)
TEMPERAMENT Actively inquisitive

BREED COLORS

SELF COLORS
Black
Sable

BREED HISTORY

In the 1950s, Kentucky breeder Nikki Horner embarked on an attempt to create a "mini black panther" from black American Shorthairs and Sable Burmese. By the 1960s, she had produced cats with shiny black coats, muscular bodies, rounded heads, and copper eyes. The Bombay was first recognized in 1976. Over the years the breed has developed its own distinctive look, with features of both ancestral breeds. Litters still produce sable-brown kittens with sepia pointing, although these are now rare.

Bombay head
The Bombay head has vacillated between the Burmese and American Shorthair types. Because of the Burmese heritage, some Bombay lines suffered the Burmese head malformation; breeding to avoid this may lead to a look more like the American Shorthair.

Head
Rounded in all aspects, with a short to medium muzzle

Ears
Wide at the base with rounded tips

Eyes
Large, rounded, and widely spaced

Body
Medium, semicobby, and surprisingly heavy

Tail
Medium length and thickness

PATENT-LEATHER GLOSS

Coat
Close-lying, with satinlike texture

Legs
Medium-length and sturdy

ROUNDED PAWS

Black Bombay
The glossy, Black Bombay has always had a unique look. The body type came from its Burmese heritage, and the solid, even color from its American Shorthair ancestors. Because the sepia pointing gene of the Burmese is recessive, Sable kittens still occasionally appear.

THE ASIAN GROUP

NOT YET RECOGNIZED IN NORTH AMERICA, THE SHADED, SMOKE, self, tabby, and Tiffanie (*see page 135*) Asians are designated by GCCF as a group rather than a breed. Interestingly, Asians had the first breed standard that allowed points to be awarded at cat shows for temperament.

ASIAN SHADED

THESE STRIKING CATS, WHICH WERE THE FOUNDING MEMBERS OF THE GROUP, are also commonly known as Burmillas. Their type is inherited from their Burmese (*see page 184*) parentage and the shaded coat comes from their Chinchilla Persian (*see page 104*) side. Like all Asians, Burmillas are less boisterous than the typical Burmese, but more sociable than Persians. While Burmillas are undoubtedly attention-seekers, they remain polite, moderate in their vocal demands, and are remarkably even-tempered.

BREED HISTORY

In 1981, an unauthorized alliance took place in London between a Burmese and a Chinchilla Persian, resulting in attractive shaded silver kittens. After consultation with relevant bodies, owner Miranda von Kirchberg began a planned breeding program. The original litter was of Burmese type, and initial policy was to breed back to Burmese every other generation. Both in Britain and elsewhere in Europe, other Burmese-Chinchilla crosses were made: backcrossing still helps to enlarge the genetic base. The Burmilla was recognized by GCCF in 1989 and FIFé in 1994; bloodlines in the two associations differ.

Brown Shaded Silver
A striking characteristic of the Burmilla is its natural dark "eyeliner" or "mascara." With the line of color around the nose and the almost red, rather than pink nose leather as well, these cats look like they have just returned from a full makeup session.

Lilac Shaded Silver
The Burmilla, or Asian Shaded, includes both shaded and tipped cats, although the coat should not be so lightly tipped that it appears white. The undercoat should be pale, almost white in silvers. Tabby markings are restricted to the face, legs, and tail, and broken necklaces.

Body
Medium-sized and firmly muscled

Shading
Varies from medium-heavy to tipping

Tail
Medium to long, tapering to rounded tip

Ears
Medium to large, widely spaced, angled slightly outward

Head
Short wedge, gently rounded on top

Eyes
Neither almond-shaped nor round; any color from gold to green

Coat
Short, fine, and close-lying

Legs
Medium-length with oval paws

ASIAN SMOKES

SMOKES ARE THE HALFWAY HOUSE BETWEEN THE Shaded Asians (*see opposite*) and the solid Asian Selfs (*see page 180*). They combine the white undercoat of the former, caused by the inhibitor gene, with the solid coat caused by the non-agouti allele in the latter. They come in all the colors of the selfs, and Burmese color restriction is also permitted; the Smoke already differs from the Burmese enough by virtue of its white undercoat for there to be no question of confusing the two breeds. With a coat slightly longer than that of the Burmese, the smoke undercoat shows in a faint gleam over curves when the cat is still, and a gentle shimmer when it moves. This coat type appeared in the second generation of crosses from Shaded Asians.

Black Smoke
In many cases it can be hard to tell a sepia Smoke from a black Smoke, because Smokes naturally tend to be darker on the short hair of their "point" areas. Black Smokes, however, are not sepia-pointed; if they were, the color would also be affected, becoming a deep sable-brown.

ANY COLOR FROM GOLD TO GREEN

UP TO HALF OF HAIR LENGTH IS WHITE

KEY FACTS

DATE OF ORIGIN 1981
PLACE OF ORIGIN Great Britain
ANCESTRY Burmese, Chinchillas, nonpedigrees
OUTCROSS BREEDS Burmese, Chinchillas with restrictions
OTHER NAMES Burmilla; Smokes were once called Burmoires
WEIGHT RANGE 9–15 lb (4–7 kg)
TEMPERAMENT Relaxed and engaging

BREED COLORS

BURMILLA OR SHADED COLORS (SOLID, SEPIA)
Black, Chocolate, Red, Blue, Lilac, Cream, Caramel, Apricot, Tortoiseshell, Chocolate Tortie, Blue Tortie, Lilac Tortie, Caramel Tortie

SILVER SHADED COLORS
Colors and patterns are as for shaded

SMOKE COLORS (SOLID, SEPIA)
Black, Chocolate, Red, Blue, Lilac, Cream, Caramel, Apricot, Tortoiseshell, Chocolate Tortie, Blue Tortie, Lilac Tortie, Caramel Tortie

SELF COLORS (SOLID)
Bombay (Black), Chocolate, Red, Blue, Lilac, Cream, Caramel, Apricot, Tortoiseshell, Chocolate Tortie, Blue Tortie, Lilac Tortie, Caramel Tortie
Sepia colors

TABBY COLORS (ALL PATTERNS IN SOLID, SEPIA)
Brown, Chocolate, Red, Blue, Lilac, Cream, Caramel, Apricot, Tortoiseshell, Chocolate Tortie, Blue Tortie, Lilac Tortie, Caramel Tortie

SILVER TABBY COLORS
Colors and patterns are as for standard tabbies

Chocolate Smoke
Although Asian Smokes are genetically non-agouti cats, they should show ghost tabby markings, which give the coat the look of watered silk. Silvery frown marks are apparent on the forehead, and there may be lighter "spectacles" or "clown marks" around the eyes.

ASIAN SELFS

INDEPENDENT OF THE BREEDING PROGRAMS THAT WERE INITIALLY
underway in the Asians, black Burmese-type cats, called Bombays
in Britain (distinct from the American Bombay), were being bred
in the 1980s. Although the Bombay development program had
used nonpedigreed cats, it was then integrated into the continuing
development of the Asian group as a whole. Other self colors were
also developed, and there is now a wide range of colors. The
sepia pattern is not allowed for showing in any Asian self colors:
this helps to preserve the identity of these cats as distinct from the
Burmese. Self breeders, in particular, tend to see selfs as distinct
from shaded cats, and some do not use cats from Chinchilla
lines in their breeding programs. There are some breeders,
however, whose philosophy is that all the colors are one breed.

Black Tortie

*As in the Burmese, the standard for
tortoiseshell Asians allows for colors to be
either subtly mingled or dramatically blotched.
Distinct facial blazes and solid legs and tails are
all accepted. The color should be even to the roots
of the hair: in the Black Tortie the standard calls
for jet black mingled with varying shades of
red. The eye color may range from
gold to green.*

PATCHES ARE DARK
AND LIGHT RED

DARKER
COLOR ON
FACE

Burmese variant Cream

*The recessive gene for Burmese pointing
is still present in the gene pool of these
cats. A sepia-pointed self such as this
one cannot appear in cat shows, but it
may still be used in breeding programs
because this pattern is allowed in other
cats within the Asian group.*

British Bombay

*Characterized by a sleek black coat, the Bombay is one
of the original Asian selfs. This color should not be
confused with the North American breed with which
it shares its name (see page 177). The British Bombay
resembles the European Burmese (see page 184);
the American Bombay has American Shorthair
and Burmese features.*

ASIAN TABBIES

As well as the recessive selfs and smokes, tabbies also began to appear in the second generation of Asian crosses. They appeared because the Chinchilla Persian (*see page 104*), one of the group's founding cats, has an agouti coat, although its tabby markings are rendered invisible by the inhibitor gene. It was then found that some breeders had also been bringing Abyssinians (*see page 172*) into their programs to introduce the ticked gene, and this work was also incorporated into the Asian breed. The result is that the Asian tabby is one of the few cats recognized in Britain in which all four tabby patterns are bred; the ticked pattern is the most popular of them. The slightly disparate origins of these various coat patterns were another factor in the unusual decision to grant the Asians status as a group, rather than as a single breed.

EDGES OF EARS
ARE DARK

STRONG TABBY
MARKINGS

PENCIL MARKINGS
ON CHEEKS

Black Ticked Tabby

Ticked tabbies are allowed in both standard and silvered coats, in all the Asian colors. The Asian Ticked Tabby standard allows no unbroken necklaces, but it does call for tabby markings on the legs and tail. The intensity of the color may be reduced in silver tabbies, but there should always be at least two bands of darker ticking on every hair. Underparts are paler than the rest of the coat, but should harmonize in color.

NECKLACES MUST
BE BROKEN

TABBY MARKINGS
ON LEGS

Blue Ticked Tabby kitten

The blue in Asian standards is medium to dark, rather than the light color preferred in many other breeds. This helps to provide good contrast in the tabby colors. The ticked pattern is the most commonly found tabby pattern in Asians, but tabbies are less common than the other coat types.

DARK TIP

BLACK RUNS UP
TO HOCK

AMERICAN BURMESE

RICHLY COLORED AND WIDE-EYED, THIS BREED HAS BEEN DESCRIBED AS "bricks wrapped in silk." Although it is fond of human company, the Burmese is less vocal or demonstrative than other Oriental breeds. The North American Burmese differs from its European counterparts (*see page 184*), in that its standard emphasizes roundness, notably in the shape of the head. The extremely round "contemporary" look was born out of Good Fortune Fortunatus in the 1970s; unfortunately, so was the Burmese head fault, an inherited deformity of the skull that is often lethal or requires euthanasia. As late as the 1980s, Sable was the only color universally accepted. Other colors had occurred since early breeding programs, but were known within CFA as Malayans. CFA and TICA now recognize four colors.

Burmese head
In spite of carrying the Burmese head fault, the contemporary look ruled CFA until 1995. In that year, their top three cats were of the less rounded "traditional" type, which does not carry the fault.

BREED HISTORY

The Burmese begins with Wong Mau, a brown cat from Rangoon in Burma (now Myanmar), brought to the United States with US Navy psychiatrist Joseph Thompson in 1930. She was to found a breed of which, ironically, she was not a member. Thompson bred Wong Mau to a Siamese (*see page 188*), the most similar breed, and bred the kittens back to Wong Mau. Three distinct types emerged: Siamese-pointed; dark brown with minimal pointing (the first true Burmese); and a dark body with darker points, like Wong Mau. She herself was a Burmese-Siamese hybrid, and a natural Tonkinese (*see page 186*).

Champagne
Despite the slightly idiosyncratic terminology of the Burmese colors, this is actually the sepia equivalent of the color more generally referred to as chocolate. Some degree of darkening in the mask area is almost unavoidable in this color; the main coat is a warm, even, honey brown.

Body
Medium-sized, muscular, and compact

Coat
Short and fine, with satinlike texture and glossy shine

CLOSE-LYING COAT

TAIL IS DARK

LEGS SHOW LEAST POINTING

Sable
This was the first, and for a long time the only, Burmese color. It was recognized in the 1930s, and ruled in splendid isolation for decades. Kittens are often born lighter than the standard requires, their coats darkening with maturity. The standard calls for a solid-colored cat, with the genetic masking or pointing so minimal as to be imperceptible.

EYES BROWN IN YOUNG CATS

Blue
The genetic dilute of sable, the American blue Burmese is not the cool, frosted color of many other blue cats. The standard calls for warm, fawn undertones, in marked difference to the standard for the European Burmese.

Tail
Medium in length

EARS TILT FORWARD

ROUNDED TIPS

Eyes
Rounded in shape
and golden in
color

Ears
Medium-sized
and widely spaced

DISTINCT NOSE BREAK

Head
Pleasingly rounded,
with full cheeks

Muzzle
Short and
broad, with a
rounded chin

WELL-DEVELOPED NECK

Legs
Moderate in boning
and length

ROUND PAWS

SLIGHT MASK APPARENT

COAT LOOKS FROSTED

KEY FACTS

DATE OF ORIGIN 1930s
PLACE OF ORIGIN Burma (now Myanmar)
ANCESTRY Temple cats, Siamese crosses
OUTCROSS BREEDS None
OTHER NAME Some colors previously Malayan
WEIGHT RANGE 8–14 lb (3.5–6.5 kg)
TEMPERAMENT Friendly and relaxed

BREED COLORS

SEPIA COLORS
Sable, Champagne, Blue, Platinum
All other self and tortie colors

SABLE TORTIE (NOT CFA)	RED (NOT CFA)	CARAMEL (NOT CFA)	CINNAMON (NOT CFA)

Frost or Platinum
*This is the color referred to in other cats
as lilac or lavender; the Burmese names
for it are unique to this breed.
As with the Blue, the tone of the color is
warmer in the Burmese than in other
breeds, with pale fawn undertones.
The sepia-influenced shade is also
lighter than in other breeds, accounting
for the metallic name.*

Burmese ancestor
*The Thai Cat Book Poems include
copper-colored "Thong Daeng" cats,
which are possibly ancient Burmese.
Mutations are rarely completely isolated.
Siamese pointing occurred elsewhere in
Southeast Asia – Wong Mau carried it –
and the Burmese pattern may similarly
have been known in Thailand.*

EUROPEAN BURMESE

THIS BREED HAS DIVERGED INTO TWO TYPES, ALMOST TWO BREEDS, on either side of the Atlantic. While the American side of the family (*see page 182*) has developed into a rounded cat, European breeders, followed by those in South Africa, New Zealand, and Australia, have opted for a well-muscled but more angular shape. This more Oriental look has a moderately wedge-shaped head, oval eyes, and long legs. Both planned and accidental matings expanded the color range to ten, whereas a more limited range of four colors is commonly seen in North America. Regardless of color or type, the Burmese is ideally suited to living in active households.

BREED HISTORY

The European Burmese is descended from the American breed: American cats were imported into Europe after World War II, and the brown was recognized in 1952 by GCCF. Here, the story takes a new turn. Firstly, the Europeans preferred a more Oriental look, and secondly, they were interested in a wider range of colors. GCCF, for example, took only eight years to recognize the Blue, while in North America CFA took decades to do so. This seems to have started a trend; the wide range of colors seen in the European breed was developed by the introduction of the red gene (from a red-point Siamese, a tortie-and-white farm cat, and a ginger tabby), and in the 1970s this range was broadened to create tortie versions of all the recognized colors. A further change came in 1996, when FIFé amended its breed standard to allow green eyes.

Burmese head
This Lilac shows the typical European Burmese head and eyes. Burmese eye color can appear very different in different lights. A golden yellow is much preferred: South African and Australian cats are particularly noted for their excellent eye color.

Brown Tortie
Deep brown with shades of red and cream, this is the tortie version of sable. In the Burmese, tortie patterns may be quite dramatically blotched, as in this cat. Facial blazes and solid areas of dark or light color are also allowed.

HARD BODY

SOLID-COLORED LEGS PERMITTED

ROUNDED TIP

HIND LEGS LONGER THAN FORELEGS

Chocolate
This color is more accurately detailed as a shade of "milk chocolate" in the breed standard. An even overall color is preferable, but elusive. Although the nose leather matches the coat, the paw pads are pink, shading to brown.

Legs
Slender legs in proportion to body

Blue
The British breed standard recognizes the Burmese as a pointed cat, but requires that the shading be slight, gradual, and confined to the face. The underparts may also be lighter than the rest of the coat. The standard for blue calls for a soft color, with a distinct silver sheen showing on any rounded areas of the body.

Lilac Tortie

This subtly mingled lilac-and-cream coat is not rated above the more blotched mixtures in the Burmese, although it would be in other breeds in Britain. Because tortie results from the presence of the red gene, it is unknown in the more traditional American cats.

NOSE LEATHER MOTTLED

Red

A tangerine shade is preferred in Burmese, with less rufousing than is seen in other breeds. Exposed skin may show some freckling, and tabby markings are tolerated on the face, although they are a fault elsewhere. The short Burmese coat will not camouflage vestigial tabby markings, so a good Red is to be prized.

EARS TILT FORWARD

Head
Short, blunt wedge

Ears
Medium-sized, rounded at tip

Body
Strong, muscular, surprisingly heavy

Color
All colors must be solid to roots

Eyes
Large, widely spaced, and slightly slanted

WIDE-SET EARS

Muzzle
Blunt, with deep chin

OVAL PAWS

Underparts
May be slightly lighter than rest of coat

Coat
Short and fine, lying close to body

KEY FACTS

DATE OF ORIGIN 1930s
PLACE OF ORIGIN Burma (now Myanmar)
ANCESTRY Temple cats, Siamese crosses, household cat crosses
OUTCROSS BREEDS None
OTHER NAME None
WEIGHT RANGE 8–14 lb (3.5–6.5 kg)
TEMPERAMENT Friendly and relaxed

BREED COLORS

SELF AND TORTIE COLORS
Brown, Chocolate, Red, Blue, Lilac, Cream, Brown Tortie, Chocolate Tortie, Blue Tortie, Lilac Tortie

CHOCOLATE TORTIE

CREAM

BROWN

LILAC

TONKINESE

SOME BREEDERS DISPUTE WHETHER THESE CATS CAN IN FACT BE called a breed. As a hybrid of the Burmese (*see page 182*) and the Siamese (*see page 188*), Tonkinese inevitably produce variants in the pointing patterns of both their parent breeds. But this is hardly the first breed to produce variants, and the softly pointed "mink" pattern is not the only distinguishing feature of the breed. Their type is a blend of their parent breeds, less angular than one but lighter than the other, and their temperament has all the lively curiosity and affection of an Oriental breed, without the more vociferous traits. They also possess an attractive and distinctive eye color that is often referred to as "aqua." With its pleasing looks and friendly temperament, it is small wonder that the "Tonk," although it has yet to achieve full championship status in some registries, is already one of the more popular breeds.

BREED HISTORY

Some breeders believe that the "Chocolate Siamese" of the 1880s were in fact Tonkinese-type Siamese-Burmese hybrids, but this is unprovable. The first documented Tonkinese seen in the West was Wong Mau, the mother of the Burmese breed imported from Rangoon. Her natural hybrid characteristics were bred out of her offspring, however, and not until the 1950s did work begin to recreate this blend through controlled breeding programs. Early work was carried out in Canada, and the breed was first recognized by the Canadian Cat Association. Today it is accepted by all major registries, although there is still considerable variation in the acceptance of colors. British authorities, for example, accept all the colors that already exist in the Burmese. There have been two attempts to produce a longhair of this pattern, the Silkanese and the Himbur, but neither gained the popularity of the Tonk.

Brown or Natural Mink
Called sable in the Burmese and seal in the Siamese, this color has two names in the Tonkinese – natural mink in North America and brown elsewhere. It should be a light brown with darker seal points and matching seal nose leather and paw pads. The type of the Tonk is well muscled and medium-foreign. There is a slight difference between North American and European cats, perhaps reflecting the difference in Burmese type: European Tonks tend to be slightly more angular than their transatlantic counterparts.

Ears
Slightly taller than wide, with broad base and oval tips

Head
Moderate wedge with slight nose break and whisker pinch

Eyes
Upper edge oval, lower edge rounded, blue-green in color

Pattern
Darker points merge gently into lighter body

Body
Medium to long, muscular, surprisingly heavy

Coat
Short, silky, and close-lying

Tail
Equal to body in length, neither heavy nor thin

Legs
Slim, well-muscled, and in proportion, with oval paws

Chocolate Tortie

The pointing is less apparent when overlaid with tortie or tabby coat patterns, but the mask and legs should still be darker than the body. Tonkinese eyes may be a light aqua blue, as in this cat, but Siamese-blue eyes are not allowed.

Cream

The standard for this color in the Tonkinese calls for a "rich, warm" tone, shading to paler cream. The points may be less even than in other colors, with the legs being lighter than the mask and tail. As in all breeds, it is difficult to eliminate tabby markings completely from creams and reds, and slight markings are allowed in cats that are excellent in other respects.

KEY FACTS

DATE OF ORIGIN 1960s
PLACE OF ORIGIN United States and Canada
ANCESTRY Burmese and Siamese
OUTCROSS BREEDS Burmese and Siamese
OTHER NAME Once called Golden Siamese
WEIGHT RANGE 6–12 lb (2.5–5.5 kg)
TEMPERAMENT Sociable and intelligent

BREED COLORS

SELF AND TORTIE MINK COLORS
Natural, Blue, Chocolate (Champagne), Lilac (Platinum)
Red, Cream, Cinnamon, Fawn, Torties
Pointed and sepia patterns

TABBY COLORS (ALL PATTERNS)
Colors are as for self and tortie

BLUE	BROWN TABBY	CHOCOLATE	LILAC TORTIE

Lilac

The body of the lilac is a pale, dove gray with a pinkish cast, and the points are a darker shade of the same color. Kittens are often lighter than adults, although they should develop distinct pointing fairly early. Eye color can range from light blue to the green seen in this individual, but any tinge of yellow is unacceptable. The exact shade is not related to the coat color.

Red

The light red body shades to darker points, although the legs may not show much shading. Slight freckling may appear on the nose leather, lips, eyelids, ears, or pads of reds and creams: this is not penalized in mature cats. Reds and creams are not universally accepted in North America.

SIAMESE

POSSIBLY THE WORLD'S MOST INSTANTLY RECOGNIZABLE CAT BREED, the Siamese has had its share of controversy. The first cats often had crossed eyes and kinked tails; the early breed standards even required these traits, as well as legs that were "a little short." Since then, selective breeding has altered the cat considerably – crossed eyes and kinked tails are now rare, and regarded as a serious fault – but the build of the cat is a matter of dispute. North American cats take the GCCF Siamese look – a svelte body, long, slim legs, and a long head with slanting eyes and a fine muzzle – to greater extremes. All Siamese still have the gregarious, chatty nature for which they are famous: this is the most vocal breed, even strident in its talking. It is also one of the most sexually precocious, often mating by five months of age.

BREED HISTORY

Siamese originated in a mutation in Asia over 500 years ago. The mutation may have been widespread; in the late 1700s, the naturalist Pallas described a white-bodied cat with dark ears, feet, and tail in central Asia. In Thailand, however, these cats were revered by Buddhist monks and royalty. They made their way to the West in the late 19th century, appearing at a British show in 1871. Originally the Siamese included solid colors; these are now known as Oriental Shorthairs (*see page 192*). New colors have been bred (*see page 190*), and the longhaired Balinese (*see page 136*) has won recognition. The popularity of the breed peaked in the 1950s. Some attribute a decline in the fortunes of the cat to the move toward an "extreme" look. In 1987, a group of breeders formed TCA to breed "old-style" or "applehead" Siamese.

Prestigious pet

The Siamese has long been among the preferred pets of stars from Jean Cocteau to Anna Pavlova, seen here with her kitten. Even today, the Siamese can still count celebrities such as actress Anjelica Huston among its fans.

Lilac Point

In 1896 a cat was disqualified from a show for being "not quite blue" – some shows did accept blue points. It is possible, but by no means certain, that the cat was an unrecognized lilac point. The American standards call for a white body, while the English allows slight shading.

Chocolate Point

With points the color of milk chocolate on a ground of ivory, this color was not accepted in the United States until 1951. It may have been carried recessively from the start; dark chocolate points could have passed for poor seal points.

GLOSSY SHINE

Body
Medium-sized, long, and svelte

Coat
Very short and fine, with no undercoat

FINE TIP

Tail
Long, tapering, and free of kinks

Legs
Hind legs longer than forelegs

Paws
Small and oval

Changing looks
This 1930s lithograph by Jacques Nam, although slightly stylized, shows a Siamese far heavier than the show cats of today. Artists' works are open to interpretation, but old photographs and films also suggest a less fine-boned cat.

Siamese head
The long head should have good width between the ears, tapering down to a fine muzzle. In profile, the nose is straight, with only the slightest change in direction at eye level. The head is carried on a slender, elegant neck.

PRICKED TIPS

WIDE BASE

Ears
Follow lines of face outward

Eyes
Oriental in shape, slanted in set

DEEP, BRILLIANT BLUE

Head
Long, narrowing to muzzle in straight lines

Mask
Clearly defined, covering whole face

Blue Point
Records of blue points go back at least as far as 1903; given that Thailand's other famous cat, the Korat (see page 176) is blue, it is likely that the dilute gene came to the West with the Thai cats, rather than being introduced after arrival. The blue of the Siamese points is lighter than that found in solid-colored coats.

Seal Point
The classic color, this is the Siamese that has appeared in films, advertisements, and cartoons. Genetically, this color is black, translated into a dark seal brown by the Siamese pointing gene. For a time, this was the only Siamese accepted; other colors existed, but were usually classified as "any other variety," and records are unclear as to what they may have been. For some, this color remains the only "true" Siamese.

Original standard
The Thai Cat Book Poems (see page 92) show a short-legged cat with a pure white body and dark ears, tail, and paws only; this is because the Siamese is paler in warm climates. The first Siamese to reach the West were Seal Points that resembled the book's renditions.

Legs
Slim, in proportion to body

Points
All dense and matching in shade

KEY FACTS

DATE OF ORIGIN Pre-1700s
PLACE OF ORIGIN Thailand
ANCESTRY Household and temple cats
OTHER NAME Royal Cat of Siam
OUTCROSS BREEDS None
WEIGHT RANGE 6–12 lb (2.5–5.5 kg)
TEMPERAMENT Energetically enterprising

BREED COLORS

SIAMESE POINT COLORS
Seal, Chocolate, Blue, Lilac,

OTHER COLORS (COLORPOINT SHORTHAIR IN CFA)
Red, Cream, tortie and tabby versions of all colors
Cinnamon, Fawn, Smoke, Silver and bicolor versions

CHOCOLATE TORTIE POINT | CREAM TABBY POINT | LILAC TORTIE TABBY POINT | CHOCOLATE TABBY POINT

NEWER SIAMESE COLORS

NEW COLORS AND TABBY STRIPES HAVE AUGMENTED THE original four Siamese colors (*see page 188*) since the 1960s. "Shadow-points" and silver-points also exist, but have never won wide recognition. These pointed cats live under two names. In Britain and mainland Europe, all colors are classified as Siamese, and pointed Oriental Shorthairs are also classified and registered as Siamese. In North America, TICA also follows this method, but CFA classifies only the eumelanistic colors as Siamese and calls all others Colorpoint Shorthairs, relegating pointed Orientals to the "any other variety" category. One body of opinion suggests that, as with the Asian Group, there could be an Oriental Group, with pointed, solid, shorthair, and longhair divisions. This is the strategy taken by TICA. Regardless of name, these cats are Siamese both in spirit and in conformation. Actively inquisitive, often resoundingly vocal in their demands, they are absurdly gregarious in their relationships with people. Like the Siamese, these cats live long lives, but they may be more prone than other breeds to inherited heart disease (*see page 66*), and amyloidosis, which causes lethal deposits in body organs.

Chocolate Tabby (Lynx) Point
Tabby points, called lynx points in North America, have been known since the turn of the century, but were generally ignored. A litter of seal tabby points was shown in 1961 in Britain, bringing renewed interest, more active breeding, and acceptance a few years later.

SOLID-COLORED TIP

Cinnamon Point
The cinnamon point is one of the newest colors. The body is ivory and the points a warm cinnamon brown; as in the chocolate point and the caramel point, the legs may be slightly paler than the other points.

Red Tabby Point
Tabby versions of all the point colors are now generally accepted. In all, especially the red and cream, the legs may be paler than in solid points. Shading on the body should be no more than in solid points, but it should follow tabby patterning.

Blue Tortie Point
The introduction of the red gene inevitably led to tortie points; one of the first outcrosses produced a half-Siamese tortoiseshell. Each point must show some mingling of color, even if only on pads. Colors need not be evenly broken.

Lilac Tabby (Lynx) Point

The points should all show tabby markings, but these should not extend over the body; in particular, the frown lines on the forehead should not extend over the rest of the head. The lilac tabby lynx point has pinkish gray markings on a magnolia ground, with faded lilac or pink nose leather and paw pads.

Fawn Point

Another very recent color, this is the dilute of cinnamon. The standard calls for "rosy mushroom" points against a magnolia body color. As in many lighter colors, the legs may be paler than the mask and tail.

Cream Point

Crosses to Red Tabby Persians brought this gene into the Siamese in the 1930s, but the controversial color faded into obscurity. It was re-created in the late 1940s, but the loss of body type from the outcrossing was a problem for a time. This color gained general recognition in the mid-1960s.

FRECKLING ON FACIAL SKIN ALLOWED

Seal Tortie Tabby (Lynx) Point

In these cats, the coloring may be mottled, mingled, or patched. The degree of patching is not a prime consideration, as long as it is present; the tone of the colors is more important.

COAT SHADING DEEPENS WITH AGE

ORIENTAL SHORTHAIR

EVERY OWNER CAN TELL YOU THAT THIS BREED'S FAVORITE PLACE is between you and your book, or newspaper, or keyboard. These active and athletic cats are also outrageously gregarious – breeders call them shameless flirts. In physique and temperament, the Oriental is a Siamese (*see page 188*), but in solid coat colors. There is some dispute over the status of the pointed Orientals that do crop up; most fancies classify them as Siamese, but the CFA in North America does not allow this. Like Siamese, Orientals can suffer from inherited heart problems, but they have impressively long lives, belying their appearance as a delicate breed.

BREED HISTORY

The historical *Cat Book Poems* (*see page 92*) show Siamese or Thai cats in varied colors. Today, over half of their descendents are self or bicolor, and fewer than a quarter are pointed. There were solid cats among the first Siamese to be brought to the West, but in the 1920s the Siamese Club of Britain vetoed "any but blue-eyed Siamese," and their numbers declined, although blacks and blues may have been bred in Germany until World War II. Work on a solid chocolate in Britain in the 1950s led to the Chestnut Brown Foreign, recognized in 1957 and the origin of the Havana Brown (*see page 171*). Until recently, the breed was called "Foreign" in Britain and "Oriental" in America: the British change will remove confusion.

Ears
Large, pricked, continuing lines of head

EARS WIDE AT BASE

Eyes
All Orientals have green eyes

Head
Long, triangular wedge, described by straight lines

SLANTED, WIDE-SET EYES

Brown Spotted Tabby
Oriental Spotted Tabbies were once called Maus, but they were confused with the Egyptian Mau breed in the United States (see page 204). Their spots should be round, clear, and evenly distributed.

KITTTENS MAY HAVE SOLID SPINAL LINE

LONG, SLENDER NECK

NECKLACES ARE ACCEPTABLE

Blue Oriental
Blue cats were imported from Thailand in the 1800s, but these could also have been Korats (see page 176). There could be no confusing the breeds now; the blue Oriental has the characteristic elongated build and slanted eyes of the breed.

Legs
Long and slim, but muscular

SMALL, OVAL PAWS

TRIANGULAR FACE

Tail
Long, tapering to point

Chocolate (Havana or Chestnut Brown)

This rich, warm-toned brown, genetically a chocolate, was called Havana by early breeders, but then recognized as the Chestnut Brown Foreign, reverting to its present name in 1970. This color is still referred to as chestnut by CFA, although TICA uses chocolate.

NOSE AND
CHIN ALIGN

KEY FACTS

DATE OF ORIGIN 1950s
PLACE OF ORIGIN Great Britain
ANCESTRY Siamese, Korat, Persian, Shorthairs
OUTCROSS BREEDS Siamese
OTHER NAME Previously called "Foreigns" in Britain
WEIGHT RANGE 9–14 lb (4–6.5 kg)
TEMPERAMENT Devoted and demanding

BREED COLORS

SELF AND TORTIE COLORS
Black, Chocolate, Cinnamon, Red, Blue, Lilac, Fawn, Cream, White, Tortie, Chocolate Tortie, Cinnamon Tortie, Blue Tortie, Lilac Tortie, Fawn Tortie
Caramel, Apricot, Caramel Tortie

SMOKE, SHADED, AND TIPPED COLORS
Colors are as for self and tortie, excepting White

TABBY AND SILVER TABBY COLORS (ALL PATTERNS)
Colors are as for self and tortie

BICOLORS
All recognized colors with White

SILVER SPOTTED TABBY BLUE AND WHITE CHOCOLATE TORTIE RED MACKEREL TABBY

Body
Medium-sized, long, and svelte

Coat
Very short, fine, and glossy

Lilac or Lavender

The dilute of the chocolate, this color was one of the first to be developed in the 1960s. Historically it has been called lavender and frost as well as lilac. As with all dilute colors, any faint tabby markings are more easily seen, so good color is quite an achievement.

COAT IS FROSTY, PINKISH GRAY

COLOR OF COAT MUST BE EVEN

HIND LEGS LONGER THAN FORELEGS

Foreign White or Oriental White

This color is the last one where different names still exist. It is called Oriental White in some countries, and in most countries it may have green or blue eyes. In Britain, only blue eyes are allowed, and the designation "Foreign" has been retained to acknowledge this.

Black or Ebony

In sleek, solid black, the Oriental build resembles nothing so much as an Art Nouveau poster come to life. The entire cat must be solid, jet black, from the tips to the roots of the coat and from the eye rims to the paw pads. Eyes of brilliant, unflecked green stand out dramatically against this background, making a very striking cat.

NEWER ORIENTAL COLORS

NEW COLORS AND PATTERNS CONTINUE TO BE DEVELOPED within the Oriental Shorthair breed. Many of the genes for these cats have been present since Our Miss Smith, the breed's Siamese founding mother, gave birth to green-eyed, brown-coated kittens in the 1950s. Since then, other genes have been intentionally added. The smoke coat, which has a shimmering presence only apparent in the short, close-lying fur when a cat is moving, and other silvered types resulted from the accidental crossing of a Siamese to a Chinchilla Persian (*see page 104*), an outcross that also introduced the longhair gene responsible for the Oriental Longhair (*see page 142*). Today there are over 50 recognized coat colors, and this number will probably continue to increase. Bicolors are accepted by North American associations, but not in Britain; matings were made in Britain in an attempt to create a "Seychellois" breed, with Van patterning on an Oriental body, but the program never reached fruition.

Red and White
Because pointed Orientals are registered as Siamese, some British breeders are reluctant to develop bicolors, fearing that very slight spotting might pass unnoticed in a Siamese out of bicolor lines, only to emerge more strongly in future generations.

Red
As in other Oriental breeds, sex-linked red colors made a late appearance, even though this gene does exist in the cat populations of Asia. The coloration should be as even as possible, but tabby markings are tolerated in otherwise good cats.

FRECKLING ALLOWED

Apricot
A recent addition to the Oriental color range, apricot should be a reddish cream. It is darker and warmer in tone than a true cream. The genetics behind this color are still disputed among breeders.

TABBY RINGS

LONGER HAIR
ON BELLY THAN
ELSEWHERE

Chocolate Silver Tabby
In silver tabbies the color is restricted to the tips of the hairs, and the undercoat is white. Although the contrast between the markings and the base is quite clear, the color may be so restricted that the pattern cannot be distinguished on the flanks.

WHITE
UNDERPARTS

Cinnamon
Although the cinnamon color was not present in the earliest Orientals, it was one of the earlier colors added to the range. The gene was introduced in the 1960s, by crossing Havanas to Sorrel Abyssinians (see page 172), which are genetically cinnamon.

Chocolate Classic Tabby
The earliest Oriental tabbies were of the spotted pattern, but since then classic, mackerel, and ticked patterns have all been added to the range. Oriental tabbies often have white lips and chins, but this should not extend over the muzzle or throat.

WHITE
LIPS

JAPANESE BOBTAIL

PLAYFUL AND AFFECTIONATE, THIS BREED IS A DISTINCTLY ATTRACTIVE companion. The Japanese Bobtail's ancestors were portrayed in ancient art (*see page 38*), and superstition may have played a role in the perpetuation of its most notable characteristic, its short, 3–4 in (8–10 cm) tail. In Japan, a cat with a bifurcated tail (one with two tips) was considered a demon in disguise (*see page 30*). Cats with normal tails may have been persecuted, but those with short tails left alone, which would have led to more successful breeding among Japan's short-tailed cats. The Bobtail is seen everywhere in Japan as the famous *Maneki-neko*, or beckoning cat, popular as a good-luck symbol (*see page 31*).

BREED HISTORY
In Japan, legend holds that cats arrived in the Japanese Archipelago from China in AD 999, and that their ownership was restricted to aristocrats for the next five centuries. In reality, cats had arrived hundreds of years earlier, and ownership was more general (*see page 24*). Among the original feline immigrants from mainland Asia there were individuals with stumpy or "bobbed" tails. Within the restricted gene pool that existed in Japan, the recessive gene for the bobbed tail flourished in the cat population. In 1968, American breeder Elizabeth Freret established the first breeding program outside Japan. Recognized in North America, the breed is not yet accepted in Britain.

Red Tabby and White
The Bobtail has undergone some changes since its arrival in the West. Like this male, the original cats were less delicate in appearance, with broader faces and shorter legs. Breeders have worked to refine these features, and the breed is now quite distinct from simple bobtailed cats from Japan.

KEY FACTS

DATE OF ORIGIN Pre-19th century
PLACE OF ORIGIN Japan
ANCESTRY Household cat
OUTCROSS BREEDS None
OTHER NAME None
WEIGHT RANGE 6–9 lb (2.5–4 kg)
TEMPERAMENT Vibrantly alert

BREED COLORS

SELF AND TORTIE COLORS
Black, Red, Blue, Cream, White, Tortie, Blue Tortie
All other self and tortie colors, pointed, mink, and sepia

TABBY COLORS (ALL PATTERNS)
Colors as for self and tortie

BICOLORS
Above accepted colors with White
All other colors and patterns with white

BROWN MACKEREL TABBY

BLACK AND WHITE

Eyes
Large, oval, and distinctly slanted

HIGH CHEEKBONES

Ears
Large, widely spaced, and upright

Head
Balanced triangle with curved sides and long nose

Body
Long, straight, and slender

Coat
Medium-short, with negligible undercoat

Legs
Long and slender, but not dainty

Tail
Short, with fanned hair resembling pom-pom

Mi-ke
Tortoiseshell and White Bobtails, known as Mi-ke in Japan, are the most prized coat color and pattern. Odd-eyed Mi-ke cats are even more valued than their blue- or gold-eyed counterparts. The cat should resemble a porcelain figurine, with a pure white coat and dramatic splashes of rich color.

LA PERM

FOR CENTURIES, REX MUTATIONS HAVE OCCURRED AND THEN vanished into the random-breeding feline population. The advent of breed registries changed the situation. Since the first major rexed breeds, the Cornish (*see page 198*) and the Devon (*see page 200*), became established, many more have appeared. The La Perm is undoubtedly the most quirkily named of these, and in some ways the oddest in expression. The coat goes through many changes in appearance early in life before it settles into the distinctive adult curls, which resemble a new permanent wave, hence the name. The La Perm is descended from farm cats, and the standard describes them as working cats and "excellent hunters." There are both longhaired (*see page 143*) and shorthaired versions of La Perm: the soft hair of the shorthairs may be more wavy than curly.

BREED HISTORY

In 1982, a working farm cat in The Dalles, Oregon, produced a litter of six kittens that included a single bald kitten. In spite of this disadvantage, the kitten survived, and at the age of eight weeks she finally grew a coat. But this coat, unlike that of her littermates, was curly and soft to the touch. Linda Koehl, the owner and founder of the breed, named this kitten Curly. Over the next five years, Koehl produced more curly-coated kittens, which became the basis of the breed. The gene is dominant, so wide outcrossing to increase the gene pool can be done while still producing reasonable numbers of rexed kittens. The breed has been recognized by TICA.

KEY FACTS

DATE OF ORIGIN 1982
PLACE OF ORIGIN United States
ANCESTRY Farm cats
OUTCROSS BREEDS Nonpedigreed cats
OTHER NAME Also called The Dalles La Perm
WEIGHT RANGE 8–12 lb (3.5–5.5 kg)
TEMPERAMENT Affectionate and inquisitive

BREED COLORS

SOLID COLORS
All colors/patterns, including sepia, pointed, and mink

SILVER TORTIE TABBY | BLUE | BLUE-CREAM | CINNAMON SILVER

Ears
Medium-sized, with wide base and rounded tip

Eyes
Large, almond-shaped, and slightly slanted

Head
Broad, modified wedge, with prominent muzzle

Neck
Long, and carried vertically

Body
Medium-boned, muscular, and heavy for size

Coat
Short, thick, and silky, with moderate undercoat

Legs
Medium-length and well-muscled

Paws
Medium-sized and round

Tail
Long and tapering, with wavy hair

FULL WHISKER PADS

Brown Tabby kitten
With its softly wedge-shaped head, the La Perm has a foreign look, especially apparent in kittens. Some kittens may go through an almost bald phase, yet will become very curly as they enter adulthood.

Red Tabby
Rexed coats tend to obscure the clarity of tabby markings, and the La Perm is no exception. Frown lines on the forehead and "mascara" lines on the temples and cheeks remain clear, as do the rings on the tail and bars on the legs, where the hair is shorter or less curly. There is no relationship required between the eye and coat color.

CORNISH REX

EXTROVERTED AND CURVACEOUS, WITH WASHBOARD WAVES OF HAIR, the Cornish Rex is a showstopper. The coat lacks guard hairs and is gloriously soft to touch, much like cut velvet. But the breed also has a distinctive physiognomy; dramatic, large ears are set high on a relatively small head, and the arched body is set on fine, lean legs. Although the coat is the same on both sides of the Atlantic, the conformation is slightly different. In contrast to the less delicate appearance of their British relatives, American cats have a "tucked-up" torso, which makes them resemble the feline equivalent of a greyhound, an impression in keeping with the breed's lively behavior. This is an Olympic jumper, which thinks nothing of springing from the floor to your shoulder to greet you.

BREED HISTORY

In 1950, Serena, a farm cat from near Bodmin, Cornwall, had a litter with one curly-haired male kitten, Kallibunker. Her owner, Nina Ennismore, recognized this as similar to the "rex" mutation in rabbits. Breeding Kallibunker back to his mother confirmed that the trait was recessive. Descendents were crossed to British Shorthairs and Burmese. In 1957, the Cornish Rex arrived in the United States, where Oriental Shorthair and Siamese lines were introduced. A similar rexed breed was known in Germany, developed from a stray adopted by breeders in 1951. Crossing with the Cornish produced rexed kittens, revealing that both breeds had the same mutation; the German breed has since dwindled. The Cornish Rex is not related to any other rexed breeds.

Ears
Large and cupped, set high on head

HIGH CHEEKBONES

Eyes
Oval, set at slight slant

Head
Egg-shaped, with curved skull and Roman profile

Neck
Slender and elegant

Body
Small to medium and muscular, with fine boning

Coat
Short and velvety, with regular waves

Legs
Long and very slender

Tail
Long and slender, tapering to fine tip

Paws
Small and oval

Tortoiseshell

In finely built breeds, such as the Cornish Rex, the breed standards favor female cats. This Tortoiseshell shows the typical Cornish arch of the spine and upward tuck of the belly which is visible as part of the Cornish Rex normal stance.

HIND LEGS LONGER THAN FORELEGS

SLENDER, TUCKED TORSO

Black Smoke and White

The absence of guard hairs makes the white undercoat of Smoke and Silver colors particularly apparent in the Cornish Rex. This cat shows the typical North American conformation, with dramatically large ears, finely chiseled facial features, and a racy build.

Ears
Large, wide at base, with rounded tips

EARS SET HIGH ON HEAD

Head
Medium-length, with rounded muzzle and strong chin

Eyes
Medium-sized and oval

British profile
In contrast to the curves of North American cats, the British standard for the Cornish Rex head requires a wedge shape with a flat skull, a curved forehead, and a straight nose. British cats also have smaller ears.

White
This male typifies the moderately foreign look of the British type. While the build should be slender, the body is strong and distinctly muscular, and the legs should not be overly long and fine. The original Cornish Rex, Kallibunker, had a distinctly foreign appearance, but the look of the breed was defined by the cats used in the early development of the breed, as well as later breeding choices on each side of the Atlantic.

Body
Medium-sized, hard and muscular

Coat
Short, plushy, and silky

Tail
Long, fine, and tapering

HAIR CURLS ON TAIL

Paws
Small and oval

Red Smoke
Cornish Rex carry their bodies very high on their legs, with the spine in a gentle arch. The waves of the coat are most apparent over the back and rump. The red gene was present in the breed from Kallibunker's own offspring.

KEY FACTS

DATE OF ORIGIN 1950s
PLACE OF ORIGIN Great Britain
ANCESTRY Farm cat
OTHER NAME None
OUTCROSS BREEDS None
WEIGHT RANGE 6–10 lb (2.5–4.5 kg)
TEMPERAMENT Enterprising acrobat

BREED COLORS

All colors and patterns, including pointed, sepia, and mink

CINNAMON SILVER   TORTIE AND WHITE   CHOCOLATE POINT

DEVON REX

STARTLING, DRAMATIC EYES AND STRIKINGLY OVERSIZED, LOW-SET ears give the Devon Rex the look of an elfin clown. Its coat ripples, unlike the waves of the Cornish Rex (*see page 198*). Good breeding has greatly improved the coat; it now matures in four months rather than a year, and is very rarely patchy. Due to outcrossing with a variety of breeds, including the Persian, in the 1960s, longhairs sometimes occur. The coat has led to claims that the Devon is nonallergenic, but this can never be guaranteed. Breeders are unanimous that Devons never sit around looking elegant and bored; they are seldom elegant and always find life amusing. This, together with their coat, earned them the nickname "poodle cats." Typical breeder descriptions are "lovable slobs" and "love babies." Perhaps they should add "extraterrestrials"; a Devon was the chosen pet in the otherworldly epic *Dune*. Superman also rescued one from a tree in the 1984 film, so Hollywood certainly likes this breed.

BREED HISTORY

In 1960, Beryl Cox found a curly-coated cat near an old mine in Devon, southwest England. A mating to a local female gave a normal litter with one curly-coated kitten, named Kirlee. The gene has been shown to be recessive; Kirlee's parents were almost certainly closely related, and inbreeding was needed to perpetuate the Devon Rex. The Coxes bred Kirlee to several Cornish Rex females, but all the offspring had straight hair; the Devon Rex gene is a different mutation, and the breeds have been developed as distinct types. The Devon was recognized in Britain within the decade; in North America it was not separated from the Cornish until 1979. Unfortunately, early inbreeding brought to light a genetic spasticity syndrome, which is being studied as part of the Feline Genome Project.

Silver Tortie Tabby
Wide outcrossing in the development of the Devon Rex gave it almost limitless patterns and colors. The curl shows up shaded colors well, and softens the markings.

Brown Tabby
The tabby markings on a Devon Rex will be most evident on the legs, where the hair is both shorter and less curly. All kinds of tabby patterns are allowed, but the ticked type is seen less often.

Ears
Large and very wide at base, tapering to rounded tips

BASE OF EARS "JUGGED"

EARS SET WIDE APART

GUARD, AWN, AND DOWN HAIRS ALL PRESENT

SLENDER NECK

Head
Wedge-shaped, with full cheeks and well-defined chin

CRINKLED WHISKERS MAY BREAK EASILY

BROAD CHEST

BODY CARRIED HIGH ON LEGS

Legs
Long and slender

Paws
Small and oval, with pads of any color

KEY FACTS

DATE OF ORIGIN 1960
PLACE OF ORIGIN Great Britain
ANCESTRY Feral and household cats
OUTCROSS BREEDS British and American Shorthairs (until 2003 in CFA)
OTHER NAME Nicknamed "poodle cats"
WEIGHT RANGE 6–9 lb (2.5–4 kg)
TEMPERAMENT Appealing clowns

BREED COLORS

All colors and patterns, including pointed patterns

WHITE

BLACK SMOKE AND WHITE

Red Tabby

This Red Tabby was a top show cat. He was kept unneutered for breeding, and has developed the "stud jowls" that are often seen in older toms. Neutered Devons keep the classic elfin face, and never have this very full-cheeked appearance.

STUD JOWLS

Devon Rex profile

The short, wedge-shaped profile, seen here in a blue, has a curving forehead, and a well-defined stop to the nose. The whisker pads are prominent; the whiskers themselves are coarse and brittle, and are easily broken.

Cream Point

The pointed colors are the result of crossbreeding with Siamese cats in the early development of the breed, now no longer allowed. The broad-chested body conformation of the Devon and its very distinctive "bulldog" stance are quite different from the Siamese, however. These colors were once called "Si-Rex," a term not used today.

Body
Slender, but hard and muscular

Coat
Very short, soft, and rippled or swirling

Black Smoke

The first Devon Rex to be bred, Kirlee, was a black smoke. Because of its curly coat, the Devon shows the smoke shading better than any straight-coated shorthair will, and the darker the color is, the more striking the contrast with the silvery white undercoat will be. An Oriental look has been a characteristic of these cats since the early days of the breed, but the elfin appearance of the face can belie the solidity of the body.

Tail
Long and tapering, the tail must be well covered but not bushy

UNDERPARTS DOWNY BUT NOT BALD

HIND LEGS LONGER THAN FORELEGS

Blue-Cream and White

The broad chest of the Devon Rex can be clearly seen here. Combined with its quite slender legs, this can make the cat appear bowlegged, but the legs do not really curve. There are no skeletal deformities associated with the breed.

SPHYNX

HAIRLESS CATS HAVE APPEARED WORLDWIDE AT DIFFERENT TIMES. Not truly hairless, the Sphynx is covered with short, silky, "peach-fuzz" down the texture of soft chamois or suede. Without the insulating protection of a coat, Sphynxes are vulnerable to both cold and heat and must be housed indoors. Each empty hair follicle has an oil-producing gland. With no hair to absorb the oil, Sphynxes need daily rubbing with a chamois. Proponents of the breed feel that its devoted and playful nature is just as unique as its attention-grabbing hairlessness.

BREED HISTORY

The first Sphynx, Prune, was born in 1966, but his line died out. In 1978, a longhaired cat and her hairless kitten were rescued in Toronto. The kitten was neutered, but his mother subsequently had other hairless kittens. Two were exported to Europe, where one was bred to a Devon Rex. Hairless offspring implied that this recessive gene was at the same locus as the Devon gene. One, nicknamed E.T., was agented by Vicki and Peter Markstein at the Madison Square Garden Cat Show in the 1980s. Today the breed is recognized only by TICA; many other groups fear potential health problems. In Britain, GCCF registers the Sphynx to ensure that the gene is not carried into Devon Rex lines.

Blue-Cream and White

Sphynx show colors on their skin just as other breeds do on their hair; with no tweezing out of stray white hairs possible, these cats show the naked truth. The natural absence of hair apart from "peach-fuzz" down is vital – any evidence of hair removal is strongly penalized in shows.

Blue

Colors in the Sphynx are often warmer than they are in cats with coats, because the natural pink of the skin shows through. A Blue like this one may, in some lights, look closer to a Lilac in other cats.

Ears
Very large, wide at base, and open

Head
Slightly longer than it is wide, with high cheekbones

FINE HAIR ALLOWED ON EARS

Eyes
Large and slightly slanted

Coat
Apparently hairless, but has fine down

POWERFUL NECK

Sphynx head
The jugged ears, large eyes, and elfin face of the Sphynx show the influence of the Devon Rex. Its whiskers, if there are any, are often brittle and broken.

Body
Rounded, hard, and muscular

Tail
Tapering and whiplike

Legs
Firm and muscular

Paws
Oval, with long toes and thick pads

KEY FACTS

DATE OF ORIGIN 1966
PLACE OF ORIGIN North America and Europe
ANCESTRY Nonpedigreed longhair
OUTCROSS BREEDS Devon Rex
OTHER NAME Once also called Canadian Hairless
WEIGHT RANGE 8–15 lb (3.5–7 kg)
TEMPERAMENT Mischievous

BREED COLORS

All colors and patterns, including pointed, sepia, and mink

WHITE   BLACK   TORTOISESHELL

CALIFORNIA SPANGLED

THIS SOCIABLE AND ACTIVE CAT IS A SOLIDLY MUSCULAR BREED. The body is long and lean, but surprisingly heavy for its size. The round head is reminiscent of many small wild cats, and the dense double coat was developed to mimic leopard markings, with spotting over the back and sides, and striping between the ears and down the neck to the shoulders. The wild appearance of the California Spangled indicates that the diversity of coats in the cat family has not been lost in the domestic cat. The breeding program has produced a kitten black at birth, except for its face, legs, and underbelly, maturing to show a coat that is similar to that of the rare African king cheetah.

BREED HISTORY

This breed is the creation of Californian Paul Casey, who set out to create a wild-looking spotted cat without wild cat bloodlines. Using nonpedigreed cats from Asia and Cairo and a range of pedigreed breeds, he produced the desired cat. It was launched in 1986 through the catalog of a department store, a move unpopular with other breeders. "Spangled" is an ornithological term for spotted. Rosetted and ringed coats mimic those of the ocelot, margay, and jaguar. The breed has not as yet gained wide recognition at home or abroad.

Gold kitten
All spotted tabby California Spangled kittens are born with their spots. Kittens with the "snow leopard" pattern are born white, and those of the "King Spangled" pattern are born black. Blue eyes will become green or golden as the kitten matures.

Royal mutation
The spots of the African king cheetah are joined together in rosettes. The same mutation has come to light in the Spangled gene pool. These King Spangled cats are not shown, but are being used in breeding studies.

Ears
Upright, with rounded tips, set far back on head

DARK RIMS TO EYES

Eyes
Oval and slightly slanted

Head
Wild in appearance, with broad, high cheeks and full whisker pads

Blue
The spots on a California Spangled vary in shape from round to oval or triangular: the wilder the appearance of the coat, the better. Investigation of patterns and development is still ongoing. The blue is not as cool as it is in many other breeds; in the paler areas some rufousing may be seen.

Body
Long and muscular

Coat
Short and sleek, but not close-lying

Legs
Medium-length and muscular, with tabby bars

Tail
Tapering from heavy base

KEY FACTS

DATE OF ORIGIN 1971
PLACE OF ORIGIN United States
ANCESTRY Abyssinian, Siamese, British and American Shorthairs, Manx, Persians, African and Asian street cats
OUTCROSS BREEDS None
OTHER NAME None
WEIGHT RANGE 9–18 lb (4–8 kg)
TEMPERAMENT Gently sociable

BREED COLORS

TABBY COLOR (SPOTTED)
Black, Charcoal, Brown, Bronze, Red, Blue, Gold, Silver

SNOW LEOPARD COLORS
Colors and pattern are as for standard tabbies

BROWN   SILVER   GOLD

EGYPTIAN MAU

MAUS LOOK SIMILAR IN MANY WAYS TO THE CATS FEATURED
on ancient wall paintings and scrolls in Egypt,
and in fact Mau is the Egyptian word for cat. Body
and face are both moderate in form, and the coat
has a spotted pattern in shades of the original brown
color. Only the eyes do not tally: early portraits have
wild-looking eyes, while the modern Mau has wide,
round eyes with a decidedly worried look. The helpless
expression is deceptive, however: this is an effervescent
and gregarious cat with a tendency to "chortle" to itself,
and an innate self-reliance carried from its ancestry.

BREED HISTORY

While all domestic cats trace back to ancient
Egyptian ancestors, the Mau is possibly the
breed that resembles them the most, and its
ancestors can still be seen on Egyptian streets.
Nathalie Troubetskoy, an exiled Russian, was
taken with the spotted markings of street cats
in Cairo and imported a female to Italy to mate
with a local tom. In 1956, she traveled to the
United States, where the kittens were registered
and shown the following year. The breed
received full recognition from CFA by 1977,
and is also shown in TICA, but remains almost
unknown in Europe. It has often been confused
with Oriental Spotted Tabbies (see page 192) in
Britain, since these were called Maus for a while.

Mau face
Moderate in shape, the face is neither
rounded nor wedge-shaped. The nose is
the same width from brow to tip, and
the muzzle flows smoothly from
the lines of the head. Strong
"mascara" lines
accentuate eyes.

Smoke
Mau Smokes differ from
smokes of other breeds.
Instead of being selfs with no
tabby markings, they show
tabby patterning. The result is
a charcoal gray cat with jet
black markings and a white
undercoat. The white undercoat
shows just enough to provide
contrast, and no more.

HIND LEGS
LONGER THAN
FORELEGS

Unique spots
Breed standards for the Egyptian Mau claim that
it is the only natural spotted breed. The various
definitions of what is a "natural breed" make
this a difficult claim to assess, but it is
certainly true that the Mau's spotting is
unique. Ideally, the spots, which may be of
any shape or size as long as they are clear,
should be distributed randomly on the
torso, not following the configuration of
either marbled or mackerel stripes.

Head
Medium, rounded
wedge without
flat planes

Ears
Medium to large,
upright or slightly
flared in set

YELLOW CAST IN YOUNG CATS

Eyes
Large, rounded,
and gooseberry
green in color

Nose
Smooth curve from
tip to forehead, with
no distinct break

Paws
Small and
dainty, very
slightly oval

LEGS ARE STRIPED

DARK TIP

Tail
Medium-length,
tapering from
base to tip

Body
Medium-sized,
well-muscled, neither
cobby nor foreign

Coat
Fine and silky, close-
lying, but not too short

Ancient model
*In ancient Egyptian art, such as
this depiction of Ra as a cat in
the Book of the Dead, cats are
striped or spotted. The classic
mutation became prevalent in
Europe and the United States,
but spotting remained common
in the cat's original home.*

Bronze
*There are only three color forms of the
Egyptian Mau, and bronze is the
most ancient-looking. Markings on
the flanks are random, but spots
along the spine run in symmetrical
lines, often joining into a dorsal
stripe at the start of the tail.*

Legs
Medium-length, with
good musculature

KEY FACTS

DATE OF ORIGIN 1950s
PLACE OF ORIGIN Egypt and Italy
ANCESTRY Egyptian street cats, Italian
domestic cats
OUTCROSS BREEDS None
OTHER NAME None
WEIGHT RANGE 5–11 lb (2.25–5 kg)
TEMPERAMENT Friendly and intelligent

BREED COLORS

SELF COLORS
Black occurs but is not accepted

SMOKE COLORS
Black

TABBY COLORS (SPOTTED)
Bronze

SILVER TABBY COLORS (SPOTTED)
Silver

OCICAT

MORE THAN JUST ANOTHER NEW BREED WITH UNUSUAL SPOTTING, the Ocicat is an excellent blend of the attributes of its Siamese (see page 188) and Abyssinian (see page 172) blood. Playful and curious, with a love of laps, Ocicats enjoy company, respond well to early training, and are not suited to prolonged solitude. They are muscular and surprisingly solid; males are much larger than females. The most distinctive feature of the breed is its spotting. The distribution should follow the classic tabby pattern, swirling around the center of the flank. Show-quality Ocicats must have perfect spots; cats with imperfect spotting are sold as pets, but numbers are still limited.

BREED HISTORY

The Ocicat is a happy accident. Virginia Daly of Berkeley, Michigan, crossed a Siamese with an Abyssinian, aiming to develop an Aby-pointed Siamese. The kittens looked like Abys, but when one was bred to a Siamese, the litter included not only Aby-pointed Siamese but also an odd, spotted kitten. Daly's daughter, noting its resemblance to the ocelot (see page 14), called the kitten an "ocicat." This first Ocicat was neutered and sold as a pet, but the mating was repeated, producing Dalai Talua, the foundation female of this still-rare breed. Another breeder, Tom Brown, helped to continue the Ocicat's development, introducing American Shorthairs (see page 160), and in 1986 the breed received its first recognition, from TICA.

The Ocicat head

The facial markings of Ocicats should be clear and detailed. The frown lines on the forehead are balanced by "mascara lines" on the temples and cheeks, and the dark-rimmed eyes are surrounded by "spectacles."

Head
Modified wedge with broad muzzle

Ears
Moderately large and set out at an angle

Eyes
Large, almond-shaped, and slightly tilted

Cinnamon
Breed standards for the Ocicat call for a distinctly wild appearance, with a graceful, athletic build. The markings, which show most clearly in the darker coat colors, start with intricate lines on the face, progress to spots on the body and bracelets on the legs, and end with brushstrokes and spots on the tail, which has a dark tip.

Neck
Graceful and arching

Body
Large, solid, and powerful, but graceful

Coat
Short, fine, and sleek

Legs
Medium-length and well-muscled

Paws
Oval and compact

Tawny or Brown
Genetically a brown tabby, this color is called tawny by CFA. It has black or dark brown spotting on a warm, ruddy background, showing the rich rufousing of its Abyssinian ancestors.

Lilac or Lavender
This dilute version of chocolate has lilac spotting on a background of pale buff or ivory. Allowance is made in the breed standards for the slightly softer appearance of the tabby markings that is almost inevitable in the dilute colors.

BROKEN
NECKLACES
DESIRABLE

KITTENS HAVE
DEEP EYE COLOR

KEY FACTS

DATE OF ORIGIN 1964
PLACE OF ORIGIN United States
ANCESTRY Siamese, Abyssinian, American Shorthairs
OTHER NAME Oci
OUTCROSS BREEDS Abyssinian (until 2005 in CFA)
WEIGHT RANGE 6–14 lb (2.5–6.5 kg)
TEMPERAMENT Social and responsive

BREED COLORS

TABBY COLORS (SPOTTED)
Tawny or Brown, Chocolate, Cinnamon, Blue, Lavender, Fawn
Classic and mackerel patterns

SILVER TABBY COLORS (SPOTTED)
Colors are as for standard tabbies
Classic and mackerel patterns

SELF COLORS
Colors as for tabbies

SMOKE COLORS
Colors as for tabbies

SILVER   FAWN

Blue Silver
The silver gene came into the Ocicat from American Shorthair outcrosses during the early development. All silver colors have a white ground, which shows off the markings dramatically.

Tip
Color of coat is shown most truly here

Cinnamon Silver kitten
Ocicat markings take time to develop. Kittens and young cats may show solid lines along the spine, which resolve into separate spots as the cats mature.

Tail
Fairly long and slender

BENGAL

STILL RARE WORLDWIDE, THIS BREED HAS A DISTINCTIVELY THICK and luxurious coat. Because of the wildcat origins of the breed, a dependable temperament is a vital feature of breeding programs. Although not recognized by all associations, Bengals are rapidly increasing in popularity. In Britain, for example, there are three separate breed clubs, although there are only a few hundred cats. Early breeding introduced genes – for dilution, long hair, and self color (non-agouti) – but also the Siamese coat pattern, which has resulted in the extraordinary "Snow" shades. With its robust good looks, the Bengal's future is promising.

BREED HISTORY
When Jean Sugden bought an Asian leopard cat (*see page 16*) in California in 1963 and bred it with a domestic cat, her concern was the conservation of the leopard cat. Ten years later, Dr. Willard Centerwall at the University of California continued this hybridization in order to examine the Asian leopard cat's resistance to feline leukemia virus. The research was disappointing, but out of these beginnings came the Bengal. Dr. Centerwall passed eight of his hybrids to Sugden, now remarried as Mill. The first Bengal, Millwood Finally Found, was registered by Jean Mill in 1983. Initially this was a nervous feline family, but development has led to a more outgoing breed. Early crosses were to nonpedigreed cats, but when the leopardlike coat appeared, individuals were crossed with an Indian street cat and Egyptian Maus (*see page 204*).

"SCARAB" LINES

GOLD, GREEN, OR HAZEL EYES

Bengal head
Slightly longer than it is wide, the Bengal's face has high cheekbones and a full, broad muzzle. The chin is strong, and widely set canine teeth help to produce pronounced whisker pads. Frown lines and broken streaks of color cover the head, and the "puffed" nose leather is pink outlined in black. In profile, there is a gentle curve from forehead to nose, rather than a break.

Blue-Eyed Snow Marbled
The Snows come from pointed lines in the nonpedigreed cats used in the Bengal's development. Breed registries are controlled to avoid such unexpected occurrences, but Bengal breeders have used this happy accident to create truly stunning cats. The color restriction should give an impression of "pearl dusting" to the coat; the pattern for these cats is as for their full-colored counterparts.

Brown Marbled
This pattern should suggest the coat of a wildcat, not the blotched or classic tabby pattern, and it should be distinct but not symmetrical. The markings should be clear, but, uniquely to the Bengal standard, cats should show three shades of color: the base, the dark markings, and darker outlines.

KEY FACTS

DATE OF ORIGIN 1983
PLACE OF ORIGIN United States
ANCESTRY Asian leopard cat, household cats, Egyptian Mau, Indian street cat
OUTCROSS BREEDS None
OTHER NAME Once called Leopardettes
WEIGHT RANGE 12–22 lb (5.5–10 kg)
TEMPERAMENT Elegantly conservative

BREED COLORS

SELF COLORS
Black color exists but is not accepted

TABBY COLORS (SPOTTED, MARBLED)
Blue, Brown, Snow

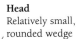

Head
Relatively small,
rounded wedge

Ears
Short, with wide
base and rounded
tips, no tufts

Tail
Thick and even,
with rounded tip

Eyes
Large and oval, with
slightly slanted set

Brown Spotted

The first coat to be stabilized, the Brown Spotted resembles that of the Asian leopard cat, right down to the light-colored "ocelli" on the back of each ear. The base color is buff and the markings are deep brown or black. Facial features are outlined in black, and the spots on the coat should be large, forming rings or rosettes, and randomly distributed; any resemblance to the vertical stripes of the mackerel pattern, the pattern behind many breeds, is to be avoided.

LARGE, BROAD NOSE

THICK, MUSCULAR NECK

BROAD
CHEST

Body
Large, very
muscular,
and sleek

Coat
Dense, soft,
glittery

FUR IS SHORT-
TO MEDIUM-
LENGTH

HIND LEGS
LONGER THAN
FORELEGS

Legs
Strong and muscular,
medium-length

LARGE, ROUNDED PAWS

AMERICAN BOBTAIL

THERE WERE, UNTIL RECENTLY, ONLY A COUPLE OF BOBTAILED or tailless breeds. But in the last few years, breeds from the former Soviet Union such as the Kurile Island Bobtail (see page 144) have become better known, and two new bobtail breeds have been registered in North America. The American Bobtail was the first of these. The genetic background of the breed is uncertain; bobcat parentage is unconfirmed, but both Manx (see page 154) and Japanese Bobtail (see page 196) genes may be present, since both completely tailless "rumpies" and cats with kinked tails appear. In contrast to the Manx breed standard, these rumpy Bobtails are not showable: the Bobtail should have a short tail that stops just above the level of the hocks.

BREED HISTORY

This breed can be traced back to a random-bred bobtailed tabby kitten that was adopted from an American Indian reservation in Arizona by John and Brenda Sanders from Iowa. Early work with the breed aimed to produce bobtailed cats with a pattern resembling the Snowshoe (see page 165), but the cats became inbred and unhealthy. Later work, led by Reaha Evans, reintroduced more colors and patterns, and improved the breed's health. TICA allows American Bobtails in the New Breed and Color class.

Classic Tabby longhair kitten

There are both longhaired and shorthaired divisions for the American Bobtail; because the longhair gene is recessive, there are fewer of these. The coat is semilong, and longer "muttonchops" on the cheeks are desirable. The Bobtail coat does not mat easily, although it appears shaggy.

KEY FACTS

DATE OF ORIGIN 1960s
PLACE OF ORIGIN United States
ANCESTRY Uncertain
OUTCROSS BREEDS Nonpedigreed cats
OTHER NAME None
WEIGHT RANGE 7–15 lb (3–7 kg)
TEMPERAMENT Friendly and inquisitive

BREED COLORS

All colors / patterns, including sepia, pointed, and mink

FAWN AND WHITE	BLUE TABBY	RED TABBY	WHITE

Spotted Tabby shorthair

The American Bobtail breed standard calls for a brawny, hearty, and wild-looking cat, with a strong head and a hunting look to the eyes. American Bobtails are a slow-maturing breed, and may take as long as three years to reach their full potential. The shorthair coat is long enough to stand away from the body and appear slightly shaggy.

Eyes
Oval and angled, with heavy brow

Ears
Medium-sized, wide at base, and set high on head

Head
Broad, modified wedge with curved contours

Coat
Resilient and double

Body
Semicobby, with substantial muscling

Tail
Must be present, but stops above hock

Legs
Heavy, with large, round paws

PIXIEBOB

Domestic-sized cats with a wild appearance have become increasingly popular over the last two decades; it was perhaps inevitable that North American breeders would eventually develop a cat that resembled the native bobcat (*see page 14*). Despite their wild looks, Pixiebobs are claimed to have the temperament of faithful dogs; breeders recommend that owners consider carefully before acquiring one, since they do not readily change homes, and are often happiest as a single-cat "ruler of the roost." The wild look is described as "essential to the uniqueness of this breed."

BREED HISTORY

The origins of the Pixiebob are reputed to be wild bobcat-to-domestic "barn cat" breedings that took place in rural areas, although DNA profiles have not provided supporting evidence. The assumed hybrid kittens are called "legend cats" because of the claims of wildcat ancestry. Two such cats were acquired in 1985 by Carol Ann Brewer in Washington State, who bred them to produce Pixie, the founding cat who gave her name to the breed. The breed was first allowed by TICA in the New Breed and Color class almost 10 years later, but is not known outside North America. "Legend cats" are still found in rural areas, and may be refined to produce Pixiebobs: no other pedigreed breeds or wild cats can be used.

KEY FACTS

DATE OF ORIGIN 1980s
PLACE OF ORIGIN North America
ANCESTRY Domestic cat, possibly bobcat
OUTCROSS BREEDS Brown tabby nonpedigrees
OTHER NAME None
WEIGHT RANGE 9–18 lb (4–8 kg)
TEMPERAMENT Quiet but affectionate

BREED COLORS

TABBY COLORS (SPOTTED, ROSETTE)
Brown
Any other tabby pattern, other colors

Brown Spotted Tabby kitten
Most kittens acquired for breeding have been given, rather than sold, to breeders by farmers who would usually have culled them. The hybrids seem to inherit the tractable natures of their mothers, rather than the wild characteristics of their putative fathers.

Brown Spotted Tabby
Any brown spotted tabby of suspected "legend cat" heritage can be used in breeding Pixiebobs. The look of these cats can vary, due to the parentage of domestic cat and possible regional varieties of bobcat. Coat markings are regarded as secondary to the physical conformation.

Pixiebob head
The facial markings must be strong in Pixiebobs, with "mascara" lines on the cheeks and light "spectacles" around the eyes. Lynx tips on the ears are desirable, but not essential. The lips and chin should be creamy white.

Ears
Wide at base, slightly rounded, and set far back on skull

Head
Wide, medium to large pear shape, with slightly curved contours

Eyes
Prominent brows above medium-sized, deep-set eyes

Body
Medium to large in size, substantial in build

Coat
Luminous quality, with much ticking

WIDE NOSE

Tail
Generally carried low

Paws
Polydactyls are accepted

Legs
Long and substantial

RANDOM-BREEDS

THE RANDOM-BRED CAT HAS NO ROMANTIC HISTORY OR ROYAL connections to beguile the public, yet the "household pet" is still the most popular and widely owned cat worldwide. Type tends to vary from place to place, with stocky, sturdy cats found in cold countries and lighter, more slender cats much in evidence in warmer climates, but the extremes of cobbiness or elongation that have been selectively bred into the pedigreed breeds are most unusual in these cats. Typically Oriental colors and pointed patterns remain rare in Western nonpedigreed cats, although these genes have occasionally filtered from pedigreed breeds into the general population through the determined ingenuity of all felines in matters of mating. Occasionally, nonpedigreed cats may closely resemble particular breeds but, for the most part, these felines are only reminiscent of the breeds that emerged from their stock.

Cream Tabby
In the first pedigreed cats, creams were often regarded as poor reds, because their color was warm and orange, but too light for a real red. Over the decades, breeders have bred out the red tones to produce paler, cooler coats in pedigreed creams. However, random-bred individuals will still show the orange hues of those early cats.

Brown Classic Tabby and White
In Europe, the classic tabby came to outnumber the mackerel tabby by the 18th century. It has been suggested that, because it is darker than the mackerel pattern, the classic coat provided better camouflage in the urban environment. Breeds such as the European Shorthair (see page 166) are not so very far from their roots in these cats.

Red Classic Tabby and White

Because the white spotting gene is dominant, bicolors are common in domestic cats. Reds vary in distribution from area to area within most countries, and can help to indicate whether adjacent cat populations are interbreeding or not. Breeds such as the American Shorthair (see page 160) grew from sturdy domestic cats like this one.

Blue and White

Blue is a common color in many areas of mainland Europe, and the Chartreux (see page 168) was developed from such stock. Many random-bred cats are a much darker blue than pedigreed breeds, and lack the intense and varied eye colors achieved by dedicated selective breeding. The build of this cat is heavier than that of mainland European breeds, but would not disgrace a British Shorthair (see page 152).

Tortoiseshell and White

Northern European cats tend to have small amounts of white in their coats; in southern Europe predominantly white patterns, reminiscent of the Turkish Van (see page 126), are more common. Without selective breeding, polygenic factors have a large influence on coat: this cat's plumy tail might indicate that it is genetically a longhair, even though the coat on its body remains short and soft even in winter.

CHAPTER SIX

CARING
FOR
YOUR CAT

CATS THAT ARE KEPT FOR COMPANIONSHIP
depend upon us for food, shelter, and
freedom from illness or suffering. Choose a
cat that fits into your family life. Some
require extensive grooming, others
demand considerable attention, while all
need balanced nutrition and both mental
and physical stimulation. Be very careful if
your cat goes outdoors; natural predators or
cars are likely to be the greatest dangers.
Understand the principles of first aid and
train your cat to meow when you call its
name. For most cat owners, these are
satisfying responsibilities, forming the basis
of our bond with this fascinating creature.

ABOVE KITTENS SHARING A SAUCER OF MILK

LEFT KITTENS NEED A PLACE TO CALL HOME

CHOOSING A CAT

YOUR CHOICE OF CAT DEPENDS UPON AESTHETIC AS WELL AS MORAL decisions. A cat's looks are important: the choice of size, color, coat length, even sex, is highly personal. Equally important are your moral decisions. Do you want to offer a home to a lost or unwanted feline? Do you want your cat to live safely indoors or have more risky but potentially more exciting outdoor life? Do you want your cat neutered or do you feel that this is "unnatural"? Owning a cat is a considerable commitment, and it is important to answer these surprisingly difficult questions before making your decision on who to choose as your feline companion.

Perhaps the most common way for cats to enter our homes and lives is on their own terms – arriving at our doorsteps, willing acceptors of both food and affection. If, however, you have decided to acquire a cat, you have the luxury of making your own personal choice.

INDOORS OR OUTDOORS

Your first and perhaps hardest decision is whether to keep your cat indoors or allow it to roam outdoors. Until the 1950s, when cat litter became widely available, owners had little choice but to allow their cats outdoors. Surveys in the United States indicate that approximately 50 percent of cats now live exclusively indoors, a figure that surprises even the experts. Indoor living is partly a cultural phenomenon: American pedigreed cat associations strongly advise cat owners to keep their cats indoors. Dr. Nicholas Dodman, director of the Behavior Clinic at Tufts University School of Veterinary Medicine,

Feral cats and strays
If you acquire a stray from a shelter, find out about its background. Ferals, born and raised away from humans, will usually be apprehensive. Strays, which were initially raised with people, will be much more companionable.

notes that American cats have a much higher incidence of anxiety-related problems, such as urine marking, than British cats. He suspects that the reason for this is that many more British cats, pedigreed or not, are allowed outdoors.

Your choice of cat should be made on the foundation of its lifestyle. Raised from kittenhood, most cats willingly and contentedly live indoors, but cats that have experienced the thrills of outdoor life often find them difficult to give up.

RESCUED CATS

Cat rescue shelters often have feral cats needing homes. Mature ferals, raised outside human contact, are apprehensive. If you crave contact and feline affection, these individuals are not suitable pets for you. If, on the other hand, you enjoy the satisfaction of offering an independent creature a secure home and a regular supply of nourishment, it is highly rewarding to take on an adult feral. Initially, feral kittens under seven weeks old may hiss and spit, but will still have sufficient adaptability to accept and eventually enjoy some human companionship.

CATS AND OUR HEALTH

Many more people are likely to be allergic to cats than to dogs, because of their sensitivity to a protein in cats' saliva and skin. Cats are naturally hygienic animals, and cover their hair with saliva as part of their fastidious grooming routine. People with an allergy to cats should always keep them out of the bedroom, and wipe them at least daily with a clean, damp sponge to reduce the amount of saliva left on the hair.

Ritual cleansing
Cats wash themselves in a ritual fashion. First they lick their body, then paws, then use their licked paws to clean each side of their head.

Pedigreed cats
Pedigreed varieties of cats, such as this Korat, offer considerable advantages: known looks, size, and personality. To a limited extent, however, they have a higher incidence of inherited medical problems.

Nonpedigreed cats
Nonpedigrees, such as this red spotted tabby, form the genetic root stock for all pedigreed cats and exhibit most of the varieties of coat colors and textures.

Once they are beyond this age, it is more difficult for them to overcome their ingrained fears. Rescue shelters also have strays – cats that are familiar with people, born in other homes but now needing new ones. These cats can make extremely satisfying but often nomadic companions.

Happy families
Cats raised together from kittenhood make the best companions. If you are planning to introduce a kitten to your cat, find one that has stayed with its littermates until it is 12 weeks old.

NEW ADDITIONS TO THE FELINE FAMILY

If you think your resident cat will benefit from a feline friend, it is often advisable to think again. Not all cats want friends. A resident cat can be disconcerted when a new person or dog walks through the door, but indoor cats in particular are likely to be severely affronted if they find their territory being invaded by another feline.

When you bring your new cat home, restrict it to one room, leaving your resident cat to roam the rest of the home. Leave food near the closed door of the room for your resident cat to find; it will eventually associate the pleasure of food treats with the scent of the new cat. After a few days, allow your resident feline to enter the new cat's room, only when the new cat is in a deep sleep, and only for a look. Increase these exposures, leaving nothing to chance. These gradual introductions reduce the likelihood of fights, or of one cat simply leaving for new pastures.

MALE OR FEMALE

Most pet cats are neutered (called spaying in a female), but if you choose an unneutered male, remember that cats use urine to mark their territory. Male cat urine is particularly pungent. Some males are content to leave their urine only in their toileting sites, but others use it to spray objects such as fences, trees, or if indoors, curtains and walls. Unneutered males can be very affectionate with people but are most likely to fight with other cats. This is a serious problem, because fighting is the most successful way for potentially lethal viruses such as feline leukemia virus (FeLV) and feline immune deficiency virus (FIV) to spread from one adult to another. Unneutered males are more likely to be carriers of these viruses than neutered individuals. Neutering only moderately affects temperament and behavior, making both males and females slightly less excitable and more affectionate.

GROOMING REQUIREMENTS

The cat is "self-cleaning"; its barbed tongue is ideal for standard coats, fairly good for longer coats of heavy guard hair, but unfortunately inadequate when long coats consist of fine down. Cats with Persian-type coats are high-maintenance pets, and require careful, daily grooming. They are also prone to hairballs and need preventive attention for this problem.

Thin coats
Thin coats evolved in hot climates. Consequently, breeds such as the Singapura retain their thin coats only in temperate or warm climates.

Long coats
Some longhaired breeds need moderate grooming, but this Longhair requires daily, whole-body grooming.

Short coats
When allowed outdoors in cold climates, the British Shorthair naturally develops a thick, insulating down.

Neutered cats
The neutered cat, male or female, is more easygoing, friendly, hygienic, playful, and affectionate than unneutered individuals.

Unneutered cats
Unneutered males develop visible secondary sex characteristics such as cheek jowls, thick neck skin, and heavier muscles. Unspayed females are much more excitable in temperament than spayed females.

HOUSEHOLD HARMONY

When choosing a cat, consider the reaction of the whole household to a new feline and vice versa. If you have a dog and acquire a new cat, plan its introduction carefully. Train your dog to accept the cat's presence. Regardless of size, your dog is likely to be dominated by the cat but remember that even the best-trained dog will sometimes give chase to its "own" cat.

HEALTH CHECKUP

Ask your vet to examine your chosen feline's eyes, ears, nose, mouth, and body for any signs of disease or parasites. If your cat is pedigreed, ensure the viral health status of its parents by asking the breeder for proof of their virus-free condition. Most pedigreed cats will have been vaccinated before leaving the breeder; ask for a vaccination record and show it to your vet.

Living with other animals
Most dogs accept cats into their homes, but some, especially terriers, can be troublesome. It is wise to supervise all initial contact. Restrict your cat to one room, and when it is asleep, allow your dog to see and sniff it.

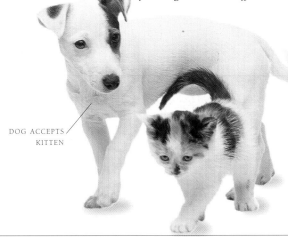

DOG ACCEPTS KITTEN

EQUIPMENT AND SAFETY

CATS NEED LESS ATTENTION THAN DOGS BUT THAT DOES NOT MEAN they should simply be ignored. We are always responsible for their safety, health, comfort, and security. Although we are seldom legally responsible for our cat's actions, as cat owners we have moral responsibilities to our neighbors. Ensure that outdoor cats are controlled as best as possible. This is most easily accomplished through neutering and by providing a litter box that your cat finds appealing. All cats need mental as well as physical stimulation. Spend quality time playing with your cat; it is invigorating for your pet as well as relaxing for you, and reinforces bonding.

Cats like to have their own bowls, bedding, and toilet. Food and water bowls should be easy to use and simple to clean. In multiple cat households, each cat should have its own bowl. Most cats willingly select cat litter over hard floors because it feels natural, and allows them to bury their droppings. Many types of cat litter are widely available. Some contain deodorizers, while others are reusable and washable.

OUTDOOR SAFETY

Most injuries to outdoor cats are caused by road accidents. In cities, "high-rise syndrome" (*see page 65*) is also common. Falls from four to seven floors are usually lethal but some cats survive even greater falls because they have sufficient time to relax. Avoid this risk by making windows cat-proof. Many outdoor cats get lost; ensure that your cat can be identified.

TYPES OF CAT LITTER

Cat litter should be an absorbent substance with a pleasant odor, but cats and owners are likely to have differences in olfactory opinion. The best way to control odor is by frequent cleaning. If cats are used to one type of litter, they often prefer its continued use.

REUSABLE   FULLER'S   LIGHTWEIGHT   WOOD-
       EARTH   BASED

Suspended "spider"
Virtually all cats are captivated by movement. Dangling a suspended toy just out of reach of your cat will provide it with endless excitement.

Feline utensils of choice
Research shows that most cats prefer to eat from shallow plates or bowls. Use utensils made specifically for feeding cats rather than dogs.

KITTENS SHARING LITTER BOX

TOYS FOR MENTAL STIMULATION

Outdoor cats find mental stimulation in natural activities such as hunting or simply patrolling their territory. Indoor cats have the same needs which, if they are not met through planned activity, can be released in behavior that might seem reasonable to the cat but is unacceptable to its owner: activities such as stalking, biting ankles, or pouncing on precious objects.

Creative toys offer an enjoyable release for these behavioral needs. Invest in a selection of toys that will stimulate your cat's natural inclination to stalk, chase, grab, and bite in a safe context.

Fun and games for felines
Cats will play happily with a variety of toys, but the common denominator in their enjoyment is movement, whether it is from a brightly colored ball that skids across the floor with a deft flick of the paw, or a high-tech toy mouse that is activated either by paw or battery.

GLOVE TOY

"FISH" ON ROD

"SNAIL" ON ROD

CAT TRIES TO CATCH MOUSE

CAPTIVATED KITTEN

BRIGHTLY COLORED BALLS

PREVENTIVE MEDICINE

Prevention is always more effective than cure. Ensure that your cat is vaccinated against feline diseases, use safe and effective methods to prevent flea eggs from hatching and biting, and worm outdoor cats according to veterinary advice. Cats that hunt and eat wild prey can carry toxoplasmosis, a condition they may pass to humans in their feces. This is a potential health hazard to unborn babies; pregnant women should wear rubber gloves while gardening and cleaning the litter box.

PROTECTING THE YARD

Training your cat to use a litter box should deter it from fouling the yard. If it persists, place chicken wire under the soil. In established yard areas, lay strips of chicken wire, plastic mesh, or gravel between and under plants.

MICROCHIP

Vital information

All cats, even indoor cats, should carry identification in case they become lost. Engraved tags or canisters containing vital information can be worn on the collar, or identifying microchips may be inserted under the neck skin.

IDENTIFICATION TAG   IDENTIFICATION CANISTER

Safe and easy access

A cat-flap is better for home security than an open window. Some cat-flaps are "personal," and are only activated by a small magnet on the cat's collar.

Artificial nails

Declawing is restricted mostly to North America and is rare in Europe, Japan, and elsewhere. Stick-on nails are a painless alternative, and will last for about six weeks. With just a little practice, they are easy to apply.

CLAW IS SHEATHED BY ARTIFICIAL NAIL

Starting from scratch

All cats scratch, both to renew their nails and to leave visible marks on their territory. In the home, provide attractive scratching posts and locate them in prominent places where your cat can use them undisturbed. Once your cat has started to use the scratching posts, move them almost imperceptibly, day by day, until they are in the position that you find most convenient.

SAFETY IN THE HOME

ATTRACTIVE GREEN LEAVES

House plants

Most cats will want to chew on house plants, so avoid toxic ones. Provide grass in pots or non-toxic plants such as the spider plant for safe chewing.

Always check your clothes washer and dryer before use, in case your cat has hopped in for a snooze. Train your cat not to jump on the stove by leaving double-sided adhesive tape on all work surfaces; landing on it should deter most cats.

Spray electric cords with commercially available nontoxic taste deterrents. Deny your cat access to garden chemicals, antifreeze in the garage, and your car engine compartment.

Most cats are uninterested in babies, but some are attracted by their warmth; netting over a baby's crib will keep a cat at bay. Observe how children behave with your cat: young children can be annoying and risk being scratched, while older children may tease and endanger cats. Never use a "dog" flea spray, powder, shampoo, or liquid on your cat unless it is specifically licensed for use on cats. Many of these products, although safe for dogs, are potentially toxic to felines.

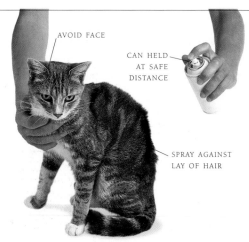

AVOID FACE

CAN HELD AT SAFE DISTANCE

SPRAY AGAINST LAY OF HAIR

Flea-spraying safety

Always use a recommended flea spray on your cat. Avoid organophosphate sprays; they are poisonous when ingested, and your cat will naturally want to lick itself after spraying. Never spray your cat's face; spray onto a cloth, then wipe over the facial area.

FEEDING AND NUTRITION

THE EVOLUTIONARY DEVELOPMENT OF THE CAT HAS CREATED SOME exacting nutritional requirements. It must eat meat to survive, and it needs the essential amino acid taurine. Whole rodents and birds offer excellent nutrition but are not practical foods for most pet cats, and a diet based on our food is invariably inadequate.

Cat food manufacturers have carried out extensive research into feeding demands; well-balanced commercial cat food ensures nutritious, tasty diets for cats at all stages of life. Most cats prefer to eat from shallow bowls; many dislike eating from plastic dishes because they retain the smell of food and detergent.

There are two types of diets: homemade and commercial. Homemade diets, unless based upon sound nutritional knowledge, rarely provide a sufficiently balanced diet for a feline. Cats will not naturally select what is best for them; they will select what they like and will sometimes refuse to eat anything else. If a cat becomes "addicted" to a single fresh food, such as tuna, it may develop a nutritional deficiency disease. Commercial diets are formulated to be complete; manufacturers blend carefully chosen ingredients to provide the optimum nutritional content in their cat foods.

PREPARED FOOD AND FOOD FORMULAS
Dry "premium" brands are the most palatable and energy-rich, a combination that may lead to obesity if offered on demand. All reputable manufacturers test their foods in feeding trials to determine palatability, digestibility, and their effect on cats with widely differing energy requirements.

Some cat foods are based upon variable recipes, others on fixed formulas. So-called premium foods always have fixed formulas, but this does not necessarily mean that their nutritional content is superior to varied-formula foods.

UNDERSTANDING CAT FOOD LABELS
Most labels on cat food include a contents analysis and an ingredients list. Nutritional recommendations are given on a dry-matter

Unfair competition
Although most domestic cats will eat together without jealousy, it is sensible to feed them separately. This reduces the inclination to gobble food and ensures that even the smallest cat gets a sufficient share of the meal.

Food treats
Cats, like humans, enjoy snacks. Major cat food manufacturers produce a variety of dry or semimoist treats. It is claimed that some of these complementary food treats keep a cat's teeth clean and tartar-free.

TYPES OF COMMERCIAL FOOD

Commercial cat foods are available in three different textures: canned or wet, semimoist, and dry. Each type of commercial food is similiar in nutritional value. Canned or wet foods, especially those with a high jelly content, are often the most appealing to felines; jelly is a texture that cats seem to enjoy. Some cats do not find dry foods particularly palatable, while others will eat nothing else. Semimoist foods

are generally considered less palatable to cats than canned or wet food. Dry foods may help to prevent tartar buildup on the teeth, which can lead to gum disease and tooth decay, but they are also associated with more concentrated urine production. When deciding on whether to feed your cat one or several forms of commercial food, consider its personal tastes and preferences, as well as your lifestyle and financial resources.

CANNED WHITE FISH
CANNED POULTRY
CANNED TUNA
CANNED LAMB

Dry foods
These foods contain about 6–10 percent water. They are the most convenient type of commercial food, but water must be freely available. The dry foods shown above are a complete dry food for a cat (left) and a complete dry food for a kitten (right).

Semimoist foods
Varieties of semimoist foods contain 25–40 percent water. They used to contain the ingredient propylene glycol, which is now known to lead to blood problems in felines. The semimoist foods shown above are beef-flavored (left) and chicken-flavored (right).

Canned or wet foods
These commercial foods contain 75 percent water, often providing enough for a cat's daily fluid requirement. Canned or wet foods are the most palatable to cats, but will not stay fresh in the bowl for more than a few hours. In hot weather they dry and attract flies.

The glories of catnip

Most cats adore the aroma of catnip (Nepata cataria). When rubbed or chewed, catnip provokes a "pleasure" response in cats, such as rolling around or purring ecstatically. Catnip contains a mild hallucinogenic chemical, nepetalactone, which might cause the apparent euphoria.

Special kitten needs

Kittens need food that is high in energy, both to grow and to maintain good health. Many large pet food companies produce special foods formulated for a kitten's specific nutritional requirements. Most kittens can be fed on demand, because they will stop eating when their stomachs are full.

FELINE ENERGY REQUIREMENTS

KITTEN AGE	ENERGY REQUIREMENT KCAL/DAY		
TWO MONTHS	175		
THREE MONTHS	260		
SIX MONTHS	280		
ADULT WEIGHT	**6 LB**	**9 LB**	**14 LB**
INACTIVE	125–175	200–280	325–455
ACTIVE	175–225	280–360	455–585
PREGNANT FEMALE	250	400	650

basis, without any water content. Adult cats need a diet containing 30 to 45 percent protein and 10 to 30 percent fat. Growing kittens need 35 to 50 percent protein and 17 to 35 percent fat. Analyses on labels are not on a dry-matter basis, but you can request information from the manufacturer to check whether the food meets feline nutritional requirements. Cat food labels often include statistics on ash, once suspected of contributing to feline lower urinary tract disease (FLUTD). It is now known that one specific component of ash, magnesium, contributes to FLUTD, so check labels for a low magnesium content.

HOME-PREPARED FOOD

With a little help from a veterinarian or an animal nutritionist, you can design a well-balanced, homemade diet for your cat. This must be meat-based, to provide essential fats and amino acids; a feline cannot survive on a vegetarian diet. Do not make major substitutions to the ingredients in the diet without consulting your nutrition advisor first.

SPECIAL DIETS

A variety of special diets are available. Some manufacturers specialize in "natural" diets; these foods are expensive because of the cost of the best-quality ingredients and sophisticated manufacturing processes. Other companies provide a range of foods specifically formulated for cats with a range of medical- or age-related conditions. Such special diets include low-calorie foods for overweight cats; low-phosphorus, low-protein foods for cats with kidney problems; and diets that ensure acidic urine production or the smooth functioning of the digestive tract. Special diets should be fed only under veterinary supervision.

Occasional salads

Plants are part of a cat's diet; they are a satisfying foodstuff, and may also be used to induce vomiting. Indoor cats should be provided with boxes of fresh grass to chew. In its absence, most felines are likely to chew on household plants, an expensive and potentially toxic habit.

DIET FOR THE OLDER CAT

Obesity is not a significant problem for older cats; they tend to lose weight in old age rather than gain it. Weight loss might be caused by medical problems such as overactive thyroid glands or failing kidneys but it also occurs because the digestive function simply declines. Senior cats should be offered energy-dense diets consisting of easily digestible protein and fat.

A natural diet

If your cat hunts and eats its prey, take this into consideration when calculating its food requirements. A mouse provides almost ideal nourishment for a cat: protein in the muscles, and essential fats, vitamins, and minerals in the bones, intestines, and internal organs. Eating the bones will also help to keep the cat's teeth clean.

GROOMING

CATS WITH LONG, LEAN BODIES AND SHORT COATS NEED ONLY A little grooming for hygienic reasons; brushing the coat once a week will stimulate the oil glands, remove dead hair, and keep the coat lustrous. Cats with dense or long coats need more frequent grooming, while older cats need more attention to their teeth, nails, and anal regions. From the time your feline arrives in your home, train it to accept combing, dental attention, and nail clipping. Always use food treats and play as rewards for good behavior. Grooming reinforces your cat's relationship with you, reducing your blood pressure and that of your cat, a potent sign of relaxation.

GROOMING A LONGHAIRED CAT

Routine, simple grooming is an excellent opportunity to bond with your cat; it is an activity that should always be relaxing and pleasurable for both parties. Regular grooming keeps your cat in pristine condition and warns you of possible medical problems. Evolution has equipped the cat with its own grooming tool: the barbed tongue. Consequently, cats are magnificently self-cleaning and self-grooming.

However, this evolutionary grooming tool is inadequate for felines with dense or long coats; these individuals require their owners' aid in the judicious use of a wide-toothed comb and a bristle brush. Older felines with dense coats will require even more grooming assistance from their owners. Longhaired breeds with heavy, predominantly guard-hair coats need frequent brushing, and grooming around the ears and legs is necessary at least weekly.

All cats with soft, Persian-like coats are high-maintenance pets. They have long, fine down hair, which can easily become matted. This requires daily, whole-body grooming in order to prevent serious tangles. These felines are also prone to hairballs, which are potentially dangerous if ingested; therefore preventive grooming is necessary. Although the grooming steps in the sequence below are for a longhaired cat, they can be followed for all types of coats.

1 Use a wide-toothed comb to comb the fur between the hind legs, behind the forelegs, and behind the ears; knots are common in these regions. Next, comb the fur on the abdomen; many cats are sensitive in this area, so be gentle.

2 Tangles develop at the wispy ends of the hair on the top of the neck and back. Working on one section at a time, part the hair and comb gently upward from the roots. This removes loose hairs at their source and helps to eliminate knots.

3 As you complete each section, part the hair and ensure that the skin is healthy. Tease out remaining tangles by hand. Check for tiny specks of shiny, black dust. If you find any, your cat and its environment need treatment for flea infestation.

4 Comb the hair upward behind the ears and over the ruff to enhance this area and remove any tangles. Knots and mats are common in both these regions, because a cat cannot groom them; they are inaccessible to the reach of its tongue.

5 Finally, groom the tail. Do not simply brush along its length; many cats resent this method. Parting the hair and gently brushing it to either side is much less traumatic. Always finish grooming sessions with rewards of food and play.

GROOMING EQUIPMENT

For grooming, use a wide-toothed comb, then a bristle brush; a fine-toothed comb can be used to expose fleas. A child's toothbrush fits comfortably into a cat's mouth. "Guillotine" nail clippers cut nails without crushing.

TOOTHBRUSH

WIDE-TOOTHED COMB

BRISTLE BRUSH

"GUILLOTINE" NAIL CLIPPERS

TRIMMING THE NAILS

Outdoor cats benefit from sharp claws; they are part of its natural defenses, and assist it in climbing. If you keep your cat indoors, trim its nails routinely. Older cats often grow long nails, which may curl in and penetrate the paw pads. Although nail trimming is painless, cats rarely enjoy it, so start training early. Accustom your feline to having its paws handled and its nails extended. Always use a comfortable "guillotine" nail clipper, but if the nail has grown into the pad, consult your veterinarian. If your feline is a "wriggler," vary the location in your home where you clip its nails so that it does not learn to associate a particular site with the activity. Trim the nails when your cat is relaxed and reward compliance with food treats and play.

1 Cats naturally retract their claws. To extend each nail, press gently behind the claw to expose the brown to white tip and pink central core or "quick" of the nail. The "quick" is living tissue and must be avoided when cutting the nail.

2 Position the clippers over the nail and in front of the "quick." Squeeze firmly, cutting straight across the claw. Speak reassuringly to your cat while you are trimming its nails, and reward it with food treats and play when you are finished.

BRUSHING THE TEETH

Overwhelmingly, the most common reason why cat owners visit the veterinarian is tooth and gum disease. Tooth enamel erodes, exposing the living pulp within; gums become infected, producing disease and foul breath. The most effective way to prevent oral problems is by brushing your cat's gums and teeth. Begin with mock brushing, then graduate to cleaning the teeth several times each week. Always reward good behavior.

1 A cat usually resents oral attention, so train it to associate teeth and gum cleaning with simple rewards. Using a cotton swab scented with pet toothpaste or even tasty food, gently massage the gums and teeth.

2 Once your cat tolerates the cotton swab in its mouth, graduate to using a soft, child's toothbrush. Gently massage the gums and brush the back teeth, the region where tooth resorption and gum disease most commonly occur.

CLEANING THE EYES, NOSE, AND ANUS

Most felines have superb anatomy but human intervention has led to eye and nose problems in some breeds. In the relatively flat-faced breeds, tears overflow and normal nasal secretions crust around the nostrils. Tear overflow produces a mahogany-colored discoloration to the hair around the eyes. A cotton ball dampened with antiseptic eyewash solution can be used to remove excess tears, clean the nasal fold, and remove crust from the nostrils. Consult your vet if your cat has a chronic tear overflow, or suffers from frequent sneezing or nasal discharge. Excessive licking of the anal region indicates that the anal sacs are blocked. Your vet can show you how to empty impacted anal sacs manually.

CLEANING THE EARS

Ear mites are the most common cause of gritty, dark wax in a cat's ears; consult your vet for treatment. An excess of normal but oily and irritating ear wax is common, particularly in indoor cats. Use a recommended wax remover, then remove the excess wax with a soft cotton ball. Never poke a cotton swab into the ears: it pushes the wax into the ear canal.

TRAVELING AND TRAINING

CATS ARE REMARKABLY GOOD TRAVELERS, AND MOST OF THEM FIND trips interesting. Even those that prefer the security of home will simply hunker down and withdraw into themselves until the cat carrier is opened and normality returns. Because they are so adaptable, sedation before journeys, even those by airplane, is unnecessary, even counterproductive. New vistas will bring new risks, and cats are more likely to stray on new territory. By training your cat to come to you on command or to meow when it is called, you increase the likelihood of finding it if it disappears in fright. Begin training at an early age to ensure success.

Vacations are always a difficult time for pet owners. While dogs will happily travel long distances with the family, most cats tend to prefer their own territory, and unless your cat is particularly adaptable it is easier to leave it either at home or in a well-managed cattery. However, it is important that your cat is at ease with traveling, if only for those important visits to the vet. Plan ahead by accustoming your cat to its carrier. Use it as a cat bed at home so that the cat feels secure and content when in it, and considers it part of its own territory. If you do intend to travel frequently with your cat, you should get it used to car travel when it is young. This might entail taking the cat on short trips, or even driving around the block occasionally. Of course, never leave your cat in the car in hot or sunny weather. Because it cannot sweat it is at risk of heatstroke, and death can occur very quickly. Once you reach your destination, simply open the cat carrier and allow your cat to get its bearings at its own pace. Its natural curiosity should soon overcome its initial wariness, and it will emerge from the carrier when it is ready. Because cats can get lost in unfamiliar territory, you should always ensure that they wear a collar and an identification tag bearing up-to-date information.

BOARDING ALTERNATIVES

Alternatives to catteries include leaving your cat with friends, or asking neighbors or house-sitters to keep an eye on it. It is usually best for your cat to stay in its own home with a reliable person visiting each day to feed it, clean its litter box, and occasionally play with it. Leaving your cat with friends can be problematic if it is an outdoor cat. It will be unfamiliar with the new territory and if close enough to home may try to return there. Others may simply stray.

Wherever your cat stays, make sure that it is protected against contagious diseases and fleas. If traveling abroad, be aware that some of the necessary vaccination documents will need to be dated several months before departure.

Comfortable carrier
You should always use a travel carrier when you take your cat out of its home. Increase your cat's enjoyment of its carrier by leaving it open at home, filled with soft bedding and a few hidden food treats. If you use the carrier only to take your cat to the vet or the cattery, your cat is likely to disappear each time you take out the carrier.

TRADITIONAL WICKER CARRIER

DELUXE CARRIER WITH FEEDER

EASY-TO-CLEAN PLASTIC CARRIER

Hygienic accommodation
Good catteries are designed to permit a cat to move in and out of doors. Some will also have larger units for groups of cats that are used to living together. Cats that are not from the same household should never be kept in the same unit. Each unit should include both perches and hiding places, and central heating should be available when necessary. Always inspect a cattery for cleanliness. Feeding and drinking bowls should be spotless, and bedding should be disinfected for each new occupant. Be sure your cat is vaccinated against contagious diseases.

Types of cat carriers
Wicker carriers are attractive to you and your cat but can be extremely difficult to clean when soiled. Molded plastic cat carriers are easy to disinfect, not attractive to fleas, and easy to disassemble for storage.

TRAINING TO "COME" ON COMMAND

Cats can be trained, and training is fun for both of you, provided that you understand that cats do not respond to touch and kind word rewards in the way that dogs do. Cats really respond well only to food rewards. Needless to say, they never respond to punishment. Successful training involves conditioning your cat, using food treats, to respond to your command. Initially, the cat is rewarded each time it performs the behavior – coming forward to eat a food treat, for example. As it moves forward you say its name and the word "Come." When your cat understands what it must do to earn its reward, switch to intermittent rewards. Professional trainers often use "clickers." As the cat comes for its food reward, the trainer clicks the clicker. The cat learns to associate the click noise with the reward. After a while the food reward is phased out. The cat simply responds to the click sound. Training your cat to "Come" on command is vital to entice your outdoor cat indoors when you are going out. Train your kitten as soon as it arrives in your home.

1 Through trial and error, discover a food treat that your cat craves. Professional trainers often use pieces of liver, fried to a crisp. It is easy to accustom a young kitten to the flavor of yeast-based vitamin tablets. Begin by feeding treats from your hand, then raise your hand so that your cat rises up to get the treat. You may wish to incorporate a clicker noise as professional trainers do.

CAT RISES UP TO HAND

RAISE HAND ABOVE CAT'S HEAD

STAND BACK AND CALL CAT

CAT COMES FORWARD FOR REWARD

2 Once your cat has learned to love the food treat, show it the treat, then take a step back and say "Come" as it moves toward you. If you are using a clicker, click it as your cat takes the necessary step forward. Over successive training periods, increase the distance until your cat comes from another room. Each training session should never be more than a few minutes long.

CAT IS ATTRACTED TO REWARD

REWARD NOT GIVEN EVERY TIME

CAT MEOWS IN RESPONSE TO HEARING ITS NAME

"MEOW" ON COMMAND

Life is endlessly interesting for a cat, but sometimes its curiosity can lead it into situations that it finds frightening. A cat's natural response to fear is to hide, usually in some small, dark corner. Unfortunately, cats sometimes find it easier to get into hiding places than to get out of them, and may need to be rescued from an awkward spot. A cat may also be so frightened that it simply does not want to leave the security of its hiding place. Fortunately, cats recognize human voices and can differentiate known from unknown ones. If your cat has been trained to meow when it hears its name called, it is likely to do so, even from its hiding place, when it hears a friendly voice that it knows.

1 Just as when training for any other activity, find a treat your cat adores and habituate it to that treat. If you have had success with the clicker, use it here, too. Call your cat's name and/or use the clicker as it comes forward. Always train in the quiet of indoors and never with any other animals around; otherwise, the cat will be easily distracted.

2 After your cat has learned to associate hearing its name or the click sound with the food reward, tease it a little with the food. Your cat may try to bat the food from your hand, but many cats that already use their voices to demand food will meow. Give the treat immediately. Reinforce the meow response by giving the food only intermittently during subsequent training. Gradually increase the distance between you and your cat until you are in separate rooms. Finally, move outdoors to continue training.

BEHAVIORAL PROBLEMS

MARKING TERRITORY WITH URINE, DIGGING TOILET SITES IN YARDS, preying upon songbirds, climbing curtains, scratching furniture, and even creating "Grand Prix" racing circuits in the living room are all natural feline behaviors. Cat owners, however, are likely to consider them problematic. True behavior "problems," such as compulsive grooming, obsessions with articles, or even psychosomatic illnesses, do exist but are relatively rare, compared with natural behaviors that we want to modify because we find them offensive. Use common sense and originality, never harsh discipline, to change your cat's behavior.

In most countries, cats historically have had the freedom to roam outdoors. In many countries, such as the United States, half or more of all cats never go outdoors; however, their need to hunt remains. In Australia, fears about the cat's predatory effects on ground-nesting birds and other species have led to laws restricting cats indoors during dusk and dawn, their favorite hunting times.

FORMS OF AGGRESSION

If a cat cannot hunt, it may satisfy its natural predatory needs by stalking, pouncing, and biting its owner's ankles or a resident dog's wagging tail. This unpleasant, antisocial behavior can be diminished by giving indoor cats an acceptable predatory outlet. Toy manufacturers have created a vast array of stalk-and-capture toys for felines, but even a simple table tennis ball with a few grains of rice inside will make a satisfying toy.

In Aesop's fable, *Belling the Cat*, mice try to outwit a cat by putting a bell on its collar, but there is no evidence that a "belled" cat is any less successful as a predator. Dr. David Paton at the University of Adelaide in Australia found that belled cats were just as successful as hunters as those without bells, perhaps because rodents and birds have not learned to associate the ringing of a bell with danger.

Predation is not the only form of aggression; others include aggression between two cats in a household (*see page 82*), maternal aggression, dominant aggression, fearful aggression, and, perhaps the most exasperating to owners,

Playing rough
The vast difference in comparative size does not stop this ginger cat from mock-biting its canine companion's leg in a predatorily aggressive but inhibited, playful manner.

Fearful aggression
This feline, ready to roll over and use all its claws, and with its ears folded back flat against its head for protection, shows fearful aggression.

petting aggression; having seemingly enjoyed being stroked, a cat suddenly lashes out with teeth and claws and jumps away, only to return seconds later for more petting. A possible cause of this behavioral quirk is conflict in the feline's mind. Being stroked is pleasurable; it is reminiscent of its mother's grooming. However, cats have evolved to have no body contact with other cats in adulthood other than during mating, an occasion particularly fraught with conflict. Petting aggression can be avoided by restricting your stroking of prone individuals to short episodes.

Jailed frustration (left)
When an indoor cat spots natural prey but cannot stalk and pounce, its teeth may chatter. This unusual response does not occur when predation is possible.

Scent marking (right)
Cats spray urine on upright objects such as walls, chairs, and curtains to mark their territory. Neutering can diminish this behavior.

Scratch happy
All cats scratch, both to unsheathe their claws and visibly mark their territory. Unfortunately, an indoor cat is likely scratch furniture, carpets, or curtains. This natural behavior can be prevented by training your cat from an early age to use a scratching post, and by trimming its nails regularly. Use blunt, stick-on "artificial nails" on felines that persistently prefer to scratch your furniture rather than their own.

Although most cats willingly eat together in a multicat household, feeding can become competitive and potentially intimidating. If your cat eats quickly and then vomits its food, feed it smaller quantities more often.

PSYCHOSOMATIC ILLNESSES

Dr. Tony Buffington, a veterinarian at Ohio State University, has described a form of bladder inflammation in cats that is not related to diet or microbes, but responds to "anti-anxiety" drugs. In certain felines, even mild stress can bring on an episode of cystitis (painful urination sometimes accompanied by bleeding into the urinary tract). Some veterinarians believe that cats can exhibit other medical manifestations of stress-induced anxiety, such as itchy skin or a tendency to vomit easily. The behavioral component of these medical conditions has not yet been studied, but it is possible that there are various feline behavioral problems that mask themselves as chronic medical conditions.

ELIMINATION PROBLEMS

Overwhelmingly, the most common behavior problems that frustrate cat owners are those concerned with elimination. Cats might decide to use places other than the litter box for toileting, possibly because they associate the tray with the pain of cystitis or blocked anal sacs. When medical considerations have been ruled out, examine the circumstances in which the problem occurs. Try different forms of litter to discover which your cat prefers. Keep the litter box clean and place it in a quiet location.

MARKING TERRITORY

Many cats scent mark their territory with urine. The urine marker does not squat in the normal bladder-emptying fashion. Instead, the cat backs up to a vertical object, raises its quivering tail, then pulsates a spray of urine against the object. Urine is intentionally left as a "calling card" for other cats. Scratching furniture serves a similar purpose. A well-scratched piece of furniture is a visible way of marking territory. These problems can be diminished or eliminated using "aversion" methods; a squirt from a water pistol or a sudden loud noise just as your cat takes aim or begins to scratch can be sufficiently offensive to stop the behavior. Neutering is the most effective way to reduce urine marking.

EATING PROBLEMS

Refusing to eat is the most common feline eating problem. Cats are adapted to go without food longer than we can; in a battle of wills between cat and owner, the owner usually gives in first, offering a *smorgasbord* of tempting delights.

When your vet has concluded that your cat's behavior is due to stubbornness, not illness, concentrate on the reasons why it will not eat. Never place food too close to the litter box. Do not position the feeding bowl in busy areas; cats like peace and quiet while they are eating. Ensure that the feeding bowl does not have an unpleasant smell; certain plastics hold odors that cats do not like. Feed two cats in separate areas to avoid rivalry.

Feline food obsessions (above)
When medical considerations have been ruled out, a refusal to eat tasty and nutritious food should be considered a behavioral problem. It often occurs when owners offer their cats a selection of foods from a large menu. Eventually, the cat may develop a food obsession, and refuse to eat anything but its favorite food.

In the genes (left)
If a kitten is taken away from its mother before completing its 12-week suckling period, it suckles its owner instead, "kneading" with its paws and sucking skin or clothes. Wool sucking in the Siamese breed is slightly different. Restricted to specific genetic lines, this activity begins in adulthood in cats weaned normally, rather than continuing from kittenhood in individuals weaned early.

SIGNS OF ILLNESS

IN THE PRESENCE OF SEVERE OR SOMETIMES EVEN DEVASTATING illness, felines will often pretend that nothing is wrong. From an evolutionary viewpoint, this has been a successful adaptation; they hide their illnesses and injuries from predators until they recover. In the newer context of living with us, however, this is unfortunate.

Without acute observation on our part, a cat may not be treated for an illness until the condition has reached an advanced stage. This makes a successful outcome less certain. All cats develop natural rhythms of life; be alert to even the slightest changes in your cat's behavior, and contact your veterinarian for advice.

The understanding of feline medical problems has increased dramatically in the last few years. New methods of diagnosis and treatment mean that, increasingly, it is possible to assess the nature of a problem accurately, and then successfully treat and correct it.

VIRAL COMPLICATIONS

The cat is the natural host to three potentially serious viruses: feline infectious peritonitis (FIP), feline leukemia virus (FeLV), and feline immune deficiency virus (FIV). Your cat may have bad breath caused by gum inflammation.

This could be caused by a soft diet, a flu virus, or any of the three serious "slow-acting" feline viruses. Without knowledge about the presence or absence of these three viruses, there is always an undercurrent of uncertainty, even when diagnosing seemingly minor medical problems.

Maternal danger

A female cat can transmit potentially lethal infections to her young just before, during, or shortly after birth. She may be a symptom-free carrier of feline leukemia virus (FeLV), feline infectious peritonitis (FIP), or feline immune deficiency virus (FIV). All cats, male and female, should be tested for these viruses before being used in breeding programs.

SIGNS OF DISORDERS

CLINICAL SIGNS	CAUSES	ACTION
SCRATCHING/ EXCESS LICKING	External parasites are the most common cause of scratching, but allergies to food or environmental causes may also be responsible. Cats lick most wounds thoroughly. Impacted anal sacs cause a cat to lick its anal region.	Check the skin thoroughly for signs of parasites such as specks of black, glistening flea droppings, and treat accordingly. If there is a small wound, see your vet. It may seem insignificant but there might be hidden damage.
EYE CONDITIONS	Viral, bacterial, and chlamydial infections cause inflammation and discharge. Many of these diseases transmit easily to other cats. Eyes may be injured or become inflamed through environmental irritation or allergy.	Vaccinate your cat to prevent against transmissible infections. Treat affected individuals with appropriate antibiotics or other drugs. Always have your vet examine any physical injuries to the eyes.
EAR CONDITIONS	Ear mites cause dark, gritty wax to build up in the ears. Cats scratch and shake their heads. Infections are common. Many older cats have benign tumors of the ear canal called ceruminomas.	Eliminate parasites with appropriate medications. Break down built-up ear wax with olive oil. Untreated chronic ear infections lead to ceruminomas, which may need surgical removal.
BAD BREATH/ DROOLING	Gum infection is the most common problem suffered by felines. Fetid breath is caused by bacteria multiplying at the tooth margins. Severe gum inflammation, which may be virus-induced, causes drooling.	Prevent gum disease by permitting your cat to exercise its teeth and gums; chewing on bones is the most effective and natural method, but beware of possible splinters. Viral gum disease needs veterinary attention.
SNEEZING/ NASAL DISCHARGE	A variety of viral and bacterial diseases cause sneezing or nasal discharge. Allergies and foreign objects such as blades of grass in the nose may also be responsible. Older cats can develop irritating nasal polyps or tumors.	Vaccinate your cat to prevent against transmissible diseases. If your cat has allergies, avoid allergens when possible or use antihistamines and other treatments to reduce irritation.
COUGHING/GAGGING	Coughing may be caused by a variety of medical conditions, including allergies, parasites, chest and upper respiratory infections, more serious chest complaints, or forms of heart disease.	Although it may simply be an allergic bronchitis, cats can suffer from a wide range of more serious chest complaints. If your cat is coughing, always consult your vet for an accurate diagnosis.
BREATHING DIFFICULTIES	Chest and upper respiratory tract infections may cause breathing difficulties. So too does asthma, a serious, even life-threatening problem. Trauma to the chest or diaphragm seriously affects breathing.	All breathing difficulties are serious. Your cat should be seen immediately by a veterinarian. Intervention with drugs or surgery is often vital to restore ease of breathing.
VOMITING	Occasional vomiting is often caused by diet or eating grass. Cats regurgitate hairballs, an action seemingly similar to vomiting. Persistent vomiting often has a metabolic cause elsewhere in the body.	Use cat laxatives for cats suffering from hairballs. Offer grass to eat. All cases of persistent vomiting should be seen by a veterinarian who will make an accurate diagnosis of the cause.

APPETITE CHANGES

Any change in eating and drinking habits is significant. Refusing to eat can indicate pain in the mouth, but it is often of greater significance. Asking to eat but then refusing is always a serious cause for concern. A cat may simply not like what it has been offered, but this behavior is sometimes associated with tumors in the abdomen's lymph nodes, a fairly common condition called lymphoma. Excess eating with weight loss is frequently associated with an overactive thyroid gland. Affected cats are usually over 10 years old, active, affectionate, and playful. Any increase in thirst should be reported to your vet. It may only be that the environmental temperature has increased, but it is more likely to be a significant sign of illnesses such as kidney or liver problems and different forms of diabetes. All of these conditions are relatively common in older cats.

Age-related weight loss

Senior cats commonly lose weight, but rapid weight loss is cause for concern. Combined with a good appetite, it may indicate an overactive thyroid, kidney problems, or other serious conditions.

Excessive licking

Cats are fastidious groomers and clean their coats by licking in a ritualized fashion. Excessive licking, however, may indicate local injuries or wounds, or the presence of skin parasites such as fleas and ticks.

Listlessness

Cats enjoy "cat-naps" throughout the day, but increased lassitude, listlessness, and sleeping, retiring to unusual places or hiding for no apparent reason, might be caused by illness. Consult your vet if you notice any change in your cat's daily routines.

Changed eating habits

Assume that your cat is ill if it eats or drinks less than usual, or refuses food and water. If it eats or drinks more than normal, it may have kidney or liver disease, or an overactive thyroid gland.

ALTERED BEHAVIOR

With a growing elderly cat population, heart problems are increasingly common. An affected cat often shows only the slightest change in behavior, possibly sleeping more, being less inclined to patrol its territory, or flopping when lying down rather than reclining gracefully. In severe cases there is coughing, and with accompanying weight loss the heart can be seen beating quickly through the chest wall. As soon as you see any changes in your cat's behavior, report them to your vet; you may be seeing a problem at an early stage, and it is always easier to treat health conditions sooner rather than later. One of the best methods of preventing disease is to arrange for routine medical examinations for all individuals over nine years old. With skillful diagnosis, age-related illnesses can be caught early and treated more effectively.

SIGNS OF DISORDERS

CLINICAL SIGNS	CAUSES	ACTION
DIARRHEA/ CONSTIPATION	Diarrhea is often diet-induced, but it may also be caused by parasites, infection, malabsorption conditions, or, in older cats, by masses in the intestinal wall. Do not confuse the straining of diarrhea with constipation.	Contact your vet for advice. Simple diarrhea can be treated successfully with a brief fast. The cause of persistent diarrhea needs to be known for effective treatment. Prevent constipation with cat laxatives.
LOSS OF WEIGHT	This is a general sign that a cat is sick. Starving is the most common cause in young cats. Kidney problems or overactive thyroids are the most common causes in older cats that continue to eat well.	Always see your vet if your cat is eating but still losing weight; it is usually a sign of significant problems. Changes in diet, surgery, and other medical treatments may be useful.
LOSS OF APPETITE	A brief loss of appetite is seldom a problem. A cat may be bored or have eaten elsewhere. Loss of appetite for more than a day is an important clinical sign that a cat is sick; it is associated with many problems.	Consult your veterinarian, who will carry out an examination and possibly tests to find the cause of your cat's loss of appetite. Although many causes are serious, others can be treated easily.
BIRTH PROBLEMS	Most cats experience few difficulties giving birth. Some, however, have poor contractions or are unable to deliver their kittens because of problems in the birth canal.	If your cat is pregnant, make sure that your vet is informed of the expected due date. Prepare a quiet place at home for the birth. If labor lasts for more than two hours, veterinary help is required.
URINATION PROBLEMS	Straining to urinate may be caused by mineral crystals or infection in the urinary tract. Decreased urination is caused by dehydration or a blocked bladder. Increased urination has a variety of significant causes.	Contact your vet if there are any changes in your cat's urination routines. All are significant and some changes are associated with serious conditions that need immediate medical attention.
LOSS OF BALANCE	Injuries are the most common cause of balance problems. Blood loss, strokes, middle ear infections, viral diseases, and other serious problems can cause a drunkenlike walk.	All causes of loss of balance are potentially serious; some are life-threatening emergencies. See your vet immediately. Your cat may look normal outwardly, but have very serious internal problems.
SEIZURES/PARALYSIS	Epilepsy, brain inflammation, and poisons can cause seizures. Paralysis is frequently associated with severe neck injuries, but may also be caused by infections and poisons.	Seek immediate veterinary attention for paralysis, and immediate veterinary advice for seizures. Vaccinate your cat to prevent against infectious diseases, including rabies, where warranted or necessary.
BEHAVIOR CHANGES	A variety of physical but also emotional problems may manifest themselves only through moderate changes in your cat's behavior. Trauma, infection, and metabolic conditions have behavioral consequences.	If your cat's behavior changes, no matter how slightly, always consult your vet. A minor behavior change may signify a considerable problem; cats are naturally reticent and seldom complain.

CARING FOR A SICK CAT

THE CAT'S NATURAL INDEPENDENCE USUALLY SURFACES WHEN IT IS sick. Although some cats seek the attention of their owners, the majority try to conceal signs of illness, often hiding away. When a cat is sick, other resident house cats may behave spitefully toward it, an antisocial clue to illness. Always contact your veterinarian when you observe changes in your cat's routine, and follow your vet's instructions for giving medicines and for changes in diet. Prevention is always simpler and cheaper than treatment; arrange for routine checkups to catch old-age problems early, when changes in diet can forestall development of age-related decline.

Good cat care depends upon careful observation of your cat's behavior to spot any changes in its routine. Just as important is your willingness to take your cat to the vet when necessary, and to carry out treatments that the vet prescribes.

VISITING THE VET
Early training to accept a cat carrier means that when it is necessary to use one for a trip to the vet, your cat will not resist being put in it. At the vet's, gently calm your cat and reassure it of your presence. Give the vet a detailed description of the problem. Remember, your vet relies upon you for information on how your cat is behaving and responding to treatment. The vet may want to take blood samples or carry out diagnostic tests. If this treatment requires hospitalization, arrange to leave your cat's bedding or any other item that your cat is familiar with, and tell your vet what your cat likes to eat. Follow the vet's routines concerning your possible visits while your cat is hospitalized. Generally speaking, cats should recuperate at home whenever possible.

CONSIDERATE NURSING
The typical cat does not want to be excessively fussed over. Provide it with a warm bed and follow your vet's instructions for feeding and medication. If your cat has had surgery, check the wound carefully, looking for unexpected swelling, redness, or discharge. Bandage changes can be very difficult and are best left to the veterinary staff. A sensible cat hates

Giving liquids
With your cat comfortably relaxed, insert the nozzle of a syringe or a pipette behind the canine teeth, and squeeze in a few drops. Let your cat swallow this liquid before giving more.

being given medicine, which almost always tastes unpleasant, so you may need someone to help you. Unlike dogs, cats are unlikely to eat pills buried in food. Wrap your cat in a bath towel if necessary and tuck its body under your free arm as you give the pill. A sick cat may also need hand-feeding in the same manner.

ADMINISTERING PILLS

Cats do not like being given pills. It is also uncommon for a cat to eat willingly any form of medication placed in its food. The only way to ensure that medicine in pill form is consumed is to give it directly to your cat. Speed and confidence are essential. It is usually best to have the help of extra hands: one person holds, while the other gives the pill. When this is not possible, wrap your cat's body in a bath towel, and hold it under your arm while you give it the pill.

JAW IS OPENED

1 While one person steadies your cat, use one hand to hold its head, tilting it upward. The jaw muscles may slacken slightly as its head tilts. Use your other hand to pull the lower jaw downward, gently but firmly. Push your finger on the skin in the space between the jaws.

PRESSURE FROM EACH SIDE

2 Your forefinger and opposing thumb will keep your cat's jaws open for a few seconds. With its head tilted upward, a pill can be dropped over the tongue directly to the back of the throat. Lubricating the pill with butter can be beneficial both because of its taste and its slipperiness.

3 As soon as the pill drops to the back of the throat, close your cat's jaws using one hand and keep the jaws closed. Massage the neck. When your cat licks its lips it has swallowed its medicine.

Comfort and warmth
A sick cat needs to be kept warm. Either place a hot-water bottle under its bedding, or use special cat heating pads that are activated in a microwave oven.

Giving ear drops
Ear mites frequently take up residence in a cat's ear, and sometimes unpleasant microbes thrive, causing infection in the ear canal. Ear drops should be warmed to body temperature by rolling the bottle in your hands for a minute. Invert the bottle, insert into the bottom hole in the ear, and squeeze. Massage below the ear to spread the medicine thoroughly.

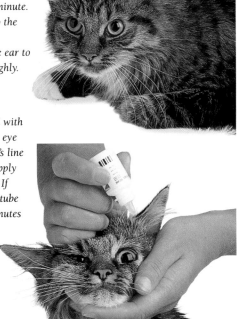

Giving eyedrops
Gently hold your cat's head with one hand and approach the eye from above, out of your cat's line of vision. When possible, apply drops at body temperature. If using an ointment, roll the tube in your hands for a few minutes to warm the ointment and improve its flow.

Warm up food to body temperature, and feed small amounts as frequently as possible. Fluids are absolutely essential and should be given by syringe if your cat is not drinking sufficient quantities by itself. Even moderate dehydration is a serious complication in any illness.

A sick cat may appear to be completely better before it really is. Always finish any course of medication. Treatments will sometimes involve altering your cat's feeding routines to prevent a recurrence of the problem. This aftercare is just as important as the initial treatment.

AFTER SURGERY
Routine surgery is usually followed by a week of indoor rest, while bone surgery may require four to eight weeks of involuntary restriction. Confinement may be boring for your cat but is essential for its recovery, and allows you to keep an eye on its progress. The surgical site should look clean with little swelling or redness. Your cat's appetite should return rapidly, as should its desire to investigate its territory. If you are concerned about its appetite, mobility, or demeanor, contact your vet for advice.

APPETITE LOSS
A short fast is of no concern but prolonged feline fasting is dangerous, and can even lead to serious liver-related disease. If your cat has lost interest in its food, consult your vet. Stimulate its taste buds with extra-aromatic foods and warm up food slightly, to make it give off stronger aromas. Stay with your cat while it

eats, as encouragement can sometimes help. If your cat refuses to eat, your vet will prescribe a liquid diet that you can feed it by syringe until it is well enough to eat on its own. If the cat becomes dehydrated, your vet will have to feed it either intravenously or by stomach tube.

CARE OF THE ELDERLY CAT
Cats are living longer than ever before, in part because of advances in disease control through vaccination, and in part because so many cats live safely indoors. In feline veterinary medicine, medical conditions associated with old age have increased in frequency. Older cats need special care. Tooth and gum disease remains the most common reason for seeking veterinary attention and routines such as tooth brushing and feeding may need to be altered. With age, many cats fail to groom themselves as well as they once did, leading to a greater likelihood of parasites. Take extra care of your elderly cat's skin and coat. Old skin loses its elasticity, so you will need to be careful not to damage it accidentally when grooming. Clean the ears more routinely for wax, discharge, or debris. Small benign tumors called ceruminomas are fairly common in the ears of elderly cats.

HOW FAR SHOULD WE GO?
Medically speaking, most of the diagnostic aids or therapeutic techniques available for us can be used on cats. Vets routinely use ultrasound, endoscopy, and imaging apparatus to make diagnoses. They have the skill to use advanced

surgery, including transplantation, to treat feline illnesses. The availability of this vast array of equipment and knowledge raises the question of how far cat care should be taken. Cost of care is a financial consideration: what a cat owner will spend is a personal decision. More important is what the patient gains from the procedure. The long-term quality of a cat's life should be the most important consideration, not the medical challenge to the vet or the emotional stress the cat's owner is suffering.

Preventing self-inflicted damage
It is sometimes necessary to prevent a cat from rubbing or scratching at its face. A protective collar permits a cat to eat and drink, and allows air to circulate around the healing region, while protecting it from further irritation.

FIRST AID

THE CAT'S NATURAL CURIOSITY IS WELL DOCUMENTED, AND OFTEN places it in danger. The need for first aid, and then for help from your veterinarian, is more common for outdoor individuals. Your objectives in giving first aid are to save life, prevent any further injuries, control damage, minimize pain and distress, and then to get your cat to the vet for attention. Follow practical steps to assess the situation. Is your cat in danger? Are you in danger if you try to help? Look for life-threatening signs, sustain life by giving emergency first aid on the spot; other people who are available can help by arranging transportation to the nearest vet.

When emergencies occur, perform a physical examination to determine the severity of the injuries. Do not be fooled by any lack of external damage: felines often suffer hidden internal injuries that are potentially life-threatening.

GENTLE RESTRAINT

If a cat is injured, its instinct is to hide and protect itself from further damage. Calm your cat with soothing talk and use as little restraint as necessary to perform your examination. Eliminate escape routes and, avoiding sudden gestures, place a soft object such as a towel over the cat, wrapping it gently to prevent escape and to minimize the risk of injuries to you. Next, gently unwrap the head so that you can watch the cat's breathing, which will normally be at a rate of 10 to 30 breaths per minute. Flaring nostrils are a sign that your cat is not well.

MONITOR VITAL SIGNS

A cat's resting heart rate varies from 100 to 160 beats per minute. Kittens have heart rates up to 260 beats per minute. To detect the heartbeat, feel the chest firmly behind the elbows. This is simple in lean cats but more difficult in plumper individuals. For those, feel the pulse in the thigh by gently pressing your fingertips into the slight groove inside the hind leg where it joins the body. Examine the gums for color by gently lifting the upper lip. Normal gums are a healthy pink color, while bluish, pale, or white gums are all causes for concern.

SHOCK

Clinical shock is a potentially life-threatening event; cats may go into this state hours after an accident. The signs of shock are pale or white gums, a rapid heart rate of over 250 beats per minute, and fast breathing of over 40 breaths per minute. Shock has many causes, including internal or external bleeding, burns, heart failure, vomiting, diarrhea, urinary blockages, trauma, animal or insect bites, electrocution, diabetes, and poisons. Treating shock takes precedence over most other injuries, including broken bones. Minimize shock by placing the cat on its side on a warm surface with its head extended, elevating the hindquarters with a pillow or towel to send as much blood as possible to the head. Use manual pressure to stop obvious bleeding. Give artificial respiration and heart massage if necessary, wrap your cat in a warm blanket, and go immediately to the nearest veterinarian for life-sustaining medical treatment.

ASSESSING AN INJURED CAT

After restraining your cat if necessary, monitor its breathing and its heart rate. Always look for signs of clinical shock, the greatest hazard to your cat. Regardless of whether your cat is conscious or unconscious, check the color of its gums to establish its physical state.

1 Gently lift your cat's upper lip to expose the gums. If they are pink, its heart and lungs are probably functioning well. If they are pale or blue, breathing or circulation has been affected; this is an acute emergency.

2 If your cat is unconscious, use your thumb and fingers around the chest just behind the elbow to feel for its heartbeat, or feel the inside of the hind leg for the pulse. If there is no heartbeat or pulse, start heart massage immediately by grasping the cat's chest between thumb and forefinger and squeezing vigorously.

PHYSICAL WOUNDS

Injuries may be open, where the skin is broken, or closed, where the skin is intact. Do not underestimate the significance of closed wounds: typically, there is pain, swelling, discoloration, or heat under the skin and possibly superficial scratches. Apply a cold compress, or a bag of frozen vegetables wrapped in a towel, as soon as possible.

RECOVERY POSITION

When assessing your cat, if its heart is beating and it is breathing, there is no need for heart massage and artificial resuscitation (CPR). Place the cat in the recovery position by laying it on a warm surface on an incline. Make sure that its head is lying lower than its body so that maximum blood goes to the brain. Unless your cat is suffering from heatstroke, wrap it loosely in a light blanket to prevent the loss of body heat, while you seek immediate veterinary attention.

FIRST AID 233

Open wounds are more apparent, with possible pain, bleeding, and broken skin, even if there is only a small puncture. If a cat is not in shock, it will increasingly lick the affected area. Treat open wounds by applying pressure with clean gauze or absorbent material. Once the gauze or material has been applied to the bleeding wound, leave it there until your vet examines your cat: removing a blood-soaked dressing disturbs the clot and can initiate more bleeding. Do not use disinfectants or antiseptics on gaping open wounds. Never rub open wounds because you may cause further damage.

Cats rarely bleed profusely from minor wounds; blood vessels in their skin clot quickly. Internal bleeding is more common, and very dangerous, because it cannot be seen. Always seek veterinary advice after any trauma. If you see bleeding, apply pressure to the wound using clean gauze. Flush minor wounds with clean water or 3 percent hydrogen peroxide. Bandage injuries only if absolutely necessary. It can be extremely difficult to apply a bandage to any part of a cat's body other than its torso.

CRITICAL INJURIES

Injured cats are often unable to move. Take extreme care when moving a cat with potentially serious physical injuries. Let the cat find its own most comfortable breathing position, then, keeping its back as still as possible, slip one hand under the cat's rump and the other under its chest, and gently slip it onto an improvised "stretcher," such as a blanket or coat, for a trip to the nearest veterinarian. A well-cushioned cardboard box is ideal for transportation. Cover the cat in the box to reduce movement and conserve body heat.

MONITOR THE PATIENT

After giving life-saving first aid to your feline, always have it examined by a veterinarian. If your cat's injuries are not life-threatening, perform a detailed inspection, looking for potentially serious, painful, or distressing conditions. Watch the cat's behavior and observe its responses to you. Listen for any unusual breathing sounds and watch your cat's movements. Ask your vet to show you how to take your cat's temperature. A normal temperature is between 100°F (38°C) and 102°F (39°C). If it is above or below normal, seek veterinary attention. Examine the eyes, ears, nose, mouth, head, and neck. Feel the body, limbs, and tail. Check the anal region for injuries or unusual odor. Monitor your cat's eating and toileting habits. If there are any changes in normal behavior, contact your vet.

FIRST-AID EQUIPMENT

Most cats resent the use of any first-aid equipment, especially bandages. This is unfortunate; bandages keep wounds dry and prevent further injuries, including self-inflicted damage. Bandages also protect open injuries from contamination, absorb seepage, and minimize pain. Unless the cat is subdued or sedated, it is almost impossible to apply an effective bandage. If bandages are required, seek veterinary attention.

THERMOMETER

TWEEZERS

SCISSORS

COTTON BALL

ANTISEPTIC CREAM

ADHESIVE BANDAGE

STERILE DRESSINGS

GAUZE

ASSORTED BANDAGES

ADHESIVE TAPE

Feline first aid
A feline first-aid kit should contain a few basics that may be needed in the event of an accident or emergency. Keep all medicines in a safe place.

ARTIFICIAL RESPIRATION

A heartbeat but no breathing means that your cat needs artificial respiration; a cat will die if its brain does not receive sufficient oxygen. Near-drowning, electrocution, choking, smoke inhalation, poisoning, diabetic shock, and allergy may all interfere with breathing. If the heart has stopped, combine artificial respiration with external heart massage.

1 Assess the cat's heart rate. If its heart is pumping but it is not breathing, place the cat on its side, clear the airway of debris, and pull its tongue forward. Elevate hindquarters above forequarters.

2 With your hand around the closed muzzle, place your mouth over the nose and blow in to expand the chest. Avert your mouth and let the chest deflate. Repeat 20 to 30 times per minute.

MOVING AN UNCOOPERATIVE CAT

Even the most amiable of felines may lash out with tooth and claw when injured. Talk soothingly to the cat to reassure it, and approach it slowly and cautiously. Drape a lightweight but thick towel or blanket over your cat, to restrain it and to prevent it from running off to hide. If possible, wear gloves to protect your hands from any bites or scratches. Pick up the entire bundle, applying as little pressure as possible. Make sure its face is exposed so that it can breathe easily. Apply gentle pressure to the towel around the scruff of the neck to prevent any attempts to escape.

GLOSSARY

Agouti The lighter areas of fur in the tabby coat; also a term for cats expressing any tabby pattern.

Awn hair Bristly undercoat hair. *See also* Down hair, Guard hair.

Bicolor Coats consisting of white hair mixed with one other color.

Boots *See* Gauntlets.

Brachycephalic An abnormally short nose and flattened face.

Breeches Long fur covering the upper part of the hind legs.

Breed An animal strain visibly different from its parent species, particularly produced by human intervention. *See also* Family, Genus, Order, Species, Subspecies. Other individual interpretations apply within the cat fancy.

Breed clubs Organizations within a registry devoted to one or more particular breeds. Several clubs may exist within a registry for one breed.

Breed standard A description of the ideal characteristics against which each cat in a breed is measured.

Burmese pattern *See* Sepia.

Castrate Method of neutering male cats by removing testicles. *See* Neuter.

Cat fancy Umbrella term for registries and the people who breed and/or show cats worldwide.

CFA The Cat Fanciers' Association, the world's largest feline registry, founded in 1906, primarily based in North America.

Chinchilla Persian with white coat tipped with black, or such a coat in any cat.

Colorpoint A cat whose face, ears, feet, and tail are a different color from the rest of its body. *See* Pointed.

Cool Colors as far as possible from red.

Dominant gene A genetic trait that if carried is always expressed. *See also* Recessive gene.

Down hair Soft, insulating hair in undercoat. *See also* Awn hair, Guard hair.

Family Group of animals within an order that share many defining characteristics and evolutionary descent. *See also* Breed, Genus, Order, Species, Subspecies.

Feline Immune Deficiency Virus (FIV) A relative of the HIV virus, which weakens the immune system, causing death. Highly contagious to other cats, but not to humans or other animals.

Feline Infectious Peritonitis (FIP) A viral disease that is usually fatal. Symptoms include fluid accumulation in the abdomen, jaundice, and anemia.

Feline Leukemia Virus (FeLV) A virus affecting the lymphatic system, suppressing immunity to disease.

Feral An animal living wild but descended from domestically bred stock.

FIFé Fédération Internationale Féline, an umbrella organization for European cat clubs, founded in 1949.

Flehmen Lifting the upper lip to bring a scent into contact with the vomeronasal organ. *See* Vomeronasal organ.

Free-breeding *See* Random-breeding.

Frown lines Dark lines forming a letter "M" on a cat's forehead.

Gauntlets White hind paws in a colored or bicolored cat, ending below or above the hock. *See also* Mittens.

GCCF The Governing Council of the Cat Fancy, founded in 1910, the governing body for most British cat clubs.

Gene pool The genetic diversity available in any given species, race, or breed.

Genus A group of species within a family that share characteristics and ancestry not shared by other species. *See also* Breed, Family, Order, Species, Subspecies.

Ghost markings Faint tabby markings sometimes seen in the coat of non-agouti cats, usually in kittens.

Guard hair Long, coarse hairs that protect the undercoat and provide a waterproof layer. *See also* Awn hair, Down hair.

Hock A cat's ankle.

Hot Colors that resemble red.

Jacobson's organ *See* Vomeronasal organ.

Kitten In common understanding, a kitten below the age of separation from its mother at about 12 weeks. In shows, cats may still be called kittens for some months after this.

Kitten cap White cats carry the dominant gene W, which masks other colors. White kittens sometimes show a hint of their underlying color in a "kitten cap" of hair on their heads, which disappears with age.

Locket Small area of white hair on chest of a colored cat, a fault in many breeds.

Manx Tailless breed of cat. The taillessness is caused by a gene that can cause fatal problems if passed on by both parents.

Mascara lines Dark lines extending from the outer corners of the eyes.

Mink A combination of Pointed and Sepia patterns, with colored body and moderate pointing. The characteristic pattern of the Tonkinese breed.

Mittens White forepaws in a colored or bicolored cat, typically stopping below the ankle. *See also* Gauntlets.

Mosaicing Random patching or mottling of coat colors, as in tortoiseshell colors.

Mutation Change away from the normal state in a genetic trait.

Neuter To castrate males or spay females to prevent reproduction and unwanted sexual behavior.

Non-agouti Any solid-colored cat showing no tabby markings.

Nose break *See* Nose stop.

Nose stop A change in direction, slight or pronounced, seen in profile at the nose top.

Odd-Eyed Cat with eyes of two different colors; in breed standards, one blue and one orange.

Order Group of animals with one defining characteristic, for example carnivora, all carnivorous mammals. *See also* Breed, Family, Genus, Species, Subspecies.

Pedigree A record of ancestry, showing a cat's parentage over several generations.

Pointed Color restricted to the extremities of the head, limbs, and tail, the body remaining pale, first known in the Siamese breed. Also a generic term to cover other less obvious pointing patterns. *See* Mink, Sepia.

Polydactyly Any number of toes above four on forepaws or five on hind paws.

Queen Unspayed female cat.

Random-breeding Process of animals choosing their own mates without human intervention. Also called free-breeding.

Recessive gene A genetic trait that may be carried without being expressed.

Registry An authority, national or international, that decides on breed recognition and standards, and maintains records of pedigree breeds. Made up of constituent breed clubs. *See also* CFA, FIFé, GCCF, TCA, TICA.

Rex Term for any mutation causing a curly coat. Also referred to as rexing.

Ruff Longer fur that sometimes appears around the neck and on the chest.

Rufousing Red tones in the agouti parts of a coat, giving rich, warm tones. In silver coats, referred to as "tarnishing," and usually regarded as a fault.

Scent marking A cat marks its territory with urine, or with scent from glands on its face, lips, and ears.

Selective breeding Human intervention to determine the partners in any breeding.

Self Coat of one color. *See* Non-agouti.

Sepia Darkest color restricted to the extremities of the head, limbs, and tail, the body being a slightly paler shade of the same color. *See also* Mink, Pointed.

Shaded A coat silvered for approximately half of its length. *See also* Silvering, Smoke, Tipped.

Siamese pattern *See* Pointed.

Silvering Inhibition of color production in part of a hair, leaving it pale or white. *See also* Smoke, Shaded, Tipped.

Smoke Colored coat with white undercoat. *See also* Shaded, Silvering, Tipped.

Spay Method of neutering female cats by removing ovaries and uterus. *See* Neuter.

Species Animals sharing common characteristics and ancestry, capable of interbreeding naturally. *See also* Breed, Family, Genus, Order, Subspecies.

Spectacles Areas of lighter hair around, and particularly below, the eyes.

Subspecies Geographically separated group within a species that has differences from the rest of the species but will interbreed with it where ranges overlap. *See also* Breed, Family, Genus, Order, Species.

Tabby Pattern of stripes, blotches, or spots, used in the wild as camouflage. *See* Agouti.

Tarnishing See Rufousing.

TCA The Traditional Cats' Association, formed in 1987, dedicated to breeding cats to old breed standards or fashions.

Third eyelid A membrane concealed in the inner corner of a cat's eye, which draws across the eye in sickness or injury.

TICA The International Cat Association, a registry founded in 1979, based on genetics.

Ticking Banding of light and dark colors along a hair.

Tipped Coat of white hairs with colored tips. *See also* Shaded, Silvering, Smoke.

Tom cat Unneutered male cat.

Tonkinese pattern See Mink.

Topcoat Outer layer of protective hairs, carrying pattern in tabbies. *See* Guard hair.

Undercoat Layer of insulating fur under topcoat. *See also* Awn hair, Down hair.

Vomeronasal organ A sensory organ in the nasal cavity that analyzes smells and tastes. Also known as Jacobson's organ.

INDEX

PUBLISHER'S ACKNOWLEDGMENTS

We are indebted to the many owners who gave up their time to allow us to photograph their cats for the breed profiles. Without their kind assistance, Chapter Five would not have been possible in its present form.

The cats used in the profiles are credited here page by page: Page numbers are given in bold, and positions on the page in terms of top (t), bottom (b), left (l), center (c), and right (r). Each cat's name is followed by that of its breeder and (in parentheses) owner.

Any awards the cat holds are given, such as champion (Ch), Grand Champion (GrCh), Premier (Pr), Grand Premier (GrPr), Supreme Grand Champion (SupGrCh), Supreme Grand Premier (SupGrPr), European Champion (EurCh), or International Champion (IntCh). Many of the younger cats that we photographed have gone on to win more awards, but the details remain as they were at the time of photography. We regret that it is beyond the scope of these credits to give the same depth of information for the photographs provided by Chanan and Tetsu Yamazaki, which were not commissioned by DK. Abbreviations are given for the photographers Tracy Morgan (TM) and Marc Henrie (MH).

104 tl Chanan, bl *Mowbray Tanamera* D Cleford (D Cleford) MH; **105** l, br both Yamazaki; **106** tr *Cashel Golden Yuppie* A Curley (A Curley), cl *Honeymist Roxana* M Howes (M Howes), cr GrPr *Bellrai Faberge* B & B Raine (B & B Raine), bl *Casalina Dolly Mixture* E Baldwin (E Baldwin), all MH; **107** l *Watlove Hamish* H Watson (H Watson), tr *Adirtsa Choc Ice* D Tynan (C & K Smith), cr *Adhuilo Meadowlands Alias* P Hurrell (S Josling), br *Bellrai Creme Chanel* B & B Raine (B & B Raine), all MH; **108** t *Impeza Chokolotti* C Rowark (E Baldwin), c *Anneby Sunset* A Bailey (A Bailey), b *Amocasa Beau Brummel* I Elliott (I Elliott), all MH; **109** Ch *Watlove Mollie Mophead* H Watson (H Watson) MH; **110** tc *Lizzara Rumbypumby Redted* G Black (G Black) TM, tr *Chanterelle Velvet Cushion* L Lavis (G Black) TM, cr *Schwenthe Kiska* FE Brigliadori (FE Brigliadori & K Robson) MH, bl *Panjandrum Swansong* A Madden (S Tallboys) MH; **111** tr *Saybrianna Tomorrow's Cream* A Carritt (A Carritt), bl Ch&GrPr *Panjandrum April Surprice* A Madden (A Madden), br *Aesthetical Toty Temptress* G Sharpe (H Hewitt), all MH; **112** tr *Chehem Agassi* (Christine Powell) TM; **113** tl *Pandapaws Mr. Biggs* S Ward-Smith (J Varley & J Dicks) MH, cr *Chehem BryteSkye* (Christine Powell) TM, b *Rags n Riches Vito Maracana* Robin Pickering (Mrs. J Moore) TM; **114** all Chanan; **115** Chanan; **116** tr *unnamed kitten*, cl *Ch Keka Ursine Edward*, bl *Keoka Aldebaran*, all D Brinicombe (D Brinicombe) TM; **117** tl Chanan, tr *Ch Keoka Ford Prefect* TM, bl *GrCh Adinnlo Meddybemps*, br *Keoka Max Quordlepleen*, all D Brinicombe (D Brinicombe) TM; **118** bl *Skogens SF Eddan Romeo* AS Watt (S Garrett) MH, r *Lizzara Bardolph* (Ginny Black) TM; **119** tl *Skogens Magni* AS Watt (S Garrett) MH, tr *Tarakatt Tia*, br *Sigurd Oski* both (D Smith) TM; **120** all Yamazaki; **121** tl Yamazaki, tr Yamazaki, br *Olocha* A Danveef (H von Groneberg) MH; **122** tl Yamazaki, br Chanan; **123** all Yamazaki; **124** t Chanan, bl Yamazaki; **125** tc Yamazaki, bl Yamazaki, br Chanan; **126** bl *Bruvankedi Kabugu* B Cooper (B Cooper), r *Champion Cheratons Red Aurora* Mr. & Mrs. Hassell (Mr. & Mrs. Hassell), all TM; **127** tl *Cheratons Simply Red* Mr. & Mrs. Hassell (Mr. & Mrs. Hassell) TM, cr *Bruvankedi Mavi Bayas* (Mr. R Cooper) TM, bl Ch *Lady Lubna Leanne Chatkantarra* T Boumeister (J Van der Werff) MH; **128** tr Chanan; **129** all Yamazaki; **130** Chanan; **131** tl Chanan, tr *Shanna's Tombis Hanta Yo* M Harms-Moeskops (G Rebel van Kemenade) MH, bl *Shanna's Yacinta Sajida* M Harms (M Harms) MH, bc MH; **132** tr *Dolente Angelica* L Brisley (L Brisley) TM, bl *Bealltaine Bezique* T Stracstone (T Stracstone) MH; **133** tl *unnamed kitten*, b *Beaumaris Cherubina*, both A & B Gregory (A & B Gregory) TM; **134** G & T Oraas; **135** tr

Favagella Brown Whispa J Bryson (J Bryson), b *Kennbury Dulcienea* C Lovell (K Harmon), all MH; **136** tr Pr *Pandai Feargal* E Corps (BV Rickwood), bl *Blancsanglier Rosensoleil* A Bird (A Bird), all MH; **137** tl Pr *Blancsanglier Beau Brummel* A Bird (A Bird), tc Ch *Apricat Silvercascade* R Smyth (E & J Robinson), tr GrPr *Nighteyes Cinderfella* J Pell (J Pell), b *Palvjia Pennyfromheaven* J Burroughs (T Tidey), all MH; **138** tr GrPr *Nighteyes Cinderfella* J Pell (J Pell), cl *Jeuphi Golden Girl* J Phillips (L Cory), br *Mossgems Sheik Simizu* M Mosscrop (H Grenney), all MH; **139** t *Ronsline Whistfull Spirit* R Farthing (R Farthing), cl Ch *Apricat Silvercascade* R Smyth (E & J Robinson), br *Dasilva Tasha* J St. John (C Russel & P Scrivener), all MH; **140** tr *Chantonel Snowball Express* R Elliott (R Elliott), bl *Lipema Shimazaki* P Brown (G Dean), all MH; **141** tr *Palantir Waza Tayriphyng* J May (J May) TM, b *Quinkent Honey's Mi-Lei-Fo* IA van der Reckweg (IA van der Reckweg) MH; **142** all Chanan; **143** all Yamazaki; **144** all K Leonov; **145** tr Chanan, b Yamazaki; **146** tr *Maggie* (Bethlehem Cat Sanctuary), bl *White Mischief* (P Brown), all MH; **147** t *Dan-I-Lion* (V Warriner), c *Dumpling* (Bethlehem Cat Sanctuary), br *Stardust* (V Warringer), all MH; **150** tr *Pennydown Penny Black* SW McEwen (SW McEwen) MH, cr Yamazaki, bl Yamazaki; **151** tl Yamazaki, tr Chanan, b Chanan; **152** tr *Tameko Tamoshanter* M Simon (R Taylor), c Ch *Sargenta Silver Dan* U Graves (U Graves), bl GrCh *Starfrost Dominic* E Conlin (C Greenal), br GrCh *Maruja Samson* M Moorhead (M Moorhead), all MH; **153** tc Ch & SupGrPr *Welquest Snowman* A Welsh (A Welsh), cr *Susian Just Judy* S Kempster (M Way), br *Miletree Black Rod* R Towse (R Towse), all MH; **154** tr GrCh *Westways Purrfect Amee* A West (GB Ellins), cl *Kavida Kadberry* L Berry (L Berry), cr *Kavida Primetime & Amethyst* L Berry (L Berry), br *Miletree Magpie* R Towse (M le Mounier), all MH; **155** tc GrCh *Miletree Masquerade* R Towse (P Allen), cl Ch *Bartania Pomme Frits* B Beck (B Beck), cr *Cordelia Cassandra* J Codling (C Excell), br *Kavida Misty Daydream* L Berry (L Berry), all MH; **156** tr *Minty* L Williams (H Walker & K Bullin), bl Yamazaki, br Chanan; **157** tc Yamazaki, br *Adrish Alenka* L Price (L Williams) MH; **158** l Yamazaki, r Chanan; **159** all Yamazaki; **160** r Chanan; **161** tl Yamazaki, tr, cr, bc all Chanan; **162** all Chanan; **163** tr Yamazaki, bc Chanan; **164** all Yamazaki; **165** all Chanan; **166** IntCh *Orions Guru Lomaers* (Mulder-Hopma) MH; **167** tl *Eldoria's Crazy Girl*, tr *Eldorias Goldfinger*, bl, *Eldoria's Yossarian* all O van Beck & A Quast (O van Beck & A Quast), br *Aurora de Santanoe* L Kenter (L Kenter), all MH; **168** tr Ch *Comte Davidof de Lasalle*, bl IntCh *Amaranthoe Lasalle*, all K ten Broek (K ten Broek) MH; **169** tr *Donna Eurydice de Lasalle*, bl IntCh *Amaranthoe Lasalle*, all K ten Broek (K ten Broek) MH; **170** tr *Astahazy Zeffirelli* (M von Kirchberg) MH, bl Yamazaki; **171** tr, br Chanan, cl Yamazaki; **172** tr *Karthwine Elven Moonstock* R Clayton (M Crane), cl GrCh *Emarelle Milos* MR Lyall (R Hopkins), bl Ch *Anera Ula* C Macaulay (C Symonds), bc *Braeside Marimba* H Hewitt (H Hewitt), br Ch *Anera Ula* C Macaulay (C Symonds), all MH; **173** tl *Lionelle Rupert Bear* C Bailey (C Tencor), c *Satusai Fawn Amy* I Reid (I Reid), br *Braeside Marimba* H Hewitt (H Hewitt), all MH; **174** T Straede; **175** tr *Silvaner Pollyanna*, b *Silvaner Kuan*, all C Thompson (C Thompson) MH; **176** tr *Phoebe* (F Kerr) TM, cl & br GrCh *Aerostar Spectre* JED Mackie (S Callen &

I Hotten) MH; **177** c Yamazaki, t, b, Chanan; **178** tr *Kartuch Benifer* C & T Clark (C & T Clark), b *Ballego Betty Boo* J Gillies (J Gillies), all MH; **179** t *Lasiesta Blackberry Girl* GW Dyson (GW Dyson), b *Vatan Mimi* D Beech & J Chalmers (J Moore), all MH; **180** tr *Boronga Blaktortie Dollyvee,* P Impson (J Quiddington), bl *Boronga Kreem Kaskuli,* P Impson (J Quiddington), br *Boronga Black Othello,* P Impson (J Thurman), all TM; **181** l *Vervain Ered Luin,* r *Vervain Goldberry,* both N Johnson (N Johnson) TM; **182** all Chanan; **183** all Chanan; **184** tr Ch *Bambino Seawitch* B Boizard Neal (B Boizard Neal), c *Impromptu Crystal* M Garrod (M Garrod), bl Ch *Hobberdy Hokey Cokey* A Virtue (A Virtue), all MH; **185** tl Ch *Bambino Dreamy* B Boizard Neal (B Boizard Neal), tr *Braeside Red Sensation* H Hewitt (H Hewitt), bl GrCh *Bambino Alice Bugown* B Boizard Neal (B Boizard Neal), all MH; **186** *Romantica Marcus Macoy* (Mrs. Davison) TM; **187** tl *Grimspound Majesticlady,* Miss Hodgkinson (Miss Hodgkinson), tr *Tonkitu's Adinnsh Xin Wun,* bl *Tonkitu Mingchen* both D Burke (D Burke), br *Episcopus Leonidas* (Mrs. Murray-Langley), all TM; **188** tr Ch *Willowbreeze Goinsolo* Mr. & Mrs. Robinson (TK Hull-Williams) MH, c Yamazaki; **189** tr Yamazaki, l Yamazaki, br Ch *Pannaduloa Phaedra* J Hansson (J Hansson) MH; **190** tr *Indalo Knights Templar* P Bridham (P Bridham) MH, c Ch *Darling Copper Kingdom* I George (S Mauchline) MH, bl *Mewzishun Bel Canto* A Greatorex (D Aubyn) TM, br GrCh *Dawnus Primadonna* A Douglas (A Douglas) MH; **191** tl Ch *Sisar Brie* L Pummell (L Pummell) MH, cl GrCh *Pannaduloa Yentantethra* J Hansson (J Hansson) MH, cr *Merescuff Allart* (E Mackenzie-Wood) TM, Ch *Bosan Carmen* S Bell (LE Martin) MH; **192** cl *Jasrobinka Annamonique* P & J Choppen (P & J Choppen) MH, bl *Tenaj Blue Max* J Tonkinson (K Iremonger) MH, r *Simonski Sylvester Sneakly* S Cosgrove (S Cosgrove) MH; **193** tl GrPr *Jasrobinka Jeronimo* P & J Choppen (P & J Choppen) MH, c ChPr *Adixish Minos Mercury* A Concanon (A Concanon) MH, br GrCh *Sukinfer Samari* J O'Boyle (J O'Boyle); **194** tr *Scilouette Angzhi* C & T Clark (C & T Clark) MH, bl *Adhuish Tuwhit Tuwhoo* N Williams (N Williams) MH; **195** tl *Sunjade Brandy Snap* E Wildon (E Tomlinson) MH, tr *Scintilla Silver Whirligig* P Turner (D Walker) MH, bl *Saxongate Paler Shades* (D Buxcey) TM, br *Parthia Angelica* MA Skelton (MA Skelton) MH; **196** bl *Ngkomo Ota* A Scruggs (L Marcel) MH, r Yamazaki; **197** all Yamazaki; **198** all Chanan; **199** l Pr *Adkrish Samson* PK Weissman (PK Weissman), tc *Leshocha Azure My Friend* E Himmerston (E Himmerston), cr *Myowal Rudolph* J Cornish (J Compton), all MH; **200** tr GrCh *Ikari Donna* S Davey (J Plumb), bl Pr *Bobire Justin Tyme* IE Longhurst (A Charlton), br GrPr *Bevilleon Dandy Lion* B Lyon (M Chitty), all MH; **201** tl UKGrCh *Nobilero Loric Vilesilenca* AE & RE Hobson (M Reed), tr *Adhuish Grainne* N Jarrett (J Burton), cr *Sailorman Hooray Henry* K Hardwick (K Hardwick), *Myowal Susie Sioux* G Cornish (J & B Archer), all MH; **202** tr *Reaha Anda Bebare* S Scanlin (A Rushbrook & J Plumb), c Yamazaki, bl Yamazaki; **203** all Chanan; **204** all Yamazaki; **205** all Yamazaki; **206** all Chanan; **207** tl Yamazaki, cr Chanan, cl Yamazaki, br Chanan; **208** tr *Gaylee Diablo* M Nicholson (M Nicholson) TM, c Chanan, bl *Gaylee Diablo* M Nicholson (M Nicholson) TM; **209** *Gaylee Diablo* M Nicholson (M Nicholson) TM; **210** all Yamazaki; **211** all Yamazaki; **212** tr *name unknown* Jane Burton, bl *Friskie* (Bethlehem Cat Sanctuary) MH; **213** tl *name unknown*, cr *Sinbad Sailor Blue* (V Lew), bl *Crumpet* (Bethlehem Cat Sanctuary), all MH.

CARTOGRAPHY

James Anderson, David Roberts

ILLUSTRATORS

Main artworks on pp 56–75, Janos Marffy
Additional artworks, Samantha Elmhurst, Malcom McGregor, Amanda Williams

AUTHOR'S ACKNOWLEDGMENTS

Early in this project, when Candida Frith-Macdonald handed me an armload of argument, gleaned from the Internet, on whether or not cats have one or two diluting colour genes, I knew this would be a fully researched effort, with one "author" seriously underacknowledged. Thank you, Candida, for devoting your self-confessed flypaper brain to this book. My grateful thanks also go to the rest of the team, especially Ursula Dawson for her fluid designs, and Sarah Wilde, Heather Dunleavy, Tracie Lee Davis, Sharon Lucas, Frank Ritter, and Derek Coombes for their additional help and suggestions.

As a veterinarian, I have worked with cats for over 27 years, but, needless to say, much of the information in this book was new to me. It was not new to those people worldwide who answered my faxes and letters with reams of information. I appreciate the assistance of the Governing Council of the Cat Fancy (GCCF) in Great Britain, and the Cat Fanciers' Association (CFA) in the United States, for providing me with their address lists of cat clubs, and thank all the cat breeders in the United States and Great Britain, unfortunately too numerous to mention here, who responded to my questionnaire. Thanks also to the Breed Club Secretaries in those countries for providing me with such detailed information on their breeds, and to the cat breed Internet website compilers. My thanks also go to individuals around the world who provided regional information about cats. These include Magister Herbert Berthold (Austria), Dr. Marie Rihova (Czech Republic), Kerstin Breyhan (Germany), Ashley McManus (Ireland), Keiko Yamazaki, Tak Muroya, Moto Arima, and Dr. Norio Kogure (Japan), Olga Sizova (Russia), Professor Eric Hurley (South Africa), Dr. Jaume Camps (Spain), Shin Dai, Wu Hung Biksu, and Dr. Du Bai (Taiwan), Dr. Ann Schneider (USA), and Dr. Frances Barr and Joan Moore (UK).

DK Publishing would like to thank the following: Patrick Roberts for the loan of feline stamps; Jan Peder Lamm of the Statens Historiska Museum in Stockholm, Katerina Ågren, and Malcolm Ross-Macdonald for help with Scandinavian research; Irmgard Schmatz for help with German research; Joan Moore of Cat World magazine for help with breed pictures; Mrs. L.K. Pring of GCCF; Gloria Stephens, TICA webmaster; the CFA Web Page committee and others involved in the CFA site; Marie Lamb, Orca Starbuck, Laura Gilbreath, Jean Marie Diaz, and Barb French of the Fanciers list and website.
Several websites have been referred to extensively in preparing this book, notably
http://www.fanciers.com/; http://www.cfainc.org/; http://www.tica.org/

BIBLIOGRAPHY

Alderton, David, *Eyewitness Handbook: Cats*, DK Publishing, New York, 1992
Anderson, Janice, *The Cat-A-Logue*, Guinness Superlatives Ltd, England, 1989
Angel, Jeremy, *Cats Kingdom*, Warner Books, New York, 1985
August, John, Ed., *Consultations in Feline Internal Medicine*, W.B. Saunders Co, Philadelphia, 1994
Boylan, Clare, *The Literary Companion to Cats*, Sinclair-Stevenson, London, 1994
Bradshaw, John, *The True Nature of the Cat*, Boxtree, London, 1993
Busch, Heather and Silver, Burton, *Why Cats Paint: A Theory of Feline Aesthetics*, Ten Speed Press, Berkeley, California, 1994
Clutton-Brock, Juliet, *The British Museum Book of Cats*, British Museum Press, London, 1988
Davies, Marion, *The Magical Lore of Cats*, Capall Bann Publishing, Berkshire, UK, 1995
Fogle, Bruce, *First Aid for Cats*, Penguin Books, London, 1995
Fogle, Bruce, *The Cat's Mind*, Pelham Books, London, 1991
Gettings, Fred, *The Secret Lore of the Cat*, Grafton Books, London, 1989
Howard, Tom, *The Illustrated Cat: Animals in Art*, Grange Books, England, 1994
de Laroche, Robert and Labat, Jean-Michel, *Histoire Secrète du Chat*, Casterman, Brussels, 1993
Loxton, Howard, *The Noble Cat*, Merehurst Press, London, 1990
Macdonald, David, Ed., *The Encyclopedia of Mammals*, George Allen & Unwin, London, 1984
Malek, Jaromir, *The Cat in Ancient Egypt*, British Museum Press, London, 1993
Mery, Fernand, *Le Chat*, Editions Robert Laffont, Paris, 1966
Morris, Desmond, *Cat World*, Ebury Press, London, 1996
O'Farrell, Valerie and Neville, Peter, *Manual of Feline Behaviour*, BSAVA Publications, Cheltenham, UK, 1994
Kirk's Current Veterinary Therapy XII, Ed. W.B. Saunders Co, Philadelphia, 1995
Cats Ancient and Modern, Sillar, Frederick Cameron and Meyler, Ruth Mary, Studio Vista, London, 1966
The Cat Fanciers' Association Cat Encyclopedia, Simon & Schuster, New York, 1993
Tabor, Roger, *Understanding Cats*, David & Charles, London, 1995
Van Vechten, Carl, *The Tiger in the House*, Dover Publications Ltd, New York, 1996
Vesey-Fitzgerald, Brian, *The Domestic Cat*, Pelham, London, 1969
Wright, Michael and Walters, Sally, Ed., *The Book of the Cat*, Pan Books, London, 1980

PICTURE CREDITS